Marie Duval

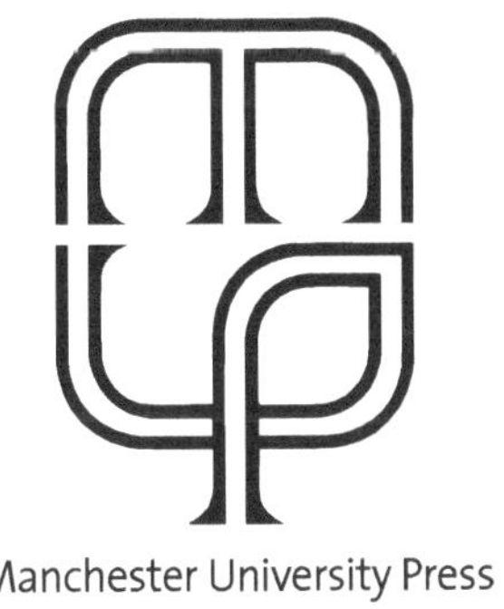

Manchester University Press

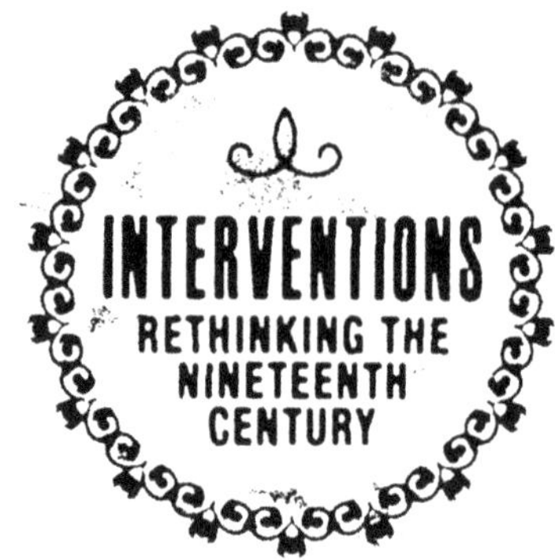

Series editors: Anna Barton, Andrew Smith

Editorial board: David Amigoni, Isobel Armstrong, Philip Holden, Jerome McGann, Joanne Wilkes, Julia M. Wright

Interventions: Rethinking the Nineteenth Century seeks to make a significant intervention into the critical narratives that dominate conventional and established understandings of nineteenth-century literature. Informed by the latest developments in criticism and theory the series provides a focus for how texts from the long nineteenth century, and more recent adaptations of them, revitalise our knowledge of and engagement with the period. It explores the radical possibilities offered by new methods, unexplored contexts and neglected authors and texts to re-map the literary-cultural landscape of the period and rigorously re-imagine its geographical and historical parameters. The series includes monographs, edited collections and scholarly sourcebooks.

Already published

Engine of modernity: The omnibus and urban culture in nineteenth-century Paris	Masha Belenky
Spain in the nineteenth century: New essays on experiences of culture and society	Andrew Ginger and Geraldine Lawless
Instead of modernity: The Western canon and the incorporation of the Hispanic (c.1850–75)	Andrew Ginger
Creating character: Theories of nature and nurture in Victorian sensation fiction	Helena Ifill
Margaret Harkness: Writing social engagement 1880–1921	Flore Janssen and Lisa C. Robertson (eds)
Richard Marsh, popular fiction and literary culture, 1890–1915: Re-reading the fin de siècle	Victoria Margree, Daniel Orrells and Minna Vuohelainen (eds)
Charlotte Brontë: Legacies and afterlives	Amber K. Regis and Deborah Wynne (eds)
The Great Exhibition, 1851: A sourcebook	Jonathon Shears (ed.)
Interventions: Rethinking the nineteenth century	Andrew Smith and Anna Barton (eds)
Counterfactual Romanticism	Damian Walford Davies (ed.)

Marie Duval

Maverick Victorian Cartoonist

Simon Grennan, Roger Sabin
and Julian Waite

Manchester University Press

Published by Manchester University Press
Oxford Road, Manchester M13 9PL
www.manchesteruniversitypress.co.uk

British Library Cataloguing-in-Publication Data
A catalogue record for this book is available from the British Library

ISBN 978 1 5261 3354 0 hardback
ISBN 978 1 5261 7893 0 paperback

First published 2020

The publisher has no responsibility for the persistence or accuracy of URLs for any external or third-party internet websites referred to in this book, and does not guarantee that any content on such websites is, or will remain, accurate or appropriate.

Typeset
by New Best-set Typesetters Ltd

Contents

Contents

Illustrations

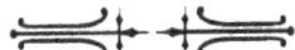

Introduction

Simon Grennan, Roger Sabin, Julian Waite

Her caricatures are full of subtle wit; and as she has been entirely self-taught, she is deserving of a peculiar gratitude, as proving the application of which most women are capable. It is to this power they owe their success. (F. H. (1894) 'Women's Work: Its Value and Possibilities', *The Girls' Own Paper*, Number 27, p. 51)

Marie Duval's life

Marie Duval was best known in her lifetime as one of the principal cartoonists on the weekly periodical *Judy*, the rival and cheaper version of the longer running *Punch*. After her apparent retirement from cartooning, the continued success of the character Ally Sloper, who she drew throughout her career, gave her limited historical fame as the main developer of this late nineteenth-century and early twentieth-century comedy phenomenon. Duval was also an actor, performing in minor productions in London and across the country, and her knowledge of the stage fed into her cartooning on a number of levels. This book aims to investigate Duval's work and put her life in context in so far as the limited historical records of her remarkable career allow.

'Marie Duval' was a pseudonym, and only one of many. Our artist's actual name was Isabella Emily Louisa Tessier, as stated on her birth certificate. She was born on 25 September 1847 at 22 Portman Place, Marylebone, London, daughter of Joseph Achille Tessier, 'Drawing Master', and Mary Adele Tessier, née Louizot (United Kingdom General Register Office Index to Births 1847: 1.156).

By the age of 13, on the date of the 1861 census, Duval was registered as living with her mother, older sister Asselle and father, then described as a 'Professor of French Language', at 52 New Church Street, Marylebone, within half a mile of her birthplace (United Kingdom Census 1861: RG 9/84 f.79 p. 3). Her father died three years later, aged 60, described on his death certificate as a 'Professor of Drawing' (United Kingdom

General Register Office Index to Deaths: 1864 December Quarter, Marylebone Registration District, 1a / 398).

At the age of 17 Duval left a job as a governess to seek work as an actor (Clayton 1876: 330). However, her first known performance was in a tiny role in pantomime at the St James' Theatre in 1868 when she would have been 21 ('The St. James's' 1868: 13).

From the following year, 1869, Duval worked with Charles Henry Ross, novelist, playwright and, from 1869, editor of *Judy, or the London Serio-comic Journal*. She provided Ross with drawings for *Judy* and spin-off publications and performed in several of his plays both in London and on tour, alongside her independent projects and collaborations with other writers, publishers and impresarios.

Aged 23, the 1871 census recorded Isabella as 'Marie Duval', living south of the Thames at 57 Nelson Square, Southwark. The same year we know her to have been having an affair with the married actor Herbert Augustus Such (whose stage name was Augustus Granville), as this led two years later to a divorce reported in national and regional newspapers where Duval is named as the co-respondent ('Theatrical Divorce Case' 1873: 8). The address recorded in the census is indeed that cited in the divorce case of '*Such* vs *Such*' (Margaret Henderson Such vs Herbert Augustus Such) in the official national records (United Kingdom National Archives 4 f.62 p. 23).

It appears that despite this scandal, three years later on 3 December 1874, aged 27, Duval gave birth to a son fathered by *Judy* editor Charles Henry Ross. Her son was also named Charles Henry, and the family appear to have lived at 4 Wycliffe Grove, Battersea (United Kingdom General Register Office Index to Births: March Quarter 1875, Wandsworth Registration District, 1d / 598). Ross was married to Mary Ross, née Atkinson, at the time of his son's birth (the marriage lasted from 1861 until Mary's death in 1876) so it would appear they chose not to divorce even though Ross and Duval were living together (United Kingdom General Register Office Index to Marriages: 1861 June Quarter, St Martin Registry District, 1a / 608). No record of a marriage between Duval and Ross has been found.

Duval died aged 42, on 11 June 1890 at 1 Pensbury, Wandsworth Road, Clapham, of 'Bronchitis and Pneumonia, and Nephritis' (United Kingdom General Register Office Index to Deaths: 1890 June Quarter, Wandsworth Registration District, 1d / 385). Ross senior died on 12 October 1897 at the same address.

Duval was buried, as 'Isabella E. Ross, aged 38', in Wandsworth Cemetery on 17 June 1890, in Grave 13, Plot 13. Ross was buried in the same plot on 18 October 1897. Their headstone survives and carries the epithet to Duval – '… and the music and the laughter ceased and there was silence' (Wandsworth Cemetery Burial Register Index).

This biography – almost all that is known about Duval's personal life – provides only the briefest sketch of the course of her life and work, whilst allowing tantalising glimpses of the realities of a career of hard work, success and failure, pleasure, and perhaps love, in the urban entertainments industries in London in the middle–late nineteenth century.

The online visual archive of her known work, some 1400 drawings made between 1869 and 1885, compiled by the authors as *The Marie Duval Archive* in 2016, adds another cache of information (Grennan, Sabin and Waite 2016). It identifies hitherto unknown work, and thereby offers an idea of her working life (her employers, her collaborators, her drawing styles and the patterns of her productivity: for example, how she rose to become one of *Judy*'s main contributors, and how her Sloper work only accounted for a very small proportion of the whole). To complete a picture of the range and significance of Duval's enterprises, much work has yet to be undertaken, to map comprehensively the details of her stage career onto both her biography and the publication of her drawings.

But we can deduce certain things about how Duval may have been perceived. For example, although she was a significant presence in late nineteenth-century British culture, she was at the same time a marginal figure – both in terms of being transgressive and an outsider. Aside from the scandal of the relationship with Herbert Augustus Such, she was also known for her cross-dressing roles both in Ross's plays and playing the popular melodrama character, highwayman Jack Sheppard. Therefore, she can be described, quite accurately, as a trouser-wearing, French-speaking, home-wrecking mother, and this book shows that in several senses she could also have been described as 'vulgar'. Such a description might provide a minor thrill for twenty-first-century readers, or even scholars, inured to the more extreme transgressions of the 130 years since Duval's death. In her own time, however, this particular mix of characteristics placed her firmly outside the aspirations of most working men and women, which were to attain a conventional respectability. It is possible that she was considered beneath the contempt of the middle classes, because of her promiscuity, her sexualised gender-swapping and her need to earn a living. However, to contrast this, her only biographer, Ellen Clayton, presents a short pen sketch which depicts her as a stylish, clever woman, elegantly dressed in black, who could delight company by her musicianship as 'on hearing almost any piece once, she can sit down and play it by ear' (Clayton 1876: 333).

As remarked, the name Marie Duval was a pseudonym. Duval adopted at least four pseudonyms during her career. Of these Marie Duval was her stage name and she retained it throughout her drawing career. In 1875 she signed a sequence of cartoons with 'Noir'. Many of these were of single female figures in fashionable or historic dress, and are all carefully worked drawings (Duval 1875c). Exclusively for her children's book, *Queens & Kings and Other Things*, she adopted the name 'S.A. The Princess Hesse Schwartzbourg' (Duval 1874b). She also used one male name, 'Ambrose Clarke', which was used for two books: once, as a co-writer for the humorous anthology *Rattletrap Rhymes and Tootletum Tales*, illustrated by Archibald Chasemore and once, as an artist, for a comedic novel penned by Ross entitled *The Story of a Honeymoon* (Clarke and Ross 1876: Duval 1869a).

Pseudonyms were and still are used by artists and performers for a variety of reasons and it is not possible to determine why Duval chose to do so. Reasons for pseudonyms and anonymity are discussed in Chapter 2, relative to Duval as a woman employee, and in Appendix 1. More generally, they included concealing gender (perhaps relevant for Ambrose Clarke and Noir), protecting family and friends from perceived shame, adopting a more memorable or overtly comic name (probably the reason for S.A. The Princess

Hesse Schwartzbourg), or distinguishing oneself from an artist in the same profession with the same name (indeed, British Actors' Equity currently allows actors to register only a stage name which is unique in the union).

Marie Duval's achievement

Duval was one of the most unusual, pioneering and visionary cartoonists of the later nineteenth century. Her work focused on the humour, attitudes, urbanity and poverty of the types of people she knew. These years were, particularly for town and city-dwellers, a period of growing and diversifying leisure activities: working people had more money and more spare time than ever before. It was an era of bank holidays, hobbies, music hall and organised sport.

Duval's positioning in this milieu was complex. Coming back to the issue of her outsider status, we can say that she was marginal in the way that the entertainments industries were marginal, because they commoditised, presented and sold transgressive sensations in a larger social environment where transgression was almost always personally and professionally disastrous. Both men and women in these industries constantly negotiated the boundaries between sensation, sales, social disapprobation and the law, although in different ways determined by gender, degrees of class and professional success and failure. As for Duval's personal life, for entertainers, whose permissiveness was socially licensed within the boundaries of their professions, adultery might no doubt be shameful in a man, whereas a woman behaving as Duval behaved could seriously be considered reckless and dangerous, to herself, to others and, if not monitored, to the fabric of society.

However, this book argues that Duval's work, for *Judy* in particular, distributed marginalised ideas (such as a woman employing masculine humour, or feminising employment in the print industries), to a wide, eager and heterogenous readership, thereby increasingly rendering these ideas and types of behaviour unremarkable, habitual and quotidian. She was part of a feedback loop, and therefore constructed the culture as much as transmitting it.

The keenness of *Judy* readers to consume the types of copy that it offered, indexed by the long trading period of the journal, lay in the fact that they belonged to, aspired to belong to or fantasised about belonging to, the social world that journalists such as Duval visualised. In turn, the daily experiences of readers were increasingly impacted by ideas and behaviour from the urban leisure and entertainments industries and so these ideas became normalised.

There is a class dimension to this. It is a commonplace to note that the readers of a periodical reflect or aspire to the condition of the periodical's producers. References made in this book to nineteenth-century debates about topics directly related to Duval's life and work derive largely from sources in middle-class papers and journals. In particular, in seeking to discover aspects of the debates about middle-class women's unemployment (focused by the results of the 1851 census, which listed such details), it appears that Victorian middle-class commentators largely set aside the contingencies of class to focus on the contingencies of gender. These commentaries overlooked the significance of a class of readers who were unlike the commentaries' authors and unlike the readers of their publications, rendering this other, working, class invisible in middle-class debates.

This book has been mindful of this oversight, seeking to consider alternative arguments in nineteenth-century discourse about the relationship between women, class and work, the significance of professional training or concepts of the ethics of the performance of masculinity and femininity.

Duval's drawings provide one source for such arguments. In this context, it is important to note that her work and the phenomenon of cheaper periodicals such as *Judy* and *Fun*, continue to be overlooked by the vast majority of twentieth- and twenty-first-century commentators and scholars, compared with the proliferation of commentary and scholarship on solidly middle-class periodical papers such as *Punch*. Thus, whereas Leech, Doyle and Tenniel, for example, continue to be republished, thereby perpetuating the canon, other cartoonists are still ignored.

Happily, this is starting to change (Scully 2018). Yet Duval's work remains under the radar, with the exception of fragmentary commentaries and a single scholarly article (Kunzle 1986). No survey of the whole of Duval's work has thus far been made, and estimates of the number of works have been in the low hundreds. Her work merits no more than mentions, or is more often completely absent from surveys of nineteenth-century illustrators, with the exception of Clayton's *English Female Artists* (Easley, King and Morton 2017; Bury 2012; Barr 1986; Houfe 1981; De Maré 1980; Clayton 1876).

The Marie Duval Archive was one way for us to address this gap. It brought together all of Duval's known output in one place, and started a conversation. On one level, it identifies drawings by Duval that have remained unidentified since publication. On another, as a new online database of images, it represents a methodology – an approach. Academics and members of the public are now able to access Duval's work (for free) and via its customised system are able to utilise it in a way that is unlike an experience of her work in *Judy*, today and in the nineteenth century. This is where fresh lines of analysis can begin, and the canon can start to be re-shaped (Grennan 2018; Scully 2018: 28; Kunzle 2019).

Our own work since the genesis of *The Archive* has been calculatedly interdisciplinary. If it has a 'core' field, then it is Comics Studies (and that is where we expect the most interest). But by necessity it has had to reach out to theatre studies, Victorian periodical studies, children's literature studies, women's studies, fashion studies, and more. This perspective has anchored our general audience book *Marie Duval* (2018), the exhibition *Marie Duval: Laughter in the First Age of Leisure* (that has toured to Berlin, London and New York) and academic papers, chapters in other books, popular articles, podcasts and lectures (see bibliography). We acknowledge that interdisciplinarity can sometimes be prone to not doing justice to every field and discipline, and naturally we welcome further research to thicken our account.

This book is another step in the process of Duval's rediscovery. It discusses key themes and practices of her vision and production, relative to the wider historic social, cultural and economic milieu in which her work was made, distributed and read. To summarise: Duval imported the licensed improprieties of the stage onto the periodical page, an aspect of which was her strategic visualising of the vulgarity of her readers and audiences. She utilised masculine humour and feminised concepts of employment. She worked by adopting the roles of both fictional men and women (paralleling her adoption of male roles) to create opportunities for employment as a visual journalist.

As a result, the book identifies Duval as an exemplary radical practitioner in a historic urban media environment, in which new professional definitions were being created for the first time, in terms of the gendering of professions, professional training and consensus, and the theorising of the roles of visual cultures, and in which new congruence between different types of media culture emerged, including performance, illustration, narrative drawing, periodicals and novels. Her success in these endeavours makes her unique.

The structure of this book

The book is divided into two parts, headed Work (five chapters) and Depicting and performing (four chapters) with two appendices discussing attribution and terminology. In the first part the authors investigate Duval in her context, giving an overview of aspects of the industries in which she worked and how she might have fitted within these industries. In the second part Duval's achievement takes centre stage, with considerations of her drawings and their importance.

In Part I, Work, the first chapter, 'Finding a voice at *Judy*', introduces the magazine, which was Duval's primary site of publication, and her place within it. Themes that emerge affecting her work relate to the serial publication of the magazine and its political orientation, and the way in which Duval's work was juxtaposed with the contributions of others, notably the cartoonist of the main 'cut' (the illustration with the highest status), William Boucher. The chapter emphasises the innovative nature not only of *Judy* but also of Duval's role within the magazine and, by extension, her role in developing cartooning itself.

Chapter 2, 'Duval and the woman employee', considers how Duval subverted the established nineteenth-century idea that employment was masculine and brutalising, by inhabiting and then manipulating the gap between supported middle-class women and working-class female manual and service workers. It suggests her stage career allowed her to develop complex metaphors in print, highlighting the mutability of gender and significance of clothing. Duval emerges as a *flâneuse* wandering through the pages of some of the most popular publications of her time.

Chapter 3, 'Marie Duval's theatre career and its impact on her drawings', traces Duval's stage performances from pantomimes to romantic dramas and burlesque, using the sparse available evidence, and relates known events in her life to specific drawings she made. Her highs and lows in Ross productions, and her use of stock characters, were inspirations for her *Judy* strips and cartoons, though less than 5 per cent are explicitly theatre-based.

Chapter 4 examines Duval's only children's book, *Queens & Kings and Other Things*, with particular reference to its relationship with Edward Lear's nonsense verse, other influences on its content and its contemporary reception. The book's lavish production values gesture to a high point in her career, and its mode of address to her willingness to experiment.

Chapter 5 concludes the section on work with an analysis of the nature of the journalistic workplace Duval found herself in. 'Marie Duval and the technologies of periodical publishing' considers the processes of periodical publishing in general and focuses on wood block engraving technology and the role of the journalist in the publishing industry in particular. This allows for reflections on the significance of gender and class in nineteenth-century employment.

Chapter 6 begins Part II, 'Depicting and performing', by considering 'The significance of Duval's drawing style', describing some of the conditions in which Duval's drawings were produced and read. It navigates her contemporaries who had a critical stance on her work despite its clear popular appeal, defining her work in a very subtle way as 'vulgar'. The chapter goes on to demonstrate the complex nature of Duval's comic achievement, through a close examination of her parodies of various artworks displayed at the Royal Academy Summer Exhibitions of 1880 and 1876.

In Chapter 7, 'The relationship between performance and drawing: suggestive synaesthesia in Marie Duval's work', the reader is introduced to the influences that may have impinged on Duval as an actor and therefore informed her drawing, including nineteenth-century performance theory and rehearsal practices as revealed through contemporary actor diaries. The chapter concludes with some thoughts on how Duval's apparently spontaneous style may relate to current notions of drawing as performance.

Chapter 8, 'The role of spectacle in Marie Duval's work', continues to examine the theatre influence on Duval's output, by noticing models other than academic drawing arising from the visual tropes of theatre spectacle. Examples of stage mechanics and human athleticism are explored for clues to her depiction of movement and novelty.

The final chapter, 'A women's cartoonist?', considers Duval's role in the developing canon of women artists and writers, and her connections with 'serio-comic' modes of female performance. An extensive survey of her strips and cartoons reveals indications of her attitudes to gender and politics, initiating a discussion of her work as potentially proto-feminist.

Acknowledgements

If our search for Duval has been difficult, it could have been more so without the pioneering efforts of many historians. Ellen Clayton's assessment of Duval's career in *English Female Artists* (1876) included Duval in a lineage that included the main female artists in history (according to Clayton) and set down a marker. Denis Gifford's championing of Ally Sloper in the 1970s brought Duval into view once more. His 1971 essay 'The Evolution of the British Comic' was an early intervention into the academy. David Kunzle's important essay about Duval (1986) was a detailed analysis of her Sloper work, and was followed by his seminal history of comics in the nineteenth century (1990) in which Duval is also featured. John Adcock's groundbreaking blog, *Yesterday's Papers* (2010), has ably demonstrated how the Internet can function as a hub for continually updated research, and which (at the time of writing) includes information about Duval and entries on Ross and *Judy*.

Other texts that have been particularly useful include, in no particular order: Beetham (1996); Campbell (2000); Balliet (2007); Campbell Orr (1995); Greenwood (2015); Epstein Nord (1995); Van Remoortel (2015); Fraser, Green and Johnson (2003); Brake, Bell and Finkelstein (2000); Brake and Demoor (2009); Macleod (1996); Richards (2014); Cherry (1996); Demoor (2000); Parsons (2000); Zakreski (2013); Flood (2013); Hall (2019); Easley, King and Morton (2017); Maidment (2017 – special thanks); Hadjiafxendi and Zakreski (2013); Leary (2010); Ledger (1997); Sutliff Sanders (2013 – special thanks); Scully (2018); Tusan (2004); Bailey (1986, 1998); Beale (2018); Smolderen (2014); Davis and Emeljanow (2001); Taylor (1989); Davis (1991). Finally, the scholarly networks for Comics Studies and nineteenth-century periodicals studies have been a constant source of support and inspiration.

Part I

Work

1

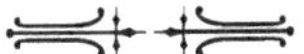

Finding a voice at *Judy*

Roger Sabin

Judy magazine (or *Judy, or the London Serio-comic Journal*, to give it its full name) occupies a central space in the Duval story. The vast majority of her output is to be found here, as collected on *The Marie Duval Archive* (Grennan, Sabin and Waite 2016). This work consists of strips, cartoons and illustrations, sometimes clearly signed, often not, and occasionally under another pseudonym, 'Noir'. She stayed from 1869 to 1885, and during her most productive time, 1874–77, was generating over 100 contributions a year – a staggering number. By dint of her work on the continuing character Ally Sloper, a working-class ne'er-do-well, she was the magazine's most prominent, and most popular, contributor.

This chapter functions to introduce *Judy*, and Duval's place within it. It explores how her work was shaped by its context in a serial publication, and raises questions about industrial conditions, her implied readership and how she negotiated the magazine's political orientation. It also throws into relief the difference between Duval's work and prevailing illustrational styles, and ultimately how her output can be seen as a riposte to an entire cartooning tradition. One subsidiary theme of the chapter is how *Judy* has been misunderstood: often dismissed as a low-level *Punch* clone, it was, in fact, innovative and often pioneering. Duval's contribution was central to this. If she was a maverick, she was a maverick in a maverick publication.[1]

Judy was founded in 1867 as a rival to *Punch*, the juxtaposition suggesting a reference to the ancient 'Punch and Judy' puppet show, but also hinting at the possibility of female-oriented content. It included a mix of prose, verse, news, reviews, jokes, celebrity portraits, cartoons, strips, illustrations, readers' letters, competitions and adverts (though in differing proportions at different points in time). Its most famous character was Ally Sloper, followed closely by Judy herself, the putative 'editor' of the magazine, whom (like Mr Punch at his magazine) readers were encouraged to think of as 'real'. It was a weekly publication, with twelve pages, in black and white, and sold for twopence, which was a penny less than *Punch*. Over time, it would generate cheap spin-off almanacs, annuals and a line of book-format volumes, which sold for one shilling (Adcock 2010a).

The magazine lasted until 1907, and in the period that Duval was there (1869–85) boasted a more-than-solid array of contributors, including cartoonists like William Boucher, Archibald Chasemore, Adelaide Claxton, Percy Cruikshank (nephew of George, who signed 'George Cruikshank Junior'), Alfred Bryan, James Brown and Hablot Knight Browne ('Phiz'). The writers were less high profile, but included Walter Parke, Clotilde Graves and Arthur Pask.[2] The editor from 1869 to 1887 was Charles Henry Ross, who also contributed writing, strips and cartoons. The owners from 1872 to 1888 were the Dalziel Brothers, a famous company of publishers/engravers.[3] Printing was undertaken in a variety of London locations, and the cartoonists would have used the traditional style of drawing directly onto wood blocks, or having their paper sketches transferred to the blocks, which were then carved into relief by a team of engravers.[4]

Judy was one of many *Punch*-like publications, with others including *Fun*, *Tomahawk* and *Will-o'-the-Wisp*. Although these competitors included some regional examples, the most prominent tended to be published within a mile of each other, in or around Fleet Street, London. *Judy* was no exception, with an address at 99 Shoe Lane. In terms of a hierarchy of publications, *Punch* was always regarded by critics as being superior, possibly because it was perceived as attracting readers from a higher social class. *Judy* and *Fun*, for their part, pictured themselves as part of the 'Big Three', and better than the other *Punch* rivals, though this may have been wishful thinking.[5] With this level of competition, the attrition rate was severe. In 1872, *Judy* included a news item gloating that 'out of ten papers of a humorous character launched in 1867 [i.e. just in that year], only *Judy* survives' (Untitled 1872).

This, then, was the 'satire boom', and indicated a huge appetite among the British public for politically aware comedy, now available in cheap publications due both to improving printing technology, and to the repeal of the taxes on paper and the stamp duty that had hitherto kept the price of publishing high (all the *Punch* rivals were priced between a penny and twopence). This boom was in turn part of a larger explosion in publishing generally, which straddled newspapers (local and national), magazines of all kinds (cheap weeklies to glossy monthlies and illustrated serials) and books. Rising literacy rates were part of this bigger picture, spurred by the Education Act of 1870, and the boom was inevitably met with debate about where it would all lead, especially regarding the political ramifications of reading among the lower classes (Waters 1990).

Judy sold well. No ledgers exist, but circulation can be estimated to have been between 20,000 and 40,000. (By comparison, during the 1860s, *Punch* was selling 40,000, rising to 65,000 in the 1870s).[6] Sales are not the same as readership, because the 'pass around' figure of people who actually read each issue would have been much higher. With this in mind, we can reasonably say that *Judy* was a significant presence in the cultural life of the country. As Richard Scully adds, the fact that several *Punch* rivals 'commanded significant readerships [...] occasioned some concern around the *Punch* table' (Scully 2018: Volume 2, 3).

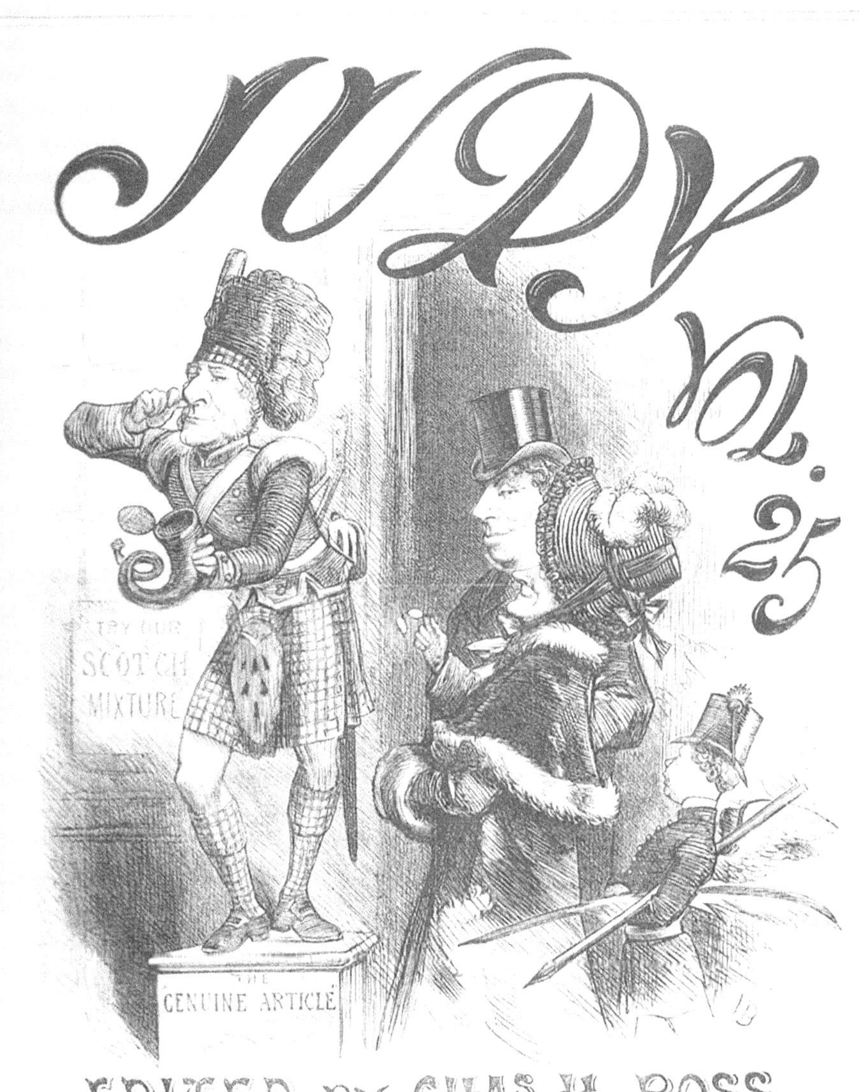

1.1   William Boucher (1879) 'Judy Volume 25', *Judy, or the London Serio-comic Journal* Volume 25, frontispiece. Judy walks arm-in-arm with Disraeli.

Selling was via subscription (making best use of the newly energised postal service), the newsagent circuit (including rail kiosks) and street vendors (a growing army of, typically, boys). Sometimes *Judy* was traded to be made available in libraries, hotels and clubs. Advertising became more important to the business model over time, as competition increased, and issues would appear in an 'advertising sheet' (i.e. a wrapper dominated by advertisements). Soap companies, tobacco firms and certain food suppliers became big investors, sometimes managed by new advertising agencies. The spin-off *Judy* books also made it into bookstores, and similarly carried advertisements.

Readers spanned a large demographic band, predominantly middle class to begin with, but with a significant lower-middle class readership as time went on (this was a class that was expanding in the last decades of the century, with the growth of the suburbs and new kinds of urban employment), and also large numbers of working-class readers. Women formed a growing proportion of all these categories, as evidenced by the kinds of advertisements that were appearing, and also the type of content (see Chapter 9). The age range for the magazine would have been teenage and above, but more juvenile readers would have enjoyed the slapstick material, and especially Sloper.

Regarding the middle class, it is clear that much of *Judy*'s content was oriented towards an educated, politics-savvy elite: for example, the news reports it was responding to came from *The Times* and the *Daily Telegraph* (and were often cited). There was also comment on urban middle-class business life (for example, the Stock Exchange) and cultural life (such as opera performances), and it was read by such bourgeois celebrities as Lewis Carroll, William Morris and even William Gladstone.[7] As the lower-middle class hove more into view at the end of the 1870s and into the 1880s, so *Judy* increasingly positioned itself as a 'commuter publication', with commentary more oriented towards this group (for example, on suburban architecture, bicycle clubs and commuting itself, with the new underground 'tube' line being an object of particular fascination).[8]

Judy's working-class readership is sometimes ignored by historians, probably on the assumption that the price, at twopence, would have put it out of their reach (this was a penny more than a 'dreadful', supposedly their literature of choice).[9] However, *Judy* circulated in non-obvious ways that were widely accessible – just like every similar publication. For example, it would have been available to read for free when discarded in cafes, pubs and railway carriages, and back issues could be picked up very cheaply, either from newsagents who sold them at a discount, or from street sellers who bundled up copies of various journals and sold them together for a penny. The other barrier to working-class readers has often been assumed to be the presence of large blocks of dense text. However, historians now recognise that literacy rates among this class were high even before the legislation of 1870; besides which, strips and cartoons could often be followed without reading the words, and there was a culture of reading aloud (Hobbs 2016: 227).

Judy's brand was built around the idea of the 'serio-comic', as signalled in its subtitle. It was a phrase that was amorphous enough to mean just about anything, and was 'all the rage', as issue 1 put it ('Judy's Opening Speech' 1867). Clearly, the main intended interpretation was that the magazine would cover both serious subjects – high politics, foreign affairs, the issues of the day – in the form of 'traditional' *Punch*-style satire, while at the same time offering 'non-serious' subject matter (fashion, sport, hobbies), often in a more lightweight form, in the guise of witty stories, comic verse, jokes, cartoons and strips. One would balance the other (and, by extension, Duval's role would be in the latter capacity). There was another meaning to 'serio-comic', however, which we will get to in Chapter 9.

This formula, by necessity, had to stay within particular boundaries of taste. These shifted over time, but were generally constructed as being 'respectful' and 'gentle', and in some ways a reaction against the 'coarseness' of the print tradition. The sort of images of abjection, and sometimes explicit sex and violence, that were to be found in the Gillray era, had no place in the new epoch of the satire magazines. Similarly, the magazine boom, because of its ability to penetrate the home so effectively, was sometimes classed as 'family entertainment', though how far this was true is debatable.[10]

Judy's content was therefore divided between politics and culture (which did not necessarily directly map onto 'serio' and 'comic', though a breezier style was used for cultural stories). In both cases, *Judy* capitalised on its positioning as a London magazine, and the affairs of Westminster were as prominent as the affairs of the Drury Lane Theatre. The word 'London' in its subtitle was a signifier in the same way as *The Illustrated London News* used the word, or as *Punch* styled itself *The London Charivari*. Why this mattered was obvious: the capital was the largest city in the world, the centre of the mightiest empire ever seen, and home to arguably the most sophisticated entertainment culture anywhere. It was both a power city and a party city, and *Judy* would gleefully exploit its access to both.

Taking politics first, *Judy* was proud to be 'Conservative – of the truest and bluest' ('Judy's Opening Speech' 1867.). This did not mean aligning itself with the ruling class, however, because Conservatism had recently been redefined to incorporate a much more inclusive vision (if not 'class-less' then at least more in tune with democracy and the welfare of the lower classes). *Judy* toed a careful line, which was consonant with new political realities. In 1867, the year of its founding, the second Reform Bill ushered in new voting categories, and thereby bestowed significant power on large sections of the male working classes. Conservative leader Benjamin Disraeli, who became a *Judy* hero, continued this direction, and his second government (1874–80) enacted reforms that were pro-working class in terms of housing, health and workers' rights. In the *1876 Judy Almanack*, a cartoon pictured Conservatism as representing 'Peace and Plenty', contrasted with Liberalism ('Doubt and Discord …') and Communism ('Theft and Murder …') (Untitled 1876).

Within this political frame, *Judy* could be hard-line on particular issues. This went for Ireland, especially (meaning the disestablishment of the Irish Church, Irish Home Rule and the rise in nationalist violence), and involved concurring with fashionable pseudo-science about the inferiority of the Irish people: Disraeli had described them as 'a wild […] race with no sympathy for the English character' (quoted in Blake 1960: 152). Indeed, ape-like caricatures of the Irish became something of a *Judy* specialism.

Similarly, on matters outside the United Kingdom, it took pro-imperialism to extreme levels, cheering Victoria's wars as proof of the invincibility of her military might, and of true born Britons' right to rule the globe (the country was at war for every year of her reign bar four).

Where this political orientation placed *Judy* in relation to her competitor publications is debatable. Certainly, it was more extreme than *Punch*, which was going through a conservative phase after its radical beginnings. Other publications spanned a spectrum, though generally this meant shades of blue: for example, *Will-o'-the-Wisp* was hardcore and occasionally matched *Judy* for viciousness on Ireland, while *Tomahawk* traded in a softer Toryism (despite its title signifying the 'scalping of politicians'). *Fun*, on the other hand, was Liberal, veering on radical at times, though it still found space to praise Disraeli on occasion.

Of course, such political stances exist within a system, and all these magazines were first and foremost commodities, inextricably bound up with capitalism. As their business models moved further from an emphasis on sales to 'delivering eyeballs to the ads', so this relationship was reinforced. Thus, *Judy* and most others were further incentivised to deem consumerism an unquestioned good, applaud captains of industry (especially if they happened to be advertisers), approve of government moves to expedite profit-making, and deride socialism.

Turning to *Judy*'s coverage of cultural matters, this too was political by its very nature, and took a position on the explosion of leisure that characterised the last few decades of the century.[11] In particular, middle- and working-class people had more disposable income, and more time to themselves (typified by the Bank Holidays Act of 1871, and the fact that the 'half-holiday' on a Saturday was becoming more widespread). Alongside cheap publishing, the music hall circuit expanded dramatically, trips to the seaside became much more of a feature of British life, the habit of smoking became ubiquitous and organised sport became established (many of the great football clubs date their origin to this period). This phenomenon became a cause of concern to some (middle-class) commentators, including at *Judy*, who asked whether leisure should be in the service of self-improvement or entertainment, a binary which unwittingly reflected upon the tension at the very centre of *Judy*'s serio-comic formula.

As for specific cultural forms, *Judy*'s forte was coverage of the theatre – meaning, inevitably, the London theatre. This spanned the more middle-class West End productions, but also less respectable light theatre and music hall, with special attention given to pantomimes (which could stretch from November to Easter). Reviews, previews, portraits of performers and gossip all served to offer critique of performance as an art form; such reportage was meant to be enjoyable in its own right, as opposed to functioning as a consumer guide (that is, to spur the reader to buy a ticket or not). Along the way, the careers of performers and impresarios were credentialised, as was the idea of the 'cultural critic'.

Elsewhere, *Judy* covered the new holiday culture, and especially the phenomenon of the 'tripper' (especially in the summer break). As the railways expanded and opened up the country, so the working class were able to afford trips out to the countryside, the races or the seaside. The middle class, and emerging lower-middle class, joined in, but on their own terms; for example, not all seaside resorts were the same, and there was a world of difference between genteel Bournemouth and downmarket Southend. (Similarly, getting there meant segregation by dint of first-, second- and third-class train tickets.) *Judy* tended to elide the worst excesses of tripper culture, such as binge drinking, in favour of more anodyne comment on promenading and bathing.

Other leisure coverage included sports, which also had a definite class character. For example, hunting was obviously for the wealthy, bicycle clubs had a lower-middle-class aura and football was increasingly for the lower classes. Perhaps the dominant *Judy* perspective on sport was as spectacle for trippers: that is, how big fixtures functioned as 'outings', and as a place for the classes to mix. Thus, Derby Day and the Boat Race provided opportunities for cartoonists to depict punters dressed up for the occasion, flirting with each other, and generally not paying much attention to the sport itself. Later, the start of the rugby, cricket and football seasons was the cue for satire (for example, football as legitimised hooliganism) and for portraits of celebrity players (with cricketer W. G. Grace the greatest celebrity of all).

Then there was leisure in terms of art and literature. *Judy* included reviews of both, ranging from short consumer guides to longer 'think-pieces'. The publication of a new poem by the Laureate, or a novel from a top writer, was a newsworthy moment, and was often accompanied by a portrait. The big art event in the cultural calendar was the Royal Academy Summer Exhibition, a jamboree attended by all classes, which was covered with a mix of reverence and sarcasm, an attitude partly informed by the fact that some *Judy* cartoonists themselves were exhibitors.[12] (For more on relationships to the art world, see Chapter 6.)

This, in essence, comprised the serio-comic mix. But it needed to be organised coherently, and this was achieved in two interlinked ways: by capitalising on seriality and by careful design. In terms of the former, the entire *Judy* product was geared towards creating expectations among readers, essentially so that they would buy the next issue. It consciously strove to garner a loyal following, and this was crucial to its survival in a crowded field. Continuing characters were useful in this regard: there was Sloper, of course, but also Duval's 'Waddimans' and 'Doveturtles', two pairs of lower-middle-class newlyweds (see Figure 1.2); Archibald Chasemore's 'Lunatic Contributor', an upper-class twit with a conical head and pointed nose; and James Brown's hugely popular (and rare non-London character) 'The McNab', a whisky-fuelled Scotsman prone to bouts of fury. The other continuing character, always there, always guiding things, was Judy: she would write the editorials and respond to letters, make guest appearances in strips and stories, and dominate the advertising (more about her in Chapters 5 and 9).

Seriality also meant following the calendar, or, rather, 'the *Judy* calendar' of dates that were deemed important enough to riff upon. Thus, as well as gentle comment on the passing of the seasons, there would be Valentine's Day, the summer break, 5 November (Guy Fawkes Night), Christmas, and, as mentioned, race days, sports season openings,

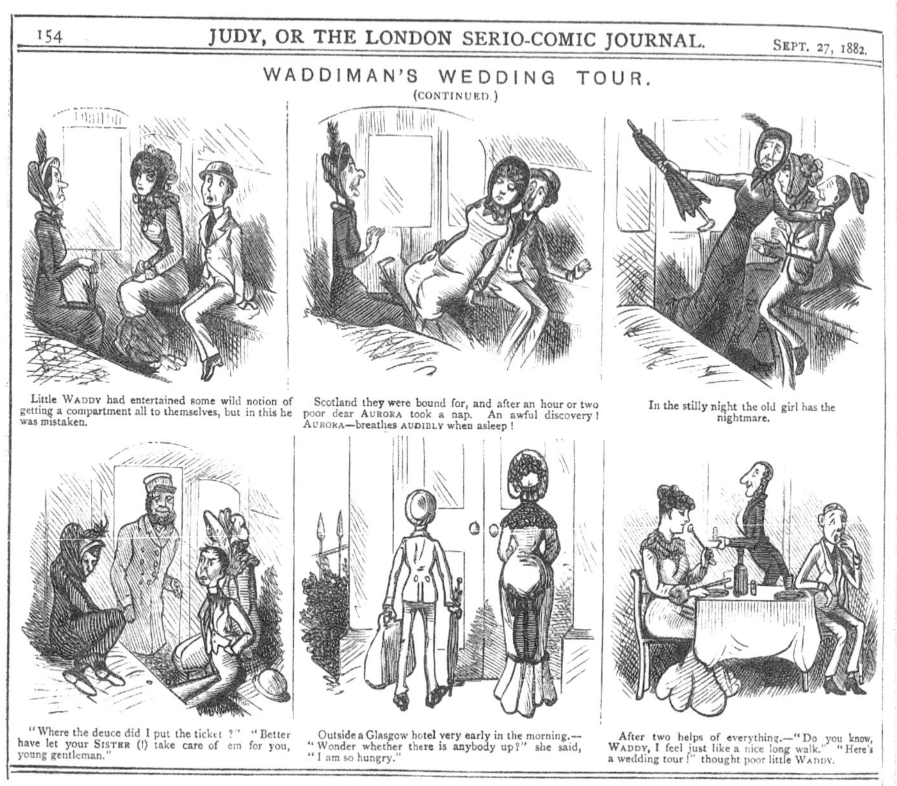

1.2   Marie Duval (1882) 'Waddiman's Wedding Tour (Continued)', *Judy, or the London Serio-comic Journal*, Volume 30, p. 154

the Royal Academy Summer Exhibition and so on. This all gave the magazine a rhythm that kept it in step with readers' lives, and a formula that was both comforting and that could be anticipated. It also meant that *Judy* writers and artists could plan in advance, with advertising arranged for the relevant issues (with Christmas becoming a consumer jamboree). All the satirical magazines followed this basic template.

The coverage of topical events would therefore have to find its place in this cycle, and be dealt with spontaneously. Commonly, the main 'cut' signalled the angle (the editorial point of view), and *Judy* included some remarkable reportage, involving, for example, Livingstone's expedition, the death of Dickens and the advent of electric lighting (as well as Ireland and the imperial wars). If a story had 'legs' (that is, if it continued to arouse reader interest), it would be followed over several consecutive weeks, sometimes with Judy herself passing opinion. By the late 1870s *Judy* was including a diary of news entitled 'Our Weekly One' (with cartoons by Chasemore).

The design of the magazine finessed these imperatives. Although it borrowed much from *Punch* (the grid system, typeface and general branding were largely indistinguishable) and was mostly dictated by available technology, it did innovate in certain regards. Notably, this included the routine nature of the double-page spread devoted to the main cut, by Boucher (even *Punch* used double-page spreads sparingly, chiefly for special occasions). The placement of individual items tended to be subservient to this main visual event. To generalise from a browse of issues from 1876, we can say that Judy's comment (if she made one) would be on page 1; the regular column of theatre reviews (by 'The Only Jones') would be around page 2; the main cut would be on pages 4 and 5; Sloper would be somewhere around page 9; and the adverts would be on the back page and on the wrapper/sleeve.

Such magazine design in general had benefits beyond the purely organisational, and related to sensory pleasures. For example, readers could 'feel' their way through the publication, working out 'how many pages in' they had got, and whether they had reached their favourite feature. This was all part of the experience, as was the smell of the paper and ink. This may sound like a minor point, but to divorce any contributor's work from such a context leaves it 'un-anchored': as periodical theorists are coming to recognise, a magazine constitutes a specific material vehicle, with all the potentialities and limitations that entails.[13]

Before moving on to Duval, it is necessary to say a little more about the other producers of *Judy*. Although most of the material in the magazine was anonymous, some star contributors were foregrounded, and this went for Ross, Boucher, Chasemore, Phiz and Cruikshank in particular. (Duval was also elevated, but sometimes in oblique ways.) Although specific employment arrangements are unknown, surviving letters and circumstantial evidence suggest that most work would have been freelance, but with retainers for valued individuals.[14] It is also clear that contributors supplemented their income by working for other employers, simultaneously producing, among other things, prose and illustrations for books and other journals, theatre plays and pantomimes, designs for performance costumes and scenery, and gags for music hall performers.

Of all the creatives at *Judy*, the cartoonist William Boucher had the highest status. He produced its main cut, and was touted as the magazine's equivalent of John Tenniel at *Punch* (other satirical journals had their own stars, for example Matt Morgan at *Tomahawk*). Boucher's mode was high political satire, and his double-page spread was the marker of his standing. In one way he was conventional in the sense that he was a highly trained illustrator, trading in a style that was detailed and realistic, and utilising all the visual metaphors of the day: his cartoons include stock figures such as Britannia and John Bull, alongside traditional religious imagery (doves, snakes), and portray countries and powers as animals – Germany as an eagle, Russia as a bear and the British Empire as a lion. But in another sense he was a maverick himself, owing to the extremity of his views: he was evidently allowed to say pretty much what he liked, and took *Judy*'s 'truest and bluest' ideology to its edge. Boucher's anti-Irish material was notably vicious, he drew Zulu king Cetshwayo as a vile savage with a bone through his nose and he turned unfriendly European heads of state into bloodthirsty monsters. (Indeed, a Boucher cartoon ended up being the subject of a libel case, in 1883.) We return to him for a case study at the end of this chapter.

Judy's best-known editor was the aforementioned Ross, who took over in 1869 (Adcock 2010b). He was a former civil servant who had always supplemented his income by other means, including writing plays, pantomimes, penny dreadfuls, theatre criticism, novels and even sermons. He continued to juggle jobs after he took over at *Judy*. He was also a cartoonist, greatly influenced by Cruikshank, and had contributed illustrations, cartoons and strips to a variety of publications. He cultivated a (not altogether fanciful) image of himself as a Renaissance man, and became known as a bohemian. Why *Judy* took him on is unknown, but it is certain that he had no previous magazine editing experience, thereby adding to the argument that *Judy* was a somewhat maverick publication. His tenure there was marked by an editorial style that was strikingly hands-on compared to his counterparts on other magazines, and he contributed columns and cartoons on a weekly basis. He was particularly known for his 'Only Jones' theatre reviews, but his masterstroke was to invent Ally Sloper.

Judy was initially owned and published by William Spencer Johnson, who may also have taken the role of the first editor (never named); and then by the Dalziel Brothers, the celebrated family of engravers and publishers, who bought it in 1872. The Dalziels were known for collaborating with some of the great artists of the day (including members of the Pre-Raphaelite Brotherhood), and having established their own printing works, the Camden Press, were able to commission their own books. As illustrated books had moved into their 'golden age' in the 1860s, so the Dalziels were at the forefront (see Chapter 4). Their subsequent move into journals was a sign of their success and eagerness to diversify. They owned *Fun* as well as *Judy* (meaning that they collectively owned more market share than the *Punch* proprietors), and they cannily played them off against each other (their politics contrasted, as we have seen). In 1872, a Dalziel nephew, Gilbert, was installed as 'Conductor' of *Judy*. Gilbert was only 19 years old at the time. His relationship with Ross was allegedly fraught.[15]

Judy's other 'producers' included those on the 'mechanical' side, for example engravers and printers. These were top quality professionals, but never name-checked. The engravers often worked in dismal conditions in various sites in London, and although their relationship with the cartoonists is not clear, it is unlikely they knew them personally. (It should be noted that thanks to the work of researchers like Bethan Stevens, we are now beginning to understand engraving as being 'artistic' as well as mechanical.)[16] Individual printers were also anonymous, but the listing in each issue tells us that a number of companies were involved – Nassau Press, then Woodfall and Kinder (based in The Strand, near Fleet Street), and then the Dalziels' Camden Press. Photomechanical techniques were taken up in the 1880s, and even then, traditional wood-block methods endured (for more on the business of periodical publishing, see Chapter 5).

So how did Duval fit in? It has taken us a long while to get to that question, but hopefully we can see immediately that she belonged to a '*Judy* system'. She had to work to its rhythm, adhere to its taste standards, negotiate its politics, respect its technology and, above all, acknowledge her place within commodity culture and the need for her to be entertaining, week after week, in order to attract readers. The parameters of the magazine were also hers. The fact that Duval minded those parameters over such a long period indicates a high level of professionalism, and underpins her position as one of the journal's chief contributors, and arguably its main cartoonist. The following paragraphs are intended to highlight Duval as '*Judy* employee' without pre-empting other chapters in the book.

Her start at the magazine in 1869 is slightly hazy. Chronology suggests that she was hired before Ross became editor, possibly by William Spencer Johnson, the proprietor.[17] Her first signed drawing appeared in March 1869, and Ross took over in October of that year. Although Duval and Ross became life partners, it is impossible to say if, by this time, Ross was already having an affair with her (the only definite evidence of a romantic engagement is the birth of their son in 1874). Doubtless they met through theatrical connections: as a leading theatre critic, Ross would have known her as an actor, and she ended up acting in several of his theatrical productions (indeed, she was appearing in his plays in the early 1870s, while cartooning for *Judy*). In terms of knowing her as a cartoonist, Ross was a fan of her drawing, and, in a letter to another magazine ('Letter to the Editor' 1869b),[18] referred to her as an artist and a better cartoonist than he. Once he became editor of *Judy*, her position was made all the more secure.

In these early days, *Judy* was not Duval's only 'gig'. As well as acting, she contributed (unsigned) strips and illustrations to *Will-o'-the-Wisp* through 1869, and illustrated a humorous booklet about fashion, *Smiles and Styles* (1870a). Later, when she had acquired more of a reputation, she would produce a children's book, *Queens & Kings and Other Things* (1874b) – see Chapter 4 – co-write the humorous anthology *Rattletrap and Tootletum* (Clarke and Ross), and illustrate a comedic novel by Ross, *The Story of a Honeymoon* (Duval 1869a).[19] It is important to mention these other endeavours because they indicate that Duval, like her fellow practitioners, was part of the Victorian swirl of hustling and entrepreneurship. If you had a skill, you used it.

How helpful was Ross's patronage to Duval's career? We would have to conclude, very; even if he was the not the person who initially hired her at *Judy*, we can speculate that he sustained her career once she got there. Aside from being a fan and possible lover, there were likely other reasons: there is now a body of academic literature about how women in the nineteenth century, with ambitions in a job, used networks and connections among male colleagues to give themselves an advantage, and about how men exploited that situation for economic gain and to make themselves look good: for example, 'to make implicit cultural statements about their own relationship to the modern age', according to Stetz (2001: 276).

Even if Ross and Duval were not romantically involved before 1874, they were certainly professionally involved, both in an editor–contributor relationship, and as sometime co-creators of *Judy* content. At some point, they made a home together, and, so far as can be ascertained, lived happily in south London for the rest of their lives. The likelihood is that they were never married. Did this relationship mean that Duval was any nearer the levers of power at *Judy*? On one level, obviously yes, but she was probably excluded from editorial decision-making (see Chapter 9).

Ross's support was doubly important because Duval was an 'outsider' in other ways. For example, it is clear that she was never part of the Dalziels' inner circle. This included cartoonists who had been with the firm 'man and boy', having served an apprenticeship at the Dalziel 'studio'. As we have seen, Duval never had that kind of advantage or training. Similarly, neither she nor Ross were as 'clubbable' as some of the more 'serious' *Judy* contributors. Richard Scully's important history *Eminent Victorian Cartoonists* (2018) maps the informal networks that existed between the creative practitioners on the London satire magazines, but the names of Ross and Duval are absent (see Scully 2018: Series Introduction). Possibly part of the explanation was her perceived 'vulgarity' – a theme taken up in the Introduction to this book.

Sloper was far and away Duval's best-known character, though the bulk of her output (maybe around 85 per cent) was directed elsewhere, as *The Marie Duval Archive* has revealed (Sabin 2014: Kunzle 1985).[20] Sloper had been invented by Ross in 1867, as essentially a variant of a particular London type: a reprobate, boozer and scam artist. Sloper was already recognisable as a developed personality by the time Duval arrived, having appeared in almost-weekly strips. But crucially his adventures involved him as part of a double-act with his Jewish friend Iky Mo (later Ikey Mo).[21] As Duval gradually took over artistic duties from 1869, she redirected the energy of the stories towards Sloper, downplaying the double-act. In addition to this she developed a 'Sloper family' of supporting characters – a wife (unnamed), daughter (Tootsie), son (Alexander), cousin (Evelina) and so on, which allowed her at times to introduce an almost soap opera element (Ikey Mo was not jettisoned altogether, and was included in the family). In the very early days the Sloper strips were signed by both her and Ross. Eventually, she ended up signing more often (with an ever more emphatic signature), and it is our contention that she became solely responsible for the strips (Kunzle 1986: 28).

This was the start of Sloper becoming a star. Spin-off books of collected strip and cartoon material were pulled together with new linking text, with Duval's name often prominent on the cover as cartoonist/illustrator. These were immensely successful, and widely reviewed. If Sloper had 'arrived', then so had Duval. The most famous of these books is known as *Ally Sloper: A Moral Lesson* (Duval 1873g), which purports to tell the character's life story from birth to death. Today, some historians consider it to be a very early example of a graphic novel (the caveat, of course, is that terms like this, when applied retrospectively, are always problematic). This success was swiftly followed by attempts to bring Sloper to the stage, first by *Judy* staffer Robert Sweetman, and then by Ross himself, who devised a routine based on strips included in *A Moral Lesson*, the advertising for which did not mention Duval (Sabin 2009).[22]

There was, additionally, a limited amount of Sloper merchandising, though this seems to have been produced on a bootleg basis. For example, there were walking sticks, with Sloper's face carved into the handle, and Sloper toys. Such merchandising was referenced in a Duval strip in 1878, entitled 'Ally Sloper's Effigy (on a Stick)', about a wooden model of Sloper, with movable parts (Duval 1878c). Eventually, Sloper would be given his own comic, *Ally Sloper's Half Holiday* (1884–1923), launched by Gilbert Dalziel, but this was only after Ross had sold his copyright to the character. For the first few years of the new publication, Duval's *Judy* work was fulsomely reprinted, but always with her signature erased. She would live to see Sloper become 'the first comics superstar' (Sabin 2003), marketed across different platforms, in a way that she had been responsible for guiding: but by then she was out of the picture and fast becoming forgotten.[23]

This connection with Sloper elevated Duval's profile to an exceptional level. The fact that she was reprinted so often (in the shilling books, the almanacs, summer numbers, one-offs and in the *Half-Holiday*), and with such success, meant she was reaching audiences way beyond *Judy*'s original base. Even though Sloper's peak period came later, already by the end of her tenure he was a folk hero, and a cultural resource that the general public were drawing upon and making their own. One commentator, writing of Sloper in 1886, when Duval's work was still very prominent, claimed him as nothing less than a nationalistic archetype: 'after all, [Columbine, Harlequin] and Pantaloon were originally foreign importations; their real character forgotten in [Britain], and they can be allowed to go now that there is a genuine English creation [Ally Sloper] to succeed them' (Pennell 1886). This kind of impact was something the loftier satirical cartoonists at *Judy* could not come close to achieving.

If we extrude salient themes from this (very) brief outline of Duval's career, then we can start to apprehend how she played to the *Judy* formula. Thus, from the start, Duval's drawing style was utilised in addressing the magazine's serio-comic brief. It was antithetical to anything else in *Judy*. It was vernacular and untutored at a time when drawing skill was valued above all else for a job as a magazine artist: it was loose and gestural, as opposed to the refined and delineated technique familiar from the Hogarth-Gillray-*Punch*-Boucher tradition. In this, she was not far away from the style utilised by Ross. But, as Kunzle (1986) has pointed out, she was using cartooning techniques (emanata to depict movement, bodily distortion and so on), which would only become commonplace much later in history. Readers' shock and delight at witnessing this kind of left-field cartooning must have been considerable (see also Chapter 6).[24]

One reason her style was so different was that it drew from off-beat sources, including European magazines and children's book illustration, and especially the work of the German cartoonist Wilhelm Busch.[25] Busch commonly worked in strips, and his style was knockabout and light. Duval on occasion swiped from him directly. Other possible influences included Granville, Doré, Doyle and Cruikshank (though, please note: whether these were strictly 'influences', as such, is contentious in today's History of Art field: the preferred model is one of intertextual connections, change and hybridity, leading to 'associations' and 'parallels').

Sometimes Duval's relationship to past work by others takes on a particular complexion. For example, she was fond of using gags which might be called 'standards' in the sense that they were used frequently by other cartoonists, somewhat in the same manner as a

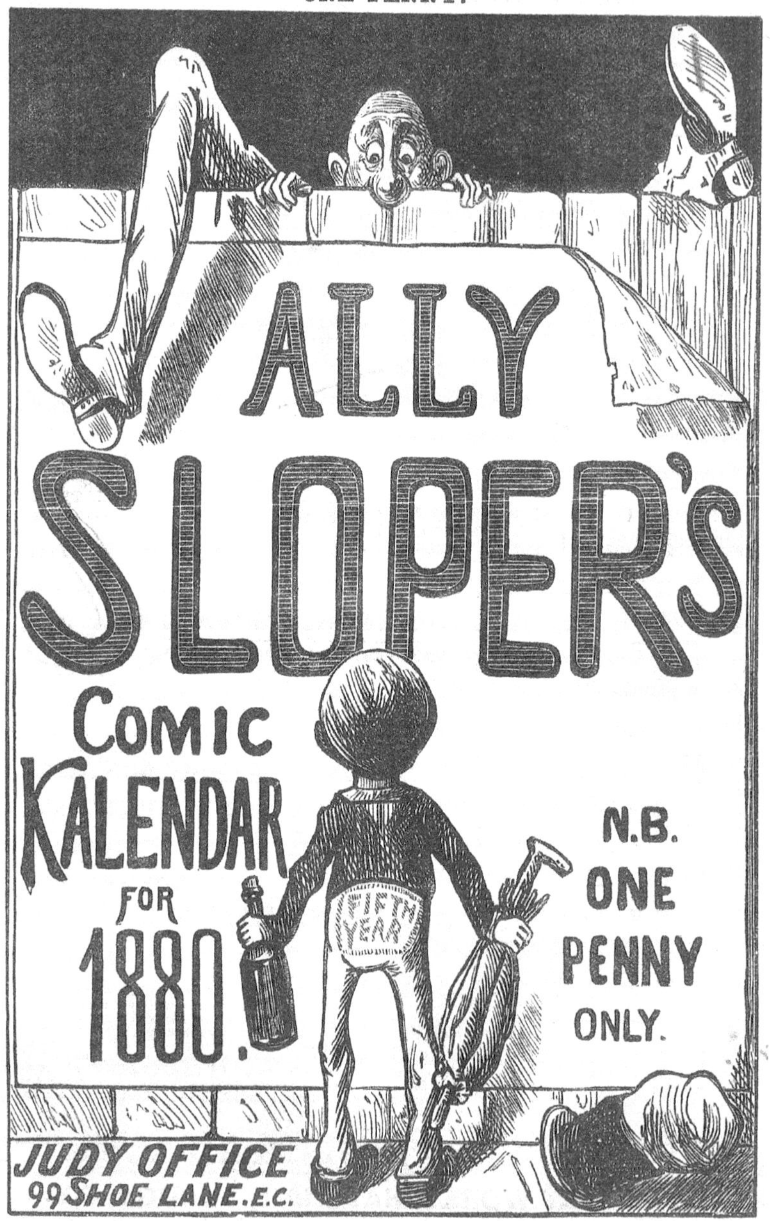

1.3 Marie Duval (1880) *Ally Sloper's Comic Kalendar for 1880*, front cover. One of the many *Judy* spin-offs to feature Ally Sloper, already a folk hero by 1880.

standard joke in a comedian's repertoire (that is, crowd-pleasers). A good example is the Sloper strip in which he accidentally sets fire to his nightcap (Duval 1871a). This gag probably originated in Europe, and was repeated many times in cheap UK periodicals.[26] It is germane that in the world of the theatre, 'borrowing' was standard practice until the late nineteenth century, due to lax or no theatrical copyright.

If Duval's style was knockabout and unusual, then it was also often expressed in strip form, and this was another aspect of the *Judy* formula that requires comment. All the other satire magazines included strips, along with illustrations and cartoons, the latter remaining the primary visual mode. But *Judy* foregrounded them, and various cartoonists proved themselves particularly adept practitioners. For Duval, sequential panel narratives fitted her style of comedic storytelling perfectly. In six, eight or more panels, she would utilise the dynamics of text–image interaction, and the rhythm of the structure, to frame her slapstick techniques and build up to a punchline. Her preposterous yarns were often masterpieces of this particular format. Over time, *Judy* became known for its strips, and spun off several volumes of shilling books that collected them together, including *Ally Sloper: A Moral Lesson*, the book that brought Duval to prominence.

But if Duval was 'the queen of the strip' at *Judy*, this does raise questions about historicisation. For, if *Judy* is to be judged on its own terms, then it cannot necessarily be seen as a stepping-stone to 'comics'. The modern emphasis on the strip form (including particularly comic books and graphic novels) has meant that antecedents have been sought, and that, as a consequence, *Judy* and Duval have acquired a special significance.[27] This approach is not entirely misguided, but to see a linear progression from print-tradition-to-satire-magazines-to-comics is only one way of 'telling history'. Retrospectively applying a grand narrative can ignore other trajectories (for example, it could be argued that *Judy* has as much in common with *Private Eye* as with a comic) and risks obscuring the distinctiveness of *Judy*'s formula (as explained).[28] How 'forward-looking' were strips anyway? Arguably, the satire magazines saw themselves as being perfectly modern in foregrounding single-panel cartoons (which allowed for subtle interplay between the drawing and the caption); strips, by contrast, may have been seen as over-long and irksome devices which looked back to a bygone era of children's books (for example, the work of Busch). By the same token, it is worth bearing in mind that Duval would not have perceived herself as a 'strip artist'; rather, she was doing a job that involved several kinds of cartooning.

Turning now to the subject matter of Duval's work, it is necessary to reiterate how it stayed within *Judy*'s limits of taste and political orientation. For example, her style may have been 'impolite', especially compared to other contributors, but it was nowhere near Gillray-esque, and rarely, if ever, ventured beyond perceived boundaries of moral decency and decorum. The (implied) readers were to be respected, and nothing she did would ever intentionally upset them, or, indeed, a potential advertiser. Similarly, if she was riffing on stage routines, then the more 'objectionable' material (maybe from the 'lower halls') would never make the transition to her stories because the expectations of her *Judy* readers were different.

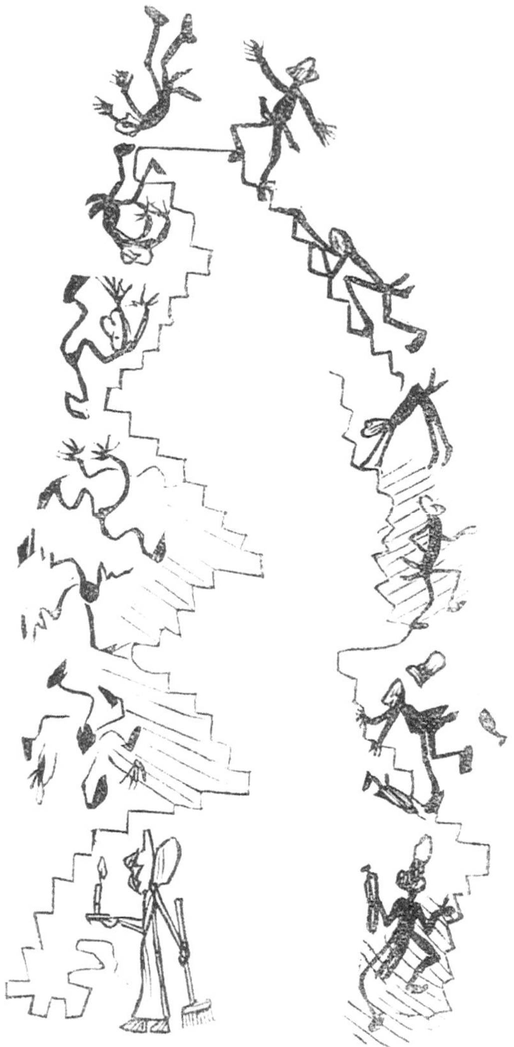

A TALE OF TERROR.

It was this way. A. Sloper had changed his lodgings, and late at night, strange to say, had forgotten the circumstance. Returning as per usual, he ascends and descends the stairs with almost exaggerated caution, only to find his late landlady, to whom a little bill is, oddly enough, still owing, quite ready for him in the hall.

1.4   Marie Duval (1884) 'A Tale of Terror', *Ally Sloper's Comic Kalendar 1884*, p. 8.

Whether Duval was policed at the magazine is not known, but we can assume that every contributor was self-regulating and self-censoring. The chances of her inspiring a Boucher-style libel case were little to none. Taste is time-specific, of course, and it is necessary to acknowledge that Duval was not averse to racist and anti-Semitic gags, which would be entirely unacceptable today. Similarly, comedy is always a balancing act, and there is often room for invention and subversion: how far Duval pushed at the edge is a topic for other chapters in this book.

Duval's (professional) politics were, to a large degree, *Judy*'s politics. She would have been under pressure to stay 'on message' and not contravene its 'true blue' outlook. On those rare occasions when she moved away from her usual slapstick milieu and parodied political figures and events, she exhibited 'approved' opinions. For example, in the coverage of foreign wars, she supports the same side as *Judy* happens to support; and when it comes to domestic politics, she knocks Gladstone, not Disraeli, and reserves special contempt for leftist radicals (Sloper is often set against them, and their 'Down with Everythink ...' banners, for example in 'Anarchy in Islington' (Duval 1870c)). Similarly, her stance on social issues is broadly in tune, and hierarchies are respected (though, as I write elsewhere in this book, her work on the topic of women and women's rights was allowed a certain amount of leeway, possibly on account of differing views within the Conservative Party itself). Even when it is possible to pinpoint moments where she was permitted to go beyond the magazine's boundaries, and even contradict conservative opinions, there is an argument that this worked for *Judy* in a self-serving manner, indicating that it was so broad-minded as to license differing views.

In other ways, Duval's subject matter was steered in particular directions. *Judy* was the 'London serio-comic journal', so she would be a London cartoonist. She was born in Marylebone, and moved to Battersea, and she would channel her intimate knowledge of the streets and people with a visual journalist's eye. Her characters are London characters – she had no interest in regional life, in farmers or miners or mill workers – and her scenarios are big city stories: about middle-class romance on the banks of the Thames, lower-middle-class trippers to Margate, working-class slaveys (domestic servants) going about their business in Kensington mansions. If dialect enters her strips, it is cockney. In sum, she offered her majority-London-metropolitan readers a chance to see a version of themselves in *Judy*'s pages.[29]

Similarly, Duval was linked with the theatre, and brought with her a lens derived from there that fitted the *Judy* brief perfectly (and which reinforced the review columns). As a sometime jobbing actor, she had unique access, and part of her talent was the ability to bring the stage to the page. As the other chapters in this book show, she borrowed not just comedy 'types' (cops, crones, swells and others), but also ideas for slapstick set-ups (possibly from watching tumblers, acrobats and other physical acts) and for 'up-to-date' surprises (borrowed, no doubt, from novelty acts). The fact that her strips are often constructed as if watching a performance, in what we'd now recognise as a 'mid-shot' (showing the whole body), is revealing. But the *Judy* perspective is ever-present, either implicitly or explicitly, and occasionally it is clear that Duval's work is being used in the service of deals done by the magazine with outside parties (as in the case of a Duval-illustrated text story which ran with the notice 'NB: The right to dramatize this narrative belongs to Mr CHARLES WYNDHAM, Criterion Theatre …' (Duval 1885a)).

Duval and *Judy*'s seriality were also enmeshed: she was a professional who could stick to a deadline, week after week, and she developed strategies for responding to events. She would riff on newspaper headlines, often quoting the original at the top of the strip, and these could be about fashion, books or manners. Similarly, she would adhere to the *Judy* calendar, and produce work as appropriate; for example, a strip about Valentine's Day cards for a 14 February edition, and one about goose fattening in the run-up to Christmas. Seriality meant she also had the opportunity to develop continuing characters (Sloper, the Waddimans, the Doveturtles) and rely on readers' memory to pick up their stories.

The final aspect of Duval's relationship with the *Judy* system is the way in which her work was used to complement or contrast with other items in the magazine. This was no small thing because the product had to work as a whole, and therefore the balance had to be right. Everything was in a relationship with everything else, and this was carefully considered. We have seen how her cartooning style provided a counterpoint to other contributor cartoonists; but this extended to subject matter. For example, her depictions of working- and lower-middle-class life can be seen as a riposte to the mannered upper- and upper-middle-class scenarios of Adelaide Claxton, while the London focus of her work was a foil for The McNab's shenanigans in Scotland.

The contributor with whom she had the most striking relationship was William Boucher. This was partly the result of their being the two most prominent cartoonists in the magazine. Obviously, their styles could not have been more unalike, and they occupied not just different modes, but different registers. Whether they knew each other in real life is not known. Boucher joined *Judy* in 1868 and his career there was roughly coterminous with Duval's. The 'dance' between them was one of the key features of the *Judy* formula, and came to special prominence when both cartoonists settled on the same topic. The best example of this happened in 1870, with the outbreak of the Franco-Prussian War, and is worth a closer look.

The war was a major conflict, which signalled the rise of German military power and imperialism. The problem was that if the Germans won, which looked increasingly possible, then the balance of power in Europe would shift, and that was a threat to the United Kingdom. *Judy*, for all its concentration on domestic affairs, could not sit idly by, and a significant proportion of its content in 1870–71 was directed towards the war. Unsurprisingly, it took the French side, as did Boucher and Duval.

A brief list of the *Judy* issues in question demonstrates the extraordinary nature of the Boucher/Duval response:

3 August 1870:
Boucher: 'Six of One – Half-a-dozen of the Other' (Boucher 1870a). War has just broken out. John Bull, blindfold, weighs the scales of justice: in one bowl, statements from Berlin, in the other, those from Paris. The French argument seems to be winning, but Bismarck is busy cheating and puffing air onto the Prussian side.

Duval: 'Ally Sloper Off to the Wars' (Duval 1870d). Sloper is 'engaged as Judy's Special War Correspondent' but has not yet left London, and dreams of glory and the admiration of the ladies. We are informed that in reality he has tried to weasel out, 'confined to bed, at the time of our going to press, extremely poorly. The promised deeds of daring are therefore put off for the present.'

17 August 1870:
Boucher: 'At Bay!' (Boucher 1870b). Marianne, symbol of France, holds up the flaming torch of 'Revolution.' Meanwhile, crows feed on the corpses of soldiers.
Duval: 'Ally to the Front' (Duval 1870e). Now in France, Sloper hides at the first sign of trouble. The French ask him to guard their supply of alcohol, with disastrous results.

24 August 1870:
Boucher: 'The Voice of the Peacemaker' (Boucher 1870c). A female symbol of peace, representing 'England, Russia, [and] Austria', tries to keep apart the Prussians and French; in the background, corpses litter the battlefield.
Duval: 'Sloper A Prisoner' (Duval 1870f). A tale of how 'the gallant Sloper fell into the hands of the foe', but how 'his courage did not forsake him'. He is pictured begging for mercy. He eventually bribes his way out of jail by offering the guard a string of sausages.

31 August 1870:
Boucher: 'Civilization's Lament' (Boucher 1870d). Framed by the smoke of the battlefield, Marianne weeps over a pile of dead French soldiers, while in the background a terrified mother protects her child.
Duval: 'Sloper's Retreat' (Duval 1870g). Relates how Sloper, again in battle, 'upon the firing of the first gun', runs away, along with the frightened locals, who collectively end up in a heap at the bottom of a hill, having tripped over, 'at the very moment that the contest was at its hottest upon the other side'.

7 September 1870:
Boucher: 'Modern Warfare' (Boucher 1870e). Bismarck, depicted as a ferocious ape in a spiked helmet, bomb in hand, destroys French civilisation.
Duval: 'After the Battle' (Duval 1870h). *Judy* declares its pride in Sloper's 'heroic deeds' at the front. There follow images of him fast asleep, reading the paper and stealing the boots of a dead drummer boy, who turns out not to be dead at all, and beats him up.

21 September 1870:
Boucher: 'Between Two Stools' (Boucher 1870f). The Pope is depicted falling on his backside, having been too cowardly to fully support the French in the war. In the background, a French soldier marches stoically off to the front.
Duval: 'Sloper and Moses Reunited' (Duval 1870i). The French army catch Sloper sloping off after the Battle of Sedan and press him into service as an infantryman. He comes under fire, and hides in a hedge, whereupon he is discovered by his old pal, Ikey, newly arrived in France.

28 September 1870:
Boucher: 'Birds of Prey' (Boucher 1870g). Bismarck, with a sack of 'plunder', tramples through France, and demands the annexation of Alsace and Lorraine. Marianne responds: 'To arms! War till extermination!'

Duval: 'Sloper and Mo go into the Spy Business' (Duval 1870j). Ikey draws up a plan for 'for taking Paris', including a secret passage 'discovered by A. Sloper', which he will sell to the Prussians for the right price. The French officer in command of Paris gets wise and 'order[s] out Mo and Sloper for instant execution.'

5 October 1870:
Boucher: 'About Time!' (Boucher 1870h). Bismarck, with a spiked helmet, kicks a Frenchman while he is down. John Bull and the Tzar of Russia look on, deciding what to do. John Bull: 'Neutrality is all very well, but if this sort of thing is going on…'
Duval: 'At Dead of Night at 73' (Duval 1870k). The scene is London once more: we are told Sloper is believed to have been killed at the front (and in a fantasy image, is depicted in a hail of cannonballs, 'riddled by the shots of his inhuman butchers'). But, lo, he returns – alive!

12 October 1870:
Boucher: 'Non-interference Policy' (Boucher 1870i). Gladstone, dressed as a policeman, stands idly by while the war rages: 'It ain't in our beat!'
Duval: 'In Re Sloper' (Duval 1870l). In London, Ikey is arrested by the secret service and interrogated for lying about Sloper's fate: that is, his last moments upon the 'ensanguined field'. Ikey eventually emerges 'without a stain on his character.'

CODA: 19 October 1870:
Boucher: 'The French Sinbad; or, "Irregular" Warfare' (Boucher 1870j). After the French defeat, Prussian atrocities have been reported. In the foreground, a newly crowned Bismarck rides on the back of a French peasant. In the background, a Frenchman is hanged from a tree, and a child weeps for her dead mother.
Duval: The strip appeared in *Judy Almanack* for 19 October, but not in the original issue. 'Sloper Sends Round the 'Hat" (Duval 1870m). In London, Sloper plays the wounded war veteran, and begs for money on the street. He gets chased off by the police.

What is amazing about this series of strips by Duval is how she fearlessly undermines Boucher's earnestness, week by week. It is as if the further he becomes obsessed with darkness and death, the sillier she becomes. (This was a stance which may have belied personal worries – it is possible she still had relatives in France.) Presumably, too, her flippant tone would have come close to being taboo for those readers who shared Boucher's investment in events (you can imagine them thinking, 'Is she even allowed to do that?!'). However, she must have made a calculation that British readers had nothing immediately at stake in the war and that she could therefore 'push the envelope': making comedy out of a tragedy was all part of *Judy's* 'serio-comic' brief, after all. It would have been a different matter if British troops or civilians were dying.

Whether Boucher was offended by Duval's impertinence is not known. Evidence suggests that he was not such a pompous personality as his cartoons might suggest, and, anyway, if he complained, he would have to go up against Duval's mentor and likely lover, the magazine's editor and his boss, Charles Ross. Indeed, even before the 1870 war, Boucher would sometimes introduce Sloper as a background character in his cartoons. This became much more pronounced as the decade progressed. In a seaside scene entitled

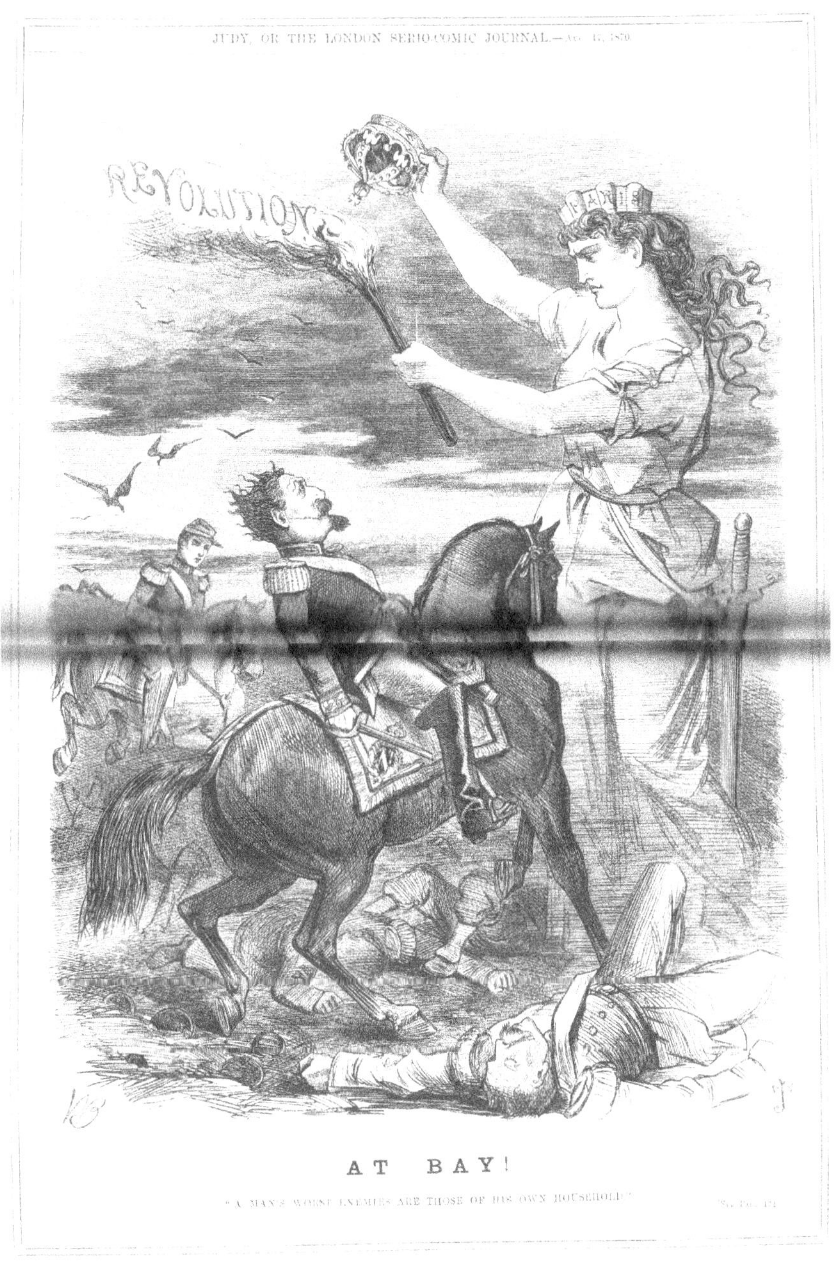

1.5   William Boucher (1870) 'At Bay!', *Judy, or the London Serio-comic Journal*, Volume 7, pp. 166–7

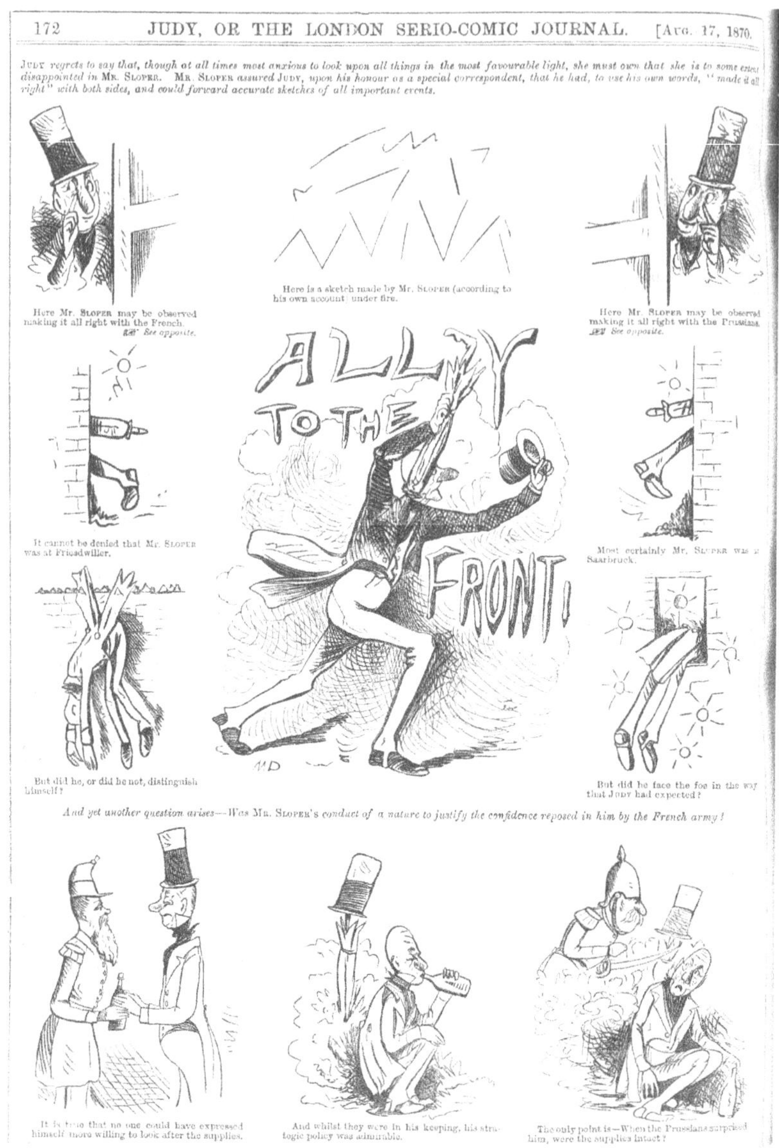

1.6 Marie Duval (1870) 'Ally to the Front', *Judy, or the London Serio-comic Journal*, Volume 7, p. 172

Two images by Boucher and Duval, from the 17 August 1870 edition of *Judy*, with a focus on the Franco-Prussian War. The contrast could not be clearer.

'Extraordinary Change in the Weather', he's there, brandishing his hat, alongside Disraeli (pictured as an angel) and other grandees (Boucher 1875). In a Boat Race drawing, 'True Blue First – Where's the Other?', complete with appearances from Disraeli, John Bull, Britannia and Judy, spectators watch the race with telescopes; Sloper in imitation (drunkenly?) raises his umbrella to his eye, thereby injuring himself (Boucher 1876b). It is no exaggeration to say that such affectionate nods to Duval and Ross marked a moment in *Judy*'s history, but also in that of cartooning generally, as two traditions came together.

To conclude this chapter, *Judy* in 'the Duval years' was a concoction made up of unstable elements: an editor with no previous editing experience, a bruiser of a satirical cartoonist, a willingness to risk reaching out to new readerships and a predilection for surprising art styles, typified by Duval herself. These elements were held together by a knowing (and sophisticated) approach to design and to sustaining reader loyalty. *Judy*'s formula was derivative, but given an effective new spin, and its success was considerable: sales were high, and as the home of Ally Sloper, it gave birth to the comedy sensation of the day. Perhaps it is time, therefore, to reconsider *Judy*'s importance in the grand scheme of Victorian entertainment culture, and indeed in Victorian everyday life: it remains a fact that *Punch* has multiple full-scale histories devoted to it, while *Judy* has none.

If Duval and *Judy* were entwined, then we have to consider to what extent. The evidence suggests she was the magazine's main contributor, its star turn. Conventional wisdom may assign this role to Boucher because his particular drawing style has traditionally been more valued, and because he more easily fits into the narrative of 'great male cartoonists' (and *Judy* itself privileged Boucher for these same reasons). But by several measures, Duval trumps him: she may not have been given a double-page spread in the magazine, and may not have been 'serious' in the same way, but she produced numerically more contributions, and made more of an impact, especially through Sloper. Her sheer presence in the last few decades of the nineteenth century, via *Judy*, should not be underestimated. In short, she made the magazine what it was.

By the same token, the magazine made Duval what she was. There are many ways of apprehending her career. *The Marie Duval Archive* brings her work together in one place, and makes evident new patterns and synchronicities. This is obviously valuable. However, it also extrudes individual cartoons, strips and illustrations from their original context. As an online resource, its egalitarian and immediate aura has the effect of flattening everything out: a strip is a strip is a strip. Only by looking more closely at *Judy* (as an organic, serial object), and Duval's place within it, can we see how she related to her industrial conditions, and, by extension, to the socio-political perspective that governed those conditions. The joy of Duval was, and is, her engagement with her times.

Notes

1 No single volume on *Judy* exists, but key secondary sources include Scully (2018), Adcock (2010a), Brake and Demoor (2009), and Kunzle (1990).

2 Scully (2018: Volume 2) covers later contributors, confirming that quality was kept up.

3 The Dalziels sold *Judy* to a younger member of the family, Gilbert Dalziel, in 1888, and he sold it on *c*.1891, though he stayed as editor.

4 Drawing onto the block was a favoured method because it saved time and avoided waste; but transfers from paper were used (in particular when it mattered that the sketches were not reversed). No paper evidence of Duval's original work survives.

5 In terms of sales, this seems to have been true (see note 6), and retrospective accounts concurred, such as the article 'Chats at the Cheese' which appeared in *Ally Sloper's Half-Holiday* in 1922, in which Sloper recites a poem: 'In the days of my youth / Father William replied / Before 'Daily Mails' were begun / On three comic papers alone we relied / Their names were 'Punch', 'Judy' and 'Fun'' (Boswell Jnr 1922).

6 Scully (2018: Volume 2, 4) gives a table estimating figures (also for *Tomahawk*, *Fun* and *Moonshine*).

7 Carroll even pitched his writing to *Judy*, but was unsuccessful. That Morris and Gladstone were associated with liberal politics may seem like a contradiction, but is a reminder that audiences should never be pre-judged (plus, they may have been primarily fans of Sloper rather than of *Judy* itself).

8 Not every *Judy* item about the suburbs was sympathetic. A six-part text story from 1883 (anonymous, illustrated by Duval), bemoans the loss of the countryside to 'hideous rows of cheaply stuck-together, sickly yellow-coloured, dwelling boxes' (Duval 1883c).

9 For a sense of the disdain with which the dreadfuls were held, see Springhall (1998).

10 See Sabin (2015). Also Scully (2018: Series Introduction, 31), and Howes (2016: 323).

11 The standard text on the leisure boom has long been Peter Bailey's *Popular Culture and Performance in the Victorian City* (1998); recently supplemented by Lee Jackson's more populist *Palaces of Pleasure: From Music Halls to the Seaside to Football, How the Victorians Invented Mass Entertainment* (2019).

12 Notably, Bernard Partridge, while others were Royal Academicians (for example, Maurice Greiffenhagen). Rival satire magazines also had their share of exhibitors, and at *Punch* names included John Tenniel and Harry Furniss.

13 In Comics Studies, the 'material turn' is associated with scholars such as Ian Hague (especially his book *Comics and the Senses*, 2014) and Jan-Noel Thon, for example Thon and Wilde (2016).

14 For example, in a letter to *The Pall Mall Gazette* (23 October 1897), A. C. Shelley, a contributor to *Judy* in 1869, writes that he was 'engaged [by Ross] to supply twenty jokes per week at a salary of two guineas'.

15 Scully (2018: Volume 2, 82) states that he took a junior role, as an 'assistant' to Ross.

16 Bethan Stevens, 'The Wood Engravers' Self Portrait: The Dalziel Brothers, 1839–1893', a talk delivered at Keynes Library, Birkbeck School of Arts, London, 23 February 2016. The Dalziels' team of engravers co-produced many of the most famous images of the period, including the illustrations to Carroll's *Alice* books (see Chapter 4).

17 The name of the editor was deliberately kept obscure in order to enhance the idea that Judy herself had this role.

18 We can conjecture another possible scenario, whereby Ross was hired at *Judy* on the understanding that Duval was part of the package (on the basis of his confidence in her work from *A Story of a Honeymoon*).

19 The provenance of *Rattletrap and Tootletum* is admittedly tenuous. The long title was *Rattletrap Rhymes and Tootletum Tales; a Book for Big Babies …*, and the art was by Archibald Chasemore. Text was by Ross and Ambrose Clarke, but the latter can only be identified as Duval via her contribution to the later book, *The Story of a Honeymoon*, for which she provided art – art which necessarily has to be determined via stylistics only.

20 But note that Sloper was never exclusively a Duval assignment, and he was occasionally drawn by other cartoonists (notably Archibald Chasemore).

21 Ross had produced a proto-version of Sloper as a bit-player in an illustrated novel, *The Great Gun* (Ross 1865). The partnership with Mo, however, was hatched in his first *Judy* strip in 1867, and in subsequent stories Mo developed an affectionate relationship with Sloper, which although never entirely free of anti-Semitic stereotyping, often meant he had equal billing as a 'partner in crime'.

22 Sloper's fame endured into the twentieth century, albeit in a steeply declining fashion, and some of his later manifestations looked back to the Duval era: in the 1920s, her son wrote a series of films part-based on her stories, and even as late as 1936 he was touting a musical play in Liverpool, under the name 'Duval Productions', though there is no evidence it was ever performed (Pettingell Collection, University of Kent Archive).

23 See Sabin (2003). Here I argue that Sloper was in many ways the template for the kind of character-driven entertainment capitalism we see today.

24 Ross's style was perhaps closer to Cruikshank, whom he claimed as a mentor. It was in evidence at *Judy* for two years before Duval arrived. For more on the general context for untutored drawing, see Smolderen (2014, chapter 2).

25 According to Kunzle (1986: 30), 'There are in Duval linear short cuts, degrees of simplified foreshortening, and a nonchalance in handling figures hurtling through the air, which can only come from the German artist.'

26 A few examples are collected on Antoine Sausverd's excellent site *Töpfferiana*: see Sausverd (2011). One pre-dates the Sloper strip (by Pepin, in *L'Eclipse*, 1869). Interestingly, a Busch example post-dates it (1873). Perhaps the most high-profile UK example post-Duval was in *Illustrated Bits* (1884).

27 Comics studies as a field is dominated by the idea of comic strips, and in particular Scott McCloud's (1993: np) definition of 'juxtaposed pictorial and other images in deliberate sequence'. Notable historical studies also imply a particular way of looking at the past, including David Kunzle's *History of the Comic Strip* (1990) and Charles Dierick and Pascal Lefèvre's *Forging a New Medium. The Comic Strip in the Nineteenth Century* (1998).

28 This is a similar argument to that of the 'cinema of attractions', a phrase coined in the mid-1980s by theorists Tom Gunning and André Gaudreault in relation to early cinema.

29 She was not the first cartoonist to depict street life, of course. As Maidment (2016: 121) points out, George Cruikshank's 1830s engravings inspired *Punch* artists to do the same (possibly then going on to influence the vogue for realism in Victorian visual arts and fiction).

2

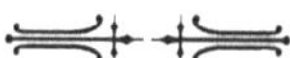

Marie Duval and the woman employee

Simon Grennan

Masculine employment

This chapter follows Roberts's assertion in *Women's Work 1840–1940* that it is 'probably over-ambitious to try and cover such an enormous topic in such a small space and the best that can be hoped for is that questions will be raised and problems aired' (Roberts 1995: 1).

The relationships between gender and work in the nineteenth century are too complex a topic for any attempt at a survey here. Rather, a broad view of scholarship describing the exigencies of women's employment, at the time when Marie Duval was working as a cartoonist and actress in the mid- to late century, suggests a handful of descriptions of the ways in which women in a range of circumstances imagined, undertook, performed and visualised both employment and themselves as employees.

Roberts, Lown, Clark and Verdon focus largely on women in manual employment (albeit in a wide range from the print shop to domestic service and from the retail shop to the farm), which paid a wage rather than a salary, who were not employers themselves and who were the domestic relatives of working men. Such were the majority of Victorian women employees (Verdon 2002; Clarke 1997; Roberts 1995; Lown 1990).

However, analysis of the contingencies of middle-class women employees (those whose employment required the purchase of education or training, as well as contradicting the other definitive circumstances of woman manual workers), establishes that the key distinction between the exigencies of male and female employment lay in the impact of women's domestic lives and the lives of children upon their opportunities for employment and the status of their employment (Mullin 2016; Thomas 2016; Delap 2011; Anderson 1988; Holcombe 1974).

Tilly and Scott's analysis of the complex relationships between the ideas and practices of domestic and nursery work undertaken by women, but not by men, points to

36

the profound significance of gendered family hierarchies in forming, reforming and driving the possibilities and impossibilities of employment for Victorian women of all social classes, not only the larger numbers of women employed in manual work (Tilly and Scott 1978). In effect, social and institutional prohibitions on women's employment arose from the continual dominance of ideas associating women with marriage, childbearing, domestic work and childcare, to the extent that the latter occupations were largely considered not to have the status of work at all (Burman 1979; Davidoff 1979).

In addition, it must be recalled that dependent women's property, including employment wages, was legally controlled by husbands, fathers and brothers until the passing of the Married Women's Property Act in England, Wales and Ireland in 1882 (Shanley 1989). This spontaneous and perpetual devolution of remuneration to men, regardless of the gender of a wage earner, for example, further reinforced the idea that employment was a masculine practice, with its concomitant financial benefit to men. Women who contradicted these prohibitions, ideas and practices, by whatever means, and hence transformed the exigencies of women's employment, were 'often regarded as unnatural, immoral and inadequate homemakers and parents [...] they were neglecting their duties at home, they were independent, they were immoral, and they were taking men's work' (Roberts 1995: 3).

Katherine Mullin also points out that the '[y]oung women of the working class, lower-middle and precariously middle classes were increasingly abandoning established occupations – domestic service, factory work, dressmaking, even governessing and teaching – in favour of alternatives of contested propriety' (Mullin 2016: 2).

This type of working woman (Mullin capitalises the term Working Girl in order to differentiate women who began to work in newly emerging types of employment, late in the century) was neither 'a "fallen woman" nor wholly respectable [...] hybrid, evasive and difficult to read' (Mullin 2016: 3). These women, transforming the orthodox gendering of work, took advantage of, and produced changes in, the status of sociability between solvent, urban men and women, creating a culture of informal exchange exemplified by the proliferations of offerings of an accessible and burgeoning leisure industry (Clemens 2006; Bailey 1998; Piess 1986).

This chapter considers a number of women and representations of women employees who created and inhabited exactly the type of situation Mullin describes, such as Duval and the fictional Miss Echo, Henrietta Stackpole and, at the turn of the century, Elsie Bengough, whilst also exploring the social contingencies that underpinned gendered ideas such as respectability, vulgarity, masculinity and femininity.

What remains significant, in the scholarship of gender and employment in the nineteenth century, is the historic association of employment with masculinity itself, rather than with men – that is, those characteristics of behaviour and practice that were socially devolved to men, the performance of which, itself, continually reconstituted masculinity (Butler 1993: 270). Palmer notes the 'balance of performativity and respectability' achieved by Isabella Beeton as editor of the *Englishwoman's Domestic Magazine* in the 1850s, that being her capacity to perform masculinity (as editor) whilst at the same time remaining feminine (respectable as a woman) and hence remaining 'inchoate and therefore flexible' (Palmer 2011: 34).

In this sense, the practices of being an employee were overwhelmingly understood to be masculine by nineteenth-century men and women and the characteristics of employment and of employees themselves evidenced masculinity, whether the employee was a man or a woman. This chapter aims to unpick some of the ways in which women employees, and Marie Duval in particular, finessed this general conception in order to transform both work and femininity.

The statement might sound broad in the extreme, given that some types of work were historically wholly devolved to women. One can immediately think of examples such as midwives, cooks, maids, seamstresses and governesses (Mullin 2016: 2). However, contending that Victorian work was largely understood to be masculine is not contradicted by examples of work that were conventionally devolved to women. Rather, those characteristics that women were understood to evidence as employed women were thought to be masculine characteristics. Even those types of employment that required the performance of femininity, in the leisure industries for example, tainted women employees with the paradox of combining the masculinity of work with another performance, of femininity (Mullin 2016: 170). For these women, this paradox caused social anxiety about their status (that is, their respectability) but was also the source of their ability to transform themselves and transform ideas of work.

This accounts in some measure for the complexities of the relationships between ideas of women's domestic and child-rearing lives and the possibilities of women being employed. For example, one school of Victorian feminist thought considered that whilst women should be allowed to undertake employment, such work was incompatible with both marriage and motherhood (Lewes 1984: 2).

This disjunction between the lives of women employees and a concept of the masculinity of work generated practical contingencies and opportunities. Hence, it remained contested terrain, as Turner elaborates in terms of the contradictions evident in the production of ideas of the male editor (Turner 2000: 188). In the publishing industries, for example, an awareness of this disjunction on the part of some women employees constituted an aspect of their own consciousness of their status as women (Palmer 2011: 8), despite the fact that women had been involved in the business of British journal publishing, in particular, since its beginning (Shevelow 1989).

The characteristics of paid work, for men and women, were a continuing topic of debate in the periodical press in the nineteenth century. Representative commentary can easily be found in *Tait's Edinburgh Magazine*, *Bow Bells*, *Printers Journal*, *Saturday Review* and *The Kidderminster Shuttle*, for example. Employment was considered to be masculine by *The Kidderminster Shuttle*. The paper considered the benefits of employment to include independence and self-reliance. For women, however, the disbenefit of employment was the effective masculinisation of employees. Both men and women, although provided with independence and self-reliance through employment, were corrupted, brutalised and rendered hard and harsh – that is, masculine – by work:

> We do not object as much to the spirit of independence and self-reliance [employment] has given [working women]; but that it has tended to corrupt and brutalise their manners and character […] the mother has lost the bloom of femininity and is often as hard, as harsh and as masculine as the father ('Women and Work' 1884).[1]

Although employment was considered generally beneficial to employees, employers and, as a result, to the social fabric – by reproducing economic and social relationships and lightening the social burden on the state, such as it was – the masculinising effect of employment on women was identified as the cause of other problems. Whereas men might suffer individual brutalisation as an effect of working, the employment of women was considered to undermine the fundamental domestic foundation of society, such that 'extra income derived from the results of female labour will never compensate for the negligence of home duties […] resulting therefrom' (W. H. W. 1867: 352).

Referring to the *Report from the Poor Law Commissioners on an Enquiry into the Sanitary Conditions of the Labouring Population of Great Britain, 1842* (Chadwick 1962), Deborah Cherry notes that the idea that women's employment upset the equilibrium of a wide range of personal and social relationships resulted in its imputation as a cause of 'improvidence, intemperance, crime and delinquency' in their families and social networks (Cherry 1996: 143). If employment was personally brutalising for men, then for women, the benefits of 'independence' and 'self-reliance' to the individual and to society were also continually set against the idea of the greater disbenefits to society, of a domestic life rendered dysfunctional by the effects of women's employment.

The inscription of femininity enabled the achievements of nineteenth-century women in their own, generic domestic lives – as managers, administrators, teachers, nurses, cooks and cleaners, daughters and granddaughters, grandmothers, mothers and wives, for example. However, employment required nineteenth-century working women to negotiate the effects of masculinisation on the practice and representation of their domestic lives and the effects that this masculinisation was considered to have upon society. The tendentious categorical distinction between work and home arose from this contradiction. It implied, for example, that work in one's own home was not work, because it was not employment. As significantly, the distinction between home and work made women personally responsible for reproducing a domestic equilibrium that was considered to carry with it nothing less than the continuing welfare of the country.[2]

The contradictions between concepts of women's domestic work, women's domestic achievements and women's lives as employees generated visualisations of femininity that unselfconsciously, even blithely, made working women's appearance a metaphor for their employment. The transformation of women, by employment, into 'harsh' and 'hard' masculine women, was also accompanied in commentary by the masculinisation of their visual appearance or the visualisation of them as adopting men's attire. Mary Howitt, writing in *Bow Bells*, encompassed this world of metaphorical inscription, utilising the image of a 'poor old gardeneress' dressed in men's old clothes as a metaphor for women's employment: 'The assumption of masculine airs or of masculine attire […] can never sit more gracefully upon us than do the men's old hats, and great coats, and boots, upon the poor old gardeneresses of the English garden' – that is, not gracefully at all (Howitt 1865: 235).

The application of visualisations of masculinity to employed women also cut across boundaries of class, from women labourers to women entertainers, middle-class women employees to the economically maintained women working unpaid, at domesticity, should they also venture to become employed. The corruption and brutalisation wrought by employment upon women labourers in industry or agriculture was accompanied by descriptions of them sharing visible characteristics with men of the same class. The effects of employment on women with other resources, such as money, education or skills, produced concomitant visualisations within their respective classes. Linton's 'pushing women' (entrepreneurial women), who themselves bordered upon the capacity to employ someone else (a domestic servant), were described as 'half trader, half fop' (Linton 1868c: 578). Linton visualised them as a curious admixture of the work and leisure activities of men of their class (Linton 1868b and 1868d). In describing the corruption and brutalisation of middle-class women caused by employment, Christian Johnstone simply elided types of work with working men, the business and the businessman, to produce an image of a masculinised woman that he 'abominated': 'we cannot help abhorring what is called a capital Woman of Business! […] It is the woman who goes out of her way to buy and sell, and plot and counterplot, whom we utterly abominate' (Johnstone 1834: 596).

In sum, these quotations succinctly outline the conditions under which women were employed and were considered as working women. Employment was thought to make women masculine because employment was considered to be masculine. As a result, employment for women challenged conceptions of the significance of domestic life, upon which the highest personal premium was placed, for women rather than men. Visual representations of women employees created metaphorical elisions between the appearances of men and the masculinisation of women, creating and perpetuating a system of representations of employed women as unfeminine and un-domestic, despite the work entailed in achieving domesticity and, frequently, in contradiction to the types of employment they undertook.

Women undertaking, performing and visualising employment

Nineteenth-century working women undertook work, performed work and visualised work. They undertook work by demonstrating their competence for work, although training for work was often not required. For example, the qualifications for becoming either an employed cotton mill worker or the maintained mistress of a middle-class home were predicated entirely on gender, age, education and means, rather than any set of acquired skills, beyond imitation of other mill workers or mistresses.

Working women performed work by creating, joining and transforming the networks of social relationships upon which work relied, beyond the tasks of work at hand. They belonged to communities of work in which concepts of femininity and masculinity might appear fixed, but which were constantly under review, relative to the work itself. Although perfectly able to undertake lace making or paper feeding for a printing press, men might be more likely to reserve these occupations to women, under the dominance of a conventional idea of masculine work, held in consensus by their peers, both men and women.

Working women also visualised work by developing, perpetuating and sharing images of themselves as women workers, through their attire, their work environments and, sometimes, as a requirement of the work itself. For example, in common with other professional stage performers, part of the definition of Duval's employment, as an actor and a dancer, was the visual representation of femininity as entertainment.

On the other hand, to be a maintained married or unmarried middle-class woman, such as the beneficiary of a private income, or the dependent relative of a solvent man, was never to be an employee. As such, employment was antithetical to significant concepts of the femininity of middle-class women. Hence, employed women were considered to be either inhabiting masculine activities and ways of behaving, or belonged to the class of industrial or agricultural labourers (including private domestic staff in the service industry), or did not conform to either of these paradigms, such as sex workers, women employed in the entertainment industries or women employed in those aspects of the retail industries with a public face.

A range of ethical, status and gender anxieties were occasioned by all of these categories, arising from the contradictions they embodied. In terms of labouring women, the contradictions of employment as a domestic servant included the unfeminine, un-domestic, that is, public, character of women's employment, when compared with public conceptions of the domestic home as the seat of private femininity. The majority of domestic servants in any house, as distinct from a house and grounds, were women. Although domestic servants were self-interested (as employees), their work appeared to require empathy, because their employers were in their domestic care. Although they had access to a relatively structured, if informal, programme of training for work, this training continued to masculinise them. Their place of work was itself highly determined, in the suppression of their femininity and, at the same time, the presentation of the homes of their employers as feminine. The distinction between 'above' and 'below' stairs expressed this contradictory relationship perfectly: for women employed as domestic servants, the domestic home was the site of employment and of masculinisation. For maintained middle-class women, it was an aspect of their femininity.

Further, the contradictions of labouring women's employment in manufacturing industries and agriculture included the reproduction of etiquettes of employee demarcation along gender lines, according to which certain tasks were reserved to men and certain tasks reserved to women, in disregard of their actual competencies. The ethically imperative idea that a man should not undertake work consensually reserved to women could be as entrenched as the idea that a woman should not 'take' a man's work. Attendant on the latter was also the idea that a labouring male employee's wage maintained a family of dependants, despite the fact that, of these dependants, the women also worked.

For women employed outside the paradigms of industrial and agricultural labour, anxieties rooted in conceptions of the masculinity of employment generated their own social contradictions. For those for whom the production of representations of femininity were central to their employment, the contradiction between the idea of work as masculine and their professional femininity was continually writ large – made explicit as well as implicit, as Tracy Davis points out (Davis 1991: 108). This contradiction often resulted in the adjudication of these types of women's employment as morally dubious or criminal. Rather than being a well-spring of the national character through the application of feminine domestic achievements, these women's employment was considered to actively assault conceptions of women, children, families, employers and state. For women entertainers, the public face of their work, in particular, also could not be reconciled to femininity. Women entertainers reproduced and represented the public milieu of the commercial stage, within which social transgressions, such as women working at being feminine, were allowed and sold, but in broader society only sanctioned on stage.

Finally, for women employees inhabiting masculine roles as part of their work, such as a middle-class women undertaking types of work that allowed them somehow to square the circle of their own class conceptions of employment, ideas of femininity and masculinity themselves became hybrid. For example, women working commercially at writing, illustration, branches of the fine and applied arts and fashion were able to manage, although not eradicate, the anxieties attendant upon middle-class women's employment, by maintaining the guise of nominal femininity resulting from hierarchical views of the relative superiority of their class, whilst demonstrating their professional competence. Education and class habituation, if not necessarily access to money, allowed this type of woman employee to remain somewhat feminine whilst becoming somewhat masculine. The perceived proportion of these two aspects of women's employment, as well as the ethics of the mix, were a never-ending topic of debate, as the levels of disapprobation in the public commentaries quoted indicates.

Duval's employment, visualising women and men on stage and page

Duval was a public stage entertainer, whose drawings for *Judy* recognised and exploited the demographic similarity between her habitual stage audiences and the targeted readers of the journal. Both the social mix and the geography of both types of employment were the same, despite the wider distribution of the journal. *Judy*'s offices and production lines, up to the point of print, were in close proximity to the London theatres where she worked.

Despite this similarity of audiences for performance and drawing, however, Duval made use of her experience as a commercial performer to conceive and develop her professional identity as a woman working as a visual artist, that is, to conceive of her 'act' on paper. As a result, she exploited the contradictions inherent in both types of women's employment (public entertaining and the inhabiting of the masculine role of visual journalist).

If Duval's stage work made social transgressions permissible, so as to entertain (as a woman working on the stage to produce femininity), her great trick and original idea was to transpose that sense of permissibility to the pages of a serio-comic journal, in her drawings. The thrilling experience of being a woman employed to be feminine on stage was transposed to the thrilling experience of being a woman working at inhabiting the role of a man, as a visual journalist.

That performance and drawing are both visual arts was significant. Duval's manipulation of the affirmations and contradictions of these types of women's employment was both actual and visually representative and, at the same time, these types of work centred on visualisations of men and women, of masculinity and femininity and of gendered work. By encompassing this Duvallian strategy, women who chose to emerge into public spaces, such as the theatre, publisher's office or journal page, through employment, were active in creating a visible urban panorama. In Duval's case, she not only undertook work, performed work and visualised work, revising femininity in the sense of appearing in the theatre and journal, but also visualised and represented this panorama in performed stage roles and as the topics of her drawings. Well-known conceptions of the antithetical nature of public and private activities and places were challenged by combinations of activities undertaken by both men and women, which effected changes to these conceptions of the gendered bifurcation of 'separate spheres' or, more profoundly, suggested that conceptions of femininity and masculinity along strict domestic versus public lines were inaccurate, class-specific or specious.[3]

Duval's work and that of urban labouring women were in some ways parallel in that both types of employment were public, although labouring women had little opportunity to maintain or revise their own femininity in the ways that Duval did. In fact, their masculinisation was both visible and public. In the performance of their work, the production of the social aspects of their work, the leisure activities of women labourers were also masculinised, so that, as Lynn Walker explains, 'the sight of working-class women standing at the bar and drinking was not an uncommon one in central London' (Walker 1995: 77) and 'there was a rapid growth in women's unaccompanied presence in the public sphere [between 1860 and 1890]: in the workforce as users of commercial and public architecture, on public transport and in the streets' (Walker 1995: 79).

However, Duval's employment differed from that of women labourers and the middle-class women who made use of the habits of their class to gain employment without entirely surrendering a nominal femininity. In working to visualise both femininity and women's employment, Duval's chosen work itself focused on the relationships between conceptions of femininity and masculinity, employment, the domestic realm and the public realms. 'Men did not impersonate women seriously on the nineteenth-century stage but women enacted non-comic male characters as well as semi- and fully-comic ones' and audiences were 'willing to accept transvestite performances of men about town […] "swells" and "mashers"' (Walker 1995: 20).[4]

Hence, on stage, a complex series of inversions and revisions of gendered roles and characteristics were commonplace, for women actors. These inversions and revisions illuminated the ways in which the contradictions of women's work were the topic of entertainment as much as being the occasion for social anxiety about the different actions and appearances of men and women. Duval the actor was a woman employee and hence masculinised and made public by work. However, her particular type of work required her to produce visualisations of femininity on stage, appearing as a woman and play-acting women. Further, her particular type of work also required her to appear as a woman and play-act men.

The wider significance of visualisations of gender inversions and revisions for Duval's employment on the stage, as well as for contemporaneous conceptions of femininity, masculinity and work, was indexed by the events of the evening of 22 April 1870 at the Surrey Theatre. Duval was performing the role of a young man, named Piccadilly Peter, in *Clam*, Charles Ross's drama of modern London. The plot of the play was itself predicated upon a strategic change of gender by a girl, who pretends to be a boy in order to survive. The play included a crowd scene at Cremorne Gardens, a commercial pleasure park and well-known site of sex work, across the Thames from The Surrey Theatre. During the performance, the male transvestites and sex workers Ernest Boulton and Frederick Park joined the actors on stage impromptu, from behind the scenes, where they had been invited from the audience. Boulton and Park were dressed in men's evening clothes, but were the focus of attention both in the front of house and on stage because they were thought to be 'women dressed as men' with 'the best make-up I had ever seen in my life, although I had been an actor for 20 years' ('Remarkable Case at the District Court' 1873).[5]

Although such visibly overt crossing of the boundaries between audience and stage was not habitual, the entry by Boulton and Park into the play as male actors, assumed to be women, alongside Duval, a woman employed to play-act a man, highlighted the mutability of the appearance of genders in a context in which mutability itself was usual, expected and monetised. On stage, a large part of Duval's job was to deliver and exploit her audiences' expectations of the excitement and pleasure gained from witnessing visualisations of female men and masculinised women visualising femininity. That was an expected and paid-for aspect of theatre-going, across all classes of theatre and theatre audience.

Duval's employment as a humorous periodical artist by *Judy* also provided her readers both with a visualisation of a woman masculinised by work – her drawings were identifiable as being hers (that is, as made by a woman), through her weekly repetitions of topics and styles – as well as visualisations of women employees as the topics of her drawings (Duval 1876d; Figure 2.1).[6] As with her employment as an actor, an aspect of Duval's job of drawing in *Judy* was the management and manipulation of her readers' expectations of an employee of a weekly paper, that is, a woman drawing professionally. As discussed elsewhere in this book, rather than seeking to minimise the possibility of readers' disapprobation of a humorous woman artist, by attempting to create a vision of women's employment that was paradoxically compatible with femininity (as Adelaide Claxton

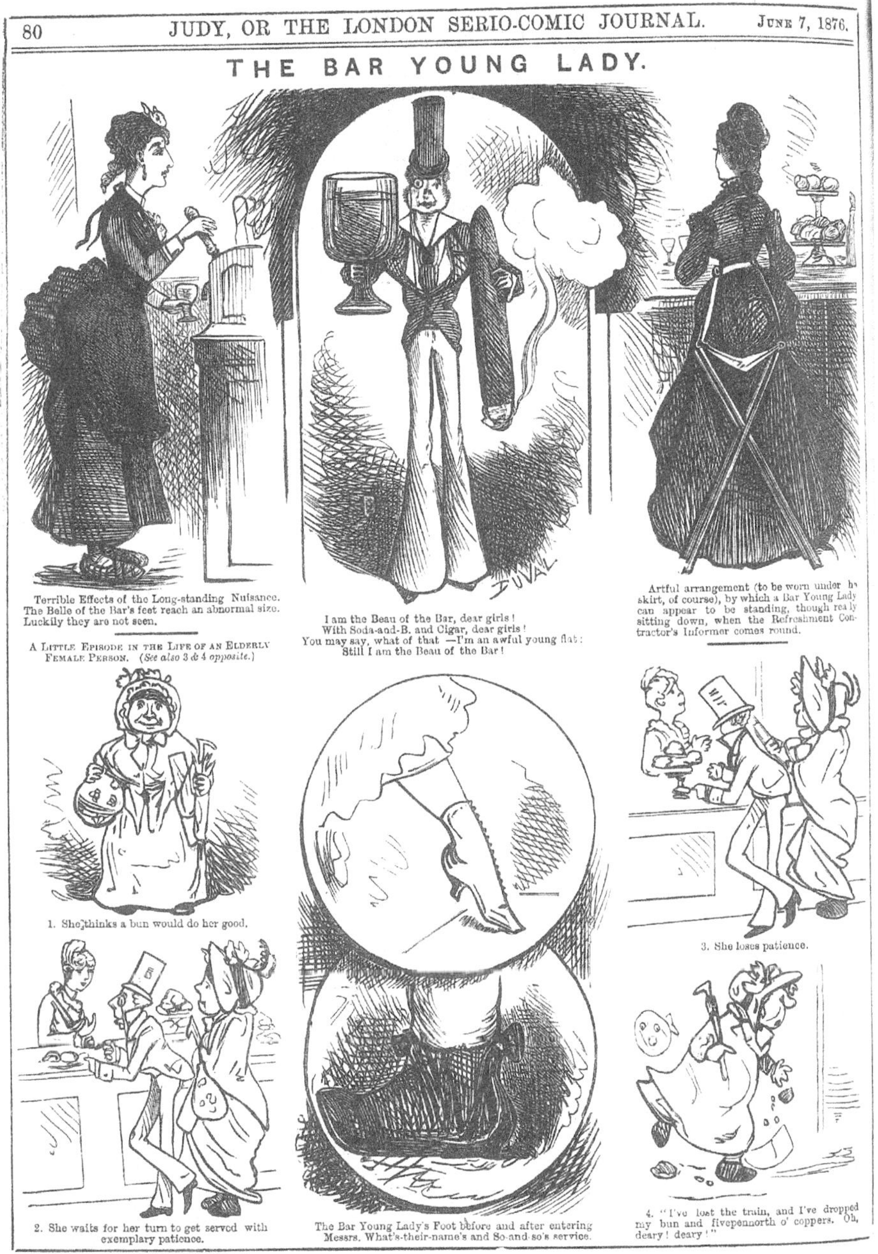

2.1 Marie Duval (1876) 'The bar young lady', *Judy, or the London Serio-comic Journal* Volume 19, p. 80

managed to do, by limiting the topics and style of her drawings to those conventionally reserved for women), Duval instead successfully sought to incorporate masculine, vulgar, humour into her identity as a working-class woman employee.

Margaret Beetham proposes that the increasing popularity of mid- and mid-late nineteenth-century periodical journals generated new visualisations of femininity, through 'a deep structure which ties entertainment and individual pleasure into the calendar and the demands of industrial society' and a 'formal relationship to time', such that visible gender and class demarcations were continually revised by the proliferation of advertisements for products directed at women readers and the regularity of the periodical's interventions into women's working lives, domestic lives and leisure (Beetham 1996: 14). She sees this recoding of femininity as future-oriented towards a visible but unreachable ideal, in which the 'promise of self-transformation is endemic in the form', establishing a new 'duality of the pain of wearing disciplining garments and the pleasure of seeing your own body rendered ideal' (Beetham 1996: 87).

However, Duval's drawings of women employees supervene upon this idea, in part because of the masculine vulgarity of her topics and drawing style. In fact, another inversion took place in Duval's drawings. This prompted readers to laugh at those women who surrendered themselves, with trouble and pain, to the dictates of shopping and fashion (Duval 1876e) and at those who were required to maintain the appearance of fashion (that is, the type of femininity prompted by advertising) as a condition of their employment, such as women employees in the entertainment industries, including herself (Duval 1873d, 'A little difference').

Beetham claims that the regular industrial production, distribution and consumption of periodical journals peddled the constraint of women, as feminine, in advertisements for corsetry, crinolines, bustles and 'cuirasse' bodices, mimicking male military armour, so that the 'uncorseted body was a social disgrace' (Beetham 1996: 85). But Duval's visualisations of women employees, at work and leisure, show that this 'social disgrace' was normative. Most of the women that she drew showed no signs of constraining or body-shaping underwear. Rather, it was those women constrained by fashion who Duval visualised as members of a minority, the extremity of their self-constraint and extent of their seduction by shopping and fashion being the focus of the joke.

Certainly, as Beetham notes, in visualisations of clothing in fashion features and advertisements in periodical papers 'the clothes assumed the body which they concealed' (Beetham 1996: 79). However, in Duval's work, visualisations of these clothes were most often visualisations of the character and identities of women employees, rather than feminine women or maintained domestic women. Women's employment in industry and agriculture could not be undertaken whilst wearing a corset. However, as discussed, women employed in the entertainment industries had to produce and visualise femininity in order to undertake their work, and hence fashionable constraints, body shaping, the application of cosmetics and use of prostheses were part of fulfilling the terms of that work.

For example, the visualisation, through their clothes, of the differences between maintained women and women employed as domestic servants was deftly shown in Duval's drawing of 15 May 1872: 'The slaveys' strike' (Duval 1872b; Figure 2.2). Panel 4 of the drawing contrasts the clothing worn by a maid-of-all-work with her mistress's clothes. Laughter was prompted by the fact that the employee and her employer had exchanged places, and the humour was sparked by the utter inappropriateness of each other's attire to the other's lives. It is obvious, but crucial, to point out that a 'slavey's' attire, in Duval's drawing, featured no corset, no fancy fabric, no cuirasse bodice, no bustle, no chignon (of false hair), no jewellery, no handkerchief, no lace, no décolletage and no false eyelashes. Rather, her cap covered all but her nose and a scrap of hair and her bosom and behind were minimised by the sheer tube of her dress. In later drawings, Duval exaggerated these aspects of the 'slavey's' attire further, so that she became literally a tube with a massive cap and massive shoes, seemingly stuck on (Duval 1879a and 1883b).

Duval's 'slavey' was a woman employee visualised as her working clothes, in exactly the way that Beetham seeks to describe the constraints placed by the imposition of corsetry on women who could choose to wear it: a type of clothing visualised and constrained a type of woman. In Duval's visualisation of the world of women's employment, however, the bodily constraint for the 'slavey' was the condition of her employment, rather than the repeated imperative of periodical advertising, to well-resourced women, to shape themselves feminine.

In effect, changes in apparel were employed across and against conventions of gender, in a range of both public and private contexts, professional and domestic. In each context, the transformation of actions and appearances from conventional to unconventional, expected to unexpected, attracted their own degree of moral disapprobation, excitement or laughter, generated their own types of social anxiety and entrenched as well as transformed the relationships between ideas of class, employment, gender and femininity.

Duval's employment as a professional periodical artist provided many opportunities to pursue unconventional roles. First, readers understood that she was employed, when employment not only masculinised women but, unlike the environment in which she worked as an actor, the publishing environment where she worked was overwhelmingly peopled by men. Her fellow employees in *Judy*'s offices, at all stages of the conception and production of the content of the journal, were largely men. If audiences understood that work on the stage masculinised Duval, then readers also understood that working for *Judy* placed her in unconventional, uncharted and hence, potentially dubious, relationships with her male colleagues, as a woman employee among men. Second, the topics and style of Duval's drawings were also rooted in this unconventional role, in that they imported aspects of her work on stage, including the relationships between stage and theatre audiences, into print.

Applying the idea that women employees visualised and performed, as well as undertook work, Duval's employment as a professional artist rendered significant both the fact that she had the job, as well as the types of visual work that she produced while employed. This congruence of incongruities described an aspect of the character of periodical publishing at exactly the time when Duval was employed. The heterogeneity of periodical content, plus the pressing, regular need to provide new content for readers, necessitated continual

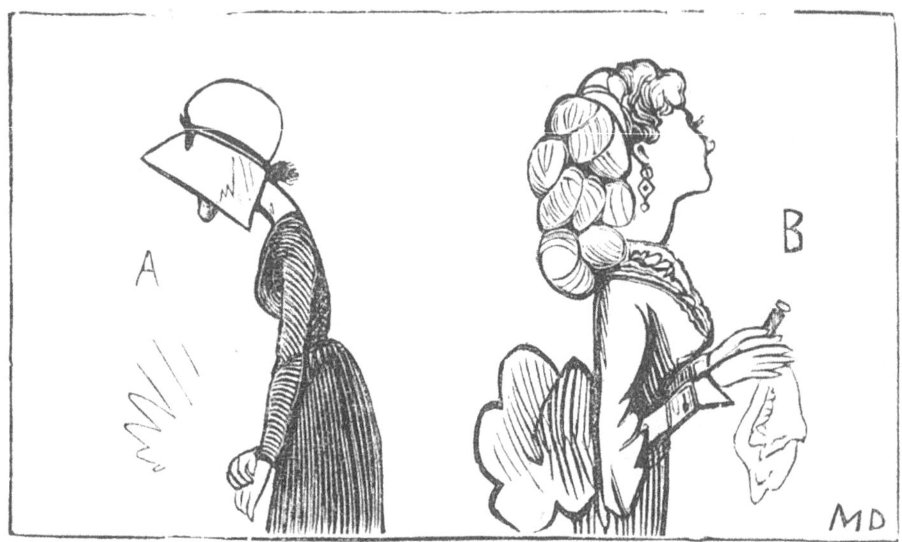

4.—That Missus should wear the Cap, if one be worn at all.
A is the Missus : B is the Maid.

2.2   Marie Duval (1872) 'The slaveys' strike', *Judy, or the London Serio-comic Journal* Volume 11,
p. 38 (detail)

revisions of the ways periodicals were conceived and directed. In the fast-moving melee
of the entertainment industries, pursuing sales, both new types of content and new types
of employment and employee visibly revised ideas of femininity.

Visualisations of maintained domestic (feminine) women and women engaged in all
types of (masculinising) employment, jostled alongside each other in *Judy*, whose readership
was extremely heterogeneous, compared with more expensive periodicals directed towards
a readership of middle-class women, such as the *Englishwoman's Domestic Magazine*. As
much as these visualisations reflected *Judy* readers' range of experiences, in their own lives,
they also provided benchmarks for the achievement and recognition of a range of types
of womanhood. When Beetham writes that becoming 'the woman you are is a difficult
project for which the magazine has characteristically provided recipes, patterns, narratives
and models of the self' (Beetham 1996: 1), the serio-comic character of a journal such
as *Judy*, revealing the expectations of its particular readers, offered a greater variety of
benchmarks for recognising and becoming this or that type of man or women, than a
narrative of commoditised domestic constraints, submitted to in order to achieve femininity.

In the *Judy* spin-off *Ally Sloper's Comic Kalendar for 1878*, this heterogeneity of visualisations of women employees and feminine women was overtly laid out between Duval's
drawing of a 'slavey' and a half-page advertisement for 'Swanbill corsets' on the facing

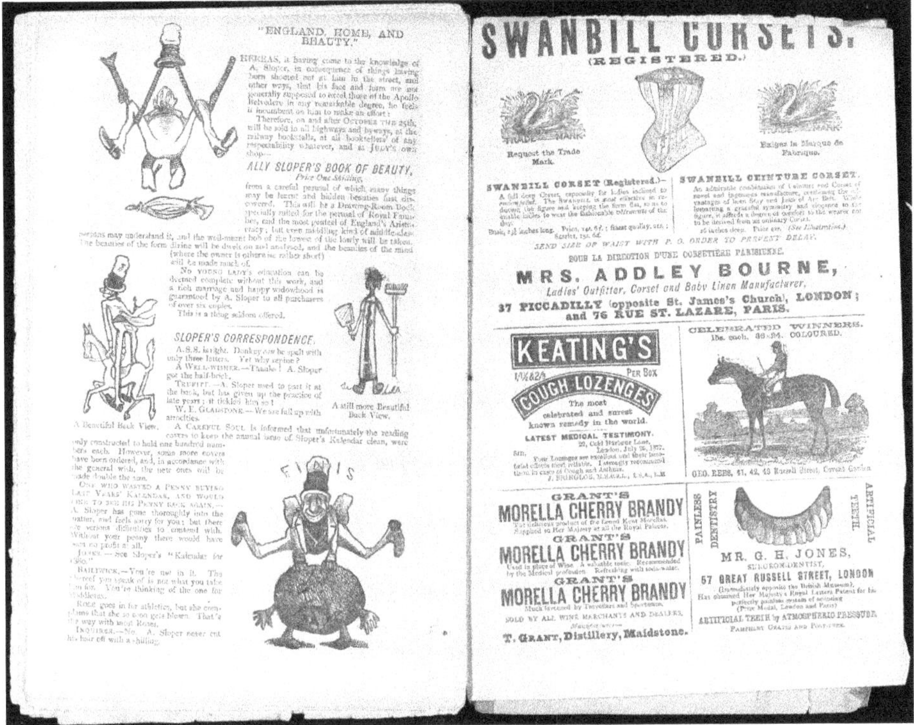

2.3   Marie Duval (1878) *Ally Sloper's Comic Kalendar for 1878*, pp. 20–1

page (Duval 1878b; Figure 2.3). As ever, Duval's visualisation of a slavey showed that the domestic servant didn't have the choice of modifying her body shape in order to be feminine, because her work prohibited it. On the other hand, the corset advertisement opposite pulled no punches in offering the woman consumer an aspirational visualisation of her body modified for femininity rather than by work. It compared the modified female silhouette to that of a swan, emphasised by French language, prompting readers' thoughts of fashion-leading Paris ('sous la direction d'une corsetière Parisienne'), although not in the sections where they had to follow instructions to pay.

It is not difficult to determine the significance of this contradiction for *Judy* readers, between visualisations of a woman employee and commoditised femininity. Readers didn't rebel at the incongruity of their pairing. Having turned the page, they had no chance not to look. Rather, the incongruity itself represented their experiences of the incongruities of their lives. Although the advertisement was directed at women readers of *Judy*, its visualisation was obviously not indelicate, or it would not have appeared. The visualisation of a 'slavey' opposite, although offering a direct contradiction to the appeal

49

in the advertisement, simply directs attention elsewhere. Readers recognised the 'slavey', as much as they were invited to laugh at her masculinity, at her being brutalised by work. *Judy* was inexpensive enough, and circulated widely enough, for a reader to be herself a 'slavey'. Together, the visualisations of an aspired-to femininity and the appearance of women employees added up to a recognisable range of types of readers' lives, both men and women. Visual benchmarks both achieved (holding down a job as a women employee) and aspired to (purchasing feminising body modification) sat easily alongside each other, their contradictions representing, in fact, a truth of readers' lives in the summer of 1878.

Duval made explicit visual jokes about this contradiction, between ideas of domestic femininity and women's employment. Beetham explains the significance of including patterns for making clothes and household items, and instructions for the pursuit of crafts, in periodicals aimed at women readers: 'In magazines like *Englishwoman's Domestic Magazine* the Berlin wool and other patterns had the double function of providing lady-like occupation and enabling the lady to embellish the house with products of her skill' (Beetham 1996: 96). Prior to the 'Swanbill corsets' advertisement in *Ally Sloper's Comic Kalendar for 1879*, Duval's drawing 'Nature and art' showed a framed homemade Berlin work embroidery depicting the family dog, frightening the family cat (Duval 1879b).[7] It follows the scale and type of embroidery patterns published in magazines such as the *Englishwoman's Domestic Magazine*. Rather than the embroidered dog, it appeared that the risibly bad quality of the home embroidery was frightening. Sloper's daughter had made it. The joke resides in the fact that not only had this visual index of domestic femininity (the embroidery after a pattern in a magazine), not been achieved, but that it had visibly, spectacularly failed. The drawing suggested that women in the Sloper household were not fulfilling the requirements of domestic crafts, and were failing to be feminine. Perhaps they were too busy elsewhere, working as employees?

Fictional women employees in *The Girl of the Period Miscellany*

In 1868 and 1869 a popular, inexpensive range of humorous periodicals presented an unprecedented fictional visualisation of women utilising femininity to leverage employment in periodical journalism. This slightly prefigures Duval's transcription of the gender conventions, contradictions and opportunities for self-creation, from her employment as an actress to her employment as a humorous periodical artist.

This visualisation was the apogee – by November 1869, the last hurrah – of a broader satirical response by the entertainment industries to a swingeing, serious attack on the morality of young urban women, made by Eliza Lynn Linton in the conservative weekly commentary journal *Saturday Review* in 1868. Linton decried what she perceived as trends in young women to be frivolous, vain, intemperate, artificial, false, stupid and tending to a dangerous and antisocial immorality. This emerging figure of young female delinquency 'dyes her hair and paints her face', and likes 'plenty of fun and luxury'. Her dress is the focus 'of such thought and intellect as she possesses' and she will forgo 'decency' and 'cleanliness' for fashion (Linton 1868a). Linton called this delinquent 'The

Girl of the Period'. She was to be compared unfavourably, Linton claimed, with a historic ideal of femininity embodying the 'purity and dignity of nature' of the 'young fair English girl' (Linton 1868a).

Far from being the caution to right-thinking men and women, politicians and cultural leaders that Linton might have desired, this description prompted a flood of new publications, unrelated to *Saturday Review* or to Linton. These publications took advantage of Linton's description to promote the idea of the Girl of the Period as an entertainment industry property, to be marketed, cross-marketed and sold. Far from decrying young women who acted as Linton described, these publications articulated and enlarged the Girl of the Period's celebrity, speculatively placing her wherever she might be expected to entertain – hence, the inexpensive illustrated publications *The Girl of the Period Almanack* (1868), *The Girl of the Period Miscellany* (1869), the *Gift Book of the Period* (1869), *The 'Spectator' of the Period* (1868) and many others, often of 24 or 30 pages, unbound. These led to the creation of the fictional Miss Echo (Miss Echo 1869), editor of the *Miscellany* and source of further diffusion products, including *Echoes from the Clubs* (1869) and *Echoes Cartoons* (1869).

Over nine monthly issues, in *The Girl of the Period Miscellany*, this fast and intense marketing of products, banking on readers' popular reception of the idea of the Girl of the Period, resulted in a detailed characterisation of an entire editorial board of fictional women journalists for the paper, all of them Girls of the Period. It also produced an overt apologia for the Girl of the Period, which counter-factually utilised Linton's description and ultimately presented a manifesto for the transcription of theatre industry conventions of women's employment to periodical publishing, in the visualisation of femininity, plus a revised inscription of femininity and work itself.

The actual writers and publishers of *The Girl of the Period Miscellany* remained anonymous, although industry conventions dictated that they were most likely men. In the 1860s, women publishers were even more rare than women professional periodical artists. As a result, it is only possible to discuss the ways in which Miss Echo's team were visualised as fictional women employees by men who were actually employed. But this was no hindrance to considering this visualisation of women's employment relative to readers, in particular. In fact, the men writing, drawing and producing the *Miscellany* in the roles of Girls of the Period play-acted women employees in order to take advantage of a series of reader-character-writer relationships in which it was obvious to readers that Miss Echo was a man.

Hence the trick that Duval later managed, to transpose the consensual permissiveness of the stage to her journalistic employment and to the topics and style of her drawings in *Judy*, in parallel to the ventriloquism of fictional Girls of the Period by male journalists in the *Miscellany*. This trick fully recognised the fact that Duval's vaulting achievement also transformed the real employment that she could undertake and perform, as well as visualise.

It was not enough to consider Miss Echo and her team as the blithe embodiment of male opinions about the Girl of the Period. The real conceit lay in the fact that the fictional women journalists were supposed to be responsible for the writing, drawing and production of the journal that readers held in their hands. Far from being stupid, ignorant and immoral, the fictional Girls of the Period were characterised as having successfully undertaken, produced and visualised a type of employment conventionally devolved to men. Much more significantly, far from being corrupted and brutalised by this work, they were characterised as extremely feminine. As with Duval's drawings in *Judy*, it was this idea, of women mutually revising and visualising ideas of both work and femininity, which was the motor that drove the entertainment for readers.

But were Miss Echo and her team undertaking paid work? Were they women employees? The question, if it occurred to readers, was easy to answer, solely on the basis of descriptions of the types of work its members undertook and where. The fictional editorial meeting, which set out the ethos, policy and contents of forthcoming editions of the *Miscellany*, was described in the first issue as taking place in a hired private room in a public house (Miss Echo 1869: 3). There was such a large amount of business to conduct that the meeting ran an hour late, to midnight. In a swift series of images of some of the contingencies of conducting an urban entertainment business in the 1860s, the meeting was only broken up when, hearing that 'the 300 guinea horses were coughing like Greenwich pensioners, the ladies cast aside their cigarettes, and, promising speedy "copy", departed smiling and happy' (Miss Echo 1869: 3). The fourteen contributors, including Miss Echo, were not producing the *Miscellany* from their homes, but rather were following an emerging industry convention whereby the places where urban leisure was publicly consumed were the same places where the business of providing and producing leisure was undertaken. Neither was the team undertaking charitable or hobby work. The *Miscellany* exploited a specific commercial market, created by the public popularity of satires of the Girl of the Period. It utilised established methods of periodical production and distribution to be delivered to readers, who paid the middling/high price of sixpence a copy, compared with the annual *Ally Sloper's Comic Kalendar* which, at 24 pages, cost one penny.

The editorial aim of the *Miscellany* was to 'display the gorgeous infoldings of [the Girl of the Period's] private opinions – whether, with poetic warble, they preferred to encourage stylish refinement, or with trenchant satire to mow down presuming vulgarities' (Miss Echo 1869: 1). It became, in the second issue, an undisguised panegyric to the possibility that the masculinisation of young women did not, in fact, contradict a more profound femininity: 'You may see girls whose walking attire shows the outline of the figure nearly as much as the dress of a common soldier does [...] They are good, kind, gentle, modest creatures to-day, just as they were a year or more ago, before they would have been wearing such dresses' (Miss Echo 1869: 34). It claimed that women could be 'delicately-masculinised' (Miss Echo 1869: 34) describing the benefits of a misunderstood social licence:

> Our lads and lasses see more, hear more, read more, and, to use an expressive phrase, 'go about' more than they used to do. There is much less vice (very much less, whoever denies

it) than there used to be, but there is more freedom; and culture, in particular the culture which comes of social intercourse and voluntary book studies, has gone on too fast for the old folks, the fathers and mothers, to overtake it.

The invocation of 'book studies' as a benefit of greater gender 'freedom', had a slightly disingenuous ring, particularly when these were the putative words of Miss Echo, whose descriptive record of the first editorial meeting devoted sentence after sentence to the fashions and cosmetic appearance of the all-women team.[8]

However, throughout the *Miscellany*'s 300 pages, the editorial thesis proposed to set aside social and ethical anxieties about the masculinisation of women in favour of recognising the existence of new paradigms of femininity and an active evaluation of the significance of these paradigms. Miss Echo often addressed the male readers of the *Miscellany* directly, pointing out that, in her opinion, the masculinisation of women in fact produced a new set of distinctions between men and women and a new set of consensually sanctioned ideas about masculine and feminine behaviour, because the 'more we pretend to imitate you the more irritatingly you feel our womanhood' (Miss Echo 1869: 34).

The challenge facing women who were masculinised by employment, as Miss Echo wrote, or women who otherwise lived on the boundaries between public and domestic activities (or might wish to do so), was the continual adjudication and calibration of social transgressions, or the continual evaluation of the social impact of women bringing about changes to ideas of femininity. This challenge was dubbed 'the Irony of the Situation' (Miss Echo 1869: 34). Within it, the *Miscellany* editorial included an overt call to arms for young women or, rather, a call to imagine, if anything was possible, what a future woman might be and how a future woman might act. 'If the Girl of the Period should only become conscious that she was accepted as the Irony of the Situation, what might not the consequences be! How far might she not push the irony?' (Miss Echo 1869: 34).

'Impressions from a thousand quarters' (Miss Echo 1869: 34)

With this imperative at its heart, there is a comparison to make between the real world activities of Duval, as a woman employee, and the activities of the fictional editorial team led by Miss Echo, even if the *Miscellany* constituted a conception and visualisation of women employed in journalism made by men, ventriloquising women in order to sell a commercial entertainment. More than the 'Girls who work' featured in the first issue of the *Miscellany*, illustrating and versifying 'The ballet girl' – play-acting femininity, 'The lady's maid', 'The refreshment girl' and 'The sewing-machine girl', working in the service industries (Miss Echo 1869: 17), Miss Echo and the members of her team resembled Duval, the humorous visual journalist, in providing readers with an exemplary object lesson in making the 'Irony of the Situation' a qualification for making the transformation of femininity itself the object of work.

Key to the character of the *Miscellany* was the pervasive idea that every aspect of the actions, emotions and thoughts of Girls of the Period represented and discussed in its pages was nothing more than quotidian truth, both in its generalisation of types of women and in the fine details it provided about their lives. If the *Miscellany* contained opinion pieces, stories, jokes and poems, these were all based firmly on an impulse to report on situations that readers encountered every day. This 'reportage' aspect of the *Miscellany* was part of its editorial ethos, to show or even persuade readers that the Girl of the Period described types of masculinised women for whom the adoption of masculine ways of behaving was beneficial whilst, as the 'Irony of the Situation', remaining feminine. Further, the *Miscellany* continually pointed out that these women were neither unusual nor rare, but were types of women who readers knew and encountered every day.

In this sense, the fictional Miss Echo and Duval brokered changing ideas and visualisations of women employees, among other Girls of the Period, through the topics and styles of their journalism and through their own employment as journalists. Their work consisted of accumulating and reflecting their own types of experiences (or the experiences of her ventriloquists, in Miss Echo's case) with the intention of providing readers with a particularly focused view of a shared world. Motivated by the desire to entertain, commercially, Duval's journalistic trade was exactly this entrepreneurship of ideas, in which an idea such as the Girl of the Period (or, as a Duvallian example, Judy, the fictional editor of *Judy*) was brokered to readers as a particular reflection of daily life. In the frontispiece to the issue published on 22 October 1873, Duval drew a mock-Roman trophy of Judy the visual artist, comprising a commemorative medal and the tools of the graphic artist's trade: a chalk and quill (Duval 1873e; Figure 2.4). Habitually, Judy was shown as a 'slavey' with a work-changed face and hair-covering cap but, as ever, the drawing exalted the fact that a woman employee was working the levers of the magazine, on this occasion as an artist. The commemorative medal says 'Queen Judy' in Latin, and the whole image followed the familiar form of a classical badge of professional employment as an artist.

In order to undertake this professional brokerage, Duval, like members of the *Miscellany* team meeting in a public house, occupied a series of public places, which provided her sources and from which she drew her material. Considering the social conflicts caused by the forcible medical examination of women sex workers during the period of the Contagious Diseases Acts (1864–86) and the ensuing catastrophes caused by the random wrongful arrest of women suspected of the crime of being sex workers, simply because they were unaccompanied, Epstein Nord writes that 'a woman's occupation of public space does more than unsettle her domestic and private identity; it threatens her respectability, her chastity, her very femininity' so that unaccompanied women in public places were considered to be 'either endangered or dangerous' (Epstein Nord 1995: 116–17, and 3).

However, between the maintenance of a domestic femininity, on one hand, and employment as a public sex worker, on the other, lay a wide range of experiences for women employees who had forfeited or negotiated their femininity according to their need to earn a living. As women employed in industry subsisted in the factory, farm or

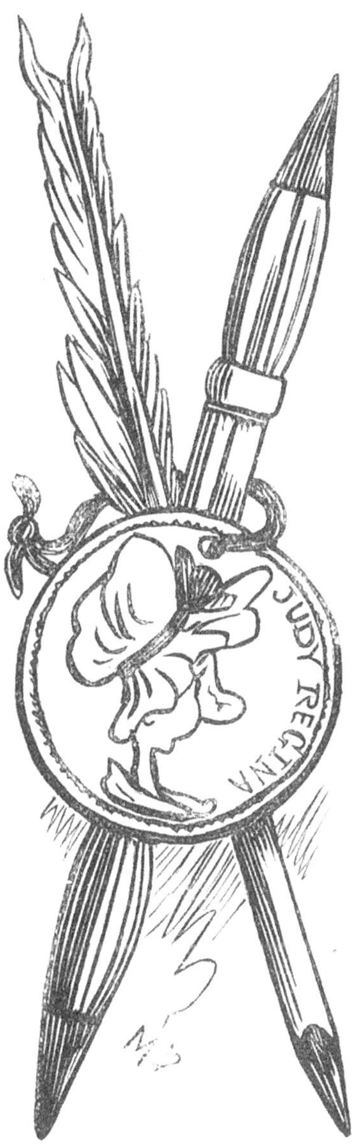

2.4 Marie Duval (1873) 'Judy medal, pencil and quill', *Judy, or the London Serio-comic Journal*, Volume 14, frontispiece (detail)

other people's houses and sought leisure in public, alongside their male co-workers, the urban public scene encompassed 'female music hall performers, shopping ladies, shop girls, glamorised "girls in business", female charity workers, Salvation Army lasses, platform women, match girls, women journalists, clerks and typists', none of whom appeared to be at general risk in the public pursuit of employment or leisure and none of whom appeared to threaten personal danger or social calamity (Ledger 1997: 155).

This was the urban environment, perhaps even the encompassing ecology, in which Duval peddled her visual journalism as a commercial provider of reflections and ideas about the public scene, and as an entertainer. As Miss Echo wrote about the Girl of the Period, she received 'impressions from a thousand quarters, and, without knowing it, assimilates, registers and reflects them all' (Miss Echo 1869: 34). In her drawings, Duval reported on lives that were familiar to her readers according to her position as a woman employee, marginal not in the sense of a criminalised sex worker, but as a performer, continually coming on from, and returning to, the wings to deliver her impressions on the page.

This description shares characteristics with Baudelaire's 1863 conception of urban '*flânerie*' – public mobility, the management of strategic anonymity, curiosity and the ability to reflect and report upon the details of an urban social scene (Baudelaire 1965). There has been much discussion of the masculine character of *flânerie* and the invisibility of the *flâneuse* (Wolff 2000; Gretton 2008) but, as Leo Hall and I have argued elsewhere (Hall and Grennan 2019), these characteristics defined a range of fictional urban women employees, for readers, making their living by commoditising their capacity for brokering urban reflections, in the literary work of Émile Zola (Madame Sidonie in *The Kill*), Henry James (Henrietta Stackpole in *The Portrait of a Lady*) and Oliver Onions (Elsie Bengough in *The Beckoning Fair One*).[9]

Tom Gretton notices the historic parallel of the emergence of *flânerie* with the growth of periodical publishing, in particular noting the importance of the regular consumption of changing ideas and visualisations of city life by readers and the normalisation and entrenchment of habits of periodical reading (Gretton 2008: 94–112). He proposes that the presentation of impressions of urban life, brokered to readers in the periodical press, was as significant for the creation of the identity of *flânerie* as the practices of the *flâneurs* and *flâneuses* from whose practices those impressions were derived (Gretton 2008: 94). In this sense, reading paralleled the negotiation of the urban environment, as readers negotiated the design, typography and practices of navigation required to read a serial newspaper graphically. As they roamed across the highly heterogeneous visual content of the paper, they followed the footsteps of the authorial *flâneurs* and *flâneuses* across the city.

The experience of reading created an understanding on the part of readers of the shifting social, cultural and financial possibilities and impossibilities of new types of urban employment and of representations of the types of people involved in them, including women. In particular, types of employment being forged anew by the necessities of changing markets for media – such as the devolving of the comic strip artist from the humorous or political cartoonist and the cartoonist from the illustrator – were founded on readers' ability to navigate complex new experiences of newspapers, periodical papers, serial novels, almanacs, annuals and souvenir publications.

With regard to *Judy* readers, knowledge that a local professional stage actress was now employed as an artist was significant in navigating, understanding and consuming Duval's drawings, particularly among the accumulated bric-a-brac of impressions provided by a wide variety of types of male co-workers. In the context of reading *Judy*, the only reason to think that Duval's employment was exceptional was that no one had previously thought of transferring the relationships between women's stage acting and its audience to the pages of a periodical paper. For readers, the fact that Duval revealed the mutability of existing ethical conceptions of gendered behaviour and managed to make a living as few women had done before, was a marketable characteristic of her professional identity rather than the object of her employment.

In this, Duval's professional identity was habituated to readers just as the fictional identities of Miss Echo, Henrietta Stackpole and Elsie Bengough were habituated to readers of the *Miscellany*, James's novel and Onions's short story. Like Duval, both Stackpole and Bengough were employed as journalists by periodical papers. Qualifications suitable to this type of employment amounted to a commercialisation of the activities of *flâneuses*: an ability to reflect details of an urban social scene, curiosity, public mobility and strategic anonymity.

Henrietta Stackpole, who appeared in James's 1881 novel, was a middle-class, educated American woman who undertook employment as a journalist, in order to support herself and her sister's children. This made her a woman of a 'modern type' in her own words (James 1963: 471), who had not negotiated the social move from domestic femininity to public employment without visible courage, as 'she went into cages, she flourished lashes, like a spangled lion-tamer' (James 1963: 88). She ranged alone, back and forth, across the Atlantic and around Europe in pursuit of impressions to broker for her readers. Stackpole inscribed the change in readers' conceptions of women's employment in journalism in the same way as, in the real word, Duval and the American visual reporter Georgina Davis did, 'in a series of illustrated travel accounts. Appearing in nine instalments from 1883 to 1885 […] as she shows herself, the artist-reporter, eagerly jotting notes and making quick sketches' (Balliet 2007).

For readers, the exceptionalism of a women turning *flânerie* into employment visualised a distinct professional identity, an aspect of which was the codification of the novelty of such a reading experience. Although Duval had a fifteen-year-long career as a professional artist and Stackpole was successful enough as an employee to be a foreign correspondent, for James, Stackpole still did 'smell of the Future' (James 1963: 15). Women employed as journalists were considered to be oriented towards emerging social conventions and away from past ideas.

For readers of Onion's 1911 short story, thirty years later, the shape of this future had been much more thoroughly mapped. In the story, Elsie Bengough is 'an unattached journalist of thirty-four' who 'pulled a better living out of the pool (as she expressed it)' than her male novelist friend Paul Oleran (Onions 2010: 15). She was 'noisy, able, practical' and, like Stackpole, monetised characteristics of *flânerie* whilst maintaining a negotiated femininity. Stackpole 'shimmers' (James 1963: 79), and Bengough 'left small whirlwinds of air behind her when she moved, in which her veils and scarves fluttered and spun'. She was 'fair as butter, pink as a dog-rose' (Onions 2010: 15), or only visibly 'delicately masculinised' by undertaking paid work, as an embodiment, in 1911, of the more urgently emerging 'Irony of the Situation'.

The underachieving Paul Oleran complained that Bengough, as a woman employee, made her business relationships a cover for a speculative and predatory romance, simply because she was a woman (Onions 2010: 42), and Stackpole was described as a 'monster' by a male character in *The Portrait of a Lady* (James 1963: 270). However, Miss Echo's 'Irony of the Situation' (or the continual squaring of the circle of employment, for example, and conceptions of femininity), was also considered in more rational and equable terms. In *A Woman of Business* (Bramston 1885), Patricia Zakreski points out that as 'a theoretical concept, the "woman of business" offers an alternative to the prevailing discourses of political economy in which self-interest formed the key motivating factor of the market' with 'a feminine restructuring of social relationships in the business world, calling for a balance between self-interest and sympathy' (Zakreski 2013: 158).

Hence, women might be considered to have the ability to feminise employment, as much as employment might be considered to masculinise women employees. As the periodical publishing industries matured, to the point of the First International Press Congress of 1894, it was possible for woman journalist G. B. Stuart to claim in a paper that women employed to provide content for the industry 'had created, not usurped their present position' (Demoor: 2000: 18).

Beetham notes exactly this creation of new identities, derived from reciprocal negotiations between entrenched and emerging concepts of femininity and masculinity, relative to the business of periodical print in particular, when she writes: 'if the periodical press may be said to have provided a theatre for cross-gender performativity, equally it may be seen as providing a stage for the performance of femininity' (Beetham 1996: 43). Beetham could almost have been describing Duval's pioneering transference to the pages of *Judy*, of her (masculinising) stage work of performing femininity, as entertainment. In Beetham's terms, the significance of this aspect of Duval's unique capacity as an employee was that she was a woman. No man could create a professional identity like Duval's, because a man was quite differently positioned by his gender.

Beetham goes further. 'Even the feminist may be said to have publicly performed feminism in the newly established women's presses, exaggeratedly enacting her personality as a woman', she writes (1996: 44). 'The production and consumption of artist personae' or, in my words, the visualisation, as well as the undertaking and performing of women's employment as periodical journalists, took place as part of the forging of new tasks for employees and the creation of new experiences for readers, so that at the 'same time that they crafted items and commodities, women drafted subjectivities and professional roles' (Hadjiafxendi and Zakreski 2013: 15 and 18).

Anonymity and pseudonym

Employees of the periodical press created fictional or fictionalised authorial identities in order to entice or reassure readers, to keep them reading, to personalise strategic relationships and to persuade them to continue buying forthcoming issues of the papers. The publication of unsigned copy was an aspect of this practice, which encouraged the idea that the periodical itself rendered multiple utterances as a single homogeneous voice. As Fraser, Green and Johnson point out, 'Victorian journalists typically employed an explicitly polemical discourse which the practice of anonymity only encouraged' (Fraser, Green and Johnson 2003: 3).

As Tighe Hopkins noted, this voice, compiled of the anonymous contributions of multiple employees, appeared to aim to produce 'the tone of a man speaking to a man', so that the ideal brokerage of the periodical paper was made between men (Hopkins 1889: 514). Although readers and, increasingly, employees of periodical papers included women, a corollary of this combination of public polemics and authorial anonymity was an ethical debate about the social responsibility of the press, discussing the need for individual authors to take responsibility for what they had written or drawn. Brake describes anonymous authorship as a characteristic of the 'subterranean practices' of the periodical press industry (Brake 1994: 25), but also notes that 'initially, anonymity was the principal guarantor' of social respectability for authors, that is, conformity to the ideas of a polite class (Hopkins 1889: 19).

Although 'anonymity enabled women to enter the writing profession without having to reveal their identity or expose themselves to criticism, [forcing] them to write [...] from the "purely masculine point of view"', this practice also 'enabled women to enter the field in greater numbers than was generally suspected and allowed them to address topics not generally through of a suitable for a woman's pen' (Fraser, Green and Johnson 2003: 27 and 11).

In fact, as Duval's work attests, whilst the trend for anonymous authorship in the periodical papers waned, both women and men employees began to create new identities in order to more greatly affect readers. These swept aside questions about the suitability of some topics for treatment by men or women journalists and periodical artists, or notions about the commercial identity of the paper as masculine. Further, in the humorous papers, this idea was itself made risible. If a reader couldn't be sure that the gender of a writer or artist followed the signature, how could they be sure of the propriety or impropriety of the topics in view, or of the suitability to ideas of femininity and masculinity of the ways in which they were treated?

Hence, Duval created a series of male and female pseudonyms under which she drew. As Maclean writes, 'pseudonyms represent an attempt to acquire "auctoritas" and "gravitas", or an attempt to shed them' (Maclean 1991). Duval did both. 'Marie Duval', the name under which she presented the largest number of her drawings, was the stage name that she imported from her employment in the theatre, as an existing commercial identity, known to *Judy* readers. In terms of the topics and style of drawings by 'Marie Duval', the idea that the stage actress had made the drawing was a significant aspect of the humour and unique character of the entertainment that the drawings provided. For readers, 'Marie Duval' brokered impressions of the larger world of leisure industries in which Duval the actress was employed: unlicensed theatres, restaurants, public houses, bars, shops, the streets, the races, the day trip.

However, throughout 1875, Duval presented a series of 31 drawings signed 'Noir', which were significantly different in topic and treatment from those by 'Marie Duval' (Duval 1875c; Figure 2.5). Drawings by 'Noir' tipped the balance between an idea of feminine domesticity and an idea of masculine humour, slightly towards the feminine. They were putative fashion illustrations or, rather, historic and current fashions were their topic. The drawings were still humorous, but their humour was charming and confirmatory rather than the physical, ribald and unsettling humour of 'Marie Duval'. For *Judy* readers, the artist's name 'Noir' itself presented as 'French', France being the home of femininity, fashion and charm, its single word prompting readers to think of the sophisticated techniques and humour of French periodical artists such as 'Cham'. It does not seem coincidental that drawings by 'Noir' appeared at the same moment that Clayton described Duval as being 'very graceful' and 'always dressed in black' (Clayton 1876: 332). In this, it might even be possible to detect some coordinated, if minor, effort at marketing the identity of 'Noir'.

In 1869 and again in 1874, Duval had created new commercial identities, as an employee, in order to ease potential readers into buying a print product. 'Ambrose Clarke' illustrated *The Story of a Honeymoon*, a comic novel by Charles Ross (Ross and Clarke 1870) and 'Her Royal Highness the Princess Hesse Schwartzbourg' authored and drew the rather lavish coloured and embossed children's book, published by Chatto, *Queens & Kings and Other Things* (Duval 1874b, Figure 2.6). Both names were pseudonyms for Duval. It is difficult to tease out the reason why Duval adopted a male identity in order to make drawings for *The Story of a Honeymoon*, apart from the rather thin notion that readers might have expected more risqué content from a comic novel about a wedding night authored by two men and, hence, more readily purchased the book. Creating the identity of a German princess for children's book *Queens & Kings* was perhaps easier to discern, considering middle-class parents' knowledge of and access to translations of works by Wilhelm Busch, which the book resembled in topic and treatment. The foreign royal identity was not to be taken seriously, by child readers or parents, but the type of joke in the name pushed distinctly into the realm of clever children rather than the French whimsy of 'Noir' and the boundary crossing of 'Marie Duval'.

Duval's self-conscious creation of authorial identities was part of her work as a media employee. As much as women employees providing content for the print industries created hybrid and entirely new identities for paid work, by undertaking, performing and visualising women's employment, they also continually negotiated with readers to provide and habituate their products and themselves. There was little difference between the creation of a commercial identity as an enduring property, by Eliza Warren Francis (editor and contributor to the *Ladies Treasury* between 1857 and 1895), for example, and Duval's

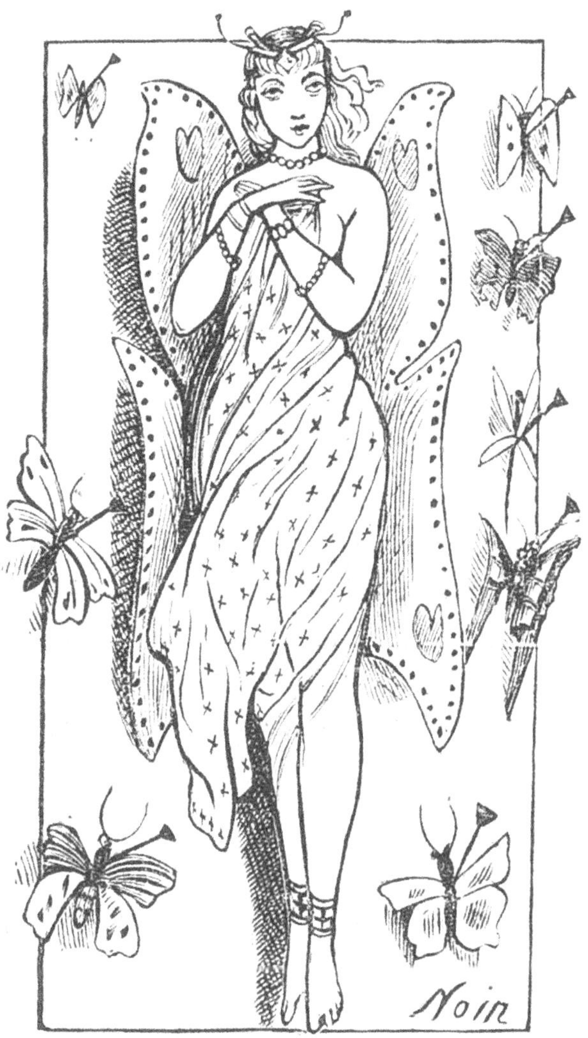

2.5   Marie Duval (1875) 'Papillonis Sillibillis: or, Sillybilly Butterfly', *Judy, or the London Serio-comic Journal*, Volume 17, p. 21

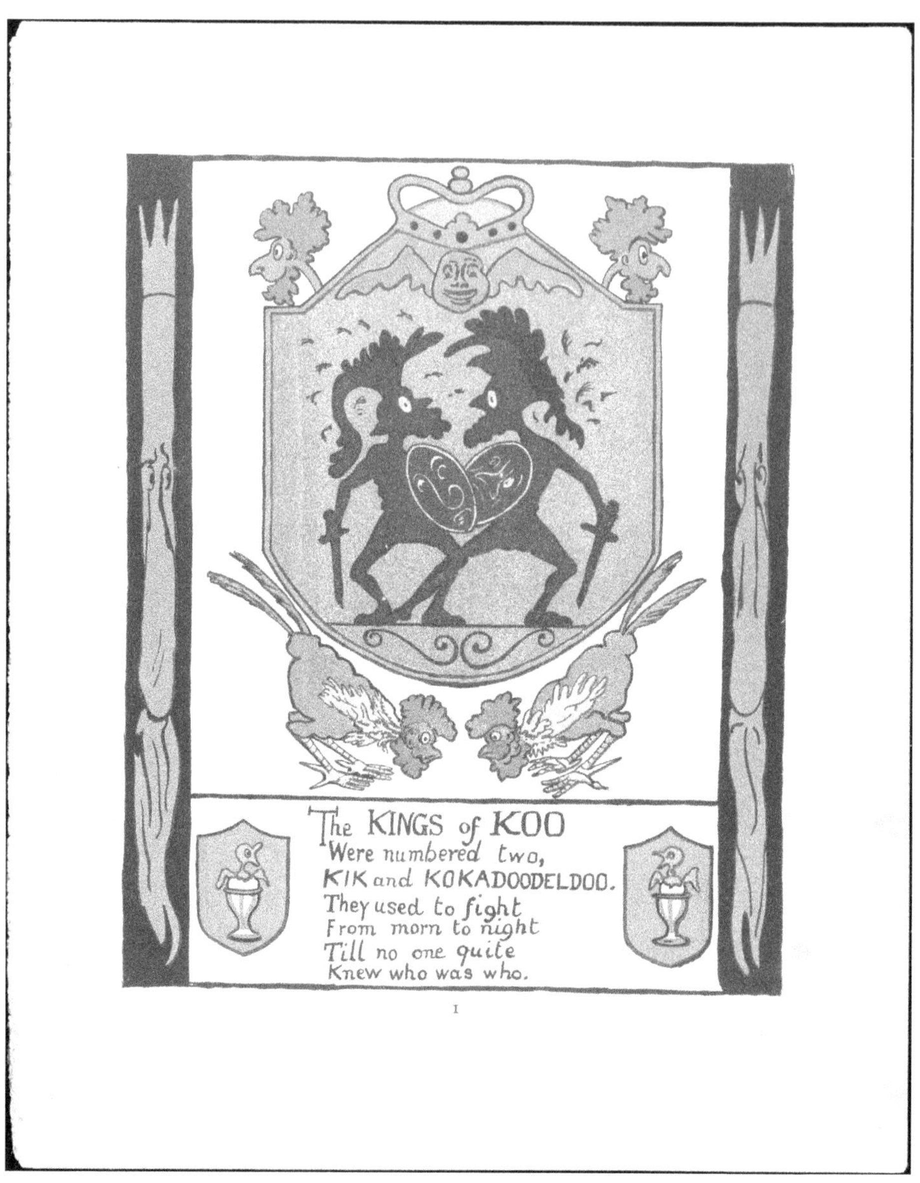

2.6   Marie Duval (1874) 'The Kings of Koo', *Queens & Kings and Other Things*, London: Chatto & Windus, p. 41

attempts to reach new readerships by adopting suitable pseudonyms. Warren variously described herself as Eliza Warren, Mrs Warren, Warren Francis, 'the mother of the family' and The Editor, as she created new voices directed at different readers, within the *Treasury* (Hadjiafxendi and Zakreski 2013: 38 and 45). The name and identity of 'Mrs Warren' survived her retirement, as the name of the editor, recognised, trusted and related to by readers, whoever was editing the paper (Hadjiafxendi and Zakreski 2013: 48).

Duval's drawings, and her career as a humorous periodical artist, were undertaken in a social environment where the masculinising effect of employment on women was frequently thought to undermine the foundation of society. Women employees challenged conceptions of the significance of domestic life and visualisations of them created meta-phorical elisions between the appearance of men and the masculinisation of women, in which employed women were also considered unfeminine.

In working to visualise both femininity and women's employment, Duval's work focused on the relationships between conceptions of femininity and masculinity, employment, the domestic realm and the public realms. Her employment as a professional artist rendered significant the fact that she had the job, as well as the types of visual work that she produced while employed. For readers, knowledge that a professional women actor was employed as an artist was a significant aspect of navigating, understanding and consuming Duval's drawings.

Duval's drawings exploited the contradictions inherent in her public entertaining and the inhabiting of the masculine role of visual journalist, transposing a series of relationships permissible between the stage and its audiences to the pages of a periodical journal. The stage environment highlighted the mutability of the appearance of genders in a context in which mutability itself was usual, expected and commoditised. As a result, Duval was able to successfully incorporate masculine, that is vulgar, humour into her identity as a woman employee of a periodical paper.

Duval's journalistic trade was an entrepreneurship of ideas, in which feminisation, masculinisation and gender shifts were brokered to readers as a particular reflection of daily life. The idea of women mutually revising and visualising ideas of work and femininity was a motor that drove the entertainment that readers found in Duval's drawings. She set aside social and ethical anxieties about the masculinisation of women, instead recognising the existence of new paradigms of femininity and an active evaluation of the significance of these paradigms, making the transformation of femininity itself the object of her employment.

Notes

1 Quoted in Huneault 2002: 8.
2 'It is the substructure from which all civilised life arises' ('Housekeeping' 768).
3 For nineteenth-century theorisations of differences of types of activities socially suitable to men and women and the idea of gendered 'separate spheres' see de Tocqueville (1840: 101); Patmore (1857); and Ruskin (1865).

4 'Swell' was the word for a wealthy or aristocratic man-about-town, or those pretending to be. 'Masher' was the word for both men and women looking for romance. Both terms were attended by stereotypical visualisations. The 'swell' displayed his class by the very high quality of his clothes and the association of his gestures and accents with aristocratic traditions (Duval 1875a). The 'masher' was dressed up, 'dressed to kill', in clothes not the best, flashing rather than spending money (Duval 1883a).

5 I am grateful to Barry Anthony for drawing my attention to this newspaper report, bringing together Duval, Boulton and Park. The report outlines how Melbourne Theatre Royal proprietor H. R. Harwood accused actor Alfred Penrhyn of being Ernest Park, in a breach of contract case. In a witness statement, the actor Boothroyd Fairclough described going backstage with Boulton and Park and their appearance in the Cremorne Gardens scene.

6 Duval was early on identified publicly as the author of her drawings, indexed by her style. See 'The Women About Town' (1872).

7 Berlin work is a type of large stitch embroidery, often used on domestic soft furnishings and upholstery.

8 Of the team members' hair, Miss Echo notes 'the startling magnificence of the chevelures, some bubbling on high in countless frizettes; some in shining plaits lustrous as quilted satin; others round and large as a Sultan's turban; others jutting out behind like a porter's knot, and one "en saucisson"'. Miss Poly Glott, the compiler of a glossary of Girl of the Period terms in future issues, 'in black velvet, looked as soft as a pussy, and classic as Hamlet', whilst Mrs Vernon Veret, the only married member of the team, was 'a little bit of a dowdy, with a strong touch of the muff': '(Conscience-stricken silence, during which the creaking caused by tight lacing was distinctly audible)' (Miss Echo 1869: 2).

9 Zola 2008; James 1963; Onions 2010.

3

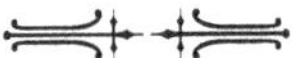

Marie Duval's theatre career and its impact on her drawings

Julian Waite

Early appearances

This chapter undertakes a survey of Marie Duval's acting career. As will become rapidly clear, this is a matter of reconstruction from surviving evidence, principally Ellen Clayton's short biography (in *English Female Artists*, 1876), newspaper reviews, advertisements and listings and surviving play-scripts from the Lord Chamberlain's collection. Sadly, even evidence from the latter is piecemeal, Charles Ross's scripts for Duval's two triumphant performances at the Surrey Theatre having been lost. However, it is hoped that this chapter will serve two purposes – giving a sense of how Duval's theatre career interlocked and supported her illustration career, and using Duval's illustration career to reflect on how a creative practitioner in the second half of the nineteenth century would have constructed what we might now call a portfolio career out of a range of skills. This theme is further developed in Chapter 7.

Underlying any historical survey of work is gender. Duval was a nineteenth-century woman working in two different industries: one where men held the power of agency and control although women had a clear and unequivocal place (the performance industry) and another dominated entirely by men at every level (illustration and journalism). It may be conjectured from the following that Duval's early success in theatre, which overlapped but mainly preceded her later success as a cartoonist for *Judy* may have given her the skills and attitude to find a place in the even more male-dominated world of journalism.

My strategy in charting the chronology of Duval's career must by necessity be based on references to her in newspapers, there being no accounts or diaries extant by Duval or her circle of her activity apart from Clayton's unique and brief biography. Her work is reported in various publications, although in terms of density *The Era*, being very much the theatre newspaper of the period, provides the bulk of references and reviews. The first mention of Duval in surviving newspaper archives is, however, from a satiric magazine *Will-o'-the-Wisp* where she is cited as being in an amateur production at the Bijou Theatre by the Notting Hill Dramatic Club ('Some Amateurs' 1868: 11). In the last performance of the evening, a farce called *The Happy Family* featured Duval dressed in:

> a pretty white frock trimmed with blue ribbons […] about whom I went home dreaming. Dear heart, how pretty she looked and how nicely she spoke, and how I wished she had had a little more to say, for I don't believe it was half-a-dozen sentences. (1868: 11)

Part of this review is quoted in a listing for her first-known professional performance in *The Era* just a few weeks later ('Mademoiselle Marie Duval' 1868).[1] The review mentions her role as Dewdrop in the 1868–69 revival of *The Sleeping Beauty in the Wood*, an operatic fairy extravaganza by English playwright James Robinson Planché. This verse pantomime had been first produced in 1840. Duval's revival was at the St James's Theatre in King Street, Piccadilly, which no longer exists (demolished 1957; Howard 1970: 210). The pantomime was a recognisable retelling of the classic story and Duval played one of the good fairies present at Beauty's nuptial party who bestowed the first gift on her:

FAIRY DEWDROP:
I first shall give the little dear my fairing –
Receive this small drop of mountain dew,
The purest mind that ever mortal knew. (Planché 1840: 12)

These are the only lines spoken by the character. However, it would appear that Duval, as in *The Happy Family* a few weeks earlier, made an impression due to her looks and deportment. The review of *The Sleeping Beauty in the Wood* in *The Era* found that 'Fairy Dewdrop, by Miss Duval, was dressed most sprucely and her whole bearing was ladylike and piquant' ('The St James's' 1868: 13). Duval's entry into public notice is here encoded in terms that suggest exactly the attitude of Victorian male voyeurism deconstructed into its fetishistic parts by writers such as Levin. She shows how the diarist Arthur Munby, writing of a fleshings-clad[2] female acrobat, explicitly states the allure of 'decency' contrasted with apparent nakedness, and of the female form with 'masculine' musculature required for circus feats:

> The female aspects of the costume were crucial in the fantasy for Munby, but so too were the fleshings and her seemingly naked, muscular legs […] The juxtaposition of gender typologies was the special thrill: As Munby notes, the acrobat was not only strong and capable of daring feats but paradoxically feminine, at risk of being '[…] perched up there, naked and unprotected, with no one to help her'. (Levin 2009: 141–2; the final words quoting Reay 2002: 148)

The same paradox is operating here, where the anonymous and presumably male reviewer chooses 'piquant' with its suggestions of stimulating taste buds as a summary of a description that is entirely prurient whilst simultaneously signalling propriety. Even more intrusively the reviewer of the *Will-o'-the-Wisp*, quoted here, found it appropriate to go home dreaming about her, a line repeated in an advertisement for the entire

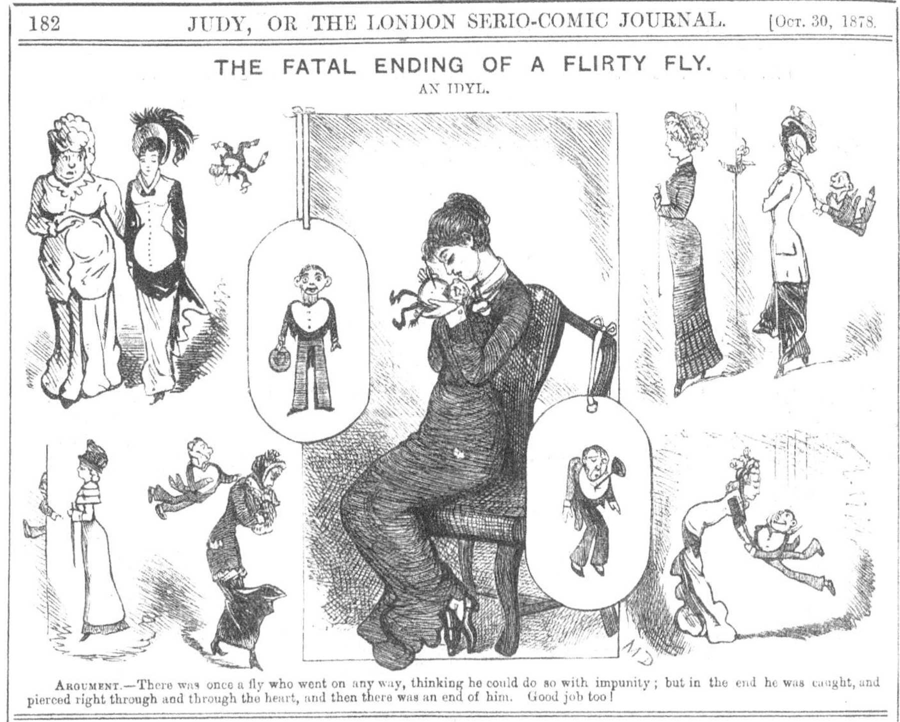

3.1 Marie Duval (1878) 'The Fatal Ending of a Flirty Fly', *Judy, or the London Serio-comic Journal*, Volume 23, p. 182

pantomime published in *The Era* the same day as its own review, also quoting other unnamed papers where Duval 'Looked and acted like a lady', 'The prettiest of Selinas' ('Mademoiselle Marie Duval' 1868: 1). Thus, a Munby-esque mixture of prurience and faux shock is maintained: Duval is 'like a lady' (1868: 1) yet 'piquant' ('The St James's' 1868: 13), playing a pure character who speaks 'nicely' yet is the stuff of sexual fantasy. Duval was later to unlock this dichotomy in proto-feminist cartoons such as *The Fatal Ending of a Flirty Fly* (Duval 1878h, Figure 3.1).

Nell Darby points out that the celebrity culture of today has its roots in the late eighteenth century and reached something of a zenith in the 1870s and 1880s. Fan mail and what would now be described as stalking was prevalent in the 1870s and 1880s. Darby quotes a schoolboy letter to a pantomime star in 1885 who exclaimed: 'I love you very much and know you do not care for me and you do not know me' (Darby 2017: 44) in a curious echo of the (presumably) adult *Will-o'-the-Wisp* reviewer. A similar hypocritical confusion is revealed when he continues: 'I love you because you are beautiful, but more because the inner man (*sic*) is displayed; for beauty is skin deep, but virtue will endure' (Darby 2017: 44)

As well as suggesting that Duval was from the first, unsurprisingly, the subject of capitalist physical commodification, this reporting demonstrates that in this commodified profession where looks and stage presence were valuable for an actor, and especially a female actor, Duval was noticed and rapidly became, in terms of these quotations at least, an object rendered by the male gaze.

Her next recorded performance was in *The Beast and the Beauty; or no Rose without a Thorn* in 1869. Her role in this pantomime, by F. C. Burnand (best known today for providing the libretto for Sullivan's *Cox and Box*), was similar in size and status to Dewdrop. The play was never printed but exists in the Lord Chamberlain's play collection in the British Library. Accounted a success by *The Era*'s reviewer, despite some hasty writing from Burnand, Duval is shown as being in only one scene, where she did not speak: 'A matronly countess and five fashionable ladies, invited to the Beast's party, found suitable representatives in Mrs Rouse, and the Misses Dubois, Marie Duval, Eversfield, Osborne, and Frances Melville' ('The Royalty' 1869: 10). This is the scene depicted in the bottom centre of her *Judy* drawing of 20 October 1869 (Figure 3.2). With the absence of a known photographic portrait of Duval, it is curious and frustrating that Duval gives no indication which of these faces is her own self-portrait. We might conjecture that her subsequent modesty in depicting her own performances in cartoons suggests she is the shadowy figure in the centre, but in fact it remains for the reader to decide, perhaps comparing the other hints of Duval's looks charted in this chapter (Figures 3.8 and 3.13).

Duval in Ross's *Clam*

Duval's next recorded appearance onstage is an entirely different level of activity. *Clam, a Romantic Drama* opened on 16 April 1870 and marks, if press activity is anything to go by, the first time Duval has a claim to be a 'known' actress. *Clam* was also written by Duval's common-law husband-to-be,[3] Charles Ross, and was to be the first of several of his plays that she appeared in. Her illustrating evidences that Duval and Ross knew each other before this time, as they had initially collaborated on panels of Ally Sloper the previous year. However, we do not know whether Ross met her though her employment as an artist (she published her first illustrations just before Ross took over as editor) or he first came across her as an actor. However, indisputably at this moment their careers both onstage and in print were entirely entwined.

Clam was to be Ross's most successful play, and sadly the text is entirely lost, never having been published, and missing from the Lord Chamberlain's collection at the British Library.[4] However, there are extensive reviews so that we can get a good idea of the nature of the play and Duval's part in it.

Clam was presented at the Surrey Theatre, which was in Blackfriars Road in Lambeth until its destruction in 1934. It was an old theatre, first built in 1782, but had been rebuilt following a fire only five years before *Clam*. It was an important theatre, being south of

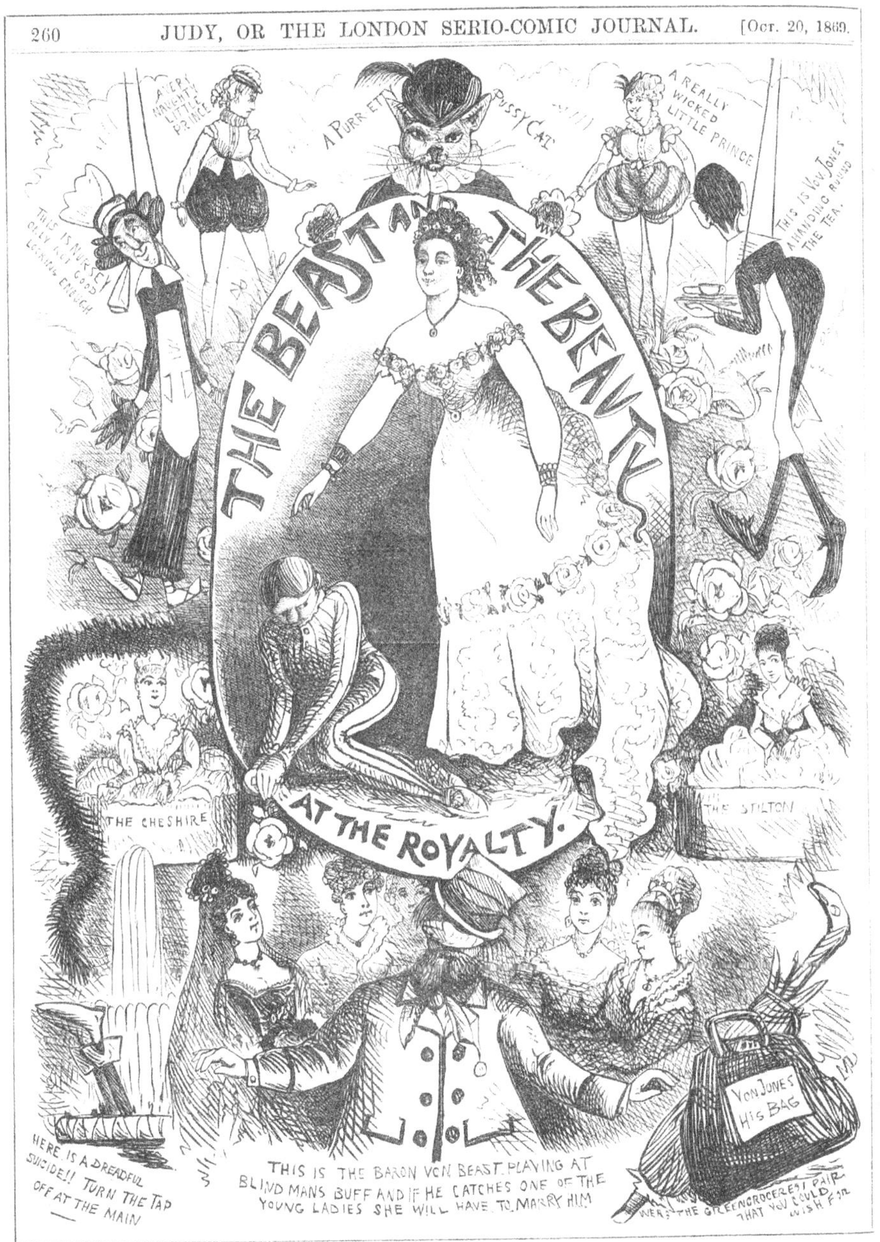

3.2 Marie Duval (1869) 'The Beast and the Beauty at the Royalty', *Judy, or the London Serio-comic Journal*, Volume 5, p. 260

the river and a well-established home to melodrama, the genre of this and Ross's subsequent plays *Ruth* and *Silence*.[5] *Clam* is identified as such by the review in the *Illustrated London News*, which described it as 'melodramatic in the extreme' ('Surrey' 1870: 18) and there is contemporary awareness of the specific nature of the Surrey audiences in the *Daily Telegraph* where the anonymous reviewer writes that *Clam* 'may be regarded as a production fulfilling every condition required by audiences on this side the water'. It goes on to say that the Surrey audience are 'ever ready to swallow an exciting draught without being critically scrupulous as to the ingredients' ('Surrey' 1870: 3). This decided whiff of snobbishness confirms that at the time Duval and Ross presented their work at the Surrey it was still a cheap theatre with benches in the pit and a crowded gallery filled with spectators eager for drama and 'sensation'. Mayhew's 1851 description of the nearby Victoria's gallery gives a vivid picture of the sort of crowd who attended mid-century melodrama:

> All around the door, the mob is in a ferment of excitement and no sooner is the money-taker at his post than the most frightful rush takes place [...] As you look up at the vast slanting mass of heads from the upper boxes, each one appears on the move. The huge black heap, dotted with faces, and spotted with white shirt sleeves, almost pains the eye to look at, and should a clapping of hands commence, the twinkling nearly blinds you [...] The bonnets of the 'ladies' are hung over the iron railing in front, their numbers nearly hiding the panels, and one of the amusements of the lads in the back seats consists in pitching orange peel or nutshells into them, a good aim being rewarded with a shout of laughter. (Mayhew 1851: 25–6)

Duval was an artist highly equipped to depict just such a crush, one she must surely have endured (see for example 'Sloper in Knots' (Duval 1881a) where a crowd who have got free tickets to the front row of an event debunking a séance burst through the door exactly as Mayhew describes). Although the description sounds chaotic, the subtle appreciation of the audience is emphasised by Mayhew, since any misbehaviour is clearly ascribed to disappointment and the engagement and enthusiasm at appropriate and appealing work is immediate: 'The shrill whistling and Brayvos that followed the tar's performance showed how highly it was relished' (Mayhew 1851: 27), whereas 'no delay between the pieces will be allowed, and should the interval appear too long, some one will shout out – referring to the curtain – "Pull up that there winder blind!"' (Mayhew 1851: 27). The same etiquette clearly still featured ten years later at the Surrey. Davis and Emeljanow quote an anonymous 1869 account describing the audience at the Surrey as 'an enthusiastic, nay a noisy audience [...] but well behaved, more cordial, and most sincere [with] visible social gradations' (Davis and Emeljanow 2001: 32). Ross's play *Silence*, in the West End, was much less kindly received.

The Surrey would appear to be the model for Duval's occasional cartoons showing the Pit or Gallery, rather than a theatre like the Bancroft's Prince of Wales, which was refurbished in 1865 to remove the rowdy pit and replace it with seating rows that would be familiar to a theatre-goer today. Booth notes that during precisely the period of Duval's two Surrey shows, this movement to 'gentrify' the West End was taking place, creating something of a split between exclusive middle-class theatre, showing small 'drawing room' theatre, and the larger theatres such as the Surrey south of the river and the Princess's and Adelphi in the West End, which were still doing large-scale spectacle and melodrama (Booth 1991: 7, 52–62). This was exemplified by the Haymarket's controversial increase of the stalls' prices from 1 shilling to 10 shillings in 1880 (Booth 1991: 52).

Duval, or the writer providing her text, refers to this explicitly the following year. The text beside one of the cartoons in 'Sloper's Mixture' (Duval 1881b) reads: 'It is not often nowadays that the white hat rests beneath the velvet cushion of the costly stall.' The white hat is Sloper's and the production, which is illustrated, a revival of *The Corsican Brothers* at the Princess's Theatre. It is instead the older style venues that generally feature in Duval's earlier cartoons, for example 'Sloper at the Play' (Duval 1874a; Figure 3.3) where Sloper interacts with decidedly working-class characters at the back of the pit, whilst by 1878 Duval appears to be more comfortable drawing seated stalls and a middle-class audience shocked at accidentally arriving onstage with the cast in 'Personally Misconducted' (Duval 1878; Figure 3.4).

The story of *Clam* as played to the appreciative crowd at the Surrey was convoluted and deliberately dense. Ross crammed incidents into his play: two young sisters of unknown parentage cross-dress their way through adventures with 'street Arabs' ('Surrey Theatre' 1870: 3) and the attentions of a money lender. Villainy perpetrated against their father is resolved and Clam herself protects her sister and then selflessly gives up her claim to the love of the rich hero, an Oxford undergraduate. If this sounds confusing it clearly was, the reviewer of the *Daily Telegraph* noting that Ross has 'supplied to overflowing his piece with adventure' and then added some in the shape of numerous set pieces, including a much encored can-can so that the piece 'is replete with incident and without one scene that flags' ('Surrey Theatre' 1870: 3). In sum, it is precisely the fare that Mayhew reports as being likely to enthral a mixed audience with a strong working-class presence, south of the river.

Marie Duval appears as 'a street outcast known as Piccadilly Peter' and is mentioned favourably in the same *Telegraph* review as coming 'conspicuously forth in the cast' ('Surrey Theatre' 1870: 3). This was a 'trouser role' (in which women actors played male roles, also known as 'travestie' roles), a common convention of the time (see Chapter 8). As described, Duval was praised for her feminine appearance in earlier work, and there is little doubt that her appearance would have been considered equally attractive and indeed erotic 'en travestie'. She appeared in male roles not only in *Clam* but also in her next two known roles, Claude Duval in *The Beggar's Uproar* and Lord Fernfield in Ross's *Ruth*. Her attractiveness as a woman in drag is also specifically mentioned in the 1873 divorce case where she was cited as co-respondent.

Duval in burlesque: *The Beggar's Uproar*

As was usual in theatre practice of this period *Clam* was accompanied by various curtain raisers and after-pieces. Towards the end of the run (7 May 1870) the evening ended

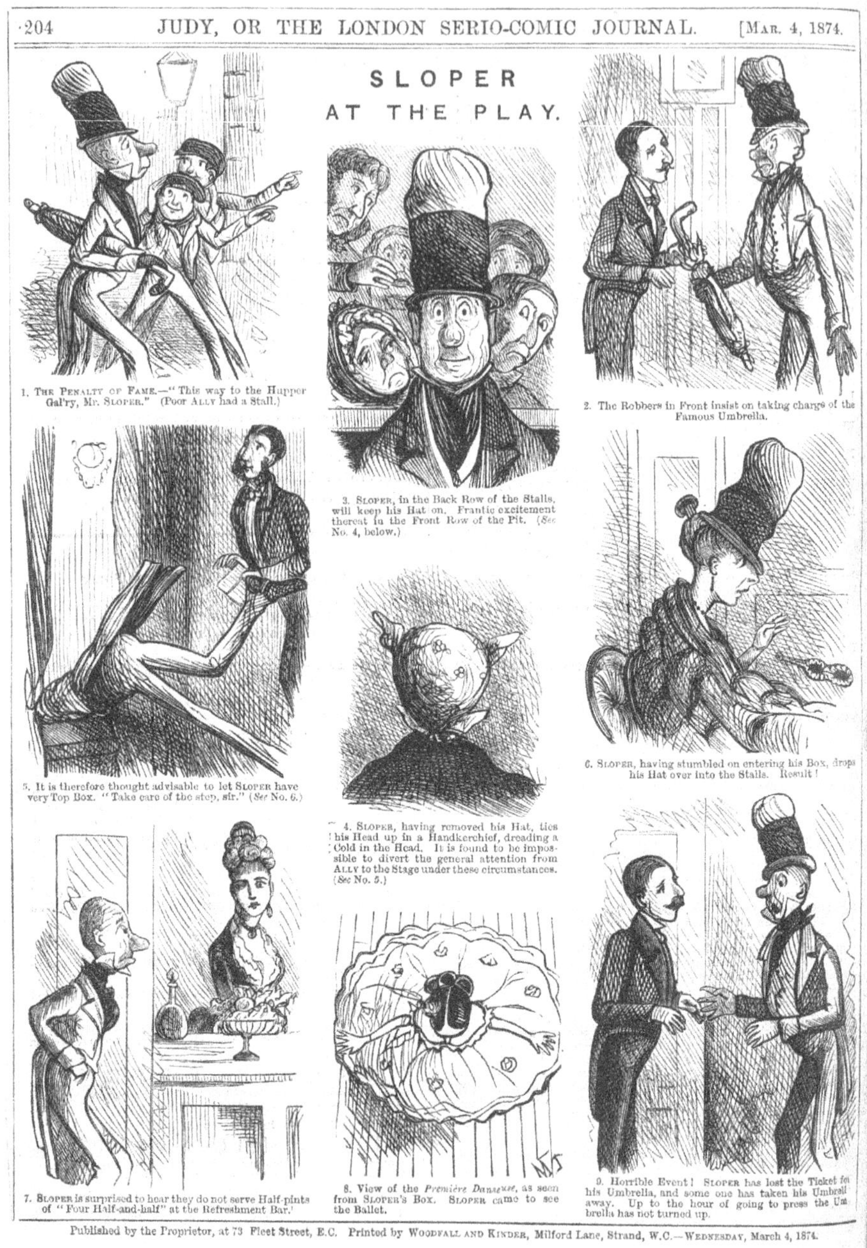

3.3 Marie Duval (1874) 'Sloper at the Play', *Judy, or the London Serio-comic Journal*, Volume 14, p. 204

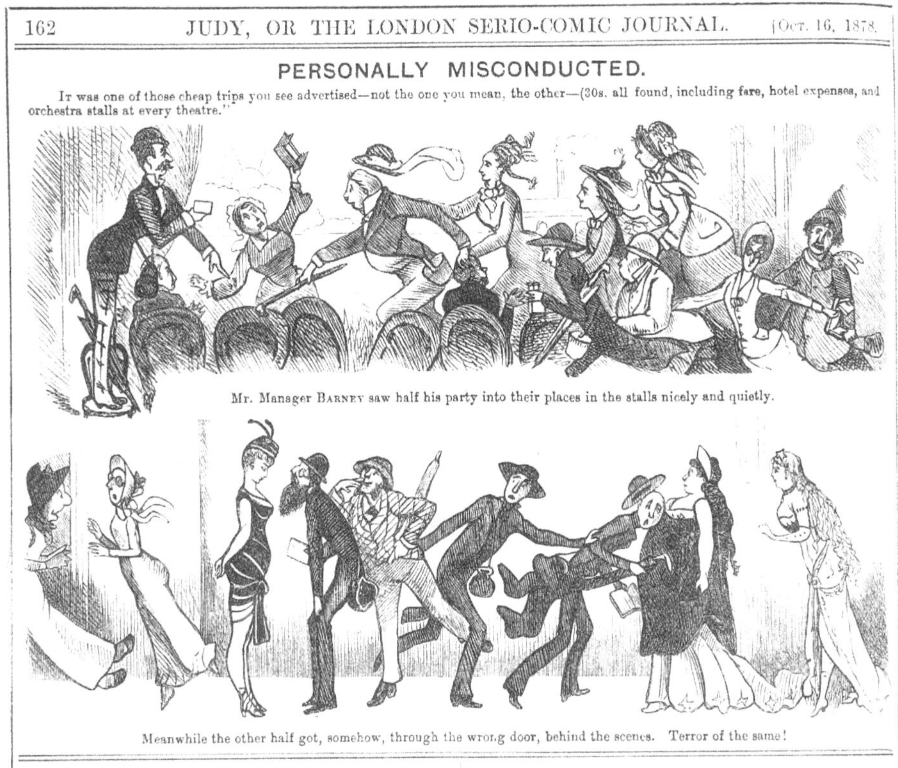

3.4 Marie Duval (1878) 'Personally Misconducted', *Judy, or the London Serio-comic Journal*, Volume 23, p. 162

with *The Beggar's Uproar* by Hubert Jay Morice in which Marie Duval played the highwayman Claude Duval (Morice 1870). On the page the piece reads exactly as described by the anonymous reviewer in *The Era*, that is something of a mess. Their comment that after the robber scene 'he would be an historian of preternatural sagacity who attempted to explain the progress of the story beyond this point' is entirely apt, and although later in the review the piece is condemned as 'a nondescript extravaganza', the writer found it a highly enjoyable nondescript extravaganza – rollicking in fact – and reports that the audience found the same. 'A very crowded audience, nevertheless, signified their perfect satisfaction with the piece, which is made the vehicle of innumerable songs and dances, and the author was called for at the fall of the curtain' (all 'Surrey Theatre – (Last Night)' 1870: 14).

In this piece, not only Marie Duval, but every single one of the long list of highwaymen were played by women (including even Macheath and forty-odd supporting non-speaking robbers). It seems highly likely this display was intended as erotic, *The Era* review emphasising the attractiveness of women in men's clothing: 'about forty young damsels, who look pretty enough in their powdered whigs [*sic*], square-cut coats and flesh-coloured tights' ('Surrey Theatre – (Last Night)' 1870: 14). In the third scene, there is a hint of Duval's exceptional good looks in that she was cast as the highwayman who is the seducer of the ladies:

MAC: Are you prepared my gallant Captains say
         To stop the Mail when it shall pass this way?
ALL: We are!
JACK: I'll to the coachman look.
DICK: The guard must me beware of.
JACK: I'll hold the horses' heads!
DUVAL: The ladies I'll take care of.
DICK: I'll skid the wheel.
JACK: I'll cut the traces.
DICK: I'll grab the swag.
DUVAL: Come, let's take to our places. (Morice 1870: 33)

There is no indication of whether there was any business associated with this aspect of her role and thus whether the potential titivation of a woman seducing a woman was purely verbal or enacted.

Another section plays on Claude Duval's supposed French nationality and suggests that Duval, although not born or raised in France, was able to speak some French due to her parentage. There is a similar ambivalence in her drawings where the 'ignorant' English mangle the French language, yet flatteringly the reader is expected to be able to understand limited stretches of French. Thus in 'At Bolong' (Duval 1869b), the English mother pestered with a child's question eventually lapses into frustrated French with 'Tai toi donc tu m'embetes'[6] (Duval 1869b). Similarly, in *The Beggar's Uproar*, Duval's French character speaks French with the assumption the audience will understand it (or, perhaps, that it would not matter whether they do or not). This section also reveals interesting levels of self-reference:

CAPTAIN: Claude Duval.
DUVAL: V'la monsieur.
CAPTAIN: You are the ladies [*sic*] Highwayman, aren't you, also the dashing,
          you speak French.
DUVAL: Mais parfaitement. C'est ma langue a moi.
CAPTAIN: But then it strikes me, Claude Duval, you lived in the time of
          Charles the Second, how is it you're here in Jack Sheppard's time
          and in this dress, this must be looked to.
DUVAL: But is so in ye book – for one penny. I am dress as they dress me.
CAPTAIN: Dick Turpin, you rode to York you say … (Morice 1870: 41)

The reference to the absurdity of these historical characters all turning up in the same play and wearing the same costumes is a clear example of the way these performances involve a knowing interaction with an audience, which is far from simplistic. Taylor cites Walter Goodman, writing in 1895, about the actress Mrs Keeley, showing how she could utilise comedy even in the midst of melodrama: 'She employed the "arch" style of comic acting that impressed one with the idea that she was enjoying the joke quite as much as the audience, and yet was unconscious of being the cause of their merriment. This gave a spontaneity to everything she did or said, making her acts and words appear perfectly natural or unstudied' (Taylor 1989: 142). Our contemporary review of Duval gives her no more than a mention, and her acting is not singled out. However, we can safely assume that she as much as the rest of the cast 'exerted themselves strenuously to promote the success of this nondescript extravaganza' ('Surrey Theatre – (Last Night)' 1870: 14).

Duval on tour

On 6 August, Marie Duval and *Clam* went on tour, starting at the Theatre Royal, Croydon and visiting Leicester, Birmingham, Newcastle and Oldham throughout the autumn 1870. The notice writer in *The Era*, presumably Ross, continued to feature Duval alongside stars Burdett and Glover, and dancer Leslie ('Mr Charles H. Ross's Provincial Tour' 1870). By September Duval was in Birmingham and continuing to receive good mentions: 'Miss Marie Duval and Miss Mary Grainger were successful as […] Piccadilly Peter and Ragged Jack' ('Birmingham' 1870: 11).

Despite the pressures of touring and the probable daily rehearsals, it would seem that Duval found time to draw. This period of intense theatre activity coexists with Duval's early publications in *Judy* (her first cartoon appeared in March 1869 and she was drawing regularly from July that year) and in *Smiles and Styles* for Lynes & Son (October 1870).[7] However, together with her output for *Judy*, which in 1870 consisted of at least 70 known drawings, this is clear evidence that Duval was by this time performing and illustrating simultaneously. Suggestively, the *Smiles and Styles* booklet is announced at almost the same time as the *Clam* tour, implying that she had time whilst engaged in her long London run to put into illustrating before heading off on tour, despite the work that would need to go into her role in *The Beggar's Uproar* and any of the other burlesques in which she may have performed.

Duval's theatre cartoons and their relationship to her performance work

However, Duval's drawings appeared pretty regularly in *Judy*, and there is no sense of her taking these months off, nor do her cartoons follow a discernible autobiographical agenda. There are explicit cartoons of the theatre, some of which appear to follow her biography. A clear example is the panel on 'The Beast and the Beauty at the Royalty' (Figure 3.2) in which she appeared (Duval 1869c). The image is full of references that are only comprehensible to someone who had seen the performance, and given that *The Era* reports that the theatre was 'crowded to excess' then this is perhaps not unreasonable ('The Royalty' 1869: 10).

It also seems reasonable to assume that Duval created this picture either from life or with the help of portrait *cartes de visite* of the actors. However, the female faces, as often, are somewhat stylised and certainly Martha Oliver, who played Beauty and whose image is much the largest, did not look very much like Duval's portrait to judge from her photograph in the Victoria & Albert Museum theatre collection (Elliott and Fry 1866). By far the most successful actor in the cast was Charlotte Saunders who played the Beast's side-kick Tiger Tim. For her, Duval depicts a cat head, even though it would seem she played the part with subtler make-up – 'with her features fashioned to a cat-like look' ('The Royalty' 1869: 10). On the other hand, E. Danvers, who played the dame, receives a recognisable caricature as 'nursey' who is given the presumably ironic legend, 'only not good looking enough' (Duval 1869c). Danvers's photograph can be seen in the Victoria & Albert Museum theatre collection. He is portrayed playing Scampa in a burlesque of Ernani (De Vere 1865). Ross's first play *Worryburry's Whims* was on the same bill, although Danvers didn't perform in it ('The Theatres' 1865: 19).

The caricature of Danvers is also interesting in having a reference that certainly requires explanation for those who had not seen the performance. From his body, and from H. Elton's opposite him, two strings are extruded, which look very much like wires, suggesting these two characters flew. In fact, it was not that. Rather, they performed a dance that became particularly famous beyond the performance, being praised by *The Era* as 'the best feature of the burlesque, a Fantoccini Quadrille, in which the dancers simulate the movements of Marionettes' ('The Royalty' 1869: 10). Like a number of other dances and songs from the show this 'was loudly applauded and deservedly redemanded' ('The Royalty' 1869: 10). This notion is very well caught, particularly in the Danvers caricature, where his body in Duval's hands assumes the limpness of a rag doll, or perhaps a Dutch doll, which was to become a signature trope. This early cartoon therefore shows a precise influence of the movement of the human body playing a puppet that recurs again and again in Duval's opus.

With this exception, mapping Duval's known theatre activity to her drawings, from her earliest productions to the rest of her career, produces only occasional correlations rather than precise connections. Thus the opening of *The Beast and the Beauty* on 10 October 1869 (Duval 1869c) – which came seven months after her first known published drawing 'The Moulsey Hurst Papers' (Duval 1869d) – coincided with a cluster of theatre-related drawings also in *Judy* on 6 October ('The Story of a Lady who Married a Walking Gent' [Duval 1869e]), 13 October ('Some of the Latest Fashions' [Duval 1869f)]), 8 December ('The Siren' [Duval 1869g]) and a whole sequence of individual images in the 22 December edition. There is then a curious gap until the following year when another cartoon appears on 13 April ('At a burlesque' [Duval 1870n]) that coincides with the opening of *Clam* (17 April 1870).

Three theatrical cartoons, among many that are not, follow during the London run of *Clam* ('Not Entirely a Fancy Sketch' on 11 May [Duval 1870o] and two cartoons 'At the Theatre Royal and at a Hall' on 15 June [Duval 1870p]). From 6 August when Duval set off on tour with *Clam* there are no theatre cartoons, and the period of this tour and the following year's production of *Ruth* are the period where we have the fewest cartoons (a mere 23 in 1871 compared with 70 the previous year. This is also the year of Duval's involvement with the married man Herbert Such.).

Whilst she was on tour, Duval interestingly produced a number of cartoon sequences. 'Paul and Virginia' started in June 1870 and ran through to 10 August. As an ongoing serialised story, she could have drawn this at any time and stockpiled the drawings. For most of the tour, and certainly during the early months of August and September, Duval only contributed one cartoon a week to *Judy* of Ally Sloper's adventures in the Franco-Prussian War. Being decidedly topical there might have been some logistical problems in getting these illustrations to London,[8] or perhaps Duval was returning to London between engagements just giving the time for this reduced output. Moss's movements confirm that actors frequently travelled by train, for short-term tasks, in this period (see Chapter 7).

Two other sequences of cartoons that emerged in this period seem biographically suggestive. On 18 August 1869, three individual cartoons appeared on one page of *Judy*, about having photographs taken, a theme that never appears again in Duval's work (Duval 1869h). She was to open in *The Beast and the Beauty* only two months later. Is it possible she was having a *carte de visite* made, which led to employment, or the cast of the performance were being photographed for advertising purposes? Second, through much of the summer and autumn there was a strong concentration of drawings about society parties, which is a theme she occasionally returned to, but never again in such profusion. This was the period of her success in *Clam*, the dates when the affair with Herbert Such originate and perhaps the time when she was establishing her relationship with Ross. Was she enjoying a 'higher class' social life for the first time in view of her sudden success in a named role in a hit play?

The cluster of cartoons in October and December specifically about theatre are particularly interesting for their variety. They show backstage details but there is also a focus on audiences (that continues throughout Duval's work). There are both narratives, such as 'The Story of a Lady who Married a Walking Gent' (Duval 1869e; Figure 3.7) and individual drawings. In a cartoon like 'Pictures from Fairyland (Not by Richard Doyle)' (Duval 1869i; Figure 3.5) a reference to the saccharine fairy cartoons of Doyle, the reader is invited to savour the realism of bitchy backstage conversations. This is surely the sort of exchange Duval, with her concurrent experience of backstage choruses, would have been well placed to invent, if not literally overhear.

Another cartoon in the same edition of *Judy* seems to depict the sort of audience Duval would have been playing to nightly at the Royalty as she performed in the burlesque *The Beast and the Beauty*. Called 'The Last New Burlesque' (Duval 1869j; Figure 3.6) the

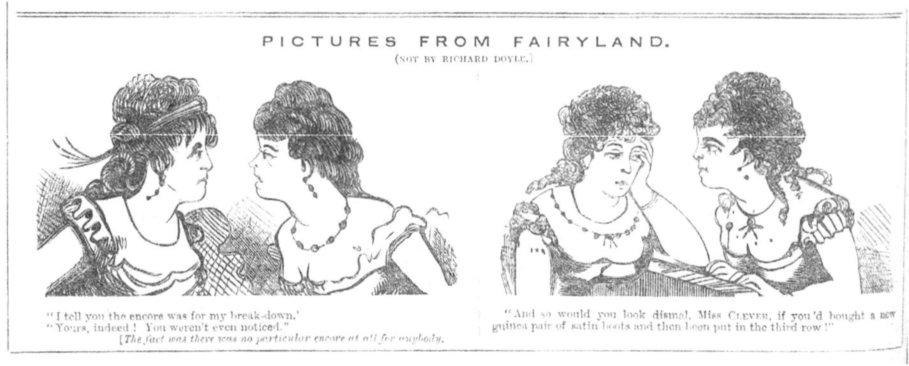

3.5　Marie Duval (1869) 'Pictures from Fairyland (Not by Richard Doyle)', *Judy, or the London Serio-comic Journal*, Volume 6, p. 80

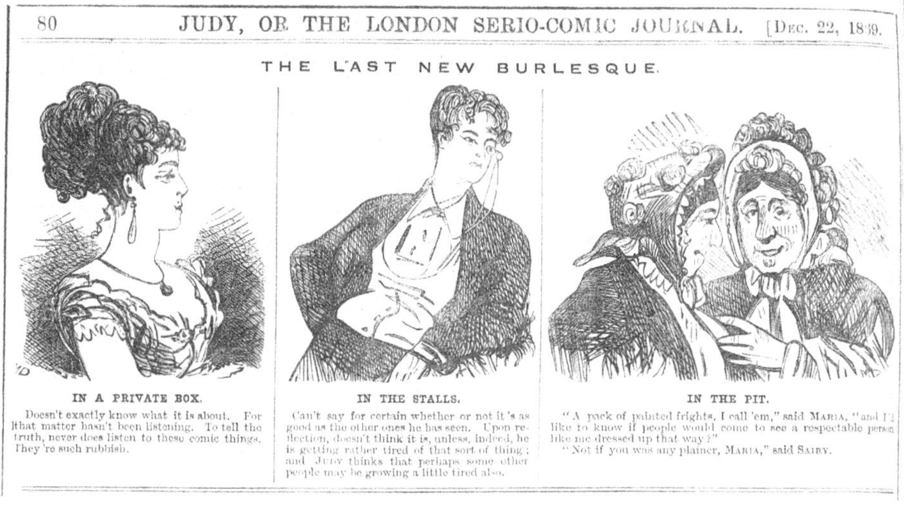

3.6　Marie Duval (1869) 'The Last New Burlesque', *Judy, or the London Serio-comic Journal*, Volume 6, p. 80

panel shows the contrasting reactions of three areas of the theatre and their inhabitants. A languid beauty in a box is not even listening to the play; a swell in the stalls is unsure if he thinks 'it's as good as the other ones he has seen' (Duval 1869j), whilst in the cheapest pit a couple of older theatre-goers gossip about the finery around them.

Duval's use of stock characters

Duval shows her knowledge of stock company characters in her first explicit cartoon about theatre, 'The Story of a Lady who Married a Walking Gent' (Duval 1869e; Figure 3.7). This cartoon refers to the category of actor in melodrama (the 'walking gentleman'), a good-looking minor character such as Horatio from *Hamlet* or Benvolio from *Romeo and Juliet* (Booth 1991: 126). Comically, Duval's Walking Gent is not what he seems, yet he is also a male on display, subject to his later wife's female gaze. In her drawing Duval gives the woman agency, emphasising her eyes – indeed in the first panel the eye is almost all that is visible. Similarly, the male is passive whilst the woman actively journeys through the rain to deliver the marriage proposal in a written communication at the stage door. In this frame neither sees the other, the woman's head being entirely covered by an umbrella, and the actor represented only by a hand and a pipe. In the last two panels the fan and umbrella are stripped away from the woman who appears 'dishabille' whilst moustache and padded tights are stripped from the actor, who is revealed as a paunchy drunkard. The whole panel is centred around a typically Duvallian image of the tights themselves, which have become personified with the actor's hat as head, standing in front of flaming footlights.

The whole is an extraordinarily sophisticated rendition of the semiotics of theatre at the service of an archetypal narrative. Even the simple, but not simplistic, manipulation of the body language of the characters in the first two acts, as she reveals breasts and he bends towards her, contributes to a play of meanings that is entirely in line with stock character and burlesque. It is perhaps no accident that Duval's second contribution to this issue of *Judy* on the facing page is a love tale of two shop toys, their romance doomed by human agency and their passage in life as symbolic as our contemporary Toy Story franchise. The principal remains the same, whilst the body language is reduced to an absolute scheme.

Duval and *Ruth*

While Duval was on tour (during the second half of 1870) the newspaper record reveals her emergence as a successful periodical artist. The following year was to bring the last major successful London theatre production that Duval was involved in. Again, a collaboration with Ross and the Surrey Theatre, *Ruth, or a Poor Girl's Life in London* opened on Saturday 18 February 1871. It would seem that the management of the theatre and Ross himself were capitalising on the success of *Clam*, which had only finished touring a few months before. Reviews for *Ruth* were similarly enthusiastic for the play, the production and Duval's part in it. As before, Ross seems to have got the combination of elements for the particular audience represented at the Surrey Theatre exactly right, combining a mix of Dickensian sentimental realism with spectacle and 'sensation' whilst not being over careful about plausibility or the structure of the plot. Like *Clam*, the play is lost, having no publication and missing from the Lord Chamberlain's manuscript collection

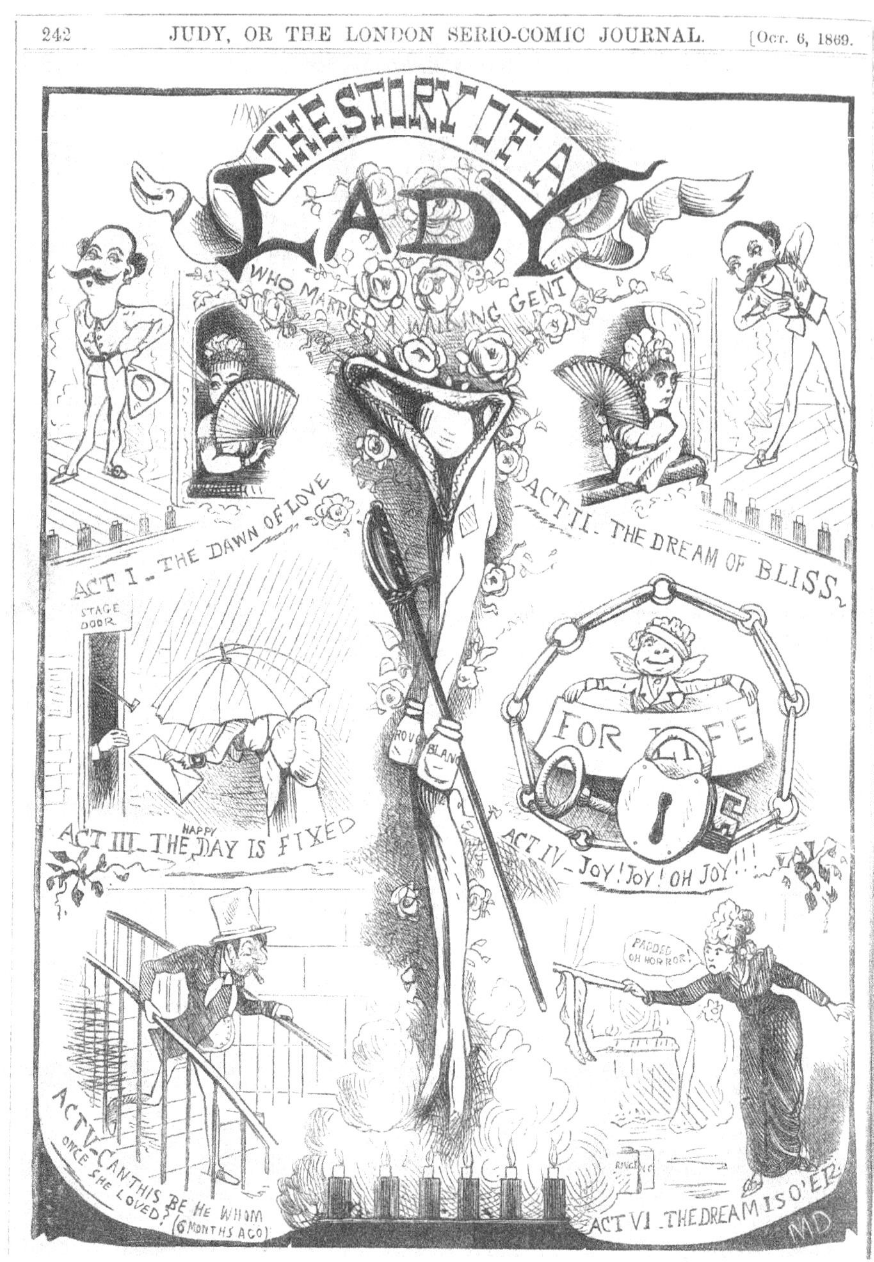

3.7   Marie Duval (1869) 'The Story of a Lady who Married a Walking Gent', *Judy, or the London Serio-comic Journal*, Volume 5, p. 242

(see previous note). However, from extensive reviews (this was Duval's most reviewed performance by far) it is easy to see that Duval played her most important role and was universally commended for it.

The character Lord Fernfield is a significant driver to *Ruth*'s plot and another 'trouser' role for Duval. Unlike the street character Piccadilly Peter, he is a nobleman who as the owner of jewellery purloined by the villain is instrumental in discovering the latter's deceptions and revealing their extent. As with *Clam*, the staging at the Surrey was spectacular, with much praised scenery depicting a number of London settings, of which a snowstorm in Hampstead Heath (where Ruth's mother dies, played by notable West End actor Marie Henderson in a successful double with the role of Ruth herself) and especially the scene of Covent Garden Market (complete with hundreds of extras) were particularly lauded by critics. Another innovation was the use of a split stage for the second act so that the audience could simultaneously follow the progress of Ruth in a lowly garret in Bermondsey and the benign nobleman Sir John Worth in a 'saloon in Belgravia' ('Surrey Theatre' 1871a).

The plot, which the reviewer in the *Morning Advertiser* admits was impeded rather than helped by comic interludes and 'the acrobatic services of the gentry retained for the favourite pantomime, running and to run at this popular theatre' ('Surrey Theatre' 1871a) forms another swirling mass of incident, treachery, pathos and absurd coincidence. The *Clerkenwell News* found it entertaining 'though full of inconsistencies and incongruities' ('London Amusements' 1871: 4). The *London Evening Standard* clearly thought the plot incomprehensible, likening it to a mess of pottage: 'Passing over any reference to the plot as superfluous, the play might fairly be termed an olla podrida [hodgepodge], in which the burlesque, comedy, farce, sentiment, idealism, realism, and broad caricature, are alternately depicted, producing greater or less effect on the sympathies of the audience' ('Surrey Theatre' 1871b). However, as typically with reviews of this period, the writers attempt various synopses from which the following plot emerges.

In the first act Ruth's father is wrongly transported as a convict, due to the machinations of Frank Lucas, then a clerk to the benign banker John Worth. Her mother treks to London to die in the aforementioned snowstorm. With the second act the baby of Act 1 is now Ruth herself, living with a pawnbroker who, for purposes of multiple settings, also owns a farm! She is affianced to Frank Lucas and is making a wedding dress for Florence who turns out to be about to marry the very same Frank Lucas who caused the death of Ruth's mother. Duval appears as the companion to Florence on what seems to be essentially her hen night, and the same morning Frank marries Florence, and Ruth faints away as the curtain falls.

Duval had comic work with Hester Penge, her landlord's housekeeper, in Covent Garden Market in Act 2 as reported in *The Era*: 'an exciting bit of fun takes place, when Hester Penge arrives in a covered cart, drawn by a pony, and gets hustled by the roughs and befriended by Fernfield' ('The Surrey' 1871: 11). Later he is again involved with comedy between the pawnbroker and his pigs (which the pawnbroker keeps in an apparent instance of city farming) at the start of Act 3. Fernfield's presence allows him to witness both the distress of the six-month married Florence (who later dies of neglect) and overhear that Lucas has pawned jewels that he, Fernfield, left with him for safekeeping. Realising Lucas is a villain, Duval's character has a pleasing scene where she jumps out from behind the counter to confront Lucas at the pawn shop. Perhaps it is more than coincidence that during the run of *Ruth* Duval drew the cartoon 'Another to Sloper' where Sloper and Ikey Mo plan a jewel heist (Duval 1871b).

In the final act Frank, still at large, attempts to steal £300 from Sir John Worth who has now taken in Ruth. They are living in another innovative set, where their cottage has the front removed so that the audience can see Ruth's bedroom above Sir John's sitting room. Sir John almost dies of a congenital fit following Frank's invasion, is saved by Ruth, the police drag Lucas back and finally Sir John adopts Ruth thus giving, as it were, restitution for the earlier accidental destruction of her family.

Interestingly, the survey of contemporary historian George Taylor (who identifies the ability of the structure and content of melodrama to appeal to the macrocosm of society that was represented in theatres of the 1870s) receives strong confirmation from the reviewer of *Ruth* in the *Morning Advertiser*. So, for example, Taylor suggests that the clown Frederick Robson's pathos was comic precisely because his audience related to his plight whilst laughing at his failures: 'There was an astonished tension between the emotional identification with the beggar's distress and amused recognition of his musical incompetence' (Taylor 1989: 75). *Ruth*'s reviewer notes that the play's appeal is visceral and ranges across the different classes present in the audience:

> A crowded and sympathetic audience, to whose minds, through their feelings, the characters and incidents of the piece made the most direct and powerful appeal. The upper classes [meaning in the physical not economic sense] in the highest circles of the gallery, representing the honest toiling costermonger section; the middle classes, in every sense, in the boxes, composed of well-to-do, industrious tradesfolk; and their assistants, shopmen with their wives and sweethearts, in the pit,– each and all found themselves typified and their manners and customs reflected with more or less truth to nature, in not a few of the dramatis personae of the melodrama of *Ruth*. ('Surrey Theatre' 1871a)

This is precisely the construction reproduced by Duval in her cartoon 'The Last New Burlesque' (Duval 1869j; Figure 3.6). The reviewer goes on to reveal, perhaps, the snobbery that was inherent in much Victorian criticism as they write, 'The lowest life was certainly most faithfully represented, divergence from real fact into romantic fiction increasing as the characters nominally ascended in the social scale' ('Surrey Theatre' 1871a), this probably reflecting the reviewer's assumptions of the 'simplicity' of the classes 'below' rather than the quality of Ross's writing.

As mentioned, 1871 was a year of intense activity for Duval in the theatre and perhaps, as a consequence, a year where she produced very little drawing. *The Marie Duval Archive* lists only 23 cartoons for this year as opposed to 70 for 1870 and 89 for 1872. Of these only two make direct reference to performance (Grennan, Sabin and Waite

2016). 'Judy's Valentines' of 1871 is, however, unique in that it contains a cartoon of 'a burlesque lady who wore her chignon and earrings when in male attire' (Duval 1871c; Figure 3.8).

Duval opened in *Ruth*'s trouser role on 20 February 1871, only five days after this drawing appeared. Her costume caused some comment in reviews mostly for its appropriateness rather than sexual connotation. Thus, the *Illustrated Times* reviewer wrote: 'Miss Marie Duval plays a boy's part, and she does not give the slightest offence either in dress or in manner' ('The Theatrical Lounger' 1871: 123). However the *Morning Advertiser* did feel the need to comment on this very established theatre convention, passing both a mild criticism and veiled reference to the fact that her costume is tantamount to nudity or at least the 'fleshings' of the less respectable burlesque: 'Lord Fernfield was represented with consummate coolness by Miss Marie Duval whose fault was that he looked too boyish in years though not in shape. This was too plainly perceptible, his jacket being very short, and his continuations [trousers] so tight that they were evidently worn merely for the sake of form' ('Surrey Theatre' 1871a).

Duval in Ross's *Silence*

The universal praise in which Duval and Ross were basking was, however, not to last. Ross's next play, *Silence*, was produced less than three months later on 6 May 1871, not at the Surrey but in the West End at the Holborn Theatre. It was an unmitigated failure. The reviewer from *The Era* actually returned two weeks later to report on the extensive changes that were attempted in order to make the entertainment acceptable. *Silence* is extant in manuscript at the British Library (Ross 1871b). It would be interesting to see if on the page *Clam* and *Ruth* read the same way, and how far the so-called 'transpontine' (river-crossing) audience of the Surrey made shows work that the reviewers found confused where a West End audience did not or would not. There is perhaps some evidence that the traditions and expectations of the audience may have contributed since *Silence* went on tour with *Ruth* later in the year, with no ill report.

That said, one of the reviews mentions that the production was made hastily. Given the recent opening of *Ruth*, this seems likely. The reviewer wrote. 'An extraordinary experiment was made at the Holborn on Saturday. With little or no preparation, the house reopened with two new pieces – One by Mr C. H. Ross, the author of 'Clam' produced at the Surrey a season or two ago' ('The Theatres' 1871: 14). After the 'fiasco' of its opening night the management also attributed blame to multiple sources, including the audience in a rather cruder way than I have attempted here. Unlike the incompetence of the backstage staff, the poor quality of the play could not be completely washed away: 'The Manager of the Theatre while admitting the fiasco of the first night, attributes it to lax management, hurried preparations, the incapacity of carpenters and scene shifters, and, lastly, to an organised conspiracy on the part of some among the audience to damn the piece' ('The Theatres' 1871).

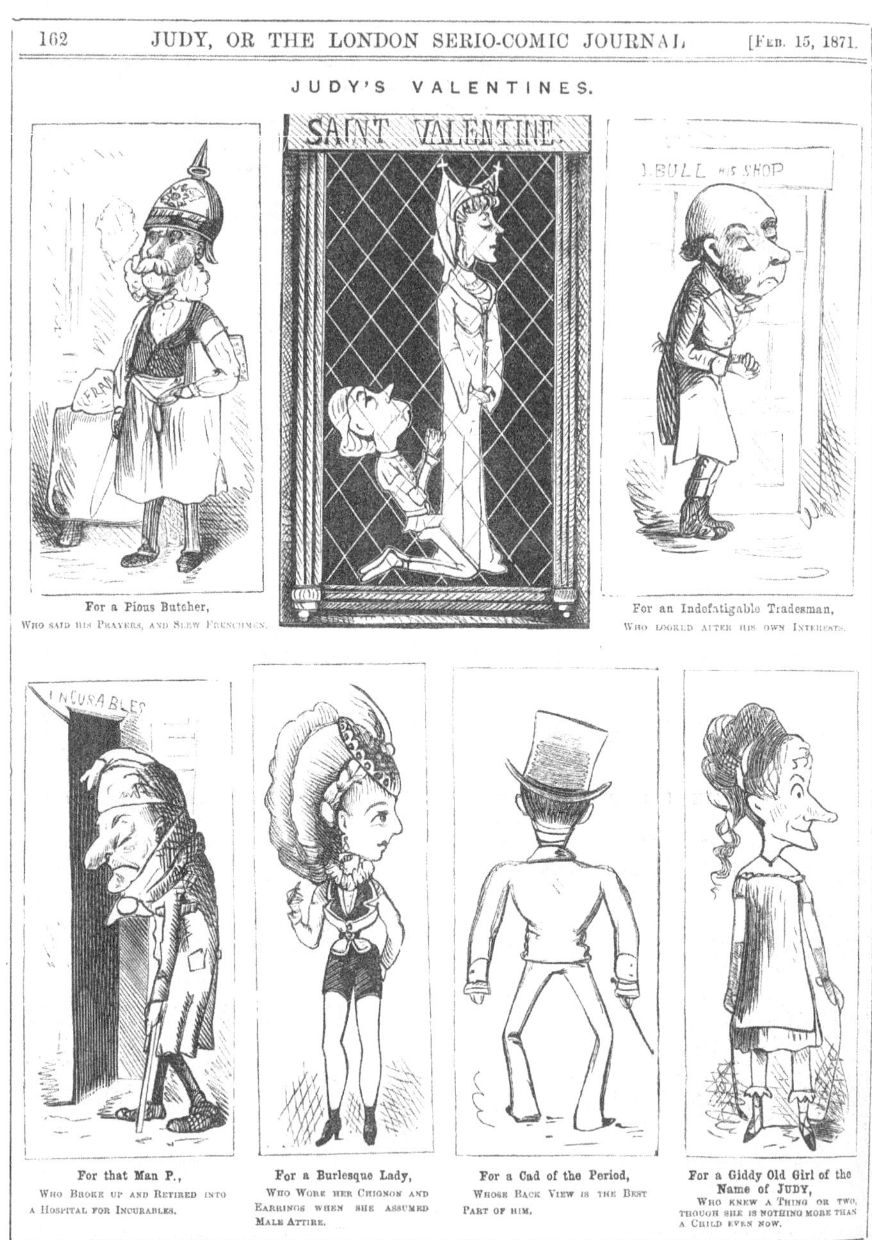

3.8   Marie Duval (1871) 'Judy's Valentines', *Judy, or the London Serio-comic Journal*, Volume 8, p. 162

However, perhaps the most surprising aspect of this set of reviews is the specific condemnation of Marie Duval's acting. Bizarrely, given the universal praise she had gleaned in the previous two years, this same reviewer is positively and personally vitriolic: 'Miss Duval, whose original name of Tinker has now been changed to Parker, *only makes herself ludicrous whenever she appears, and the sooner she resigns all pretensions to the stage the better. We have heard a child of five or six years speak with more intelligence than this young lady displays in the small part allotted to her*' ('The Theatres' 1871). What is undoubtedly true is that the part she had was much smaller (appearing only in the final scenes). Despite this, there is a kind of postscript to *Silence*, which appears in *The Referee* fully nine years later. In a column reminiscing about theatre, a writer recalls this production as a disaster, but slightly misremembers the play (citing the companion piece that Duval was not in): 'A very curious experiment was tried here about eight or nine years ago with a piece of rubbish called 'Salammbo' or 'Sallambo'. In it I remember Marie Duval appeared' ('Dramatic and Musical Gossip' 1880: 3). By 1880 this would surely be worthy of mention only if Duval was firmly established as an important cartoonist, since she was by this time almost certainly not performing.

One other footnote to *Silence* is provided by a cartoon in later 1870, called 'Mr Blank's Dramatic Agency' (Duval 1870q; Figure 3.9). In this Ally Sloper aspires to be an actor and joins an agency, which turns out to be a scam run by Ikey. This cartoon encapsulates an aspect of theatre that became very significant in the latter years of the nineteenth century and which is extensively remarked upon by contemporary historians – that is the rise of the amateur actor. For example George Taylor notes that by 1895 even great stars of the London stage such as Beerbohm Tree had risen, like many others, from amateur status: 'he worked in the City for some eight years so that when he became a professional in 1878, he was one of the many "amateurs" with no family grounding in the theatre. According to Michael Sanderson's statistics, during the 1880s 58.7 per cent of new actors came from the Professions, Commerce and Industry' (Taylor 1989: 168).

I have mentioned that Duval herself is first recorded as a performer in an amateur stage production in Notting Hill. Thus, Duval's cartoon showing a predatory theatre agent is complex, representing a current issue and being prescient in its implication. However, there is also a nice reversal, in that Ally is of course always aspiring to middle- or upper-class mores, so the strip is also a parody of the new class of actors. A further level is provided by the fact that Ross and Duval were also creative practitioners who moved fluidly between professions. It is also possible that there was a literal inspiration for the strip, if there were discussions of casting between Duval and Ross, since it emerges that at least one of the cast of *Silence* had precisely this amateur background: 'In the Esther of Miss Hathaway there is evidence that she has only very recently left the amateur stage' ('The Holborn' 1871).

There is yet one other curious autobiographical moment for Marie Duval associated with *Silence*. In the burlesque that followed (which was actually called *Salammbo*)[9] the *Illustrated London News*'s reviewer notes that the heroine's 'affections are divided between Athenaeus, her graceful husband (Mr Such Granville), and Athos, the strong man (Mr.

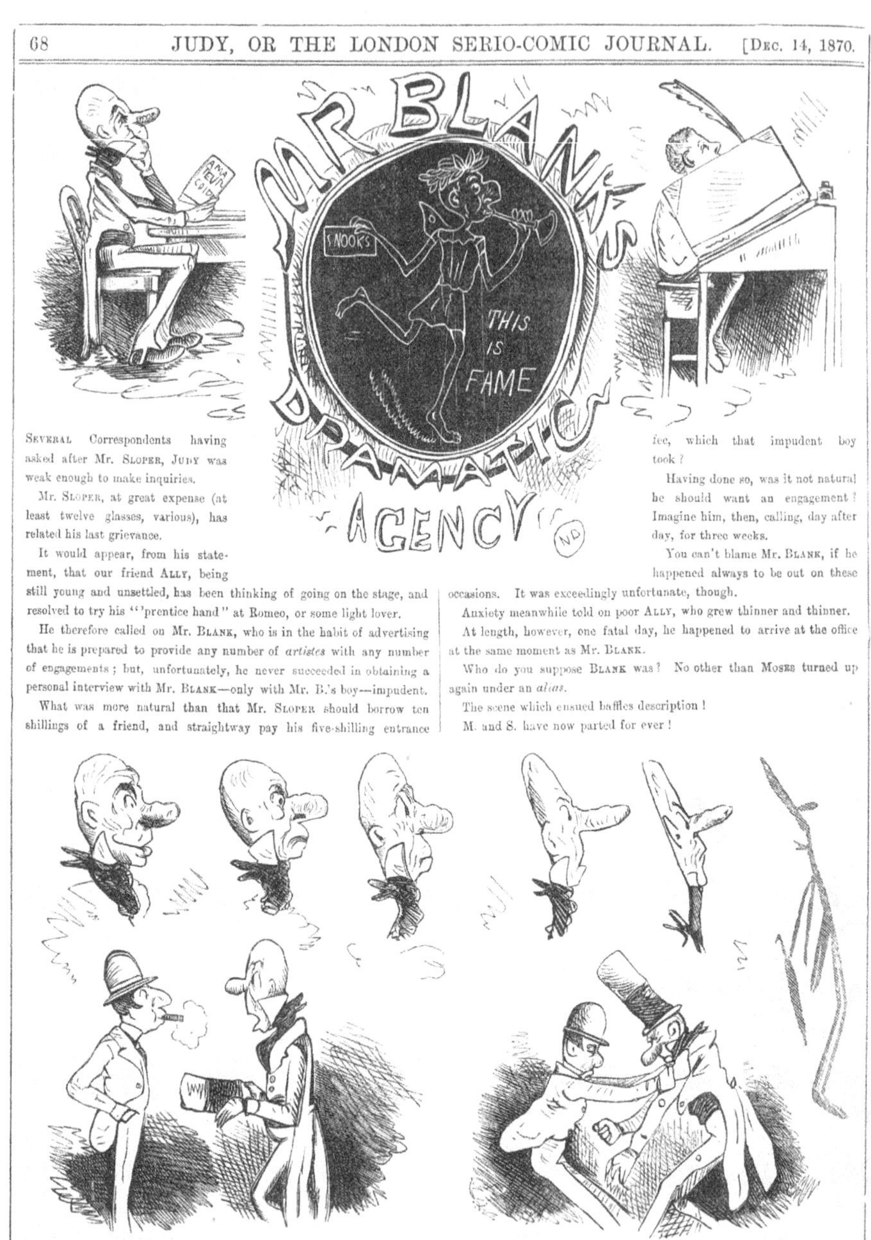

SEVERAL Correspondents having asked after Mr. SLOPER, JUDY was weak enough to make inquiries.

Mr. SLOPER, at great expense (at least twelve glasses, various), has related his last grievance.

It would appear, from his statement, that our friend ALLY, being still young and unsettled, has been thinking of going on the stage, and resolved to try his "'prentice hand" at Romeo, or some light lover.

He therefore called on Mr. BLANK, who is in the habit of advertising that he is prepared to provide any number of *artistes* with any number of engagements; but, unfortunately, he never succeeded in obtaining a personal interview with Mr. BLANK—only with Mr. B.'s boy—impudent.

What was more natural than that Mr. SLOPER should borrow ten shillings of a friend, and straightway pay his five-shilling entrance fee, which that impudent boy took?

Having done so, was it not natural he should want an engagement? Imagine him, then, calling, day after day, for three weeks.

You can't blame Mr. BLANK, if he happened always to be out on these occasions. It was exceedingly unfortunate, though.

Anxiety meanwhile told on poor ALLY, who grew thinner and thinner.

At length, however, one fatal day, he happened to arrive at the office at the same moment as Mr. BLANK.

Who do you suppose BLANK was? No other than MOSES turned up again under an *alias*.

The scene which ensued baffles description!

M. and S. have now parted for ever!

3.9   Marie Duval (1870) 'Mr Blank's Dramatic Agency', *Judy, or the London Serio-comic Journal*, Volume 8, p. 68

Irish)' ('The Theatres' 1871). Two years later Mr Granville would appear in Marie Duval's life more significantly. But before turning to Duval's involvement in a divorce scandal, we can quickly describe the other few instances of her theatre work that survive in written records.

Sangley's *The Birth of Beauty*

Duval's next recorded appearance was in pantomime at Sangley's Grand Amphitheatre (formerly and much better known as Astley's). In line with the venue this was an equestrian piece, *The Birth of Beauty*, featuring a magical horse that made its rider beautiful. There is no record of what part Duval played, but she is prominently reported as being engaged for the piece in a number of sources, one being *The Globe* of 9 November 1872 ('Art, Literature, and Music' 1872:). Her panel 'Behind the Scenes' (Duval 1873g) is clearly, like 'The Beast and the Beauty' of 1869, one of the few direct references in her artistic output to her stage work.

This exceptional insight into backstage life prominently depicts the pain of an actress on a wire, which if not drawn from personal experience must surely have been something Duval witnessed time and again in her work: 'calculated to give terrestial bodies a bad attack of Pins and Needles' (Duval 1873g). Likewise, the ambiguously predatory man (claiming to be hanging around backstage because he can't find his way out), jealous dance partners and accidents with clothing all have the ring of truth. Duval's ability to efficiently depict expression is utilised in the highly authentic and bitter little exchange between two dancers: 'Well, don't push yourself in front of me again, that's all', says the ambitious bully (Duval 1873g).

The following week, Duval's contribution looks back nostalgically but realistically on the Christmas holiday. In central images, the pantomime clown bids goodbye for another year, whilst two glamorous characters are depicted returning home in humdrum fashion, the man with his spangled costume in a bag, the woman running for a bus: 'The last of the Fairies hails the last 'bus. "Full inside, Miss. Will any gentleman ride outside to oblige the Dewdrop of the Dazzling Dell?"' (Duval 1873h). This world-weary yet affectionate portrait of both the woman and the potentially chivalrous behaviour of fellow working people is striking in its authenticity.

Duval's depiction of Irving and other performers

However, the fact that in neither of these drawings does Duval mention the name of the show she was in is consistent with her practice and, perhaps, her modesty. Similarly, she resists the temptation in her 'round up of the year's performance' in her cartoon of the previous month, 'The Drama of 1872' (Duval 1872c; Figure 3.10), where she makes no reference to the spectacular performance of 'The Birth of Beauty'. The drawing is, it would seem, a record of the popular productions that characterised 1872, of which Henry Irving's version of *The Bells* has remained a historical landmark.

Duval's image places Irving's work centre top of her spread. She reproduces Irving's face – almost certainly a copy or even tracing of the notable photo image of Irving as Mathias made the previous year (London Stereoscopic and Photographic Company 1871). Duval covers several of Irving's performances, not just *The Bells*, which actually opened in 1870. By 1872 Irving was performing in his next triumph, the now forgotten *Charles I* by W. G. Wills. Its success was described in hyperbole by the *Daily News*: 'During the last act there was scarcely a dry eye in the house. Women sobbed openly, and even men showed an emotion which comported ill with the habitual serenity of the stalls' (*Daily News* 30 September 1872, cited Pascoe 1880: 194). Indeed, Duval's drawings reveal Irving's importance at this early stage of his career, since she refers back to the 1871 production of *The Bells*; 'Do you remember the famous waltz at the end of Act II?' (Duval 1872c, Figure 3.10) and then cites his comic performance in the revival of *Raising the Wind* in April 1872: 'This old farce by James Kenney, with the principal part of Jeremy Diddler much resembling that of Jingle, gave Irving similar opportunities for comic eccentricity' (Bingham 1978: 92).

Her beautifully composed spread therefore shows the waltz from *The Bells* depicted, as often in Duval, as puppet-like figures on a turntable, Irving as Mathias, Irving as Diddler both in portrait and tumbling out of French windows, and a reference to the critical acclaim of Irving's transformation into Charles I by showing an artist (presumably Van Dyck) flying and carrying his portrait with his arm through the eye of a 'mask'. This reference to Van Dyck was recalled and explained thirty years later by Irving's biographer and stage manager Bram Stoker (better known as the author of *Dracula*) who wrote that:

> one of the notable things of Irving's *Charles I* was his extraordinary reproduction of Van Dyck's pictures. The part in its scenic aspect might have been called 'Van Dyck in action.' Each costume was an exact reproduction from one of the well-known paintings; and the reproduction of Charles's face was a marvel. (Stoker 1907: 89)

The truth of this can be attested by the National Portrait Gallery's photograph of Irving made up for the part (London Stereoscopic and Photographic Company 1873). Duval's flying artist is presumably meant to be Van Dyck, although this would appear to be a generic image of an 'old master' since Van Dyck looked nothing like this and died at 42.

Something of Duval's method is visible here, since her image of Charles I is clearly a copy of the well-known and much distributed etching by Michael Vandergucht (Vandergucht after van Dyck 1706), which would certainly have been available to Duval. The 'mask' that the artist is holding is obscure. It is perhaps meant to depict Irving out of character, since there is an 1870 portrait of Irving with a similar moustache and hairstyle also in the National Portrait Gallery, but could equally be a recalled portrait of his first London success as Digby Grant in *Two Roses*, which opened in June 1870, who also sported a drooping moustache. If the former, Duval is employing a nice conceit, showing the actual artist as a mask, and his creations as real people; if the latter, presenting a survey of Irving's London successes with a mask as the commencement of his work.

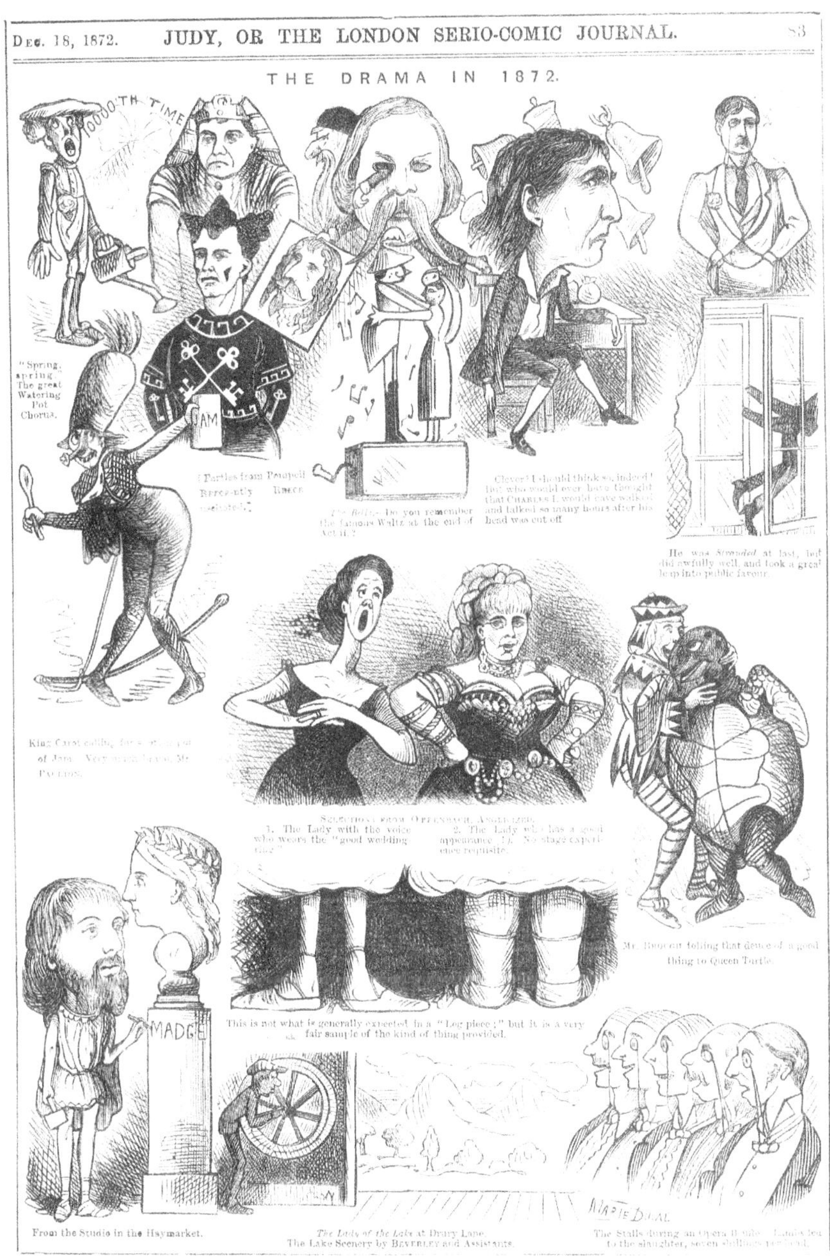

3.10   Marie Duval (1872) 'The Drama in 1872', *Judy, or the London Serio-comic Journal*, Volume 12, p. 83

Duval returns to *Charles I* in January 1873 when she provides further illustrations from the play (which was to run until April 1873) to accompany a delightful piece where *Judy*'s new reviewers, who are replacing 'The Only Jones' (Ross's pseudonym for his reviews) on account of Jones's supposed corruption. One of the two new reviewers turns out to be deaf and the other almost blind, so between them they manage to return to a different theatre after the interval and are confused that Cromwell seems to have grown taller (Duval 1873i).

Duval's 1872 review of the theatre year (Figure 3.10) includes several other successes that were celebrated contemporaneously but are footnotes or lost to history today. Thus, Lionel Brough is singled out from the stellar cast of Covent Garden's *Babil and Bijou*, a clearly incomprehensible spectacle of songs and costumes (this image is right centre in the spread). *The Spectator* describes the scene that Duval depicts:

> When Babil and Bijou arrive at the palace of King Octopus – a wonderful aquarium, where the sea-change is indeed rich and strange beyond belief – and the huge and silvery turtle pronounces for the foreign visitor, nothing more exquisitely ludicrous can be conceived than the flirtation, as conducted by Mr. Lionel Brough, with furtive asides relating to cold punch and lemons. ('Babil and Bijou' 1872)

In another image, left centre, Duval shows Offenbach's *King Carrot*, which has never been revived in modern times, memorialising it with a depiction of Harry Paulton's performance, 'a burlesque actor of considerable quaintness' according to the 1880 dramatic list (Pascoe 1880: 278). A portrait of Paulton in the part, recognisably in the costume Duval depicts, survives in the Victoria and Albert collection (Fradelle and Leach 1872). The contemporaneous Offenbach craze is confirmed with two cartoons of leading ladies (where either ability or looks are required but not both, middle centre) and a third of a row of gullible and easy to please swells as: 'Lambs led to the slaughter, seven shillings per head' (Duval 1872c, bottom right).

Duval also foregrounds a scenic artist, in William Roxby Beverley, whose sets for *The Lady of the Lake* at Drury Lane included a moving backdrop (bottom, centre). This does not necessarily reflect Duval's artistic interest, as scenic artists were regularly mentioned in reviews and their work often considered a strong reason to visit pantomimes and other spectacles. Thus, Beverley would have been as well known to readers of *Judy* as Paulton or Irving and his place in the cartoon unremarkable.

Duval's involvement in the *Such* v. *Such* divorce

Ironically, however, Duval's most pervasive appearance in the national and local press occurred in May 1873 when she was cited in a divorce case between Such and Such. The events were reported in the *Morning Post* on 2 May 1873 and *Lloyd's Weekly Newspaper* on 4 May 1873 and then syndicated to regional newspapers the following week ('Theatrical

Divorce Case' 1873). The reports expand on the bare facts of the trial records, dating from 1 May 1873, where the decree nisi was granted. The husband, Herbert Augustus Such (stage name Augustus Granville) and Margaret Henderson Such had married in March 1870 when he was 19 and she 25. Only a short time later, things began to go wrong. In her petition, Margaret reports Herbert committing adultery with unnamed women on two occasions later in the year. Then in the 'summer and autumn of 1871 the said Herbert Augustus Such carried on an adulterous intercourse and committed adultery with a woman named or passing by the name of Marie Duval at 57 Nelson Square, Blackfriars Road' (National Archives: England and Wales, Civil Divorce Records 1858–1916: 239).

Biographically this strongly suggests that Duval and Ross were not a couple at this time, since this statement is backed up by Duval's landlady, who eventually asked her to leave because she did not like her bringing Such into the house. In terms of Duval's professional status as an artist this seems significant, since far from 'giving work to his partner', both as actor and artist, through 1869 to 1872, it would seem that Duval's abilities gained her work entirely in her own right. This is confirmed by a letter that Ross wrote to the *Theatrical Journal* in 1869 when he took over as editor of *Judy*. He writes to 'correct a trifling error' from a critic who had written that Duval's pictures were 'in imitation of Mr C. H. Ross's absurd style', writing instead that her drawings 'can very easily be distinguished from that gentleman's production, because Mademoiselle is an artist and C. H. R. is not' ('Letters to the Editor' 1869b). In fact, when the relationship between Ross and Duval began is impossible to determine, since there is no record of a marriage despite Duval being identified as his wife on her death. The romantic notion of them developing Ally Sloper together as a couple must be discounted. Another curious biographical aspect of this legal document is that Duval is not given her actual name by the petitioner, Margaret Such, so it would appear she used the name in daily life or was so well known by her stage name that Margaret and her lawyers felt it best to use it.

This episode must have affected Duval both in 1871 and 1873 when it came to court. The reason for the gap was that Margaret Such needed to leave two years of separation and prove both cruelty and adultery in order to gain her divorce. Herbert Such's behaviour with Duval is described in the newspaper reports of the trial, where Margaret Such and witnesses give accounts of Herbert taking his wife to a rehearsal where he puts his arm around Marie Duval and later both praises her looks and admits he is sleeping with her.

Although he denied adultery and cruelty in the original petition, Herbert Such did not attend the trial, so the events are only described by those 'against' him. However, given Such, as Augustus Granville, was performing with Duval at the Holborn theatre in 1871 ('The Theatres' 1871) it seems more than likely the gist of the case is essentially true. Consistent with her tendency not to introduce autobiographical material into her work, there is no apparent reflection of the affair in her work of 1870–71 or 1873.

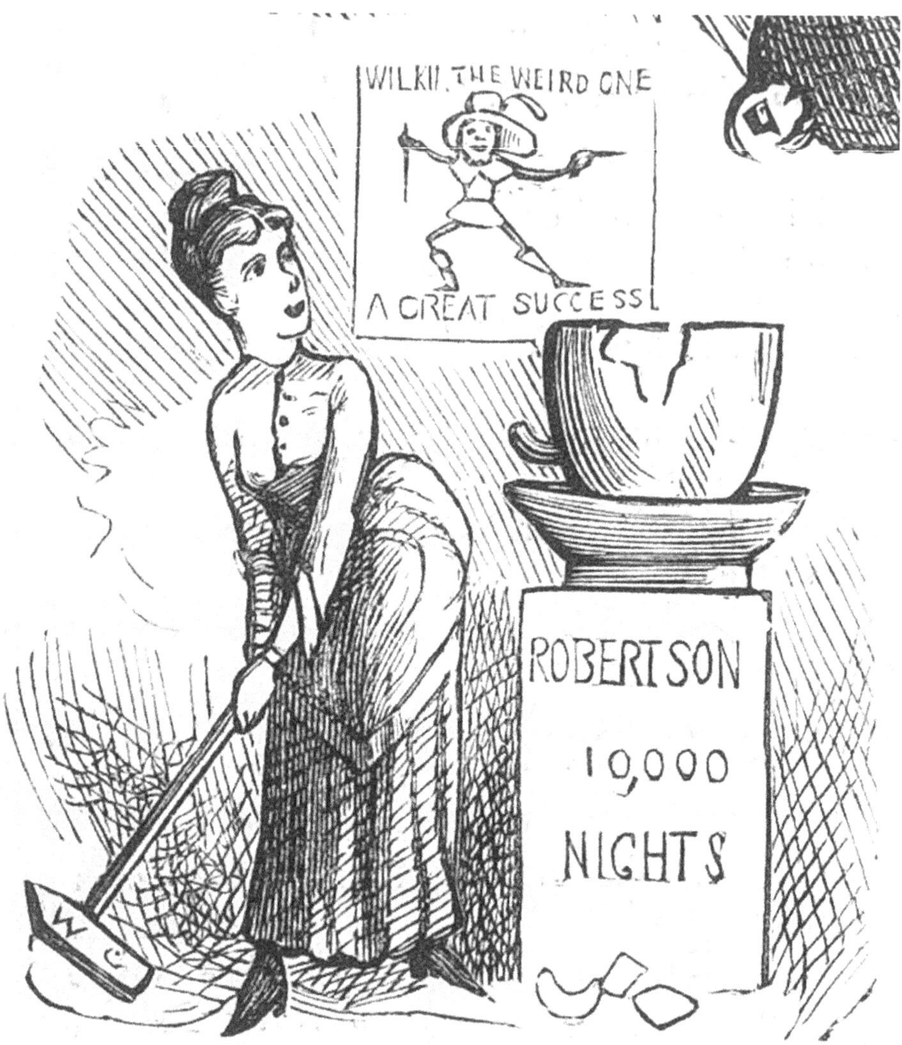

VANDALISM IN THE NEIGHBOURHOOD OF THE
TOTTENHAM COURT ROAD.

Miss M——E W——N smashes the famous
Teacup and Saucer.

3.11 Marie Duval (1873) 'Passing Events', *Judy, or the London Serio-comic Journal*, Volume 12,
p. 224

Duval's late theatre career and possible influences on her graphic work

In the period between this event and her next tour, Duval contributed relatively few drawings that feature performance. One that is historically interesting as well as relevant, perhaps to her own work, dates from early 1873 (Duval 1873j, Figure 3.11). Among the passing events is a depiction of Marie Bancroft, manager of the Prince of Wales Theatre. The image is complex. The third image down on the left shows a plinth labelled 'Robertson', which refers to the playwright Tom Robertson who had died in 1871 and had written a string of domestic melodramas that earned the title of 'cup and saucer' dramas. This explains the cup and saucer on the pedestal. By March 1873 another very long-running cup and saucer play by Bulwer-Lytton, *Money*, had also finally closed (hence the reference to an exaggerated 10,000 nights); and Bulwer-Lytton himself had died in January that year. In February Marie Bancroft had opened a drama entitled *Man and Wife* that was much more dramatic in the 'old style' – hence her character holds a sledgehammer labelled W. C. (for the author Wilkie Collins) and the poster behind her exclaims 'Wilku, the Weird One' (Duval 1873j). Having had considerable success herself in Ross's melodramas, which were very much not cup and saucer dramas, it is perhaps unsurprising that Duval might pen this cartoon with the relish she does.

Duval was on tour in a programme of works including a revival of *Clam* in mid-1873 (along with *Lantern Light and Life*, which appears to be a renaming of *Ruth*). The tour was announced by Ross in July ('Mr C. H. Ross' 1873) and Duval was performing in Cardiff by September ('Cardiff' 1873) where she received a strong commendation. The tour was given as 'Mr H. Ross's company' and continued, '… the piece [Life] has been produced effectively and is played carefully. The Lord Fernfield of Miss Marie Duval was an excellent performance' ('Cardiff' 1873).

Ellen Clayton, in her unique biography of Duval in *English Female Artists* (Clayton 1876), shows Duval as being on tour in 1874. It is possible this represents the final months of the *Clam* tour, although Clayton does not mention Ross's plays. Instead she writes that Duval 'made a very successful tour through the country, playing various roles, among others "Jack Sheppard"' (Clayton 1876: 330–1). Whilst this could refer to another tour, it seems likely that Clayton foregrounds the popular melodrama *Jack Sheppard* because of the anecdote she is concerned to tell, and that the older play may have been one of the afterpieces rehearsed during the tour. Clayton's account includes a description of a bad injury at Yarmouth, when the performance had to be stopped. Duval was climbing a rope ladder under pistol fire when 'the cartridge from one of the pistols struck the actress on the side of the face, thus obliging her to lose her hold' (Clayton 1876: 331). Clayton goes on to describe the wound being stitched up and Duval carried back to her lodgings by the company on 'a kind of sedan chair […] improvised from the stage "throne"' (Clayton 1876: 331). Despite the drama of the accident, and the fact that she was something of a celebrity as a *Judy* illustrator, there are no newspaper reports of this accident extant.

Date	Biography	Theatre – Known Productions	Illustration
1847 September	Marie Duval born		
1864	Duval leaves job as Governess to work as an actor sometime between 1864 and 1868		
1868 December 12		*The Happy Family* (Unknown) Part Unknown Bijou Theatre, Notting Hill (amateur)	
1868 December 26		*The Sleeping Beauty in the Wood* (Planche) Fairy Dewdrop St James's Theatre	
1869 March			First known published drawing in *Judy*
1869 October		*The Beast and the Beauty; or no rose without a thorn* (F. C. Burnand) Fashionable Lady Royalty Theatre	
1870 April		*Clam* (C. H. Ross) Piccadilly Peter Surrey Theatre	
1870 May		*The Beggar's Uproar* (Hubert Jay Morice) Claude Duval Surrey Theatre	
1870 August		*Clam* begins national tour	
1871 February		*Ruth, or a poor girl's life in London* (C. H. Ross) Lord Fernfield Surrey Theatre	
1871 May		*Silence* (C. H. Ross) Tinker/Parker Holburn Theatre	
1871	Affair with Herbert Such		
1872 December		*The Birth of Beauty: or, Harlequin William the Conquerer and the Pretty White Horse with the Golden Hoof* (W. M. Akhurst) Part unknown Sanger's Grand Amphitheatre	
1873 May	Divorce case Such v. Such cited as co-respondent		
1873 May		*Clam, Lantern Light, The Working Girls of London, Life* [version of *Ruth*] Various parts On tour with 'Mr H. Ross's Company'	
1874	Theatre accident in Yarmouth	*Jack Sheppard* (W. T. Moncrieff) Jack Sheppard On tour **Last known theatre appearance**	*Queens and Kings* published (only sole authored book)
1874 December	Birth of son, Charles Henry		
1885 July			Last known drawing published in *Judy*
1890 June	Marie Duval dies		

3.12 Marie Duval's Theatre Activity: A Chronology

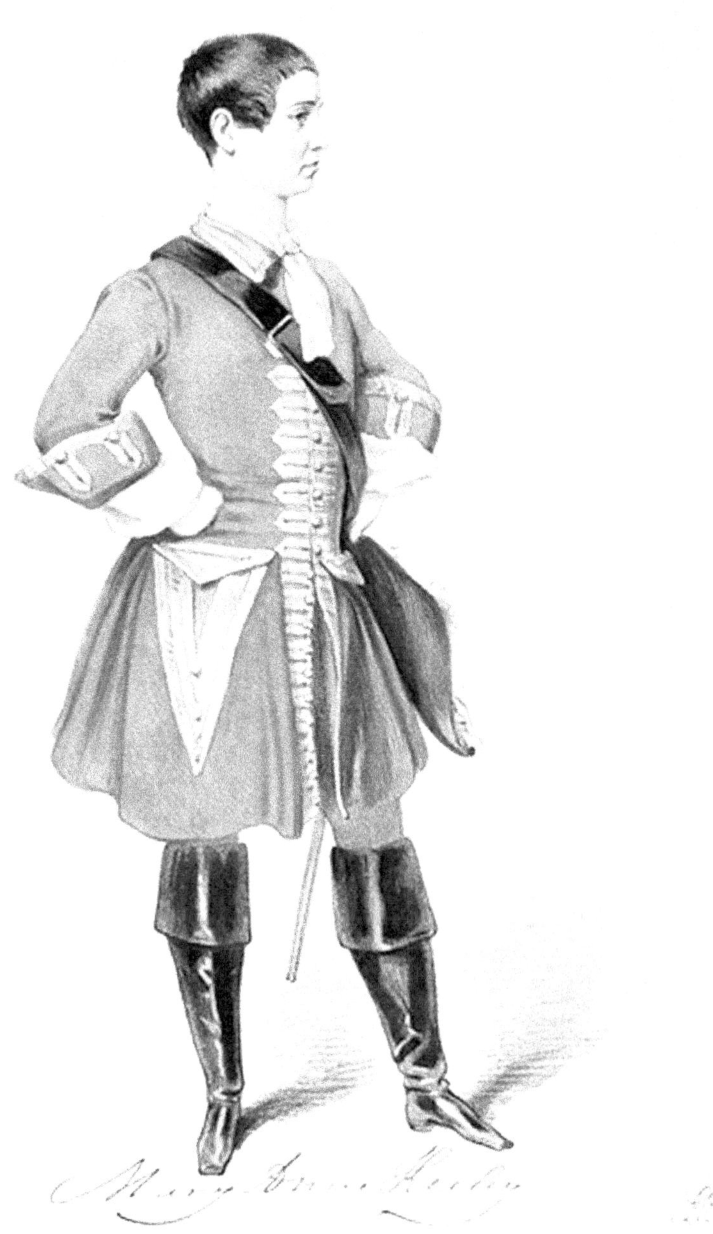

3.13 Bryan (1850) 'Mary Ann Keeley as Jack Sheppard'

If surviving contemporary documentation is a reliable guide, this was Duval's last tour, and it is plausible that this was her last performance ever, precisely because of this injury. Duval's son by Ross was born in 1875, which provides circumstantial evidence that she settled down in London as an artist and began living with Ross shortly after retiring from the stage. In the years following 1874 there are many references in newspapers to her work as an illustrator, mostly positive, and this lack of references to her as an actor would seem to confirm a cessation of performance activity.

Summary and statistics

In terms of her output of published drawings there is no real pattern statistically. Duval appears to have drawn significantly less in 1871 and 1873 (23 and 55 cartoons respectively), years of high theatre activity for her, but then she drew a great deal in 1874 when she was on tour, according to Clayton (101 drawings). However, her apparently lean year for performance work between *Ruth* and *Silence* (1871) and *The Birth of Beauty* (late 1872–73) might be consistent with the 89 images she drew that year of which, exceptionally, only one was theatrical. By 1881 her production was falling off considerably (with 44 cartoons that year and only 52 the following year) at a time when there is no recorded theatre activity. In terms of specific theatre cartoons the number appearing each year is fairly consistent in the first ten years of her artistic career (at about seven or eight a year) but falls significantly in the later years with none at all in 1882 or 1885 and only one in 1884 despite publishing a significant 92 drawings that year. Statistically, 1869, 1871 and 1873 stand out as the only years when explicit theatre cartoons reach more than double figures (about 11, 13 and 13 per cent respectively), which, given these were years of intense theatre activity for her, might be suggestive. However, these figures also show that Duval was very far from being a theatre artist. The total of explicit theatre drawings in her entire output is under 5 per cent.[10]

What did Marie Duval look like?

There are no known portraits of Marie Duval. The best guide to her appearance may be revealed by Clayton, who knew Duval personally and wrote that as Jack Sheppard she 'created surprise by the striking resemblance she bore to Mrs Keeley' (Clayton 1876: 331, Figure 3.13).

Notes

1 As can be seen in Figure 3.12, Duval is recorded by Clayton as beginning her career sometime between 1864 and 1868 having stopped working as a governess, a job she was doing at the age of 17 (Clayton 1876: 330). It is possible this role in *The Happy Family* was her first and only amateur role before her professional engagement at the Royalty. However, professional actors frequently took part in amateur productions as well as professional ones, either for the experience or for payment (Ellerslie records being offered amateur parts on both terms in her

diary) so Duval could have been acting professionally, although unrecorded, from as early as 1864 (Shuttleworth 1885).

2 Flesh-coloured tights or, in some instances, a tight-fitting flesh-coloured body suit.

3 As detailed in the Introduction there is no evidence that Ross and Marie Duval married, but they lived together, produced a son, and are both buried under the surname Ross in the same grave. I have therefore throughout given them as common-law wife and husband.

4 In theory all plays performed, or intended to be performed, in Britain from 1824 to 1968 are held in the British Library in manuscript. This is because, owing to censorship, a handwritten or printed copy of every play was sent to the Lord Chamberlain's office for approval. However, this collection was moved at various times before reaching its current location in the British Library at Kings Cross, and it is in fact now incomplete. The cataloguing currently (2019) consists of a card indexing system and paper files listing the works, and these details are present on the electronic catalogue to some extent (for example the author is often not recorded, as their name may not even be on the manuscript). A primary source is also held by the Library, in the form of the original 'day books'. These record the plays that were submitted to the Lord Chamberlain written contemporaneously. The plays that I describe as lost or missing from the British Library collection are those that appear in the day books and are reported in contemporary newspaper reviews, but which do not appear at all in the card indexing system, the paper files or the electronic catalogue. The inference, suggested to me by British Library staff, is that the plays were lost between their reception and the first paper catalogues done in the 1970s. Both of Ross's plays in which Duval played a significant part, *Clam* and *Ruth*, are lost.

5 The Surrey's status as a popular theatre is noted by Booth (1991) who explains that whilst there was change in the West End from the 1860s onwards, away from variety, for example, the Surrey was a place where older styles survived. Davis and Emeljanow make the Surrey their first case study in their excellent 2001 audience survey, showing its popularity through periods as a venue for horse entertainment, nautical melodrama, some opera, and then after the 1840s establishing itself as a house that presented both melodrama and 'legitimate drama'. They cite contemporary P. P. Hanley whose words reflect those of the reviewers of Duval's and Ross's work: 'The Surrey was my favourite house, as, like the majority of lads, I loved something stirring and exciting' (Davis and Emeljanow 2001: 15–16). The Surrey commanded more than a local audience, Hanley being happy to walk there from Camden Town.

6 Which translates as 'Shut up, you really annoy me!'

7 *Smiles and Styles* was a publication produced by the tailors' firm Lynes & Son. It was something of a media event, having frequent mentions and reviews in various papers. *Smiles and Styles* was the second of a series and Duval published further illustrations in the fourth volume *Mirth and Modes*, which came out in September the following year. The only known copy of these ephemeral volumes was in the British Library but has been designated as 'destroyed' in the catalogue, so we only have titles of the four much praised illustrations, namely: 'Original Illustrations by [...] Marie Duval (Miss Clarendon – she hurried on). (Do listen). (Good Night). (We kept on walking)' ('Smiles and Styles Ready Oct. 3' 1870).

8 In Chapter 5, Simon Grennan discusses the common practice for graphic artists to draw straight onto the wood block, although sometimes paper cartoons were transferred. Whilst the former could have been transported this would have been a logistical problem in comparison to posting drawings on paper, which Duval could have done quite easily.

9 A burlesque adaptation of *Salammbô* the novel by Flaubert which was published in French in 1862.

10 These statistics rely on *The Marie Duval Archive* (Grennan, Sabin and Waite 2016), as being the best available measure of Duval's entire oeuvre. However, *The Archive* is necessarily incomplete due to works being lost or unobtainable for scanning. There is also a measure of discretion by the author in the definition of 'explicit theatre cartoon', which includes anything where audience or backstage is illustrated, including dance and music hall, and includes cartoons with multiple images where only one is theatrical (perhaps of an actor). However, my 'explicit theatre cartoons' do not include oblique references of any sort, for example, cartoons where theatre conceits are used such as a story entirely un-theatrical, which is presented in 'seven acts', or non-theatrical cartoons where actors or productions are mentioned in the written text they illustrate.

4

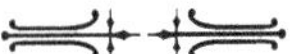

The children's book author: *Queens &*
Kings and Other Things

Roger Sabin

In 1874, a spectacular comedy book was published, *Queens & Kings and Other Things*, notable for the quality of its production and the freewheeling recklessness of its content (Duval 1874b). As a collection of highly illustrated 'nonsense poems' in the Edward Lear mould, it was ostensibly for children, but was designed for adults too. Written and drawn by the mysterious S. A. [Royal Highness] the Princess Hesse Schwartzbourg, it concerned the peculiar goings-on in invented royal households, where queens dismantle their heads to stop themselves sneezing, and kings go to sea in paper boats and promptly drown.

The book was built around 21 of these highly silly personalities: four queens, six kings (seven, if you count a pair of squabbling twins) and sundry other characters (among them two princesses, a prince, a Great Grand Duke and Duchess, and a Lord Chamberlain). Each character snapshot gets two pages: a textual introduction on one page, listing particulars and stating dates of birth and death, followed by a second page consisting of a full-colour illustration of them doing something outrageous. The colour page has a surrounding design of a parodic heraldic crest, complete with intricate marginalia (including elongated faces on either side, of kings gasping in disbelief at the story being told), which is accompanied by a silly verse or limerick ('There was a Queen called Kalli-Boo …'). Illustration and verse interweave to varying degrees, and there is some variety within the formula, though, overall, the design is uniform and predictable, in a manner reminiscent of children's alphabet books.

Not only was *Queens & Kings* published by the leading children's book publisher of the moment, Chatto & Windus, it was printed by the Dalziel Brothers, whose work on children's books was acknowledged as taking the form to a new level of sophistication (their biggest success had been *Alice's Adventures in Wonderland*). This was quite a pedigree, and *Queens & Kings'* dramatic colour (including lots of suitably regal-looking 'gilt'), large format, and hardback cover with decorative binding and embossed features, attested to

99

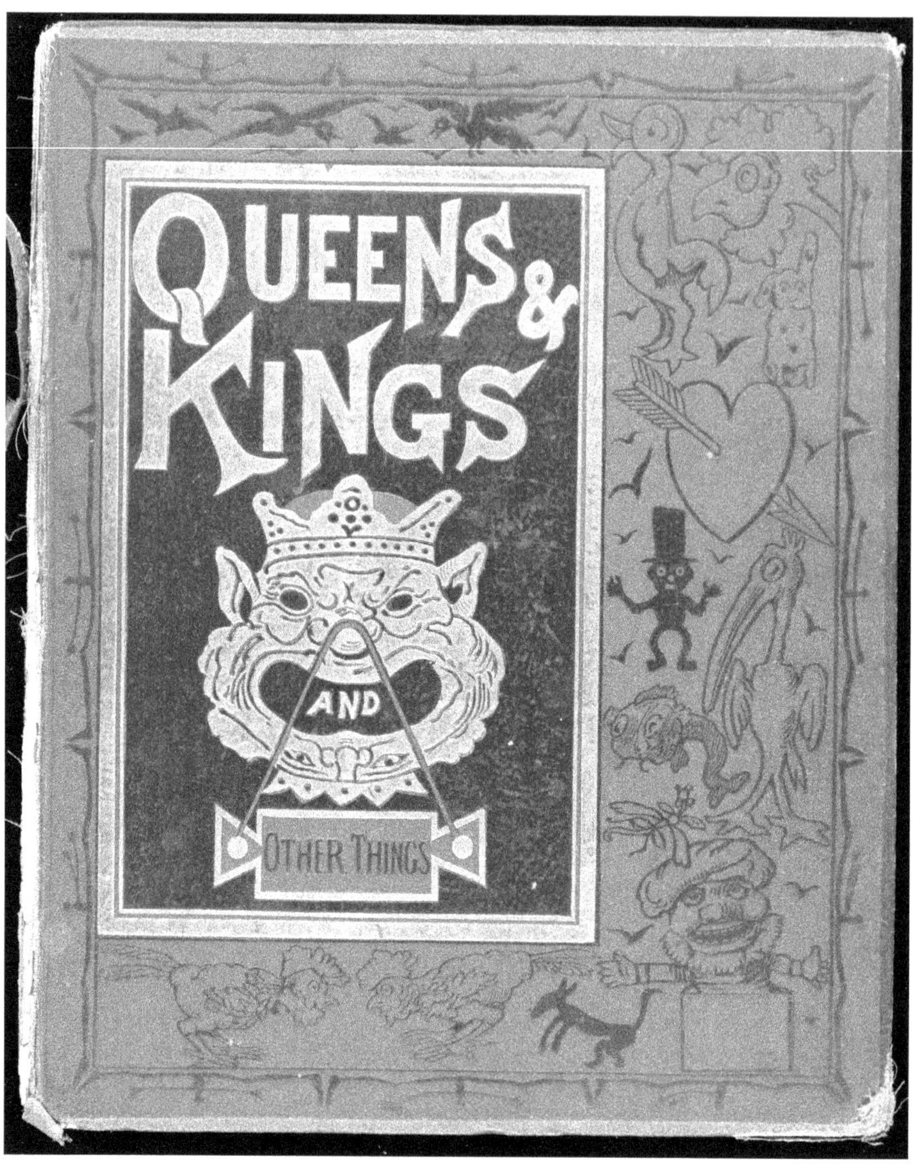

4.1 Marie Duval (1874) *Queens & Kings and Other Things*, London: Chatto & Windus, front cover its quality.[1] *The Graphic* magazine called the book 'gorgeous within and without' ('Christmas Books' 1874).

The authorial S. A. the Princess Hesse Schwartzbourg was, of course, a pseudonym for Marie Duval (as I will stick to calling her, and as she was known to most people at the time of creating the book). Duval was at the top of her game. Her job at *Judy* was going incredibly well, and she produced over 100 strips, cartoons and illustrations in the year of *Queens & Kings*' publication – her highest output to date. As discussed in Chapter 1, William Boucher tended to steal the limelight at *Judy* with his spectacular weekly double-page drawing, but by dint of the ubiquity of Duval's output, and her association with Ally Sloper (and the fact that so much of that material was reprinted and recirculated), she can justifiably be called the magazine's main attraction. The collection of Sloper strips known as *A Moral Lesson*, published in 1873, the year before *Queens & Kings*, featured her name on the cover as a co-creator, and was a huge hit, making a star of Sloper and sparking off merchandising and stage shows (Duval 1873g). It is no coincidence that the signature 'Marie Duval' became much more prominent in her *Judy* work.

More than this, the naive drawing style she had developed at *Judy* made her a natural choice for a children's book. Her untutored technique was not 'child-like' as such; to use such a term risks recruiting a culturally constructed idea. But it was typified by elastic bodies, gurning facial expressions and vertiginous perspectives, which, as we have seen, was in contrast to the much more 'professional'–cum–'illustrational' work in the rest of the journal. Similarly, she had established a corollary between her more spontaneous approach and content involving slapstick and foolish scenarios. As comedic drawing went, there was nobody quite like her.

The fact that *Queens & Kings* was not identified anywhere (on the cover, on the inside) as being 'a Duval product', therefore, did not mean it would not have been recognised as such. Her fans would have known her style, and the fact that the book had the imprimatur of the Dalziels, and was reviewed in *Judy*, would have been further clues. With this in mind, readers (or at least a proportion of them) would have been oriented to receive the book in ways that transcended its obvious genre positioning as a Lear copyist. Possibly, too, as Duval was a 'serio-comic' artist (see Chapter 9), her branding as such may have lent the book another dimension, steering it more towards women, both as female purchasers and gift recipients, that is, women responsible for children. (Girl readers are arguably foregrounded by the fact that the fictional author is female, and that queens are mentioned before kings in the title.)

Duval's diversification into quality books was thus an outcome of her growing fame. This would be her only solo effort in the world of literature: the book was attributable to her and her alone. Other firsts (for her) included the level of production investment, and the fact that this was a stand-alone book rather than a collection of previously published work, or an illustrated text (prose) work. Finally, it represented a different mode of creation, acknowledging the fact of 'chaperoned reading', which is to say it had to be read or performed by an adult, thereby requiring new ways of thinking about both the text and the art (Sanders 2013).

There may also have been a personal motivation for thinking about a switch to a juvenile readership: in the same year as the book's publication, 1874, Duval gave birth to her only child, a son, Charles, born to her and Charles Ross, the editor of *Judy*. It is possible, therefore, that when she created *Queens & Kings* she was pregnant, and thinking ahead. No doubt the book became family reading in the Ross-Duval household through the rest of the decade. But children had been a part of her life before this date. According to one source, she had worked as a governess, when she was a teenager (Clayton 1876: 330). This would have entailed being responsible for the education of the children of a well-to-do household: it is tempting to speculate that having seen the realities of middle-class expectations, and especially those of strict Victorian schooling, she may have been influenced to ensure that her book gave kids something to smile about.

Before saying more about the content of *Queens & Kings*, it is necessary briefly to explore how the book relates to late nineteenth-century publishing. First of all, this was an illustrated book, a mode which dominated the period (Maxwell 2002; Thomas 2016: 617). Literary historian Julia Thomas explains that this was largely because illustration had the effect of highlighting textual plurality, meaning that 'an illustration is an interpretation or "reading" of the text, and, as such, can conflict with other readings' (Thomas 2004: 14). For the Victorians, images often did not simply function as picturing the text, but were equivalent modes of representation. Thus, readers had to develop strategies for reading which were reflective, sophisticated, and sometimes non-linear.[2]

Within this frame, two overlapping phenomena are particularly germane to *Queens & Kings*: the rise of the children's book, and the rise of the gift book. In terms of the former, it fits into what has become categorised as the 'golden age' of children's literature, usually said to have begun with Lear's *A Book of Nonsense* in 1846, peaking in the 1860s with *The Water-Babies* (1863) and *Alice's Adventures in Wonderland* (1865), and ending in the 1910s with the *Winnie the Pooh* books.

This golden age spawned a huge number of cash-ins and knock-offs that were not so golden, of course (which category *Queens & Kings* fell into will be explored in a moment). Also, how far they were 'children's' books is contentious.[3] Many were aimed at adults as well, and the lens of 'cross-writing' has allowed scholars such as Perry Nodelman to explore how adult readers apprehend books as belonging to 'children's literature', and the way in which adult assumptions are transmitted in hidden ways in ostensibly 'innocent' texts (Nodelman 2008).[4] We should also bear in mind other assumptions behind the construction of a golden age: for example, who in particular is making that judgement, and which books are included and excluded.[5] Nevertheless, books for children were a market in the latter nineteenth century in way they simply had not been before – and a lucrative one.

This story of the rise of children's books was intertwined with that of the gift book. This category, too, had a specifically Victorian context. Flourishing in the 1860s, these books were designed to be showy and physically large. They were typically initiated by a publisher, rather than the artist or writer, and were often sophisticated combinations of text and image. They were marketed aggressively, via extensive coverage in periodicals

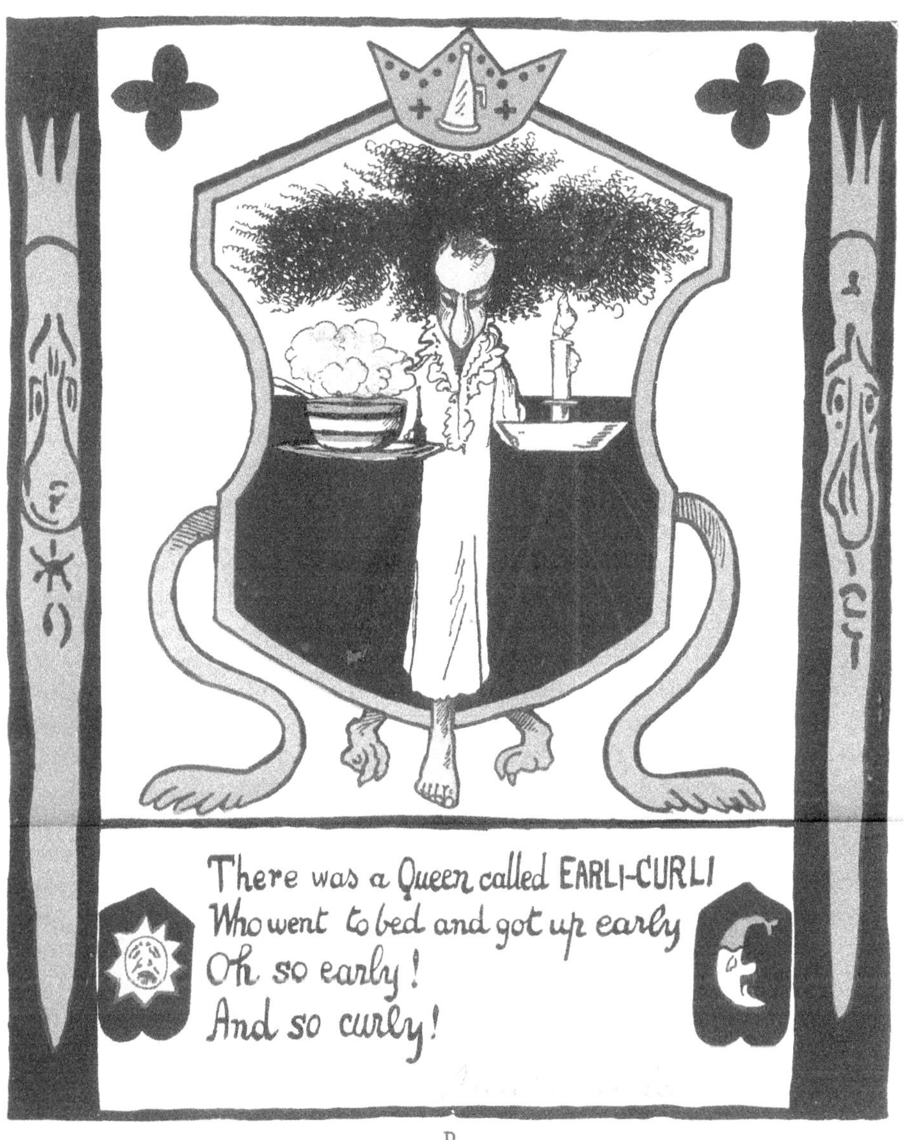

4.2   Marie Duval (1874) 'There was a Queen called Erli-Curli' *Queens & Kings and Other Things*, London: Chatto & Windus, p. 33

103

(previews, reviews and advertising) and window displays in shops. In terms of audience, they were about parading taste and disposable income, and therefore targeted the middle class. However, lower-middle-class and working-class readers were factored in, partly due to the growth of lending libraries and the second-hand book trade, but also because publishers routinely offered their wares at discount prices. Finally, they were typically bought by men to be given to women, and were assumed to be a gendered product.

To quote literary historian Lorraine Kooistra, here speaking about illustrated poetry texts for adults (which were a significant part of the market): 'The Victorian middle classes embraced the illustrated book as their present of choice because the gift book's cultural capital as a symbolic good was closely associated with notions of national identity. As a material object, the illustrated book represented the excellence of English manufacturing. As a symbolic object, it functioned as a repository of national greatness in art and literature' (Kooistra 2011: 27). But gift books were subject to the forces of commercialisation like any other print product, and it did not take long for 'the excellence of manufacture' to slide as technology enabled quicker and cheaper reproduction, short cuts were taken and the concept became democratised.

Gift books for children occupied a different material and symbolic space, of course, but were still about conveying cultural capital, and the more 'classy' the manufacture, the more this was true. (They could still have something to say about 'national greatness in art and literature', even if they were taking the 1860s template in a new direction.) Most had some kind of didactic dimension, ranging from ABC books for younger readers, to topics involving history, geography, science and maths for school-age children. Nursery rhymes and fairy tales had their own educational function, as did adventure stories.

Such publications attracted a supplementary audience of adult fans – which is to say, not just adults who bought the books for children (or read aloud to them), but adults who loved the books per se. This served to nuance Nodelman's thoughts on cross-writing and dual address, and manifested itself in ways which were sometimes almost 'underground'. For example, a round-up of children's books in *Judy* (1874), which also included *Queens & Kings*, contained a preamble that is revealing on this score: 'My head is bald, my beard is white, my waistcoat protuberates at the lower buttons [...] some of these fine days I will take you – if you are very good and pretty – into a little back room of mine, where there is a little shelf full of choice volumes, which are very dear to me [...] Every season my good bookseller, knowing my little weaknesses, sends me a huge parcel of baby literature to select from, and every now and then I add something to that sacred shelf' ('Nonsense for Big and Little Babies' 1874).

The rise of children's books and the rise of the gift book came together at one particular time of the year: Christmas. The Victorians did not 'invent' Christmas, as is often thought, but they did shape it in significant ways, and the boom in publishing was obviously a part of this (Moore 2009). Gifts were not originally part of the Victorian plan, but this became more embedded over time, as the idea of a consumption-driven holiday took over. Similarly, children became a focus, especially for conspicuous displays of family giving. As literary historian Tara Moore concludes, 'The Christmas season became a celebration of the ideology of the Victorian home' (2009: 5).

This, then was the general context for *Queens & Kings*. As a gift book, it was at the top of the quality scale, and fitted the category in other ways: it was almost certainly conceived by Chatto and the Dalziels, rather than by Duval herself, and there is an obvious trace of the 'illustrated poetry' tradition – albeit poetry and illustrations of a different kind. We can also surmise that it was a gendered product, and that the 'improving' idea that dominated thinking about books for juveniles was the context against which it rebelled. Similarly, it was clearly a Christmas book, which was reviewed in the Christmas round-ups in the periodicals. (Meanwhile, Duval mercilessly satirised the cosy Victorian Christmas in her *Judy* strips and cartoons about the Sloper family.) As for the 'textual plurality' of illustrated books, Duval was already immersed in this mode regarding her illustration work for *Judy*, where the logic equally applied.

The immediate circumstances of *Queens & Kings'* publication involved the commercial opportunities opened up by these currents. Publishing houses invested in children's books in the hope of hitting upon the next 'tentpole' title that would sustain the rest of their output for the year (often a gift book), while printers relished the opportunity to keep their presses running.[6] Artists and writers migrated from magazine work to where the best remuneration could be found, just as they had always done; *Punch* stalwart John Tenniel's success with *Alice* had shown the way forward.

Because the Dalziels were publishers as well as printers, the children's book boom had extra advantages, because it meant they could promote their stable of creative practitioners. Duval was one of these, of course, and in the fullness of time many other 'inner circle' talents would similarly go on to create or co-create children's literature (nursery books, fairy-tales, children's annuals, illustrations for adventure prose novels). These included George Cruikshank, Archibald Chasemore and Tom Hood. Charles Ross had produced several illustrated children's books in the 1860s, and continued to do so in the 1870s (once he had taken over at *Judy*).[7] Such products were duly advertised, previewed and reviewed in Dalziel publications.[8]

In this rush by creative practitioners to capitalise on what was happening, Duval was a rarity because she was a woman. True, in comparison to work on the journals, there were more women involved in book writing and illustrating, and still more involved with the children's end of the spectrum.[9] But they remained very much a minority, and were almost always paid at a lesser rate than the men.[10] Women were, no doubt, more welcome as part of the juvenile publishing world because of their supposed nurturing and motherly nature, an outcome of the prevalent 'two spheres' theory of society. The fact that *Queens & Kings* was a comedy book was doubly significant in terms of gender, at a time when women were 'not meant to be funny', a prohibition that was equally relevant to Duval's *Judy* work, as shown in Chapter 1.

The biggest influence on *Queens & Kings* was Edward Lear and his *A Book of Nonsense* (1846). Nonsense books had arguably existed since the twelfth century, but Lear's was a breakthrough, and opened up a new market for a modern audience.[11] Lear wrote the verse, and did his own illustrations, and although there was nothing new in this per se (William Blake was an obvious precursor), Lear's talent for gleeful gibberish, bizarre juxtapositions and the untutored-looking nature of both the writing and the drawing offered a new model. Clearly, it was this that Duval was following.

Her book came on the back of a Lear revival later in the century, and was one of a number of imitators. Although the *A Book of Nonsense* sold well and went through several editions (including one printed by the Dalziels in 1870),[12] it was another twenty-four years before Lear re-entered the fray, publishing *Nonsense Songs and Stories* in 1870, which involved more complex verses, often with animal protagonists, followed by *More Nonsense* in 1872.[13] With the accompanying fanfare that these new books generated, 'nonsense fever' was revived, and so too was knock-off culture. Again, Duval was a kind of pioneer for being a woman: in the same way that she was the first prominent female cartoonist, so too she was the first woman to enter the world of nonsense literature, at least, so far as is known (Hone 1888: 274). It is entirely possible that *Queens & Kings* was a calculated effort to position her as 'the female Lear'.

The similarities between Duval's and Lear's books are obvious. Both are, on the surface, 'amateurish', in terms of their art and their language (of course, neither Duval nor Lear were amateurs). This placed them in contrast both to the more 'illustrational/professional' examples of pictorial children's literature, typified by work co-produced by Tenniel, Crane and later Caldecott, and also to traditional didactic nursery rhymes and to the kind of poetry being taught to slightly older children in schools ('The Wreck of the Hesperus', 'The Charge of the Light Brigade', for example) (see Smith 2017: esp. 228–38). In terms of cultural capital, many critics inevitably took the view that one mode was sophisticated, the other unsophisticated; one was mindful, the other mindless. For such guardians of taste, neither Lear nor Duval were 'suitable' for children.

To underline this point in relation to Duval's drawing style: just as she was no John Tenniel in the world of journals, nor was she a Tenniel in the world of children's literature. If, in the profession of drawing, she belonged to a tradition that ran through Busch and other 'lowbrow' knockabout artists, rather than the tradition of print satire typified by Hogarth, Gillray and Cruikshank (and culminating in *Punch*), so in the world of children's literature, she (and Lear) belonged to a tradition of naive illustration, rather than of painterly, trained refinement.

However, the bestowing of cultural capital is a fickle business, and Duval and Lear's supposed artlessness united them in another way, because dissident critics were pleased to elevate this kind of work, and Lear in particular, to the status of fine art. They refused to see Lear as disreputable: he was in fact an extremely accomplished artist (much more so than Duval, in conventional terms), and although his nonsense books traded in an ostensibly lowbrow form, he was increasingly adored by intellectuals and bohemians. For example, he knew, and was admired by, Tennyson (author of 'serious' poetry such as the Light Brigade example), Darwin, Ruskin and members of the Pre-Raphaelite circle.[14] As it became fashionable to be an aficionado of nursery nonsense, so Lear made the transition into a new interpretive space.[15] In short, this meant upmarket houses like

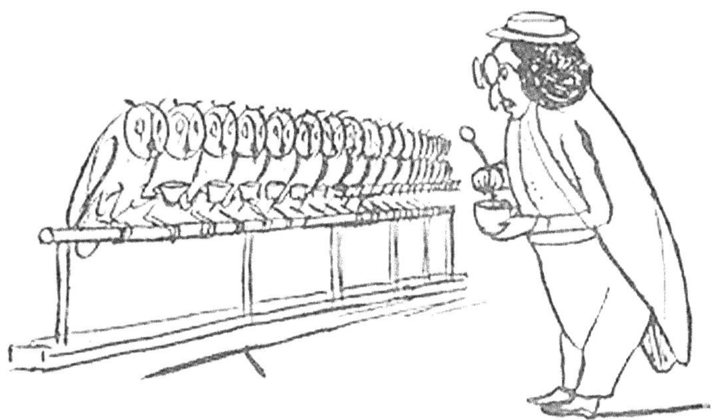

4.3 Edward Lear (1872) 'Old Man of Dumbree', *More Nonsense*, London: Robert John Bush, np. Lear mania provided the context for Duval's book.

Chatto, and equally upmarket printers like the Dalziels, could feel comfortable producing work in this vein.

A 'sine qua non' of this positioning was that books like those by Lear and Duval should be steadfast about their lack of logic. There was no moral lesson, and no educational purpose, just 'non-sense'.[16] As we have seen, in this way, they could be seen as gently subversive of the more conservative view of children's literature, which held that it should be 'improving'. This view encompassed (most evidently) versions of Bible stories, 'learn to read' books and tales of Empire, but it also included books which conditioned children into appreciating an 'acceptable' view of art. Such a perspective gained traction in the late nineteenth century, as an article in the *Magazine of Art* attests: 'Children of the mid- to late nineteenth century are poised to become the artists and tastemakers of their age […] because they are surrounded by the pictures of Caldecott, Greenaway, Crane and other notables, including John Tenniel, Gustave Doré and George Cruikshank – the 'Millais and Leightons and Tademas' of the nursery' (Untitled 1883). By the twentieth century, it was a view that was mainstream. Historian and critic Mark Girouard (1977: 139) labelled the texts illustrated by the elite artists 'secret persuaders', bought by status-conscious adults wishing to instil an appreciation of both art and the decorative arts (architecture, furniture, for example) in their offspring.

Duval, Lear and their fellow nonsense devotees were not part of this agenda, and had no interest in making this kind of taste distinction.[17] Lear was instead praised for reflecting back to children their own forms of creativity. He drew in a way that other adults recognised as childish, and thus was symbolic of the idea of a reversal of an artist's progress from 'crude' to 'polished'. Duval could be seen in a similar light, though she never got the same attention (as a sidebar, in *Judy*, she had mimicked children's drawings in many strips, including a recurring gag about a school slate). Historian Victoria Ford Smith has suggested that this desire to imitate children's art was part of a bigger shift in art appreciation whereby critics were 'beginning to pay attention to and admire the chaotic lines and palpable energy of children's drawings' (Smith 2017: 233).

Similarly, Lear's poems were reassessed by the more 'progressive' critics as belonging to a distinct literary tradition (and were therefore not 'mindless' at all). The limericks were not just clever inversions of serious poems, but were themselves a highly specialised poetic form.[18] Duval's stanzas could be so described, though as a wordsmith she was never in the same league. Indeed, when her book was reviewed, it was the verbal material that let it down, according to critics, and which was found especially wanting compared to Lear.

Both Lear and Duval were theoretically appealing to children in a very direct and innovative way. Their drawings could be copied by children, as could the verse. This was, essentially, a mode of address, and one that allowed for agency on the part of children. It also opened new perspectives on how such picture books might function in children's everyday lives, in other words, as one aspect of a broader landscape. According to literary scholar Robin Bernstein:

> When we view children's literature as something that adults produce and children consume, of course we see power emanating from the top down [...] But if we understand children's literature as persistently integrating with material culture and play, a very different picture emerges. We see adults producing children's literature <u>and</u> children's material culture, and we see children playing with and through both. (Bernstein 2013: 460)

One final point on the similarities between Duval and Lear: on a purely functional level, their books were designed to be read aloud by the adult. Parent and child were encouraged to relish the sounds of the words and the intensity of the images, as well as how these two aspects were woven together. But one had a different level of 'control' than the other, as Sanders (2013) has argued. This relationship means that the adult acts as a chaperone, and has the potential to modify the text and thereby change the meaning of the image, and also that their facility for 'performing' the text can add a further interpretative element. Regarding *Queens & Kings*, we can imagine both parties laughing together as the adult reader tries to pronounce some of the tongue-twisters, and the child negotiates the infinitely inspectable and colourful images. This is a scenario very different to somebody reading Duval's strips in *Judy* because, as Sanders points out, in contrast to such children's books, comics 'are hard to read out loud because they are designed for a solitary reader who will do the work of combining words and pictures' (Sanders 2013: 74).

There are also significant differences between Duval and Lear, and it is to these that we must now turn. The verses are not structured in the same way. Lear's primary mode is the limerick, a form he popularised. Here, the formula tends to begin with a first line, 'There was an [old / young] [man/lady/person/animal] of [place name]', which is then echoed at the end (usually as 'That [adjective] old [man/lady/person/animal] of [place name]'). The middle lines typically describe that protagonist's surreal behaviour, and a response by onlookers. But in Duval, although the first line is often similar ('There was a king called Hoddi-Doddi …'), and the middle lines describe eccentric behaviour, the final line usually does not repeat or echo (Duval 1874b: 21). The response by other people is provided by illustrations, for example, the appalled expressions on the faces in the marginalia. Duval only rarely uses the limerick form. Most of her poems are best described as silly verse.

Another difference is tone. Lear's work is often melancholic (he was a lifelong depressive), and sometimes violent (dismemberment and choking feature), whereas Duval's is upbeat and more like children's play (or, rather, is more in keeping with the emerging sense of what sort of activity was suitable for children). There is no underlying horror or sadness in her work, even though bad things happen. Perhaps partly because of the darkness in Lear, the modern academy has become slightly obsessed with attempting to decipher his meanings (the sense in his nonsense), often using the tools of psychoanalysis. Such scrutiny applied to Duval would no doubt yield lesser results.

Lear and Duval are also dissimilar because the drawings in *Queens & Kings* were much more prominent: Lear's drawings are small, black and white, and sometimes scratchy (cartoon-like pen sketches); Duval's are large, in full colour and highly designed. Her book is not in sequential images as such, but it is holistic in its repetitive architecture, and there is room for playful self-referencing: for example, a fantasy animal depicted early in the book reappears later as a motif on some background wallpaper (Duval 1874b: 9 and 61).[19] It also relies on a recurring trope based on heraldry, and this reinforces the rhythm and allows for some inspectable design elements: for example, it takes a while to pore over all the background information, and even longer to work out that the margins include faces. This attention to detail is a testament to Duval's growing reputation as an artist: the Lear books were sold as poetry, hers as a picture book.

In terms of content, beyond the fact that both Lear and Duval offer visions of adults behaving badly, there is not much common ground. Lear was fond of including animals, and animal characters. He had been a nature artist, and had once been employed by the Zoological Society. In his nonsense poems and songs, birds and beasts appear either as comedic foils or are anthropomorphised (for example, 'The Owl and the Pussycat'). Duval's animals are different. Sometimes they are symbolic in a traditional fashion (for example, crows as portents of bad luck), and occasionally they are fantastical: her 'Queekiquokes' are bizarre, huge-beaked birds, and her 'Wankipoos' are a combination of reptile and hippo, more reminiscent of Carroll's *Jabberwocky*.

The main point of difference is that Duval chose as a focus for her book a single theme, namely royalty, whereas for Lear a more eclectic approach was preferable. The only thing that unites Lear's poems is their nonsensical nature, whereas for Duval it is nonsense as applied to a collective subject. The final part of this chapter considers *Queens*

& Kings from this vantage, and asks questions about what this emphasis may have meant.

A book about royals was an obvious choice for children, both because educational history books about them were strong sellers, and because 'learning your kings and queens' was a standard rote exercise in schools. The structure of *Queens & Kings* mimicked typical early-learner history books by having one king or queen per (illustrated) page, a regular design which helped the book's rhythm, and which also had much in common with ABC volumes (there are 26 letters in the alphabet, and 20 pages of characters).

Those royals depicted are essentially upper-class twits, but lovable for their eccentricities. One king 'went to sea in a paper boat / And was surprised it wouldn't float' (Duval 1874b: 29). Another is a noted angler who 'went fishing in a tank' and gets eaten by a fish (Duval 1874b: 25). One wears his regal coat back-to-front, which does not bother his subjects, who go around naked (Duval 1874b: 37). A crazed princess on horseback hunts a fly: 'She used to call out Tally Ho! / But more than that I do not know' (Duval 1874b: 45). A prince puts his head inside a cannon and gets blown up (Duval 1874b: 53). The nobles are not much better: a Great Grand Duke asks his cobbler to make him a shoe, and kills him when it does not fit (Duval 1874b: 61). And so on.

There was no shortage of real-life examples of insane or incompetent royals to act as inspirations. Two in particular were well known in the Victorian period. There was King Ludwig II of Bavaria (1845–86), a recluse known for ludicrous behaviour and for building fantasy castles.[20] In 1870, Bavaria had sided with Prussia against France, and this may have been another reason for Duval, with her French heritage, to give her new pen-name a Germanic spin. Closer to home, there was the British King George III (1738–1820), who also had German links, becoming King of Hanover, and who suffered from mental illness to the extent that he had on occasion to be restrained by a straitjacket (a scenario reminiscent of Duval's king who wears his jacket back-to-front).

In so far as *Queens & Kings* features three strange royal deaths, involving the cannon, the sinking boat and the fish, there were oblique precedents for these, too. James II of Scotland (1430–60) was fascinated by cannon, and died when one backfired during a celebration. Other kings suffered maritime mishaps, while the fishing story probably originated in the many myths about aristocratic hunting and fishing accidents, and legends about man-eating catfish.[21] Other general models for the book's characters were everywhere in the history books: queens who went hunting and aristocrats who had their servants killed for minor transgressions. There were also fictional variations; tales of mad kings and queens were everywhere in children's books, for example the Queen of Hearts in *Alice*.

Was there a relationship in any of this to Queen Victoria herself? As we have noted, 'S. A. the Princess Hesse Schwartzbourg' is a German name, and Victoria was of largely German descent. More than this, Victoria's third child, Princess Alice, became by marriage the Grand Duchess of Hesse and by Rhine (in 1862). Whether this had any significance is again questionable: it would be tempting to infer Gallic republican intent on behalf of Duval, but it is highly unlikely.

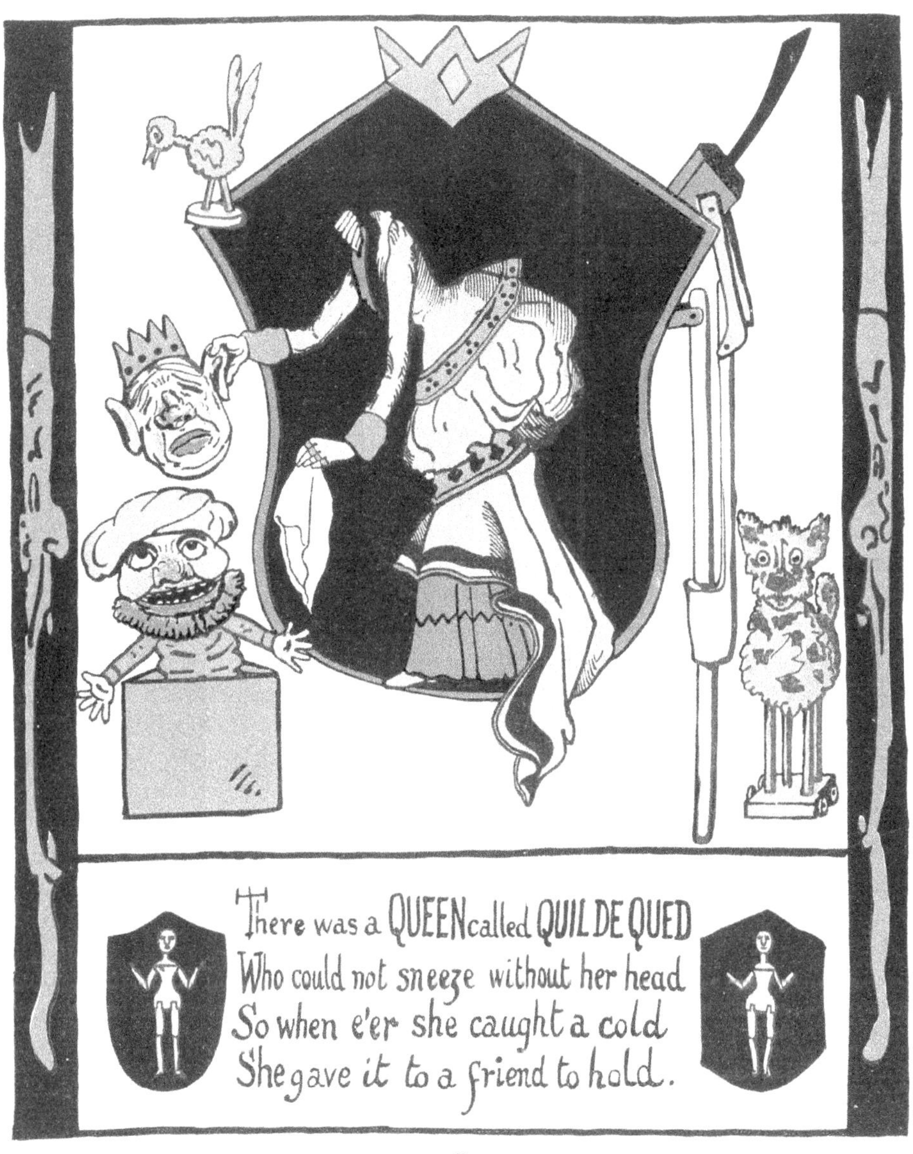

4.4   Marie Duval (1874) 'There was a Queen called Quildequed', *Queens & Kings and Other Things*, London: Chatto & Windus, p. 13

Looking closer, the depiction of the aristocrats in the book has a quality that is unmistakeably medieval (Palmgren and Holloway: 2005). The world of *Queens & Kings* is one of troubadours, courtly behaviour and medieval fashions. In this, it was part of a much bigger trend. Medieval revivalism pervaded every aspect of Victorian society, from architecture to gothic novels. In the realm of children's literature, it focused on salient personalities, especially kings and queens – exemplified by King Arthur and Queen Guinevere. For example, Thomas Malory's *Le Morte D'Arthur* (1485) was reprinted in expurgated and illustrated editions, many for children, and became a kind of 'founding myth' for the nation. *Queens & Kings* certainly owes a debt to it, if not to its nationalism (Guinevere's unpredictability, for example, is possibly another inspiration for Duval's queens and princesses).

Medieval-style fashion was a Duval forte, and *Queens & Kings* is notable for it. The female characters in particular are spectacular in their huge, patterned dresses, with ruffs and trains; in their extravagant jewellery; and, perhaps above all, in their head-dresses – steeple-, heart- and butterfly-shaped. Here, too, Malory may have been an influence, or, at least, the later illustrated versions. Duval returned to such fashion time and again in her *Judy* work, notably in 'Another Mediaeval Love Affair' (Duval 1875d).

But this medieval obsession cannot be understood without some reference to the stage, and to contemporary theatre costuming. This was a world Duval knew intimately, and medievalism in its many guises was ubiquitous. King Arthur and Guinevere (after Malory) were the topic of plays, operas, pantomimes and music hall sketches, and were duly clothed according to the prevailing view of what they looked like.[22] Perhaps even more of an influence would have been the revivals of Shakespeare's history plays: *Henry V*, *Henry VIII*, *King John*, *Macbeth* and *Richard II* were all staged by the actor-manager Charles Kean in mid-Victorian London, for instance, and were known for their attention to costume and other antiquarian detail.

Such fashion filtered down from the theatres (as well as from depictions in paintings, illustrations and other forms) to more everyday aspects of life. *Queens & Kings* may have resonated with adult readers on the basis of its associations with medieval-themed fancy-dress balls, for example, which themselves were often catered for by theatre costumiers. These were a nineteenth-century craze (as parodied by the satirical magazines, including by Duval in *Judy*); Queen Victoria herself had famously hosted such an event in 1842.

Finally, medievalism is the basis of the very design of the book. The recurring conceit is based on heraldry, with each illustrated page functioning like a coat of arms. The stories of the various characters appear framed in an elaborate heraldic design, which replaces ancient dynastic symbolism with objects a child can understand, such as toys, everyday implements and animals. One example has a Great Grand Duchess who fancies herself a tailor depicted against a crest featuring a gigantic open pair of tailoring scissors. Another has a regal lion in ironic juxtaposition to the ridiculousness of the king depicted in the foreground. A third has a maid of honour who has slipped on cobblestones and broken her bones, depicted with a symbol which replaces crossed swords with crossed crutches (Duval 1874b: 57, 21, 69).

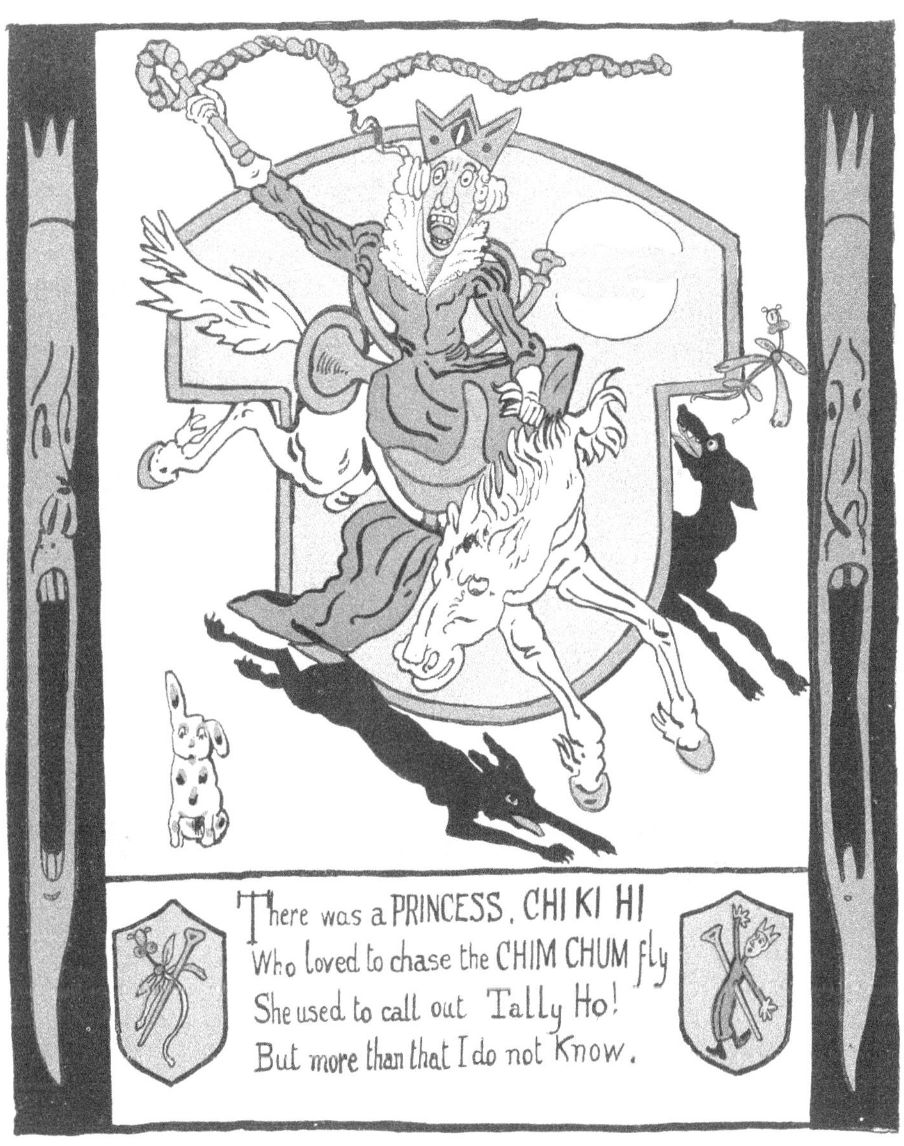

4.5   Marie Duval (1874) 'There was a Princess, Chi Ki Hi' *Queens & Kings and Other Things*, London: Chatto & Windus, p. 45

Possibly there were connections with children's play here. Scrapbooks were popular, wherein children would collect versions of coats of arms and heraldry, be they in the form of monograms snipped off envelopes and letterheads, or bought as coloured (die-cut) scraps. Kids were also encouraged to draw their own coats of arms, and to make them up using their imagination. To come back to Bernstein's point above, children's play could thus be 'creative, symptomatic, anarchic, ritualistic, reiterative, and most of all, culturally productive' (Bernstein 2013: 460).

Duval's focus on heraldry for comedic purposes was not new: humourists and cartoonists had parodied coats of arms forever.[23] Similarly, there was a lot of this kind of humour in contemporary culture, for example in *Alice*. Duval would return to it in *Judy*, in 'Some Naughty Nursery Rhymes' (Duval 1876f). But what she brought to the idea in *Queens & Kings* was unique: a gleeful, abandoned form of 'detournement' that could amuse children and adults alike, while at the same time giving her book a recurring beat. As a sidebar, there is a 'real' crest/monogram at the front of the book, that of the Dalziels.[24]

How was *Queens & Kings* received?[25] It got reviewed in *Judy*, unsurprisingly, in the aforementioned Christmas round-up. The review did not reveal that the book was by Duval, and instead went into a long, jokey rumination about how the Princess Hesse 'has a language peculiar to herself, and a solemnity in talking downright nonsense truly royal', concluding that 'Those who would [...] learn what Wankipoos, and Queekiquokes really are, and where and how you catch them, had better seek information in the proper quarter.' As we have seen, it suggests that the book can be enjoyed by 'big babies', thereby acknowledging its dual-address market, and the reviewer gleefully admits he is one, having been a collector of nursery books for a number of years. ('Nonsense for Big and Little Babies' 1874).[26]

The Graphic, an important weekly illustrated newspaper, also gave it a review, noting that 'the illustrations are undoubtedly quaint and witty', but that 'the letterpress is a feeble imitation of 'The Book of Nonsense', without its humour.' Which was pretty fair. Again, the review was part of a lengthy round-up, under the heading 'Christmas Books' ('Christmas Books' 1874).

Other press mentions tended to be one-liners, noting the fact of its existence. Elsewhere, fragments of evidence point to its gift status, and particularly to a perceived adult fanbase: for example, a copy was evidently given by the Dalziels to the painter Sir John Gilbert, who wrote on the flyleaf 'Perhaps the most idiotic book ever published.'[27]

This half-hearted reception no doubt retarded the book's sales potential. There is no way of knowing if it was a financial success, because no sales ledgers have survived. The archives relating to Chatto & Windus, and to the Dalziels, give no clues.[28] What we do know is that there were no follow-ups, no merchandising and no spin-off stage productions. Would it have done better if it was marketed as a 'Duval' book rather than 'Schwartzbourg'? Who knows? The only possible observation is that Duval quietly continued with her job at *Judy*, where she occasionally utilised ideas she had developed in *Queens & Kings* (we have noted a few already, but there was also 'Krikketekrakkle' (Duval 1878d), a fairy story with a fantasy king who is afraid of a giant insect). Meanwhile, she no doubt left dreams of becoming 'the female Lear' behind her.

The only subsequent development in the world of publishing that is worthy of note was the publication of another children's nonsense book the following year (1875), but not by Duval. This was a further Chatto/Dalziel collaboration, and was superficially similar to *Queens & Kings*. Entitled *From Nowhere to the North Pole*, it had a gold-embossed cover with illustrations, and, although text-based, included copious black and white images (mainly of fantasy animals). The inspiration was not Lear this time, but *Alice*, and the author was noted humourist and poet Tom Hood, who, as editor of *Fun*, was another Dalziel acolyte (Hood 1875).[29] So far as can be ascertained, this book, too, was a flop. Chatto had failed with a Lear copyist, and now with an *Alice* copyist: luckily for them, the following year they had a hit with an original idea from America: Mark Twain's *Tom Sawyer*.

Thus, it was left to the historians to assess the merits of *Queens & Kings*. Two years after its publication, Ellen Clayton commented favourably in her book *English Female Artists*, a self-described 'roll call of honourable names', that it was probably Duval's best work, and that she excelled in 'coloured subjects' (Clayton 1876: 330–3). But such praise fell into a sea of prejudice: this was a woman talking about another woman, and such supposed 'back slapping' was not part of the dominant narrative. Instead, it was already true that the idea of a 'golden age of children's literature' was being spun around male personalities (the quotation from the *Magazine of Art* above lists no fewer than five men). It was a view that would largely persist until the present. In Duval's case, the most egregious act of erasure occurred in the Dalziels' memoir (Dalziel 1901). Here they talk glowingly of their children's books, completely ignoring *Queens & Kings*. It is not mentioned in the text, nor in the chronological listing of 'Dalziel Books' at the end. It is as if it did not exist.[30]

Any kind of alternative legacy for *Queens & Kings* is hard to imagine, but maybe there is one. If the book's core juvenile readers were three years old in 1874, then they would have been 13 in 1884, when *Ally Sloper's Half-Holiday* was launched. This weekly was the first great British comic, and republished huge amounts of Duval's work from *Judy*, not least, of course, about the eponymous character she had helped make famous. Thus, if her children's book was not prepping her readership to appreciate the high art of the 'Millais, Leightons and Tademas' (Untitled 1883), then it may have been prepping them for something else, namely the low art typified by the comedy sensation of the late Victorian age. And for that, no doubt, they thanked her.

Notes

1 The book consisted of 43 leaves plus cover boards 345 mm × 280 mm (13.5″ × 11″), produced with covers in two colours, blue and purple/brown.

2 Duval is especially interesting for the way her work can be assessed from art historical, narratological and Comics Studies perspectives. In terms of Victorian illustrated fiction, Thomas's work has been supplemented by Leighton and Surridge (2019).

3 The classic statement of how definitions of childhood change over time is Aries' *Centuries of Childhood* (1965). For a more up-to-date survey, see Heywood (2017) and Jacqueline Bannerjee's succinct 'Ideas of Childhood in Victorian Children's Fiction: The Child as Innocent' (2007). Additionally, Joe Sutliff Sanders (2013: 68) has this to say about picture books specifically: 'Picture books, the objects of childhood, therefore enable two of the chief objectives of this culturally loaded period called childhood: nostalgia and acculturation. Nostalgia, the rewriting of childhood according to the longing of adults, and acculturation, the attempted indoctrination of children into a social order over which adults have dominance, are both built into the nature of picture books, and they have been part of the form since the modern picture book's formative years.'

4 These ideas are taken further in Beckett (1999).

5 This has led to Bourdieusian discussions about the ascribing of value, and the role of critics as cultural intermediaries. (One supplementary question has been, why bracket the period between those dates? If the idea of a golden age is maintained, then there are good arguments for extending it either side).

6 Nothing has changed in this regard: Bloomsbury thrives because of *Harry Potter*.

7 Examples include: *Merry Conceits and Whimsical Rhymes* (Ross 1883), *The Book of Cats. A Chit-chat Chronicle of Feline Facts and Fancies* (Ross 1868), and *The Surprising Adventures of Clumsy Boy Crusoe* (Ross 1867).

8 The Dalziels produced other children's books around this time, always with an eye on 'quality' – for example, Christina Rossetti's *Sing-Song. A Nursery Rhyme Book*, illustrated by Arthur Hughes (Rossetti 1892).

9 Contemporaries included Mary Ellen Edwards, Helen Allingham, Kate Greenaway and Eleanor Vere Boyle.

10 The same was true across the board. In terms of journalistic writing, even as late as 1891, W. T. Stead created an outrage when he declared that women would be paid at the same rate as the men on one of his journals. In novel writing, scrutiny of surviving publishing contracts has revealed a huge disparity (see, for example, Gaye Tuchman and Nina Fortin's study of the Macmillan Archive in *Edging Women Out: Victorian Novelists, Publishers, and Social Change*, 1989).

11 There is a wealth of literature on the topic. A very thorough introduction is given by Heyman and Shortsleeve (2011). See also Malcolm (1997), and the splendid www.nonsenselit.org website (accessed 13 August 2019).

12 This edition is discussed at some length in Dalziel and Dalziel (1901: 317–18).

13 There had been an expanded version of *A Book of Nonsense* in 1861.

14 He was a sometime illustrator of Tennyson's poems, and composed twelve musical settings for them.

15 Many critics prided themselves on pointing out that they could see through his 'unskilled' art to the trained artist underneath. See Smith (2017: 232).

16 This is a view that has been vigorously rejected both by some critics at the time (see Smith 2017: 233) and in the modern academy: see for example Antinucci (2015).

17 This fed into debates about children's leisure time, which involved new conceptions of 'leisure' versus 'recreation', 'play' and 'amusement'. This was gathering pace against a background involving

two things: the rise of socialism, and the fact that fewer children were going out to work, which coincided with legislation being introduced to curb abuse (when *Queens & Kings* was published, children as young as 5 were still being sent up chimneys to clean them). For an excellent perspective from the left, see Waters (1990), in which the socialist desire to 'encourage children to imagine a better life' (1990: 48) is interrogated.

18 For an excellent survey of literary debates about Lear, see Antinucci (2015).

19 The first appearance of a Wankipoo is on the page devoted to Queen Kalli-Boo; the second on that of The Great Grand Duke of Kalliboo [*sic*].

20 In fact, Ludwig may not have been as 'mad' as he was supposed at the time: modern historians believe he may have been smeared due to his financial extravagance.

21 Obscurely, Prince William Adelin (1103–20), son of Henry 1 of England, drowned when he and his ship's crew, drunk from partying, steered onto rocks.

22 Purcell's opera was the best known of these, revived many times in the nineteenth century.

23 A good eighteenth-century example can be seen at: https://wellcomecollection.org/works/c3wr58jt (accessed on 13 August 2019).

24 Such designs were ubiquitous: although livery crests were associated with the upper classes (queens and kings, lords and ladies, barons and knights, etc.), they were also used by corporations, and as logos for towns, churches and government offices. They were common in clubs and societies, including the freemasons, and in the military.

25 For context, see Lundin (1994).

26 The round-up includes books by, or illustrated by, Busch, Crane and Griset, but *Queens & Kings* gets the most space.

27 This copy of the book is held in Special Collections at UCLA. With thanks for this information to David Kunzle.

28 According to an archivist at Special Collections, University of Reading, which houses the Chatto archive: 'Some early correspondence files were lost when they were sent for salvage in 1915 to help the war effort, which might provide some explanation' (Personal correspondence, 7 November 2018).

29 Illustrations by W. Brunton and E. C. Barnes.

30 Elsewhere in the book Duval's work in *Judy* is offhandedly ascribed to Ross (see Appendices).

5

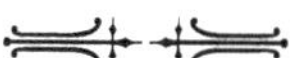

Marie Duval and the technologies of periodical publishing

Simon Grennan

Marie Duval was a professional contributor to periodical journals. She negotiated the elisions of institution, copy and person that generated the idea of the feminised journalist and the idea of the masculinised woman employee. Identifying the processes and business of periodical publishing, in the period when she worked, helps to explain the types of contribution that she made and the technical knowledge that facilitated her employment, in the network of employees that constituted a periodical publishing business or, as Agarwal and Rudolph put it, 'describing the distributed business processes and [...] functional and non-functional properties of services' (Agarwal and Rudolph 2008: np).

This chapter aims to provide a brief overview of the 'distributed business' of periodical publication in the 1870s and 1880s, in order to describe the role that Duval fulfilled, in making drawings for periodicals, and the significance of this role within such businesses. This description draws upon Davidson's concept of the 'communications circuit' in which types of reading (and the needs of types of readers) are created and fulfilled by mass-produced commodities derived from the carefully orchestrated productive practices of authors, managers, technicians and labourers (Davidson 1988: 7).

More specifically, as Easley, King and Morton point out, in periodical publishing, no employee or owner, neither author nor editor, was the absolute fulcrum of the business, precisely because of the distributed nature of the whole endeavour. Rather, 'Individuals contributed to the industry as sub-editors, designers, illustrators, photographers, printers, typesetters, newsboys, purchasers, consumers, readers, proofreaders, printers' assistants, art directors, paper manufacturers and even paper recyclers' (Easley, King and Morton 2017: 4). Beegan further notes 'the ways in which printed matter emerges as the tangible result of the often intangible labour of many people, including designers, illustrators, photographers, art directors, printers, type-setters, authors, editors, proofreaders, paper manufacturers, reproduction houses and buyers' (Beegan 2018: 115).

These taxonomies of some of the functions of a distributed business of publishing owe a debt to previous in-depth studies of specific aspects of the business. Alexis Weedon, Catherine Seville and Mary Ann Gillies have explored facets of the economic relationships between entrepreneurs, producers and audiences (Gillies 2007; Weedon 2003; Seville 1999). The significance of print technology for the production and reading of mass-produced visual images in the nineteenth century has long been argued by Brian Maidment and Peter Sinnera, alongside work on image/text relationships by Rosemary Mitchell and Lorraine Janzen Kooistra and, from another point of view, detailed descriptions of publishing as part of an expanded and heterogeneous visual culture, made by Vanessa Schwartz and Lynda Nead (Sinnera 2019; Maidment 2011; Nead 2005; Kooistra 2002; Mitchell 2000; Schwartz 1997).

However, as Joseph notes, it is important to remember that even those commentators with a focus upon aspects of the economics or technology of periodical print have broadly taken either an 'arts perspective' or have focused upon 'the outcomes of processes' rather than describing the distributed business (Joseph 2019: 19 and 12).

This chapter follows, in impetus if not in method, Hoskin and Dachler's relational approach to the reciprocal impact of individuals and organisations or, as Joseph notes, 'how organisational processes inform social relations and how taken-for-granted knowledge impacts the relatedness of human life'. This approach therefore allows for an exploration of the choices and actions made by individuals within the distributed businesses of, say, periodical publishing, and also highlights how collective social action constructed the organisational field (Joseph 2019: 55–6; Hoskin and Dachler 1995).

In the mid-nineteenth century, there were no comprehensive descriptions of the ways in which a distributed business might be constructed, as it were, from scratch. On one hand, there were published technical instructions for the production and use of machines and trade-circumscribed training in the sense of apprenticeships in specific crafts and their associated trades (*The Young Clerk's Manual; or, Counting-house Assistant* 1848; *The Mechanics' Magazine* 1871–72). For those aspects of the business that might be considered as professions, rather than trades, no qualifications or prior training were required at all. There was no instruction manual detailing how to become the boss (Murray 2006). On the other hand, there were publications containing overviews of the desired effects of business activities or studies in specific aspects of craft or profession (Baker 2012; O'Gorman 2007; Rummonds 2004; Poovey 2003). Of course, business practices themselves were heterogeneous rather than monolithic, despite the tendency of scholars of business to focus on the practices of those businesses that survived, succeeded and hence left paper trails of their own histories as evidence of the effectiveness of their work (Macmillan 1908; Dalziel 1901).

I have found no shorthand description of the intersection of business practices and technical processes that constituted commercial periodical publishing in the 1870s, which I could simply employ to precisely locate Duval's work within the distributed business of *Judy, or the London Serio-comic Journal*, for example. Such a description does not even reveal itself in the major publishing memoirs of the period, such as those of Gilbert and

Edward Dalziel, whose lives and work touched all aspects of a wide-ranging and successful print and publishing business (Dalziel 1901).

There remains a general tendency to assume that those intersections of business practices and technical processes that constituted the distributed business of periodical publishing were either understood implicitly by readers or were of little interest to them. These details also appear to have been of relatively little significance for the historic business memoirist. As a result, elisions of different practices, even in Joseph's encompassing description of the history of the Macmillan publishing house, for example, can bypass rather than reveal the quotidian structure of the work, finance, culture and ideas of a commercial publishing business as its participants strived to daily fulfil their tasks (Joseph 2019: 195–221).

Lawrence, Suddaby and Leca note that nowhere can we find a brief, encompassing description of the distributed business of periodical publishing, for example, let alone a description that claims to be typical (Lawrence, Suddaby and Leca 2011: 52). This is even more so retrospectively when information about the range of publishing and print production tasks is revealed in the entries in archival commercial accounts and is today read alongside other empirical information, such as 'the anecdotal, such as publishers' memoirs, to handbooks for printers and statistics on the tonnage of paper produced' (Weedon 2003: 5).

Extrapolating a comprehensive description of the phases and cycles of production in a distributed business, each dependent upon the other, is extraordinarily difficult. Considering how the timing of recorded purchases evidences changing levels of stock, or the wages of specific numbers of employees evidences production capacity, for example, requires a triangulation of different sources, which are most often unavailable (Weedon 2003: 23).

It might also be said that such a model as I am here imagining runs the risk of obscuring rather than illuminating the empirical detail of significant practices and tendencies. Weedon states that, in studying Victorian business practices 'the need to learn how the systems of the firm worked mean generalisations are inadequate', although he concludes that: 'Having said that, each system has a similar function' (Weedon 2003: 5).

I argue that there is value in considering Duval's work from the point of view of her role in a distributed periodical print business, because this extended social and technical environment was a primary cause and motivation of her work. This context directs attention towards both the conventional as well as the unconventional aspects of her role in the business and of her drawings. As such, I only need to outline the particular 'team production problem' posed in organising a printing business, in order to seek Duval's place within it (Alchian and Demsetz 1972).[1]

For the purpose of this chapter, it is enough to provide a syncretic outline of the functions of the distributed parts of a publishing business, encompassing the technical functions of print production, in order to identify the people who undertook each part-function as employees and to locate Duval's work in the process. The parameters of such an outline can be deduced from the causes and consequences of the range of functions that any periodical was required to perform, in order to be read, producing Davidson's communications circuit, as mentioned (Davidson 1988: 7). However, this description also seeks to avoid the kind of oversights that belong to national census classifications since 1851:

> the lumping together of different occupations in broad categories creates anomalies that are difficult to explain in class terms. Printers, for example, do not easily fit working-class models, having for much of their history exhibited above-average levels of literacy, higher wages, and a reluctance to support other workers' unions. (Greenwood 2015: 12)

A description of the roles of employees, relative to the technical functions of print production also militates against the application of anachronistic models (such as twentieth-century models) to the demarcation of tasks in the nineteenth-century publishing industry.

For example, Gifford uses the production protocols of twentieth-century American comics publishing (the 'Marvel method') to describe Duval's role in the production of drawings for *Judy*. In this model of the studio production of colour drawings, for photolithographic reproduction, tasks are allocated to a production line including an employee who draws in pencil ('penciller'), one who overdraws in black ink ('inker'), 'colourer', 'letterer' and so on. As a result, Gifford claims that Duval was an 'inker' of pencil drawings made by Charles Ross. The process of drawing on wood for engravings used in the commercial presses of the nineteenth century contradicts this idea entirely. Drawings were either transferred to the wood block by tracing or photography or drawn directly onto the block, for an engraver to cut. Interpolating an unnecessary process, such as overdrawing by a colleague, made no commercial sense (Gifford 1976: 26).[2]

Considering the lists of functions provided by Easley, King and Morton, Beegan and other commentaries on individual aspects of a distributed periodical publishing business (for example by Altick, Feather and Weedon), the enterprise of periodical publishing divided broadly into a network of distinct functions, ultimately connecting the publisher with the reader through the fulfilment of a series of team production tasks, every day, week or month (Altick 1958; Feather 1988; Weedon 2003; Beegan 2018: 115; Easley, King and Morton 2017: 4).

It is important to note, as Beetham does, that this process of team production was not linear, but cyclical, eventually generating the corollary idea that a reader could become a professional provider of content – a journalist, for example (Beetham 1996: 13). The rhythms of each type of work also followed their own cycles. Hence, it is inaccurate to say that, before anything else, the publisher had to fulfil the function of visioning the product, because publications were continually renewed, revised and transformed according to the motivating ethos of the time and its interaction with a market. Long-standing periodical brands might appear to create an ethos transcending the controlling publisher of the moment but, in fact, this effect was rather an idea than a practical principle. Shorter-lived products demonstrated that publishers' visions for their products lived less than a half-life of the commercial imperative of continuing to achieve sales. However, as the publisher's vision was never really primary or generative, we will step off from it.

As shorthand, it is also convenient to propose an elision of roles and people in terms of journalists and readers, to avoid having to give everyone in this outline a job title, which might mislead rather than clarify.

The maintenance and revision of the ethos of the publication was a function devolved to the publisher, bringing the motivational aims of the business together with the processes and people involved in making and delivering a regular experience for readers. As Feather notes, 'the mass circulation journals were generally in the hands of companies which specialised in publishing them and which often combined the processes of publishing and printing' (Feather 1988: 115). Over the 40-year life of *Judy* (1867–1907*)*, the publication in which the majority of Duval's drawings were published, the 'Proprietor' was distinct from the printer until 1879.[3]

Working to fulfil this ethos, in the form of commercial print products, were the trade and public systems of the business, articulating finances, estates, human and material resources, payment systems and value chains (Beegan 2018: 115; Easley, King and Morton 2017: 4; Feather 1988: 99 and 132; Altick 1958). The design of the product conformed more or less to the knowledge-transferred crafts of the graphic designer, plus the constraints of the technologies of print, distribution and of unit costs (Feather 1988: 87, 88, 90, 91 and 94).

The template methods and artefacts for the reproduction or revision of all of this anticipated the deadlines inherent in the chosen cycles of production and distribution, such as the ordering of paper, the payroll of staff, the payment of rents, the contracts with partners, as well as the design and production templates for the product (Weedon 2003: 15 and 18; Feather 1988). The commissioning and creation of new content and practices populated these templates, allowing the compositing of the periodical, this being the technical laying out of type and images for print, utilising a mix of new and old manual skills, methods and machinery (Weedon 2003: 15; Feather 1988: 90, 88 and 93).

Press work, being the production of the periodical itself from ink and paper, utilised a mixture of old and new press processes, both manual and mechanical, followed by the compiling, cutting and finishing of the product (Weedon 2003: 61 and 15; Feather 1988: 91). The stockpiling and distribution of the periodical, the receipt of unsold returns, plus recycling of used materials, according to established and revised templates, preceded the sale of the product via wholesale partnerships and disbursement to points of sale via retail partnerships (Weedon 2003: 61; Feather 1988: 94). Receipting and money transfers occasioned bookkeeping, legal and tax accounting and disbursements (Weedon 2003: 13 and 63).

This syncretic outline does little to describe the cycles of work at each stage, or the relationships between these cycles. Time and motion studies would allocate times of day, duration and competencies to the tasks that combined to fulfil each of these twelve functions. Alongside this outline, a description of the types of ledger costs and a note on the target receipts of the model enterprise provide a snapshot of the technical aspects of conceiving, producing and selling a periodical.

Costs to the business were incurred in the areas of dividends, fees to contributors, staff wages and training, estates and equipment, materials, transport, marketing, accounting, payroll and tax and insurance. Against these types of expenditure was set income from capital investment, sales of the product and the sale of advertising space, plus licensing and income from partnership and spin-off projects. The absence in this outline of descriptions of remuneration, costs or the social aspects required from employees in fulfilling their work does not constitute any point of view or commentary in itself. The intention is to provide a brief description of the types of production process and its systems, to which Duval contributed when making a drawing for a periodical publication.

This outline offers a broad framework for considering the material conditions, social expectations, opportunities, prohibitions and representations of the types of work undertaken in the production of periodical publications. Ultimately, the focus of our attention is the work that Duval undertook according to the relationships generated by different types of work in industrial team production, even if the focus of our attention is ultimately the work. This outline helps to describe ways in which she was identified and located by her collaboration in a business. As a result, the outline both points to 'the fluidity between wage earner and independence' (Crossick and Haupt 1995) and also avoids the 'lack of attention to trade hierarchies[,] linked to a general obfuscation of life cycle changes: workplace status was not necessarily fixed throughout a lifetime' (Greenwood 2015: 12).

Duval joined the production process as a provider of copy, which was commissioned and adjudicated by an editor and sub-editors responsible for fulfilling or revising the design templates and the commissioning practice templates of the journal, according to the demands of the publisher's ethos and the market. She responded to commissions regularly, producing drawings on topics following these practices (the editor or sub-editors were her direct managers). Her drawings were transferred to metal cased blocks of boxwood (or plaster or metal casts of these blocks), which had been painted white, by either tracing or photography, or drawing directly onto the blocks, for a wood engraver to follow in cutting her design into the wood. Her professional task was to continually conceive and make new drawings for print, according to briefs devised by or in collaboration with her editors.

Given the geographic proximity of her other habitual places of work (London 'West End' theatres) to the editorial premises of *Judy*, for example, plus the proliferation of shops of wood engravers in the same locale, cost-effectiveness proposes that Duval didn't make drawings on paper, for transfer to wood, but rather drew directly on the block. No original drawings by her survive, either on paper or on wood. This is not untypical for visual journalists drawing for cheap papers. Blocks were shaved for re-cutting with new designs, occasionally being reproduced as plaster or metal casts and saved for later reprinting ('Modern Wood Engraving' 1838: 149). Examples exist of her drawings being dismembered and the parts appearing in print at widely different times and contexts.[4]

Duval's task of making new drawings for print occupied a place in a production chain that also paralleled the place of the copy produced by verbal journalists. A writer's copy, commissioned and finalised by an editor, would form part of a sheaf of handwritten papers given directly to the compositors of the publication, who made up metal frames of moveable metal type (or, later, whole sections of cast metal type) and engraved wood blocks, for printing (Greenwood 2015: 18).

Duval's visual copy appears to have been produced through a more direct engagement with the machinery of print, even if the final drawings required the intermediary work of an engraver. The immediacy of drawing onto wood for print was often cited as an advantage in contemporaneous accounts, such that 'the greatest advantage wood engraving has over copper is that there neither need be any [...] intermediate person or process between the designer and the engraver' because in wood engraving 'the draughtsman makes black lines with a pen or pencil which the engraver leaves untouched' ('Modern Wood Engraving' 1838: 146).

This immediacy was the most significant corollary of the technology of wood engraving, resulting from the way in which wood performed when compared with copper or steel. An 1838 article in *The London and Westminster Review* described this exactly. Pieces of boxwood, which is heavy, fine-grained and extremely durable, were 'cut into slices across the grain', as distinct from the with-the-grain cutting of woodcut print techniques ('Modern Wood Engraving' 1838: 146). 'The wood engraver cuts away the part in the block which is to remain white or colourless; but the part in the copper-plate which is to be white in the engraving is to be left untouched', so that the 'wood engraver starts from black, the copper-plate engraver starts from white' and hence, the 'manner of using the ink in the two is also opposite; it is put into the hollow lines of the copper-plate, but on the upstanding lines of the wooden block' ('Modern Wood Engraving' 149 and 145). Metal type was inked in the same way and, as a result of this congruence, un-inked engraved wood blocks could be set into un-inked, made-up blocks of type and the whole structure inked and printed at the same time.

Hence, the wood engraved image could easily take any shape on the printed page, was easily 'assimilated into the typeset page' and 'could be easily situated amidst circum-ambient text to form close alliance between text and image' (Maidment 2016: 102 and 107). These technical aspects of wood engraving for commercial print, plus the economic fact that a 'plate of metal is useless after a few thousand impressions [...] while a wood-block will yield sometimes two or three hundred thousand impressions', resulted in the dominance of the medium in the nineteenth century (Maidment 2016: 147). This technology, known as the 'letterpress', incorporating the use of engraving, 'was the most prolific printing process in the early industrial period, being responsible for the bulk of books and journals as well as ephemera' (Twyman 1998: 38).

Greenwood notes the print industry standard of separation and diversification in practices and training between compositors and press workers (Greenwood 2015: 19), although *The London and Westminster Review*, focusing on wood engraving and the wood engraver, discussed the 'trio' of roles, or the collaboration between the visual journalist making drawings, the engraver and the press workers ('Modern Wood Engraving' 1838: 148). In fact, four technical roles needed to be fulfilled in order to produce prints of text and images on the page, on the journals for which Duval worked. The visual journalist worked with the engraver to make the engraved wood block. The compositor set the block into the frame with the type. The engraver, and sometimes the visual journalist, worked with the press workers to ensure that the image was being reproduced to its full advantage as paper went through the press.

Adoption of the craft of wood engraving was occasionally debated as one of the solutions to the apparent social problems caused by the lack of socially acceptable employment for middle-class women. This was revealed in the 1851 national census, where it was considered 'a means of livelihood [...] which, without severing from home, without breaking up family assemblies, is at once more happy, healthful, tasteful, and profitable than almost any other' and 'all that can be taught of the art may be learnt in a few lessons' ('Modern Wood Engraving' 1838: 152).

However, as with much of the debate about the suitability of types of work for women and the suitability of women for types of work, a generalising impulse in the media to overlook women who worked by necessity, rather than choice, obscured and distorted commentaries on the roles of women in the workplace. Social class as well as gender created distinct contingencies under which different women could consider and undertake work or attempt to train for work.

As the investigative reporters who contributed to Ramsay MacDonald's 1904 study *Women in the Printing Trades* noted, the social aspirations of working-class women employed in the print industries provided a significant counterpoint to concepts and strategies for women's emancipation, developed by middle-class reformers, because 'amongst women engaged in industry, convention is particularly potent in determining what trades are desirable and proper and what are not' and 'these notions of gentility have [...] a deeper significance [...] that the favoured trades are the lighter ones. To some extent this is true. The heavier employments are staffed by a rougher class of women' (Ramsay MacDonald 1904: 67 and 68). In the report, both the terms 'heavier' and 'lighter' refer to the physical strength required to fulfil different tasks. The 'heavier' trades referred to included manually positioning parts of the presses, such as the typeset frames, or manipulating loads of paper. The 'lighter' trades included feeding individual sheets into the press, inking or, indeed, the craft of wood engraving.

Further, concepts of marriage and child rearing reproduced existing gender relationships, so that women entered the print trades, 'not with expectations of long employment, but with hopes of a speedy release [through marriage]'. 'We were anxious to find out why they did not join [a union] [...] others frankly admitted that marriage was sure to come along', reports Ramsay MacDonald, whilst the 'custom in the trades under review undoubtedly is that married women should not work in them' (Ramsay MacDonald 1904: 102). Finally, conceptions of masculinity, as much as femininity, proved to be constraints on working-class women entering some types of work of which they were capable. In answer to MacDonald's question: 'why they did not turn their hands to simple and easy processes which were being done by men? 'Why, that is man's work, and we shouldn't think of doing it!' is the usual answer, given with a toss of the head and a tone insinuating that there is a certain indelicacy in the question' (Ramsay MacDonald 1904: 65–6).

Conflate these constraints with a sketch of 'The Factory Girl of the Period' that appeared in *The Girl of the Period Miscellany* 35 years earlier, whose 'mother never thinks of asking where she is going; she is as free and independent as her brothers. To her credit be it said, she is less likely than her brothers are to make a bad use of that liberty' (Miss Echo 1869: 185–6). However, as MacDonald wrote, 'it must be noted that when a girl's work in the workshop is finished she has often to go home to a new round of domestic tasks from which a boy is exempted' (MacDonald 1904: 66).

Hence, as Tusan claims, the 'problem of employment opportunities and working conditions for women, rather than the question of political representation, remained the central focus of late-nineteenth-century debates over women's status in Britain' (Tusan 2004: 103). Although the major projects of establishing printing and publishing businesses, including periodical publishing business, run by and employing only women, made their 'strongest impact on upper-middle and middle-class women', their 'effect on Victorian feminist reform organisations was more lasting. Women's organisations, through their continued support of institutions such as the Women's Cooperative Printing Society, became increasingly invested in the larger project of creating an economic and political space for women' (Tusan 2004: 120). The Society for Promoting the Employment of Women was established in 1859 and continues to trade. The Victoria Press for the Employment of Women was in business between 1860 and 1881 and the Women's Cooperative Printing Society was in business between 1874 and 1890.

We have no record of how much Duval was paid for her work, although work comparable in scale, if not topic, undertaken in the 1870s by artist Adelaide Claxton was remunerated at two-thirds of the cost of the work of engraving her drawing on wood for print. (Flood 2013: 113). Although we do not know how much time was allotted to Claxton to make her drawing, the engraver's task was allotted months, making the relative value of remuneration difficult to judge. The drawing in question was also of high status, as a large spread, compared with Duval's usual vignettes, half pages and occasional pages and, whatever its status as a 'Claxton', it would have taken longer to make than Duval's drawings, with their habitually rapid and slapdash techniques.

What remains key to describing Duval's relationships to the business of periodical publishing is the idea that her work conformed to the conditions, expectations and constraints of work as a journalist, providing copy. Because we have no evidence for her rates of pay, it is unfortunately also impossible to compare her remuneration to that of writers providing copy in the same period. That aside, the nineteenth-century role and image of the journalist describes Duval's situation and approach to her employment by periodical publications more precisely than any other.

The journalist in the business

As Shannon Smith points out, in common with nineteenth-century entertainments and news media of all types, from stage performances to novels, periodical publishing was a complex and dynamic collaborative enterprise in which specific ranges of technical knowledge held by different people were brought to bear upon each other, to constitute the whole (Smith 2016: 31). Although partial and brief, the above outline of periodical publishing as team production bears this out. Although Smith privileges the professional capacities of journalists, in the business of periodical publishing, as 'the centre of a demanding intersection of production technologies' (Smith 2016: 31), every member of the collaboration provided a service or undertook a craft without which the business could not run, even if their different roles occupied widely different places within a hierarchy of responsibility, control, benefit and remuneration.

Despite not necessarily being at the 'centre' of the system of periodical publishing, the journalist's role did indeed intersect a wide range of other roles in the business. The journalist's work bordered upon information management (in the form of news and content gathering from diverse telegraphic and postal networks and agents, for example), content creation (in the form of written or drawn contributions), and the technical aspects of compositing (influencing the appearance of the page), printing (influencing the production of the page), marketing, distribution and sales (paying attention to the impact of copy on readers and its promotion).

In this, only the editors' and publishers' roles superseded the journalist's in touching all parts of the periodicals business. Whereas an editor or publisher guided the ethos of the business, motivated by some aim or other, if only to make a profit, the journalist fulfilled that ethos by generating content of a particular type and style and, hence, guiding reading and driving sales. The business of periodical publishing differed from book publishing in this regard, in that the role of the book author did not require the immersive maintenance of similar sets of time-limited and dynamic relationships with the other editorial, technical and financial roles and functions.

Every role within the enterprise could be utilised as a lens with which to see the business in a slightly different way, according to the contingencies under which it was fulfilled. From a junior clerk in accounts to the owner/publisher, the motivations, constraints and opportunities constituting each role differed widely and the impact that each had upon the other also differed. The business was heterogeneous whilst always being oriented towards both the appearance of homogeneity (the commercial 'brand') and the continual consistent delivery of new products to readers, at the point of sale.

Further, the reading environments for periodical publications were also extremely heterogeneous. Far from being products with limited sites of purchase and use, periodicals were materially promiscuous, being transportable, open to re-use and multiple uses, even when 'out of date'. Even if time-limited in their production cycles, and apparently time-limited in their use by readers ('yesterday's news', 'a review of last week's play'), periodicals in fact had a long tail of use which burned bright on the day of publication, but which took some time to diminish and finally disappear.

Periodicals were shared, re-sold, discarded and picked up in public places across otherwise categorical boundaries of social class and economic capacity. What a mistress of a house might buy and read today, her domestic employee might read tomorrow. A paper bought, read and discarded on the up train from Clapham to the City might be picked up and read on the down train half an hour later. Moreover, material was often recycled – and further distributed – in compilations, annuals and 'specials'. King notes the difference between the 'value chain' of periodicals, that is, the process of production to the point of sale, and the 'value system', or the useful life of the product after sale. He writes that periodical 'economics are not then restricted to the account books of their publishers but inhere in every passage of a periodical from one place or state to another' (King 2016: 63).

Alongside this, to a greater degree than other entertainments and news media, the means by which periodical publications were produced and distributed were frequently elided by readers with the content of publications themselves, with the result that the technologies of production and distribution, the finances and the identities of an enterprise's collaborators, at every level of the business, were either purposefully or nominally obscured, to guide and affect readers in particular ways (Gitelman 2006: 5). In one sense, as a product fulfilling a number of functions, the periodical simply became normative for an increasingly wide range of potential readers, as the century progressed.

These processes and conditions not only reflected readers' sense of the normative, but also created and reproduced normative ideas and practices in the business of periodical publishing itself. Brake, Bell and Finkelstein note the importance of the idea of the ethical imperative of print products of all types, resulting from the civic promotion of literacy, creating a politically contested environment for the business of periodical publishing (Brake, Bell and Finkelstein 2000: 3). The regular and frequent appearance of new products consolidated concepts of industrial labour, in the working day, week and year, concepts of domestic life, childhood and 'the Imperial, national, gendered, economic, ethnic and sexual points of contention of the times', represented in the 'creation of new authorial identities and new professional and social roles, cutting across as well as along previously established lines' (Brake, Bell and Finkelstein 2000: 5), including the 'distinct but often mutable or unstable gendering of all aspects of the content and production of commodity print' (Brake, Bell and Finkelstein 2000: 6).

Although I have pointed away from the exceptional significance of the journalist, in the collaborative endeavour of periodical publishing, to nod to the variety of practices that constituted it, the journalist, possibly more even than the editor of a publication, came to present a cipher for the idea of a periodical, encompassing both its commercial identity and its identities in relation to readers. The terms of journalistic employment required the journalist to represent themselves, in their writing or drawing, as a fundamental qualification for the work. As a result, the impulse to elide the biographies of journalists with the styles and contents of their writing or drawing was strong, and remains a focus for current commentary on Victorian periodical publishing (Smith 2016; Fraser, Green and Johnson 2003; Brake, Bell and Finkelstein 2000; Campbell 2000; Beetham 1996, for example). Journalists were significant both for invoking an idea of who they were (which may or may not have been fictional), in the context of the business of periodical publishing, and for the representations (the copy) that they produced. Apart from the role of editor, commentary on the historic significance of other collaborators in periodical businesses, on the other hand, largely focuses on who was fulfilling the variety of roles in the enterprise, such as the class or gender of a paper-feeder or the training of boy apprentices.

Hence, whilst the *Metropolitan: a Monthly Journal of Literature, Science, and the Fine Arts* described 'the snip-snap style of penny-a-line men' catering to what *Dublin Review* called a 'feverish clamour, the hot breath of excitement […] this excited, restless craving' for the products of journalism ('Literature of the Day: – the New Magazine' 1831; 'Modern periodical Literature' 1862), it is also plausible for Fraser to note the conflation, by nineteenth-century periodical readers, of journalists with what they produced. Such 'journalistic writing, or some forms of it, involved a kind of emasculation' or, rather, the feminisation of the male journalist, because 'it was seen as a promiscuous and flighty medium, built upon the principle that ideas are as changeable as fashion […] by the end of the century the association […] with fashion and hence the feminine had become thoroughly entrenched' – the promiscuity and flightiness of copy being seen as feminine properties (Fraser, Green and Johnson 2003: 7) and 'the medium that most readily articulates the unevennesses and reciprocities of evolving gender ideologies is the periodical press' (Fraser, Green and Johnson 2003: 3).

Whereas nineteenth-century debates about the masculinising of women employees by any type of employment focused on the relationships between gender and all types of work, both male and female journalists were personally susceptible to feminisation because of the type of copy the work required. The relationship between journalist and copy, between work and the necessity to represent and comment, demanded by the work, made the periodical press 'a very particular space, both fluid and dynamic, in which women could negotiate a writing identity or writing identities' (Fraser, Green and Johnson 2003: 44).

Beetham recognises the elision of the practice of journalism, the journalist and the periodical publication, whilst also applying it as a critical device in order to describe the experience of readers, circumscribing their relationships with the product (Beetham 1996: 7 11). Hence, she describes the relative cost of a publication as determining the ways in which the visualisations and ideas that it presented gained wider social currency, according to the relative status of the readers who could afford to buy it.

The concepts of masculinity, femininity, domesticity, public life and work presented in periodical publications varied according to the price of the paper, such that 'it is possible to chart the various ways in which written and visual identities emerged and developed in the periodical press' (Brake, Bell and Finkelstein 2000: 3). Of periodicals targeted at women, Beetham writes that because 'material conditions made regular purchase of […] printed matter beyond the reach of working women, most magazines targeted the middle class and offered explicitly bourgeois models of feminine behaviour', so that there was a 'a dynamic relationship between [the] remaking of femininity and the material basis of the magazines in advertising revenue' (Beetham 1996: 7 and 8).

Hence, the heterogeneity of periodicals' contents not only provided variety and novelty of contents, but itself inculcated ideas about who was writing and reading. '[T]his diversity empowers readers of periodicals' because periodicals refused 'a single authorial voice' (Beetham 1996: 12). Readers had the opportunity to 'construct their own text from the printed version', by fragmentary reading, because the 'periodical is generically as well as physically more liable to disintegrate than the book' (Beetham 1996: 12). Beetham follows Judith Fetterley in identifying this negotiability as the opportunity for resistance to normative ideas, in understanding the experience of readers in particular (Beetham 1996: 11; Fetterley 1978).

The functional conclusion of this process of elision, of types of people (socially distinct men and women) with types of role, such as journalist and reader, was the increasing mutability and negotiability of personal and professional roles, relative to the periodical press, rather than their entrenchment. The apogee of elisions between people and types of role occurred in the invitations continually made in periodical publications for readers to become journalists. 'If the reader accepts the position of "woman" offered by the magazine, she takes on both the role and character which it defines as womanly', but she was also 'constantly invited to become [a writer]' (Beetham 1996: 12 and 13).

Also of importance, considering the visual registers of Duval's journalism, was the attention paid to the status of spectatorship, in contemporaneous commentaries on journalism. Rather than journalism being a literary craft aspiring to high cultural or civic and ethical significance, the journalist's role was not only feminised, but associated concomitantly with the commercial creation of and reporting from an ephemeral and frivolous social scene. The encouragement of readers to become writers supported this tendency, in that the personal point of view was fully elided with journalistic script, often to the dismay of cultural or literary critics and political commentators.

As Campbell points out, 'in the increasingly synaesthetic environment of late-century newspapers, visual references mostly appertained to sensory cognition generally' (Campbell 2000: 48), so that journalistic writing shifted emphasis from the categorical and analytical to the descriptive, whilst visual images, in the form of illustrations, puzzles, games, patterns, decorations and advertisements, became less an addendum to text and more an expected, crucial, adaptive, affecting and saleable aspect of periodical reading.

Journalism as spectacle articulated an accumulation of details from the passing scene, making the periodical publication 'an agency for collecting, condensing and assimilating the entire trivialities of the entire human existence' (Stillman 1891: 689), resulting in the ascendancy of the visual, such that 'the journalistic eye is now of far greater importance than the journalistic pen' (Watson 1906: 84). Journalism had completed its move 'from transcription to description and images', finalising 'the ascendency of the image, the growth of symptomatic readings, the aestheticisation and putative deterioration of political and daily life' (Campbell 2000: 48 and 42).

In all of these senses, Duval's work and her activities as an employee in commercial periodical publishing conformed to the conditions of journalism. In making this adjudication, Duval's employment and her drawings contradict nineteenth-century debates and subsequent analysis of the experiences, conditions and contingencies of women relative to the fine arts professions that, in 1861, Purnell proposed as 'twofold – partly to enable young women of the middle class to obtain an honourable and profitable employment, and partly to improve ornamental design in manufacture, by cultivating the taste of the designer' (Purnell 1861: 108).

Purnell was writing about women's access to training in the fine and decorative arts, in order to qualify them for entry into professional careers as painters, sculptors and designers, which London's The Female School of Art offered from 1842, providing training that was unavailable to women elsewhere. For example, The Royal Academy Schools prohibited women from training, on the basis both of the impropriety of them training alongside men and of making drawings from naked live models. Campbell Orr's analysis of the contingencies circumscribing middle-class women seeking to train as artists and designers, concurs with Purnell, in stating that it was 'not just a question of being admitted to art schools or the Royal Academy, but of challenging the whole notion of what an artist was' (Campbell Orr 1995: 7).

Two aspects of Purnell's commentary are significant, relative to Duval's employment and output. First, he understood The Female School of Art to be a training centre for middle-class women. The impropriety of women working alongside men was a middle-class contingency, rather than a working-class one. Although with less emphasis, Campbell Orr follows him in this. As such, training in the fine and decorative arts had little to do with Duval although, as a middle-class woman trained by her painter father, it had been a contingency of Adelaide Claxton's working life. As Purnell described:

> In the lowest classes, again, [the problem of women's unemployment] has been already solved. There, the necessity of earning their own bread is so apparent from their earliest years, that women accept their lot with patience, and are able and willing to work at whatever offers itself. Rejecting nothing, and being competent in most things, they fear nothing, except it be illness, and that only because it incapacitates them from their daily labour. (Purnell 1861: 107)

Rather, a hint of the relationship between the inflexible constraints placed upon middle-class women, by a class-rooted and patriarchal social propriety, and the licence of young working-class women, in this milieu, was the substance of a comic rhyme in *The Girl of the Period Miscellany* (the parallels between Duval and the fictional women journalists and editors of which I discuss in detail in Chapter 2):

> 'Oh, bother the children! You know
> At South Kensington, Ma, I am due,
> That exquisite cast of Apollo
> To draw with my master till two.
> 'Draw landscape, fruit, flowers.' No, thank you;
> Such tame subjects are not in my way:
> The glorious masculine figure
> Is the model I study all day. (Miss Echo 1869: 137)

Second, even the best training for men or women in the fine arts did not itself provide the skills required to make drawings suitable for subsequent wood engraving for commercial printing. Huxley recalls that *The Cornhill Magazine*'s publisher George Smith was surprised by Frederic Leighton's inability to make drawings suitable for wood engraving, in the 1860s. His surprise derived from Leighton's extremely high status as a trained professional artist and the high cost of employing him as an illustrator (Huxley 1923: 140). Leighton later became President of the Royal Academy of Arts. As a visual journalist, Duval's lack of academic training did not necessarily impede her employment as a woman working as a spectator and visual commentator in periodical publications, that is, in fulfilling the role of a journalist.

In this sense, Duval's use of visual registers was something of a red herring, due to her fulfilment of the professional conditions and contingencies of a feminised, personalised, visualising and scene-describing journalism. Like other verbal journalists employed by the periodicals for which she worked, Duval commented and described using types of slang that were familiar to readers, the only distinction being that her slang was visual rather than verbal. This similarity alone might have been all that was required, once recognised by her and by her editors, to enable her to become an employee, because the business of periodical publishing allowed it, by trading in slang. Such shifts of possible roles were not available to women seeking work in professions in which visual slang was antithetical and had no currency, such as the fine and decorative arts.

The tone, possibilities, professional relationships, conditions and contingencies of Duval's visual journalism can still be glimpsed in a contemporaneous description of a woman employed to make drawings for a periodical paper, in a comic guidebook by Charles Ross, published in 1882: the speed of work, indexing professional insouciance; the confidence and charm, indexing femininity; the significance and status of a slang drawing and, finally, a clear professional relationship to the other functions of the periodical's production and the hierarchies and practices of the business:

> having been supplied with a block ready whitened, [she] straightway dipped a pen in ink, and dashing down upon it a lopsided man toppling over into space, which, handing to me with a confident smile, she bade me take it down to the office and see the wood-cutting people didn't chop it about too much. (Ross and Wilson 1882: 110)

Quite literally, for these reasons, it could be an eyewitness description of Duval.

Notes

1 'Team production is simply production that requires various inputs of differing types from two or more individuals, and for which the output is not easily separable into the components that are attributable to the various inputs individually' (Blair 2003: 399).
2 For an example of drawing for wood engraving, see Goldman (2005: 33).
3 From *Judy*'s launch, in 1867, the Proprietor's business address, that is, *Judy*'s, was 73 Fleet Street, London, whereas the printer was Woodfall & Kinder, Milford Lane (*Judy, or the London*

Serio-comic Journal, Volume 20, 262). From 1878, print was undertaken by The Phoenix Works, Doctor's Common (*Judy, or the London Serio-comic Journal* Volume 22,136). By February 1879, Dalziel Brothers, 110 Camden High Street, had bought *Judy* and amalgamated both print and publishing 'in house'. *Judy*'s publishing office moved from Fleet Street to 99 Shoe Lane on 4 June 1879 (*Judy, or the London Serio-comic Journal*, Volume 24, 262).

4 Compare Duval (1869) and Duval (1873f), for example.

Part II

Depicting and performing

6

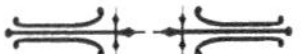

The significance of Marie Duval's drawing style

Simon Grennan

Duval's drawings were made to provoke laughter, by articulating and rearticulating social stereotypes and contradictions. Duval achieved this in her choice of topics and, more unusually, in her ideas about her own position as a humorous visual journalist: her visible lack of training, stage career, gender and social class, relative to the experiences of readers. This chapter examines this articulation, considering late nineteenth-century gender and class relationships between humour, displays of technical skill and concepts of vulgar behaviour. The chapter finally exemplifies these relationships in two Duval drawings on the topic of the Royal Academy Summer Exhibitions of 1880 and 1876.

Miserable drawing

We are fortunate that the surviving public, non-academic commentary on Marie Duval's work from the nineteenth and twentieth centuries is brief and simple to summarise. These commentaries appeared in print over a period of just under 60 years, very sporadically from 1869. Apart from the gentler comments of her biographer, Ellen Clayton (1876: 332) they either judged Duval's work to be of low quality or repeated an inaccurate platitude about her as the instigator of the professional activity of comic drawing by women.[1] An anonymous commentator in *The Sporting Times* of 18 May 1872 characteristically wrote:

> By the way, who does those horrid little woodcuts in *Judy*? The large cartoon is generally very good, and so are the sketches by Adelaide Claxton, but there are always a few wretched scratches signed 'M.D.', signifying 'miserable drawing', I suppose, though some do say it stands for Marie Duval [...]. If 'M.D.' cannot draw properly or with humour, he or she should be kicked out of *Judy's* sanctum. ('The Women About Town' 1872)

An earlier letter to *The Theatrical Journal* established the tone of the commentary, in Duval's first year as a contributor to *Judy, or the London Serio-comic Journal*, as part of a review of a performance in which she appeared, at the New Royalty Theatre:

> Is this the young lady who periodically contributes to a serio-comic journal those grotesque pictures so obviously in imitation of Mr C. H. Ross's absurd style that it is occasionally difficult to determine, with any degree of correctness, which sketches are by Miss Duval and which by Mr Ross? ('Letter to the Editor' 1869: 30:1557:325)[2]

In summary, Duval's drawings were found to be, in various ways, 'excruciatingly bad' by the small number of public commentators who wrote about them (Wilson 1927).[3] However, the scope of these commentaries is instructive as well as exemplary, in that they described exactly what was thought to be wrong with Duval's drawings by these commentators. Duval's drawings were found to be technically incompetent ('cannot draw properly', 'scratches', 'bad') and unfunny. They inculcated unpleasant and extreme sensations in the reader ('horrid', 'wretched', 'miserable', 'grotesque', 'excruciating') and were unoriginal and derivative.

The contemporaneous popularity and professional status of Duval's drawings serves somewhat to contradict the general low adjudication of their quality by commentators. More trenchantly, this contradiction indicates that opinions published in periodical papers represent a series of relationships between writers, readers, papers and the topics about which they write, rather than simply providing any authoritative analysis in themselves. The popularity and professionalism of Duval's drawings is substantiated by her production history. She published some 1400 drawings in *Judy*, as well as other periodicals, annuals and almanacs, illustrated novels and a monograph book, over a period of more than fifteen years.

Notwithstanding the consistently negative tone of the very few public commentaries that were made, these productions represented professional and commercial relationships upon which adjudications of quality more fundamentally relied, both commercially and socially. Duval's work was judged acceptable, at least, by gatekeepers such as the buyers and readers of the publications in which her work appeared, as well as professional editors, publishers and book and periodical sellers.

This chapter describes some of the significant conditions in which Duval's drawings were drawn, produced and read. I discuss the types of activities that produced the drawings, plus public opinions about these types of activities and about Duval's undertaking of them in particular. Describing these activities includes describing those questions that faced Duval in pursuing her career, making humorous drawings for the periodical press of the 1870s and 1880s, such as: to what end to draw (Duval also made a living by other means of cultural production); what, how and where to draw; how to provoke different types of laughter; and how to recognise and manipulate these activities in order to sustain the type of professional life that she created.

Consideration of these questions, relative to the answers that Duval provided in the activities that she undertook or ignored, in order to make her drawings, constitutes a method of stylistic analysis that identifies sets of specifically Duvallian circumstances – I call these circumstances her drawing style – rather than these circumstances being general for an historic period, medium, profession or drawings made by other artists comprising a list of Duval's cartooning contemporaries.

Unfit for purpose

Wilson's description of Duval's drawings as 'excruciatingly bad' meant incompetent. It was Duval's lack of capacity for making a drawing that Wilson found excruciating, in the context of Duval having fulfilled the role of published artist in a book or journal. Considering the capacity to draw as a prerequisite for having drawings published, Wilson felt, with some intensity, that her drawings were out of place. He considered them incapable of performing the function of a humorous drawing. The particular shade of meaning in Wilson's two words is difficult to ascertain. His 'excruciating' could have been arch overstatement, conspiring with his readers in an act of reverse connoisseurship (a conspiratorial wink of the eye) or it could have expressed exasperation at the effrontery of an artist unskilled in her craft. Whatever the precise meaning, Wilson's description of Duval's drawings as 'excruciatingly bad' was not simply a condemnation of their formal, stylistic properties. In being 'bad', Wilson also meant that the drawings were not fit for publication, that is, Wilson was adjudicating her drawings based upon a conception of their function in the wider ecology in which they appeared (Grennan 2017: 1–28). In other words, Wilson thought that Duval's drawings were unfit for purpose. Both Duval's drawings and Wilson's commentary shared an overriding conception of the purpose of her drawings. Duval and Wilson agreed about that. It was simply the case that Duval produced a drawing to fulfil that purpose and Wilson judged that her drawing hadn't fulfilled it.

So what was the purpose of Duval's drawings? The serio-comic journal presented current, weekly, political and social commentary and news, to be read alongside fiction, lifestyle and consumer features, visual and verbal jokes and advertising. The purpose of Duval's drawings in *Judy* was to provoke a range of types of laughter in readers and so incentivise them to buy the next edition, or to share their experiences in order to incentivise potential other readers to buy the journal, laugh and enjoy themselves. Laughter and sales appeared in a cycle.

Criticism of Duval's drawings as technically incompetent, unpleasant and derivative was congruous with their being unfunny. If they had been more technically competent, more pleasant and more original, they would have been funnier, these commentators imply. The comparison made in *The Sporting Times*, between Duval's *Judy* drawings, the centre page drawings ('large cartoon') and drawings by Adelaide Claxton, is revealing.

The centre pages drawing in *Judy* was usually a single political cartoon printed on the double-page spread. The technical capacities of the artists who drew these cartoons, such as William Boucher (1837–1906), discussed in Chapter 1, substantiated their purpose, because the laughter that they aimed to provoke derived entirely from the artists' radical visualisations of the contradictions of political punditry. Knowledge of current political ideas, debates, events and personalities was essential to finding them funny. The particular sets of properties of these visualisations, derived from technical training, were matched by readers' understanding of the status of these drawing techniques and the status of the topics of the drawings.

Similarly, Claxton's drawings articulated anticipated relationships between the way in which she drew and the topics of her drawings. They were social commentaries on topics gentle enough not to generate readers' anxiety. Claxton drew as a middle-class woman was expected to draw, by readers, if such a woman had the misfortune to have to draw professionally, for a cheap serial journal. The topics of her drawings also fulfilled these expectations, being largely concerned with the minor wrinkles of lives lived with the aid of, rather than by, servants, or presenting idealised lives in advertisements. The large cartoon and Claxton's drawings in *Judy* are, for these reasons, judged 'very good', by the commentator in *The Sporting Life*, as compared to Duval who 'cannot draw properly' and whose drawings are, necessarily, both unfit and unfunny.

Some of the circumstances of humour in the drawings of Claxton, Leech and Duval

Concepts of humour were central to the ways in which these relationships between the inferred character and social status of the periodical artist, the technical properties of their drawings and the topics about which they drew, conspired to produce adjudications of quality by readers, at least if the quoted commentary by readers of *Judy* is any guide.

Clayton, the biographer of Adelaide Claxton as well as Duval, herself associated specific topics with specific artists, drawing styles and types of humour. The contrast between the two artists' styles, topics and implied social positions is revealing. Clayton wrote that Claxton 'seeks her groups in the salon and boudoir, the croquet and Badminton lawn, and other resorts of Beauty and of the best-dressed and handsomest of the Inferior Sex. Afternoon teas, garden parties, balls and concerts, dinner parties, afford her favourite scenes' (Clayton 1876: 330). As Catherine Flood points out, Claxton's stylistic treatment of the domestic, middle-class range of topics in her drawings constituted 'a mode of discourse that assimilated [women's] professional humour with women's social duties in entering into [...] middle-class social life' (Flood 2013: 115).

Claxton's identity as a professional artist was made visible in her drawing styles and choice of topics, allowing readers to infer her respectability as a woman professional, making drawings of a section of society to which she implied that she belonged, and hence guaranteeing her own respectability. In particular, her 'style of drawing was pitched for [the] smart social end of the periodical market' (Flood 2013: 113).

Although Claxton published drawings in *Judy*, alongside Duval, she created a greater number of drawings, on both humorous and serious topics, for more expensive periodicals such as *The Illustrated London News*, *Illustrated Times*, *London Society*, *Queen* and the *English Woman's Domestic Magazine*. The latter two publications were unequivocally aimed at women readers who could afford to live with the help of servants. Duval never published a drawing in these papers, remaining in the less expensive *Judy* area of the periodicals market, more easily crossing the social and economic boundaries between purchasers who were both servants and mistresses. In Claxton's drawings, published in the more upmarket periodicals, '[p]olite humour was conceptualised as a social exchange and therefore the responsibility for generating it lay partly with the recipient' (Flood 2013: 115). That is to say, the type of person wanting (and receiving) coarser prompts for laughter bought and read those cheaper papers in which Duval's work appeared.

Claxton's drawings were sometimes technically accomplished (demonstrating techniques that were recognisable as being the result of visual arts training). However, demonstration of accomplishment in the crafts of drawing never became a display of virtuosity (in which an artist demonstrates the high level of their skill through the introduction of novel techniques). In this sense, Claxton's drawing style was as polite as her topics, her professional identity and her readership, creating the sure sense of a reciprocal and mutually assured appropriateness, including the social politeness of the type of laughter they provoked. In repeating the association between her particular manner of drawing, her middle-class topics and her own identity and that of her readers, as members of a polite class, Claxton was consolidating an established tradition of periodical drawing founded and exemplified in the relationship created with readers of *Punch*, earlier in the century by the prolific John Leech (1817–64).

Writing in 1898, fellow *Punch* contributor George Du Maurier described Leech's work as exactly constituting the desired equilibrium between style, topic and identity for drawings in a periodical paper of the 'polite' type (Du Maurier 1898). Hence, those aspects of Leech's work lauded by Du Maurier provide a useful benchmark with which to compare the styles and topics of Du Maurier's contemporaries, including Claxton and Duval. In Du Maurier's opinion, Leech was the paramount periodicals artist. Claxton's work more matches this description of Leech's abilities than not, whereas for Duval's work the opposite is the case. We must also bear in mind that Du Maurier's own drawings had followed the 'Leech' pattern for a period of almost forty years and hence his description of Leech's work tends towards a social and cultural ideal.

In provoking laughter at his drawings, writes Du Maurier, Leech avoided any hint of cultural extremism (Du Maurier 1898: 121). Drawing as an embodiment of cultural doctrine was not for Leech, pointing away from the prompting of any laughter of disdain, for example. Rather, the purpose of Leech's work was to create and consolidate the relationship between style, topic and identities in a relatively expensive humorous periodical paper. His approach to this was twofold: to charm and to affirm. In fulfilling this dual purpose, a reader's laughter arose in their understanding, in detail, the polite milieu of a drawing's story (as the milieu shared by the paper and themselves) and succumbing to Leech's stylistic treatment of the story as a charm. An important aspect of the charm was the recognition of Leech's technical accomplishment in making the drawing. Du Maurier wrote 'before all he has his story to tell, and it must either make you laugh or lightly charm you – and he tells it in the quickest, simplest downright pencil strokes, although it is often a complicated story!' (Du Maurier 1898: 23).

As with Claxton's work, the social environments of the stories in Leech's *Punch* drawings created repeated sentiments and stereotypes that consolidated and visualised ideas of the society, economics, gender, race relationships and sexualities of a polite class itself, as distinct from the classes of readers of Duval's drawings in *Judy*. Du Maurier described Leech's drawings as evincing 'upper-class British ideals of his time' (Du Maurier 1898: 26), including 'his love of home, his love of sport, his love of horse and hound – especially his love of the pretty woman' (Du Maurier 1898: 26), who is 'innocence and liveliness and health incarnate – a human kitten' (Du Maurier 1898: 31). Du Maurier commented that youthful exuberance was never vice or delinquency 'beyond smoking too much and betting a little and getting gracefully tipsy at race-meetings […] and sometimes running into debt with their tailors' (Du Maurier 1898: 33) in a world otherwise peopled by Leech's visualisations of social stereotypes, such as 'splendid lords and squires' (Du Maurier 1898: 34) and 'the good authoritative pater and mater-familias; the delightful little girls; the charming cheeky school-boys […]; the cabmen, the busmen; the policemen' (Du Maurier 1898: 39). The description is strikingly similar to Clayton's description of Claxton's topics.

Du Maurier showed exactly the consensual self-positioning undertaken by Leech and his readers, in creating the particular style, topic, humour and identity relationships by which Leech visualised his own, middle-class readers' class and the boundaries of their humour, in the more expensive periodical papers, when he wrote 'and how many people and things he loves that most of us love!' (Du Maurier 1898: 38).

This model of consensus was self-reflexive. For Du Maurier, Leech's drawings fulfilled reader expectations by showing aspects of the society to which they belonged, utilising a style of drawing considered appropriate to the sparking of polite laughter, by them. Such a series of relationships allowed Du Maurier to describe Leech's drawings as true and natural (Du Maurier 1898. 43) because readers found in them 'exaggeration, but no distortion' (Du Maurier 1898: 45) and, more than this, recognised the fact that the drawings created, as well as perpetuated, the visualisation of these specific economic, gender and social relationships, because '[t]here is always a touch of tenderness in the laughter he excites, born of the touch of nature that makes the whole world kin!' (Du Maurier 1898: 45).

Clayton's analysis of the associations and roles of different types of humour found in drawings in the periodical press is much more explicit than Du Maurier's opinions, embedded in his lauding of Leech and hidden, to some extent, behind the fact that he says nothing about Leech drawing as a man, whereas Clayton's aim was to write specifically about the exceptional circumstances of women working as professional artists.

Clayton describes the differences between the topics, treatments, circumstances and personnel of nominally masculine humour and nominally feminine humour by allocating the word 'wit' to the latter. 'Woman may be allowed to possess Wit, but except in the case of farce or burlesque actresses, when she is simply parrotising [*sic*] the fancies of man, she is denied any perception of humour' (Clayton 1876: 319). It is also worth noting Clayton's aside about the more physical types of stage comedy, particularly as Duval performed in stage farces and burlesques, because of Clayton's association of physical comedy with masculine humour. She continues: '[w]it is fine and elegant: wit shines and scintillates in drawing-rooms and boudoirs, but Humour may run the risk of stepping over the boundary lines of vulgarity', such that '[h]umour is a quality scarcely coveted by the ladies' (Clayton 1876: 319). For Clayton, humour was masculine, physical and steered a course dangerously close to vulgarity, or those qualities of public life that represented some type of exciting social crisis. Wit, on the other hand, was feminine, cerebral (it 'shines' and 'scintillates') and domestic, in that it neither caused nor represented any type of social upset or anxiety. Rather, it ultimately affirmed an existing set of economic, class and gender relationships, according to Robert Martin (Martin 1974).

For a polite class of readers of the more expensive humorous periodicals, both the pursuit of a professional life and the practice of humour were masculine activities, such that women had to struggle, socially and economically, if they wished to adopt them, whilst maintaining a nominal femininity, that is, without becoming masculine. Flood points to 'humour's apparently unavoidable tendencies to vulgarity and cynicism – qualities that [polite periodicals] will not countenance in women of the middle class' (Flood 2013: 114).

We may recall how Clayton described Claxton as managing to square this circle by choosing domestic, middle-class topics and treating them in drawing styles associated with social affirmation, by displaying an unremarkable level of technical accomplishment and by the careful curation of her own paradoxical identity as a middle-class professional woman.

An anonymous detailed apologia for the gendering of types of humour appeared in the socially conservative middle-class periodical *The Saturday Review* of 15 July 1871. The article grew from describing masculine and feminine humour to theorise limits to male and female capacities, as well defining those male capacities which were not available to women and vice versa. These, the article claimed, explained the differences between masculine and feminine humour ('Feminine Humour' 1871).

The article was less interested in defining humour itself as in apportioning types of activity to women and men. 'There is a difficulty in defining humour [...] Men as well as women are equally anxious to put in a claim for it' the author wrote, 'although [...] anybody who is capable of a horse-laugh may flatter himself that he has a sense of humour; in others, it implies a very rare and delicate faculty indeed' ('Feminine Humour' 1871: 75). Finally settling on humour as 'a certain delight in strange contrasts of mood' ('Feminine Humour' 1871: 75), the author established that this 'delight' manifested itself quite differently for men and for women, in the social milieu of *The Saturday Review*'s readers.

'[Humour involves] some variety, even at the cost of logic or reverence. It naturally follows that a very large province of the humorous is absolutely interdicted to women', the author writes, because '[t]he stories current in bachelor society [...] occasionally require […] a certain lowering of tone, before they can be repeated with perfect confidence in the drawing room' ('Feminine Humour' 1871: 75). The distinction between bachelor society and the drawing room was another identification of activities undertaken in a public (and we dare say professional) domain, by men and the identification of activities undertaken in the private and domestic domains, by men in the presence of women and by women. *The Saturday Review* writer characterised the female, private domain as antithetical to the 'variety' of public life producing the opportunities for masculine humour. 'The cause which we have already noted is sufficient to account for the feminine taste in this department being less practiced and having less opportunity of revealing itself where it exists. A monotonous and decorous life is […] unfavourable to a keen delight in sharp contrasts of emotion' ('Feminine Humour' 1871: 75).

Domestic monotony, however, was simply one of the prices to be paid by middle-class women, for being guardians of the spiritual well-being of society, claimed *The Saturday Review*. 'We cannot imagine the loftiest spiritual nature having the full appreciation of a joke' ('Feminine Humour' 1871: 75), the author wrote. As Margaret Stetz has pointed out, this tendentious eliding of the appreciation of jokes with less-than-spiritual, that is, masculine 'natures', reaffirmed the environments in which jokes could be made as public and masculine, rather than domestic and feminine ('Feminine Humour' 1871: 75).

'The humourist, in fact, has just that tendency to look at the seamy side of things, and that delight in bringing high emotions to the test of some vulgar or grotesque association' ('Feminine Humour' 1871: 75), concludes the author, '[h]ence, it may be urged that women are too good to be humourists. They are too pure and saint like and enthusiastic to understand masculine cynicism, and they hate to be told that any cause to which they have given their affections has after all a tinge of absurdity' ('Feminine Humour' 1871: 75). Hence, 'the more questionable variety of humour is practically prohibited to women of any high capacity' ('Feminine Humour' 1871: 75) because it is 'totally incompatible with the feminine sense of delicacy' ('Feminine Humour' 1871: 75), due to the fact that '[…] the atmosphere of extreme propriety in which ladies are generally brought up rather cramps their excursions into the regions of broad humour' ('Feminine Humour' 1871: 75).

The Saturday Review commentary ended with strong disapprobation for middle-class women who might have sought to undertake the socially forbidden work of transforming the relationships between humour, gender and environment, by becoming funny. It stated that such women were stupid as well as bad: 'those who signalise their independence by straying into forbidden paths are almost always inferior in intellectual, as well as moral, excellence' ('Feminine Humour' 1871: 75).

Vulgar Duval

In arguing that middle-class women who appropriated the masculine trait of humour, in order to 'signal their independence', were stupid and immoral, *The Saturday Review* was simply stating in unequivocal terms the relationships between topics, treatments, class and gender identities subsequently described by Du Maurier and Clayton in the work of Leech and Claxton.

However, the periodical papers and readerships of the last thirty years of the nineteenth century were by no means exclusively either middle class or polite. For the purpose of this chapter, there is little use in compiling a quantitative summary of the demographics of papers and readers, even if this is possible. Rather, Rowntree's definition of working-class people as those who could not afford to live with the help of a servant, provides an indication of the affordability, or not, of a range of publications, to a range of types of people (Rowntree 1901).

For the majority living without the aid of servants, *The Saturday Review*'s claim for the innate constraining virtue of women and the antithetical humour of men, was itself risible, because it was so easily contradicted by the appearance and popularity of publications that, in *The Saturday Review*'s description, were published precisely 'to look at the seamy side of things, and that delight in bringing high emotions to the test of some vulgar or grotesque association'.

As Kunzle points out, for example, *Judy*'s 'audience was fluid, restless and uncertain of its identity, a mixture of lower-middle and upper-working classes, more anxious […] to leave the working class than to identify with it' (Kunzle 1986: 28). That is to say, *Judy* was a periodical journal pitched for sale to those in social transition. These were people who were always on the boundaries of achieving middle-class life and becoming the 'pater' and 'mater' described by Du Maurier. They were on the verge of fulfilling their allocated roles as middle-class men and women and employing servants.

Otherwise, readers of *Judy* never bought the journal themselves, but were in fact those servants and working people who picked it up second-hand after being read by a mistress, handed around in a public house or theatre or discarded on a train. That this was also true for more expensive papers such as the *Illustrated London News* and *Punch* does not contradict the fact that, in *Judy*, the topics, treatments and identities of the authors, artists and readers was founded on the fact that it was relatively inexpensive and, hence, conceived and pitched to those who could afford it.

In this sense, the entire milieu of *Judy* substantiated definitions of the word 'vulgar', which *The Saturday Review* used to describe what they called the stupidity and immorality of women pretending to humour, their shows of independence and impoliteness. As Bernstein and Mitchie wrote, vulgarity did not describe a stable class of person or identify any socially dubious action in particular, but 'the act of intrusiveness constitutes vulgarity rather than the social position of the intruder' (Bernstein and Mitchie 2009: 3), where this intrusiveness was any behaviour that sought to overturn existing social relationships, or any representation of struggle by the subject. Visible self-assertion represented dissent, whilst condemnations of vulgar behaviour – that is, of self-assertive struggle – expressed anxiety about dissent itself, particularly relative to status relationships, class and gender (Chapman 1896: 632).

Hence I argue that it is apposite to use the word vulgar to describe *Judy*, a journal for people who struggled to assert themselves socially and economically, who aspired to, but had not yet achieved a middle-class existence and who were characterised perpetually by being in transition. In the public criticism of the paintings of James Tissot, in the 1870s, the charge that the painter's topic was a 'vulgar society' founded itself first on his repeated visualisations of men and women of this transitional social class, their fashions, activities and environments (Ruskin 1903–11: 161). '[T]here is inevitably […] a touch of vulgarity in his men and of the "demi-monde" in his women', wrote a commentator on an exhibition of Tissot's painting *The Gallery of HMS 'Calcutta' (Portsmouth)*, at The Grosvenor Gallery in 1877, in *The Architect* ('The Grosvenor Gallery II' 1877: 6). 'Demi-monde' meant exactly the condition of being in the transitional social milieu between the working class and the middle class, or even between the criminal classes and the middle class. A year later, the vulgar people in Tissot's paintings were described as 'parvenu' or, literally 'recently arrived' ('The Grosvenor Gallery' 1878: 2).[4] That Tissot exhibited at The Grosvenor Gallery, a private commercial enterprise with an unequivocally aesthetic brand (selling paintings by Edward Burne-Jones and Frederic Leighton to a firmly upper-middle-class clientele: those who could comfortably afford to pay for a painting more than the average annual wage of a maid-of-all-work), was a taunt to polite critics, including Ruskin. It was unusual and uncomfortable to encounter visualisations of struggle, in the context of visualisations of the ideals of a fashionable middle class and aristocratic class that was firmly established as a significant cultural industry by the 1870s.

Perhaps it would be taking a step too far to claim that the people repeatedly depicted by Tissot were those transitional folks who read *Judy* and *Fun*, because *Punch* was a little too expensive and *The Illustrated London News* a little too demanding, after a week at work. As much as Tissot painted scenes of aspiration and material display, all visualised by 'an exhibitionist of showy technique' as Marshall (2009: 205) wrote, he never depicted anyone reading a copy of *Judy* or *Fun*. But the social and economic proximity of *Judy* readers to the vulgarity of Tissot's characters, as described by critics of his own class, and hence the vulgarity of the journal and its producers, was undeniable.

The fact that the majority of Duval's drawings were published in *Judy* (Grennan, Sabin and Waite 2016) and that she was a close personal and professional associate of the journal's editor, Charles Ross (across a range of productions in different media), identified her to potential readers. Duval belonged to a group of entertainers whose productions relied upon and made visible each other's professional skills and social networks. Her public persona as a stage performer was also intimately related to Ross's identity as an author and theatre impresario. She appeared in plays that he authored and directed (Ross 1870) and illustrated a novel he had written (Ross and Clarke 1870). As a result, more than any other publication or spin-off, when it came to drawing, Duval was recognisably a *Judy* artist. It was largely from *Judy* readers that she aimed to provoke laughter with her drawings.

For *Judy* readers, the comments of critics in more expensive papers notwithstanding, Duval's humorous drawings were neither unfit nor unfunny, precisely because those readers were vulgar or parvenu, that is, striving to, or almost able to, or just able to afford a servant, or being servants and working people themselves. Because of this, it made perfect sense that Duval's visual humour was also vulgar, in both the topics that she chose and her stylistic treatments of them. Like Leech and Claxton (although with a largely different, if overlapping, set of readers), Duval draw about the society she knew and the society that her readers knew and to which they belonged. Just like Leech and Claxton, her identity as an artist was predicated upon this relationship between specific types of reader, topic and treatment. The difference between Duval's humour and techniques and those of Leech and Claxton sprang from the differences between her readership and theirs, exemplified by the differences between *Punch* enterprises and customers and *Judy* enterprises and customers, because 'both Duval's own persona and her work seem to have been more loosely moored to the middle-class ideal, and her difference suggests something of what determined vulgarity in the female illustrator' (Flood 2013: 144).

For topics, Duval depicted social stereotypes as much as Claxton or Leech, but hers were not polite. They were vulgar or 'demi-monde', like Tissot's. Instead of the drawing room, Duval's comedies took place amongst rackety women and mongrel pets in a tiny back room with a smoking fire (Duval 1872a). Instead of the vicissitudes of the squire at the county hunt, she drew the scrapes of aimless urban youths on miserable days out of London (Duval 1877a). Instead of the mistress's 'servant problem', she drew the maid-of-all-work, or 'slavey', on strike – what bliss would that be! (Duval 1872b). Instead of brokers at the city club, she drew the Jewish *flâneur* and his scheming, work-shy best friend (Duval 1882). Instead of the dowager and her mislaid pearls, she drew the middle-aged woman afraid of the seaside (Duval 1874a) and instead of the young heiress and her eligible men, she drew the flashy young woman and the 'masher' polished to as high a shine as he could manage on his day off (Duval 1883a).

The readers of *Judy* were distinct from the readers of more expensive periodicals and recognised themselves in more vulgar stereotypes than appeared in *Punch*, for example. Despite this social difference, a reader of *Judy* might almost have been able to point to the truth of Duval's stereotypes and say, as Du Maurier wrote about Leech's readers and his own class, 'there is always a touch of tenderness in the laughter [s]he excites, born of the touch of nature that makes the whole world kin!' (Du Maurier 1898: 45).

Duval's treatment of her topics adopted the appearance of struggle, as well as representing struggles. The absence of any display of technical training in her drawings substantiated intuitions on the part of readers about her professional biography. There is no biographical evidence that she ever undertook any technical training during the course of her drawing career. There is no visible progression from one group of techniques to another, no transformations produced by visual trial-and-error and, hence, no visible learning. Rather, her technical capacity, her craft, remained unusually circumscribed if compared with the development of the techniques of Archibald Chasemore, for example, whose drawings started to be published at the same time as Duval's, in *Judy*. The changes in Chasemore's drawing techniques make visible a steep learning curve pointed unequivocally in the direction of achieving the effects and the status of training. Rather, Duval started as she meant to go on.

Duval's drawings display an antithetical approach to Chasemore's, in this sense. The perpetuity of her visible lack of training both established her unique authography and an unconventional, even ground-breaking identity for a humorous women artist. Unlike Claxton, who strived to reinforce her own professional identity through a display of the levels of technical capacity and concomitant types of laughter allocated to professional women by a polite class of readers, Duval's untrained treatment of vulgar topics provoked those types of laughter allocated to men. 'Her figures are humorous to grotesqueness, though the "drawing" is often incorrect: but this defect has been judiciously utilised in heightening the burlesque', wrote Clayton, adding that 'Mlle de Tessier may be pardoned for not drawing in academic proportion when it is understood that she is self-taught. Perhaps the carelessness may be sometimes intentional' (Clayton 1876: 332–3) and '[t]here is a sense in which formal coarseness of drawing was a type of vulgarity in itself' (Flood 2013: 114).

In part, this was due to the type of laughter her drawings provoked from *Judy* readers. As Nick Holm has argued, in the twenty-first century, it was entertaining and exciting for a vulgar class of person to be provoked to laughter by the flouting of polite professional and social standards that were inherently exclusive, hierarchical and prejudicial to the lives of the 'pushing' society (Holm 2018; Chapman 1896: 632). More prosaically, it was exciting for *Judy* readers to laugh at the topics and treatments of their own society in the work of a woman they recognised as like them, 'parvenue' and impolite, because she was making her own living – on these occasions by drawing – and making all this visible by drawing with the humour of a man. As Clayton deftly noted, comparing Bowers' and Claxton's feminine wit with Duval's masculine humour: 'The others are undoubtedly witty and graceful, but rarely provoke laughter' (Clayton 1876: 333).

Duval's drawings visibly evidence a career that appeared reckless, dangerous or impossible, in her continual manipulation of readers' expectations of the propriety and purpose of the actions and outputs of a woman professional humorous artist. She made a career utilising and making visible the social contradictions of her situation. She recognised economic, gender and professional boundaries and drew attention to them, so as to provoke laughter in her readers and thereby transform these boundaries. Her recklessness and fearlessness can be enumerated simply, according to the polite conceptions of vulgarity, masculinity and femininity that were current in the 1870s and 1880s. As an aspirational working woman, she drew vulgar topics with masculine humour and eschewed the considerable protections provided by those displays of technical competence, feminine wit and an adherence to polite subjects that constituted the routes to work taken by her contemporaries.

Duval's devices and The Royal Academy of Arts Summer Exhibitions

Duval's choice and treatment of topics deriving from the Summer Exhibitions at The Royal Academy of Arts, London, indicate the significance of the relationships between conceptions of polite and vulgar activities and people, male and female humour, the significance of degrees of technical competence in making drawings and the expectations of different media, on the part of readers.

The Summer Exhibition, instituted in 1769, was an international commercial showcase, in London, for new artworks by Royal Academy members and an open submission Exhibition for aspiring artists. In common with public events such as the races at Goodwood and the Henley Regatta, the Exhibition articulated one of the key functions of the city's social season in bringing most strata of urban society into mutual view. The Exhibition was also instrumental in visualising the social milieux of the fine arts: generating representations of artists, dealers, publishers, critics, historians, institutional staff and collectors.

There was a highly specific relationship between a vulgar public, the mutual views of each other afforded to different classes of people, at the Summer Exhibition as social events, and the high cultural status of the artefacts of contemporary art on display. Unlike the Derby horse race or Henley Regatta, the focus of public viewing that constituted the Summer Exhibition was of avowed and unequivocal high social and cultural status. Although the excitement of visiting the Exhibition might have involved experiencing the spectacle of the newest, most lauded, most expensive and often largest artworks in the country, most visitors were not expected to buy anything but an admission ticket and were not expected to do anything but undertake passive viewing.

That said, the Exhibition brought together extremes of economic and social difference and their visualisations, and self-consciously made a public spectacle of these extremes. Anna Jameson, commenting upon the relationship between a vulgar public and contemporary fine art in 1844, highlighted the extreme inappropriateness of viewers' behaviour to their situation although, in this commentary, the vulgar class are interlopers in a polite situation (the admission of the public to view a private collection at Bridgewater House, rather than the commercial Summer Exhibition). 'We can all remember the loiterers and loungers, the vulgar starers, the gaping idlers, we used to meet there – people who, instead of moving amid these wonders and beauties "all silent and divine", with reverence and gratitude, strutted about as if they had the right to be there, talking, flirting, peeping, and prying' (Jameson 1844: 34).

Staring, gaping, talking, flirting, peeping and prying were not activities to be undertaken by members of a polite class, in the presence of the 'divine' 'wonders and beauties' of high-status fine art, according to Jameson. Her disapprobation of the responses of vulgar people is fully embodied in the inappropriateness, for her, of their physical gestures and attitudes, their noise, distractedness and self-obsession, all of which forfeit their right to view, or even be in the presence of, high status art.

In somewhat similar ways, twentieth-century discourse analysis has focused upon middle-class cultural life working exactly those engines of patronage, doubt, coercion, anxiety and hypocrisy that characterised the social relationships and ideas articulated in Jameson's 1844 commentary. In particular, in 'the middle class's protean attempts at self-definition', Dianne Macleod connects the behaviour of particular types of social class to approbation for some genres of depiction. She uses this idea to evidence class antagonism, such that '[t]he enthusiasm demonstrated by the working class for narrative painting was considered a strike against the middle-class patrons whose money had stimulated its growth' (Macleod 1996: 62). Key to this antagonistic co-option, or even 'détournement' of an approbation of story showing, on the part of a vulgar class, was 'the middle class's genuine love of mimesis. The shrinking of the distance between pictorial delineation and optical reality was celebrated as another of the achievements of the progressive ideal that inspired all phases of society, from the industrial to the aesthetic' (Macleod 1996: 15–16). For Macleod, in esteeming technical accomplishment in depiction, a vulgar class usurped the preferences of polite society and thereby made use of politeness itself to antagonise it. A 'love of mimesis' was one of the types of the behaviour that Ruskin described as an index of vulgarity in Tissot's *The Gallery of HMS 'Calcutta' (Portsmouth)*, alongside the depiction a vulgar class as the object of the painting itself (Ruskin 1903–11: 161).

However, contemporaneous commentary in polite periodicals, such as *Blackwell's Edinburgh Review*, could be more expansive, describing as well as adjudicating the vulgar class's pleasures in fine art and mixing consideration with patronage. Writing about the 1876 Summer Exhibition, Margaret Oliphant described the pre-eminence of the social aspects of the event, relative to the works of art displayed, or the greater significance of making a visit, compared with the significance of the object of the visit. Visitors were not characterised by knowledge of the fine arts. She wrote: 'Not only do the spectators often know nothing about the special excellences and capabilities of pictorial art, but they are often ignorant even of the well-worn subjects in which painters delight' (Oliphant 1876: 753). But this was not a fault simply devolving to a vulgar class. Rather, according to her, a charge of visual philistinism could be made against the whole nation, in which generalisation she candidly included herself: 'Art has never attained any very lofty development among us, and [...] we are confessedly devoid of that finer appreciation which is supposed to belong to races more delicately organised', she wrote (Oliphant 1876: 753).

Of greater significance, for Oliphant, was the identity of the Summer Exhibition in a national collective imagination, which she characterised as curious and pleasure-seeking. The Summer Exhibition was a leisure destination establishing a benchmark of shared experiences across regions and classes. 'There is no public event which creates more general interest [...] throughout all classes, not only in London but in England', she wrote, '[e]veryone takes an interest, more or less understanding or ignorant, in the periodical show', so that 'even the hastiest excursionist [...] thinks it necessary to take a hurried glance, if no more, at "the pictures"', concluding 'there they go, patiently, cheerfully, with warm interest and pleasure' (Oliphant 1876: 753).

As a social event, the inclusive and expansive public identity of the Summer Exhibition also gave rise to more astringent commentary, focused on the relative status of the artworks displayed. In the same year that Oliphant was describing and lauding the social aspects of the Exhibition, *The Examiner* noted that '[e]veryone is beginning to see that Burlington House does not by any means represent the artistic force of the country [...] Some of our greatest artists do not exhibit at all' ('Variorum Notes' 1876).

The relationship between conceptions of the Exhibition as a leisure destination and of the Exhibition as a national cultural high-water mark was exemplified by the proliferation of independent commercial guides, such as *The Royal Academy Album: a series of photo-prints from works of art in the Exhibition of the Royal Academy of Arts 1876*, which sought, for a small price, to aid a wide range of types of visitor to navigate the heterogeneous and sometimes challenging variety of contemporary fine artworks and to enhance the pleasure of a visit by becoming souvenirs.

On the boundaries of polite public commentary and more vulgar public entertainment, the Royal Academy Summer Exhibition was a national review of fine art with a long-established tradition as a national media event, as well as a social and high cultural one. But there was no strong visual tradition of fine arts that was equivalent to the Condition of England novel and its public criticism in the mid- and late century.[5] Ethical debates about the nation that utilised the Exhibition or the works on display as a forum, or as examples, were rare.

Duval published ten humorous drawings on topics related to the Summer Exhibition, in May 1870, 1873, 1875, 1876, 1879 and 1880 and in June 1880 (Duval 1870, 1870b, 1873a, 1873b, 1875a, 1876a, 1876b, 1878a, 1880a, 1880b, 1880c). These topics not only focused on visits to the Exhibition by the public (Duval 1873b, 1876a, 1876b, 1880c) but also on the plight of artworks and artists rejected by the Exhibition selection committee (Duval 1870, 1880a) and parodies of actual exhibited artworks (Duval 1880b), as well as the process of submission (Duval 1873a) and the hanging of selected work by artists (Duval 1878a). The parodic representation of artworks in the Exhibition in humorous drawings was commonplace in both politer and vulgar humorous periodical papers. For example, in *Judy*, both Chasemore and Cruikshank Jr often presented a page of visual bowdlerisations of some of the works on display in that year's current Summer Exhibition, accompanied by a tall story of the experience of these pictures by a risible fictional visitor or participant, such as the 'Office Boy's mother' or 'our artist' (Chasemore 1873; Cruikshank Jr 1867).[6]

The parodic intent of this tradition of drawing was evidenced by the inclusion of Summer Exhibition catalogue numbers in the depictions of bowdlerised artworks. Knowledge of the original work was required for the ludicrousness of the drawing to prompt laughter. This type of humorous drawing encouraged readers to connect a visit to the Academy, which provided a numbered catalogue of artworks on display with the price of admission, with reading the papers in which they appeared. It was possible to visit the Exhibition with one's copy of *Judy*, for example.

Duval followed this established approach in her *Judy* drawing of 19 May 1880 (Figure 6.1), parodying exhibited paintings by John Pettie, Charles West Cope, Frederic Leighton, Briton Rivière, William Quiller Orchardson and Walter Tynedale, whose artworks she identified by artists name as well as catalogue number (Duval 1880b; Figure 6.1). Duval's treatment of the paintings followed her usual strategy: she was an identified woman artist, applying masculine humour to a topic familiar to her readers, in the reckless use of her untrained technique.

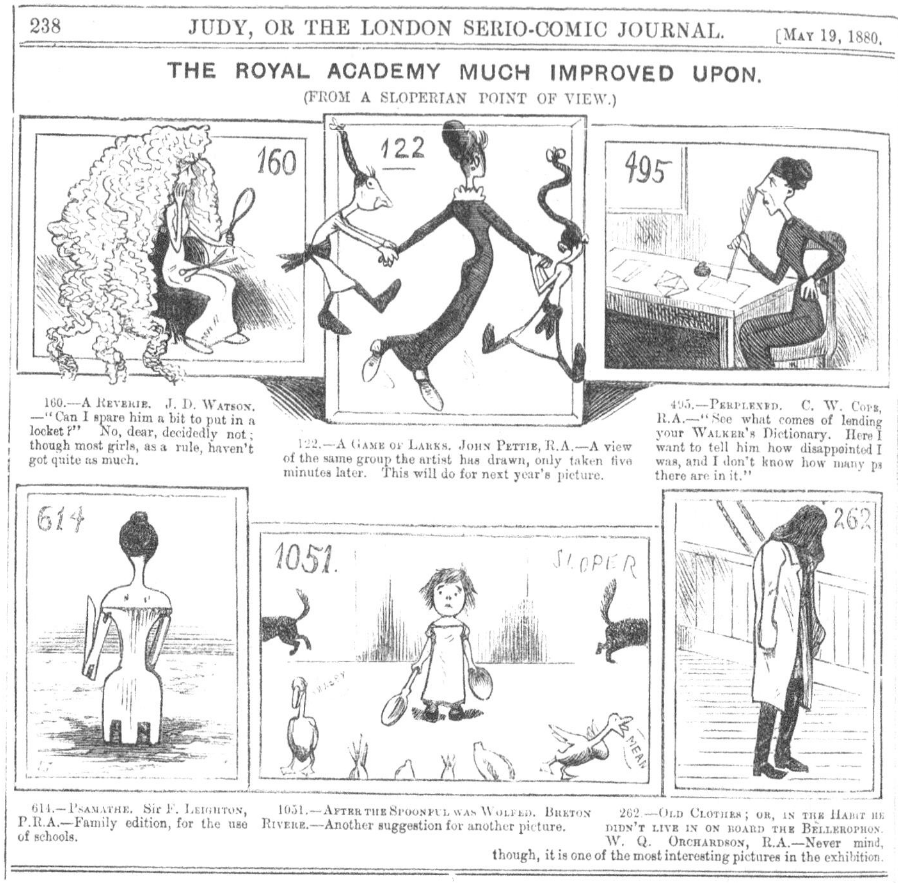

238   JUDY, OR THE LONDON SERIO-COMIC JOURNAL.   [MAY 19, 1880.

THE ROYAL ACADEMY MUCH IMPROVED UPON.

(FROM A SLOPERIAN POINT OF VIEW.)

160.—A REVERIE. J. D. WATSON.—"Can I spare him a bit to put in a locket?" No, dear, decidedly not; though most girls, as a rule, haven't got quite as much.

122.—A GAME OF LARKS. JOHN PETTIE, R.A.—A view of the same group the artist has drawn, only taken five minutes later. This will do for next year's picture.

495.—PERPLEXED. C. W. COPE, R.A.—"See what comes of lending your WALKER's Dictionary. Here I want to tell him how disappointed I was, and I don't know how many ps there are in it."

614.—PSAMATHE. Sir F. LEIGHTON, P.R.A.—Family edition, for the use of schools.

1051.—AFTER THE SPOONFUL WAS WOLFED. BRETON RIVERE.—Another suggestion for another picture.

262—OLD CLOTHES; OR, IN THE HABIT HE DIDN'T LIVE IN ON BOARD THE BELLEROPHON. W. Q. ORCHARDSON, R.A.—Never mind, though, it is one of the most interesting pictures in the exhibition.

6.1 Marie Duval (1880) 'The Royal Academy Much Improved Upon (From a Sloperian Point of View)', *Judy, or the London Serio-comic Journal*, Volume 26, p. 238

In particular, Duval's treatment rendered the bathetic sentimentalising of agricultural life, in Rivière's *The Last Spoonful*, more literally truthful, as well as funny. The visible status of Rivière's picture in the Exhibition, and of the artist, was made obvious to readers and visitors simply by its inclusion. In terms of his treatment and topic, Rivière's farm girl was pretty and coy, commanding the attention of birds and animals, which will do her bidding for a bite of whatever she is eating. His treatment displayed technical expertise and hence training, indexing both the artist's economic class and, by convention, gender status and the value of his topic, to be treated by such a well-trained expert in painting and to be painted with those techniques.

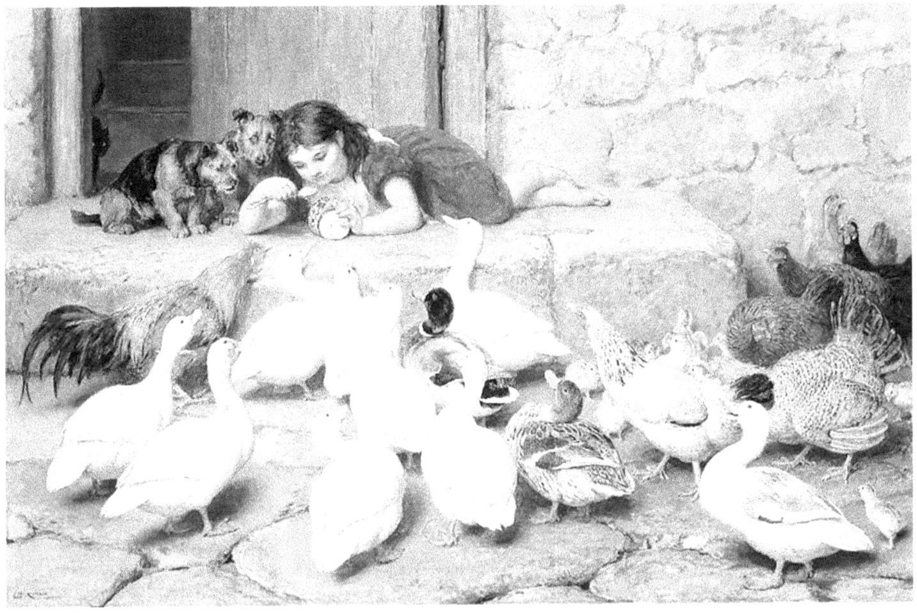

6.2 Briton Rivière (1880) *The Last Spoonful.* Oil on canvas

In contrast, in the ephemeral *Judy*, Duval's drawing depicted the moment just after that shown in *The Last Spoonful*. The title of her bowdlerisation was *After the Spoonful was Wolfed*. Duval depicted a scrappy farm girl in shapeless clothes, dismayed by the animals and birds, which shun her for having finally eaten the last spoonful. Duval's technique summarised the relative points of view in the depiction: everything was wonky, the girl's appearance and emotion, the animals and their sentiments, Duval herself (as a woman drawing incompetently, that is, with masculine humour) and the readers raising a laugh, as they applied Duval's depiction to their own experience of Rivière's polite, high status painting (Figure 6.2).

If Duval's parodic bowdlerisations of polite exhibits were essentially familiar to readers of *Judy*, as visual devices for provoking laughter on the topic of the Summer Exhibition, in two further innovative pages published in 1876, the device of her wholesale ventriloquism of the character Ally Sloper, both visual and verbal, became unique. These drawings, from 10 May and 24 May 1876, both titled *The Royal Academy. (From a Sloperian point of view)*, at first appeared to be examples of the familiar device of parodying paintings displayed in the 1876 Exhibition (Duval 1876a, 1876b). However, the visible incompetence of the artist who made these drawings exceeded even Duval's unabashed and strategic lack of technical skill. The epithet 'from a Sloperian point of view' often indicated to readers the proximity of the topics of some of Duval's drawings to the story world inhabited by Sloper, if not strictly indicating Sloper's opinions. In the 1876 Summer Exhibition drawings, Duval made the epithet literal. Following a series of 1875 drawings by Duval titled *The Statues of London* (Duval 1875b) and individual drawings such as *The Kenealy Procession. – From a Sloperian point of view* (Duval 1876c; figure 7.10), among a small number of others, she adopted the visual conceit that Sloper had produced these drawings as a roving visual reporter for *Judy*, an eyewitness to the Exhibition, rather than her.

Sensational ventriloquism was not unseen in the pages of *Judy*. After all, Charles Ross often fulfilled the role of editor of the journal by performing the character and characteristics of Judy, as a hard-bitten, ironical, shape-shifting and gender-shifting old 'slavey' (Duval 1873c). But the visual ventriloquism undertaken by Duval in these pages, the device of presenting drawings as though made by a distinct and complete fictional character, was a radical, if systematic, step beyond her depictions of characters whose visual characteristics were founded on Duval's stylistic treatment.

The device was complex, although easy to comprehend. Owing to Duval's visually unequivocal adoption of a nominally masculine humour, her drawings demonstrated something new in periodical drawing in Britain, in that, exactly as Thierry Smolderen describes, in 'wordless pantomimes (drawn on paper), the real author of the story is the graphic character engaged in a world of mechanical forces. The body builds a visual discourse in which the chain of cause and effect provides syntax' (Smolderen 2014: 173). Duval's shift from making drawings of her characters to making drawings as a character was founded in her strategic use of technical incompetence, in that she was able to draw in the character of Sloper because she remained self-consciously unfettered by training and all that it signified to readers, including politeness, social status and professional, rather than humorous masculinity.

The paintings parodied in Duval's Duval/Sloper drawings of 10 May 1876 were parlour paintings in scale and topic, that is, they were sized for domestic use and for domestic budgets, albeit of the more affluent of servant-assisted households. However, two weeks later, on 24 May, Sloper/Duval reported in *Judy* on Sloper's experiences of two of the largest, most expensive and publicly celebrated paintings in the 1876 Summer Exhibition: Edward Poynter's *Atalanta's Race* and Frederic Leighton's *Daphnephoria* (Duval 1876b; Figures 6.3 and 6.4). *Atalanta's Race* depicted a Greek mythological topic, the moment when Atalanta the hunter is distracted from winning a race, by a golden apple thrown by her competitor. *Daphnephoria* also had an ancient Greek topic, the procession to a festival held at Thebes in honour of Apollo Ismenius.

Although both these paintings were in fact the products of private commissions, their size, cost, the established identities of the artists and their visibility in the press rendered them de facto public paintings, positioned, more than any others that year, to gauge the temperature of national visual high culture and potentially to provide benchmarks for achievement, spectacle and celebrity. Resold in 1893, *Daphnephoria* commanded a price of £3937 10s, in the context of an average annual wage for British manufacturing workers of around £35, according to Allen (1994: 121). *Atalanta's Race* was the mainspring of what would now be called a diffusion line of commercial decorative

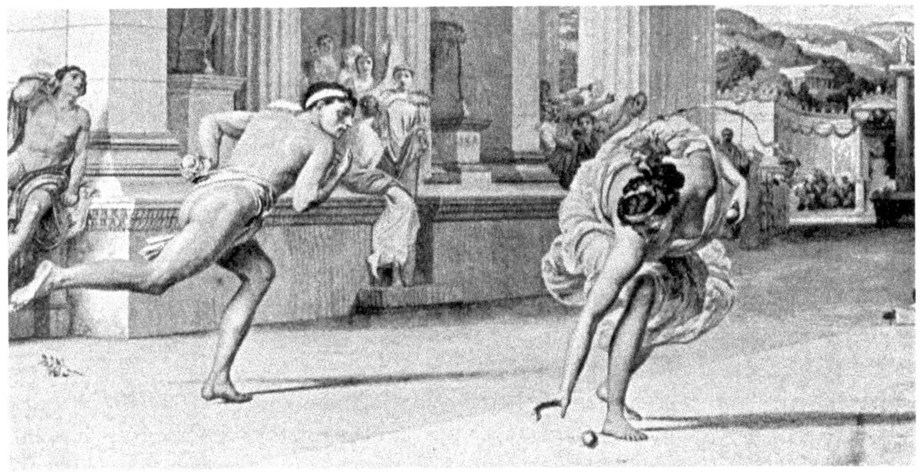

6.3 Edward Poynter (1876) *Atalanta's Race* (lost). Oil on canvas. Engraving by Joubert

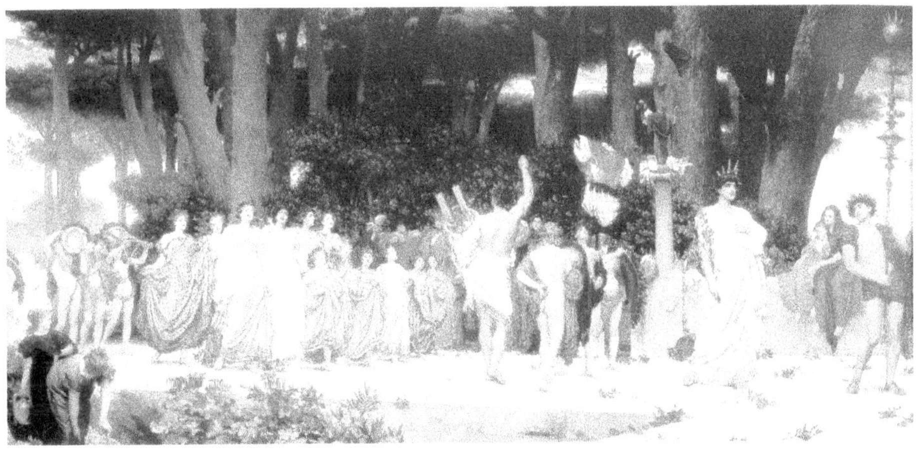

6.4 Frederic Leighton (1875) *Daphnephoria*. Oil on canvas

engravings, chromolithographs and mass-produced ceramics. In this sense, both of these paintings were exceptional and provided contemporaneous examples of the function of the Summer Exhibition as a national social event.

The British periodical press and its readers were generally unable to produce or articulate a self-aware theory of fine art, according to *The London and Westminster Review* ('Modern Wood Engraving' 1838) and later evidenced by the incomprehensible and possibly rackety character of commentaries by Sir Edward Poynter and the obfuscation offered by Oliphant (Poynter 1879: 122; Oliphant 1876: 759).

The commentary on *Daphnephoria* in *The Graphic* was typical, claiming that it was '[i]mpossible to carry luxurious refinement further [...] Decorative art might easily be stronger and nobler, it could hardly be lovelier, with that order of beauty' ('Exhibition of the Royal Academy' 1876b: 7). Although alloyed somewhat, for polite readers, by the vulgarity of special pleading, in this case for the geographical proximity of the periodical's readers to Poynter's celebrity, *The Ipswich Journal* took the same tone in its comments upon *Atalanta's Race*: 'I remember nothing in modern art more exquisitely beautiful in form, in grace, in pose, or in delicacy of treatment [...] the very perfection and triumph of art for generations to come. Your readers will be interested to learn that Mr Poynter was in part educated at [...] Ipswich' ('The Royal Academy' 1876: 3).

And yet, criticism of both paintings in the periodical press also focused on the relation-ships between the painters' technical capacities and the achievement or not of a polite high cultural ideal, however imprecisely defined. *The Examiner* noted that in 'Mr Leighton's execution there is something that seems to impoverish the life of every tint' ('Royal Academy' 1876: 17), whilst in *Blackwood's* Oliphant brought attention to Poynter's anatomi-cal inaccuracies, such that '[w]e are told that Atalanta herself is a marvel of arrested movement, and that everything is anatomically correct [...]; but it requires a very educated eye to perceive this' (Oliphant 1876: 760).

Further, that love of mimetic verisimilitude that had been usurped from a polite class to become a mark of a vulgar class, also founded criticism of the objects depicted in both paintings that, considered alongside an ill-expressed and presumed ethical ideal of fine art, began a precarious slide into masculine, impolite humour. *The Leicester Chronicle and Mercury* described the sacred members of Leighton's procession to be 'as if singing, but awkwardly suggestive of fly-catching' ('Sights of London' 1876: 10) and *The Yorkshire Herald* expressed a belief that '[e]xception will, no doubt, be taken to many things, such as the poised head of the racing figure of Malanion; the cumbersome, though airy, garments [...]; the impossibility of the apple being still in mid-air [...]; the unlikelihood of a race being run on bare marble' ('The Royal Academy Exhibition' 1876: 6).

Even Oliphant, writing in the politer range of periodicals, teetered close to vulgar humour on the topic of the verisimilitude of Leighton's depiction of ancient Greek clothes, asking: 'How any human creatures in their senses could be made to worry themselves with such flimsy and troublesome semi-clothing, it seems very hard to divine, for grace is not in it, nor does it suggest anything but embarrassment and annoyance to the wearer. If this is true Greek drapery, the mother country of art must have been sadly left to herself in the matter of clothes.' She concluded that 'they would be but too happy to drop their garments altogether – thought that would not do, would not be nice, not very fit for the eyes of the Academy, as Mr Leighton evidently feels!' (Oliphant 1876: 761).

As in her prior drawings as Sloper/Duval, of Sloper's report from the Summer Exhibition, Duval revised the topics of *Daphnephoria* and *Atalanta's Race*, treated them with masculine

THE ROYAL ACADEMY. (From a Sloperian Point of View.

A. SLOPER begs respectfully to announce that he does not intend to dilate upon every one of fifteen hundred and twenty-two pictures, upon many of which it is not his intention to cast even a passing glance. Bribes, therefore, will have no weight with A. SLOPER. (Letters containing cheques should be directed to A. SLOPER, marked "Private," and carefully fastened up.)

As, of course, all A. SLOPER's readers have enjoyed a classical education, and have their LEMPRIÈRES at their fingers' ends, if not even handier than that, it would somewhat savour of impertinence were A. SLOPER to enter into minute details respecting the exact meaning of the word "Daphnephoria," or describe at length the private life of Atalanta. Under these circumstances A. SLOPER will do so.

There were, it would appear, two Atalantas, both of them young ladies of a vigorous turn of mind. LEMPRIÈRE will inform you that "two women of this name have been often confounded by the ancient mythologists;" and no wonder. Confound them both! says A. SLOPER, for they were both of them very objectionable strong-minded hussies. The first one, who was deserted (and no wonder) by her father, took kindly to archery, and killed a couple of men and a wild pig. She also wrestled, and I believe played skittles prettily, and smoked long clay pipes. I don't think this treasure was ever married, but if not, there was a good wife lost to somebody.

The other Atalanta had a taste for pedestrian exercise. Had she lived now-a-days, she would most likely have taken the Agricultural Hall, and made a good thing of it, but she didn't. It would appear that she determined to live in celibacy, but her papa wishing her to marry, she consented to select him for her lover who should overtake her in running. This idea will naturally strike an unreflective maiden as being sweetly pretty and romantic, but the reflective mind of A. SLOPER comes to the conclusion that she must have looked unbecomingly warm when the race was over; and, besides, it may be mentioned that the dear girl also stipulated that she should have the privilege of slaughtering the unhappy young men who didn't run fast enough,

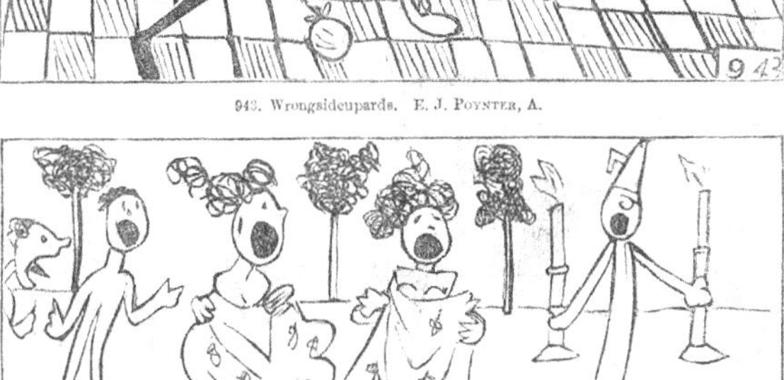

943. Wrongsideupards. E. J. POYNTER, A.

41. The Hard Word. F. LEIGHTON, R.A.

and whom she overtook. One can easily understand that it is a nice thing to kill a fine young man, and be done nothing to for it, but history does not inform us whom the amiable male flats were who ran such risks for so small a gain. You may take you roath ALLYERIUS SLOPERIUS primus was not in it. A party by the name of Melanion (some say Hippomenes) is the only one mentioned, and he, resorting to artifice, let fall, as he found Atalanta gaining on him, two golden apples he had procured for that purpose, which she stooped to pick up, and thus enabled him to first reach the winning post. I have merely to add that she and the young man were turned into lions shortly after their marriage, for some reason I am not acquainted with. Serve 'em right!

The way in which Mr. POYNTER has depicted Atalanta in the act of grabbing at the apples shows much ability. Many girls would have lost their balance. The reason why Melanion is behind instead of in front of Atalanta does not appear.

Mr. LEIGHTON has painted a long picture, and has very properly chosen a long name for it. By "The Daphnephoria" was meant a singularly uninteresting procession of simple-minded young persons of both sexes, who sang hymns and waved laurel branches, followed by boys who carried "votive tripods." Having only time to take a hasty sketch, and being particular about accuracy, A. SLOPER has thought it best to leave out the branches and the tripods. If they should be missed, however, A. SLOPER will give them a picture to themselves next week. The noticeable point of Mr. LEIGHTON's picture is costume. The gentlemen, it may be observed, don't wear much, whilst the gowns of the Theban maidens are of so loose a fit, it is all they can do to keep them on at all. The party in front is called the Daphnephoros, and deserves it. He is carrying the bed-room candles, as it is high time that these young people said good night, and retired to their respective dormitories. You may observe their mouths are mostly open. Mr. LEIGHTON says they are singing. A. SLOPER says they are yawning.

A. SLOPER, *Artless Critic.*

MR. GLADSTONE AT IT ONCE MORE.—An enormous beech-tree so large that it required seven horses to draw it away, was felled in Hawarden Park, a few days ago, by Mr. GLADSTONE, who, "notwithstanding that it measured 13 feet in circumference, accomplished his laborious but agreeable task in six hours. The tree contained over 200 cubic feet, and weighed nearly nine tons." In the art of "cutting things down"—national expenditure, national churches, trees, and so on—the late Premier must, by this time, be about the most experienced "feller" there is.

On Wednesday Next, Price 2d., Post Free, 2½d., JUDY's DERBY DOUBLE NUMBER. Sixteen Pages full of Pictures, by the best Comic Artists of the Day.

"Q" IN THE CORNER.

I AGREE with Tristram Shandy, that there is no disputing against hobby-horses! *De gustibus non est disputandum.* Did not KUNASTROKINS, that great man, at his leisure hours, take the greatest delight imaginable in combing of asses' tails and plucking out the dead hairs with his teeth, though he had tweezers always in his pocket! The wisest men in all ages, not excepting SOLOMON himself, have had their hobby-horses. Even Members of the British Parliament are not free from the weakness. There is Mr. WHALLEY. Does he not trace all the ills to which flesh and mind are heir to official disregard of the machinations of the Society of Jesus, and the ungrateful treatment experienced by a certain Nobleman who shall be nameless? Does not Mr. O. MORGAN think England will soon be num-

6.5 Marie Duval (1876) 'The Royal Academy. (From a Sloperian Point of View.)', *Judy, or the London Serio-comic Journal*, Volume 19, p. 59

humour and hence provoked laughter at the series of comparisons, between paintings and drawings, which created and consolidated her own identity as a professional woman humorous artist and the identities of her readers (Figure 6.5). *Atalanta's Race* was titled *Wrongsideupards*. It was a drawing of two ungainly household servants, a man and a woman, falling over their own feet and dropping what they were carrying. Atalanta, in particular, was dressed in characteristic 'slavey' clothes and the male silhouette had the thin limbs and big hands, feet and nose of a member of a vulgar class. Leighton's painting was re-titled *The Hard Word*, due to the fact that no vulgarian could speak Greek. The women in the procession struggled to keep their robes on, as noted by Oliphant in the source. The leader was a self-portrait by Sloper/Duval in that modern version of ancient Greek attire, his nightshirt and nightcap, holding two candles to light his way to bed.

According to these periodicals, it appeared that a fundamental challenge for British visual artists of the 1870s (humorous or otherwise) was the adjudication of the equilibrium between phenomenal experiences (that is, of quotidian life) and the artifice of visual representation. *The Pall Mall Gazette* found that, in *Daphnephoria*, Leighton's 'lines, with all the refinement of their grace, are wanting life; they register some gesture that is familiar and fit for art to interpret, but they do not retain the subtle impression of vivacity that gives the gesture its significance' ('Exhibition at the Royal Academy' 1876: 12). Whereas the paintings had been criticised in the press for their occasional failures in visually mimetic verisimilitude, their 'wanting life', Sloper/Duval's drawings made the concept of verisimilitude itself a joke. What could be truer to life than the activities and the results of untrained drawing? In Sloper/Duval's hands, visible training, politeness, feminine wit and the ideal body lacked verisimilitude, because Duval's treatments and topics proposed that these properties were not true to the vulgar lives of *Judy* readers, sharing with a later commentator, for example, the idea that the unclothed body could not conform to polite ideals of beauty in that, without clothes, the 'lines of the body are lost or deformed; there is none of the suggestion of ordinary costume, only a grotesque and shapeless image, all in pits and protuberances, for which Nature should be ashamed to accept responsibility' (Symons 1896: 88).

More than the drawings of 10 May, further inversions in the drawings of 24 May were highlighted by the neoclassicism of the source paintings: body parts that were small in Leighton's and Poynter's paintings were big in the Sloper/Duval drawings and vice versa. The 'grotesque' aspect of the wide-open mouths of the singers, noted by Oliphant in Leighton's painting, was exaggerated (Oliphant 1876: 760). In the same way, this sense of the vulgar hint of untrammelled bodies in *Daphnephoria* ran riot in Sloper/Duval, being absolutely counter to polite concepts of ideal form. Those properties in the drawings that were the focus of censure in the press were the specific properties highlighted by Sloper/Duval in order to raise a laugh – the shameful 'pits and protuberances' of vulgar life.

In her Summer Exhibition drawings, Duval's adoption of Sloper's identity, founded in her technical incompetence, constituted a profoundly radical creative vision of the relationships between humour, gender, professionalism and vulgarity, in which the imaginative projections of the fine arts worlds were deftly revealed to be contingent and mercilessly parodied in style, object and context, by being brought into the world of *Judy* and its readers and, still more radically, into the world of Duval.

In her drawings, Duval chose masculine humour, continually indexed stylistically by her displays of technical incompetence and her precarious status as a professional woman, to show recognisable stories of the familiar lives of vulgar readers. According to the ideas of femininity, masculinity and vulgarity of a polite class, she made a living recklessly, by drawing attention to the contradictions of a working life that she shared with her readers, so as to provoke laughter and, in doing so, to sell the next publication, bring on the comics register and create a new visual culture.

Notes

1 Annie M. Hone, writing in *Myra's Journal of Dress and Fashion*, three years after Duval's last published drawing, did not pay much attention to her subject. She described Duval as 'the first lady comic artist' and misspelled Duval's given surname as 'Lessier'. These slips were repeated verbatim in *The Girls' Own Paper*, six years later (Hone 1888 and F. H. 1894). I am grateful to John Adcock for drawing my attention to commentaries from 1869, 1872, 1888 and 1894.

2 Ross replied, in the next edition of *The Theatrical Journal*, that it was easy to differentiate between his drawings and Duval's, 'because Mademoiselle is an artist and C. H. R. is not' ('Letter to the Editor' 1869: 30:1558:331).

3 'Marie Duval, who invented Ally Sloper, was [*Judy's*] mainstay [...] The drawings were excruciatingly bad, but the legends were always amusing, and they led up to the establishment of Ally Sloper's Half-Holiday.' Quoted in Kunzle 1986: 26.

4 Quoted in Marshall 2009: 205 and 210.

5 For discussion of the 'Condition of England' novel, see Weber 2005 and Simmons Jr 2002.

6 The word derives from the surname of Thomas Bowdler (1874–25) and has come to mean the expurgation of a text by the application of an external rule, post hoc.

7

The relationship between performance and drawing: suggestive synaesthesia in Marie Duval's work

Julian Waite

Line is action become visible. (Roland Barthes)[1]

This chapter considers whether there is evidence that Duval's interest and abilities as a performer influenced her work as a cartoonist and illustrator. I approach this from two angles: nineteenth-century theories of acting in relation to visual aspects of the craft such as stage proxemics and the physicalising of character; and twenty-first-century theories of physical movement in relation to the production of images. These elements are distinct, but it is hoped that through examining them, the reader will be allowed to construct insight into the qualities of Duval's work, particularly her images of drawings 'made by' (rather than of) Ally Sloper. This latter group of drawings best represents the post-modern sensibility of artists such as Cy Twombly and David Shrigley and theorists such as Roland Barthes or Ernst van Alphen, who in different ways provide contemporary lenses through which to view the evidence of how Marie Duval translated her late-nineteenth-century somatic practice as an actor and dancer into gestural drawing.

Drawing the actor's gesture

In this section I intend to examine existing evidence to suggest how a highly visually orientated actor may have exploited her knowledge of the gestural qualities of her profession in creating cartoons and other graphic works. I refer to evidence by performers who wrote detailed diaries of their lives in the theatre. Some of these are famous, such as the reminiscences of West End stars such as *Mr & Mrs Bancroft On and Off the Stage* (Bancroft and Bancroft 1889) for example, but more relevant for our purposes are the diaries of obscure performers whose professional lives would more closely have resembled Duval's.

One of these is an unpublished manuscript of the 1880 diary of Hugh Moss, a minor touring actor whose unexpurgated account is refreshing. Another diary, that of Alma

160

Ellerslie is particularly useful, as she was a 'jobbing' actor of a similar status to Duval, working exactly contemporaneously. Her work, *The Diary of an Actress, or, Realities of Stage Life* (Ellerslie 1885) reveals the struggle a female actor had and the need for a provincial 'apprenticeship', in exactly the same way as a generation earlier Peter Paterson (the nom de plume of actor James Glass Bertram) found after a disastrous attempt at Hamlet in his late teens (Paterson 1864: 33).

Thus, on starting as a performer, Duval would have found herself part of a system that suggested acting relied on apprenticeship, practice and tradition (often within a family). These were stronger than theoretical constructs on one hand or training on the other. It is as certain that Duval received no formal theatre training as it is that she received no formal art training. Indeed, there was no theatre training of the type represented by the Royal Academy of Art in Duval's time. Even the oldest drama school in the United Kingdom gradually emerged in the 1880s (The London Academy of Music and Dramatic Art, LAMDA, which offered examinations in elocution) whilst the first specific acting academy, the Royal Academy of Dramatic Art (RADA), was not founded until 1904. Training for music was, in contrast, more developed. Most theoretical pronouncements relating to drama had a basis in singing, instructors often also teaching 'declamation'.

This lowering of drama's status below music led theatre critic Lewes to complain in 1875 that 'while everyone understands that it is a primary requisite in a singer that he should not only have a voice, but know how to *sing*; very few seem to suspect that it is not less a primary requisite in an actor that he should know how to *speak*. The consequence is that very few actors do know how to speak, and scarcely any of them can speak verse' (Lewes 1875: 267–8).

However, this is not to say that actors were unable or unwilling to define and codify their craft. On the contrary, criticism of acting in newspapers was frequently sophisticated and subtle and actors, in their reminiscences, make judgements and give reasons for those judgements. Moreover, in Duval's youth there were a range of reflective works, essays and practical manuals offering systematised instruction and exercises for the benefit of amateur and professional actors alike. Whilst it is impossible to know if Duval ever consulted any such works, it is reasonable to assume that the theoretical ideas advocated were taken fundamentally from practice, perhaps with the interference of music and fine art practice, or to put it more positively, the idea of cross-media visualisation (see Meisel 1984).

Nineteenth-century acting manuals present an interest in codification and the belief that there are specific gestures that can be assigned tightly designated meanings, even those in the late nineteenth century when the interest in 'scientific' methodologies had begun to thrive in drama as in medicine. Thus the critic Lewes (who worked briefly as an actor in his youth in the 1850s) produced a guide (*On Actors and the Art of Acting*, Lewes 1875), which is organised specifically through a critical and practical examination of great actors of his time, and international styles of acting, such as the drama in Paris, Germany and Spain for example (Lewes 1875: 178–263).

Garcia's 1888 manual *The Actor's Art* is a much more specifically practical guide, with copious illustrations to exemplify the gestures and facial expressions required in acting (Garcia 1888). In this it sits in the tradition of Siddons's enormously influential *Practical Illustrations of Rhetorical Gesture and Action*, first published in 1822, but still in print throughout Duval's active period (Siddons 1822). I would argue that Siddons can be seen as the Stanislavski of Victorian acting, in terms of the breadth of his influence. Alongside these the early nineteenth-century pseudo-scientific movements that spawned the complex systematisations of activities such as phrenology and homoeopathy had a parallel in work produced by practitioners such as Delsarte, whose work received promotion in English from Stebbins in 1885 in *The Delsarte System of Expression* (Stebbins 1885). Nonetheless, Stebbins was still firmly wedded to the notion that there are essentialist poses, emphasising that Delsarte has distilled these from ancient classical models rather than the less pure gestures of contemporary stage practice. Thus, for attitudes such as 'vital repose' the actor should 'look over my shoulder at this collection of photographed statues. We will select one for each of the foregoing attitudes […] What have you found? Ah. Hebe, the bewitching little waitress upon Olympus. She stands, with both lovely arms upraised. Her two dear little feet nestle close together. It is our second attitude' (Stebbins 1885: 149).

Whilst they may have been aware of such current challenges to the acting styles of their day, it seems unlikely that Duval and Ross would have embraced these ideas. However, it is incontrovertible that, as journalists and consumers of the popular contemporary culture of their time, they would have been aware of the theoretical stance of writers such as Lewes, Siddons and Garcia, implicitly if not explicitly.

With this in mind, I survey aspects of acting theory as exemplified by works between 1822 and 1885, which suggest what sort of theatrical visualisation an actor working in Duval's time would have internalised. The consistency of this theory is striking, and the visual imagery likewise remarkably consistent. Indeed, this very ubiquity is confirmed by the force of the realist challenge presented by the next generation of theorists (Michael Chekhov 1952/2014; Boleslavsky 1933/2013; Stanislavski 1926/2013a/2013b and their followers)[2] and there are visual structures in nineteenth-century theatrical proxemics,[3] which appear to be unaffected by the changes in codification that have taken place between the late nineteenth century and the present day. Thus, the modern reader of Duval's cartoons is often presented with a sign system that relates to theatrical practice rather than renaissance perspective in a way that is accessible through behavioural positioning and relationships and the ways in which these impact on the telling of a story.

There are two clear strands, two patterns of didactic activity, in acting manuals of the nineteenth century. One is well exemplified by advice to represent nature, and for the actor to have the flexibility truthfully to depict impulses and communicate emotions. With the exception of an increased emphasis on the need to communicate narrative, the language and examples of this strand of thought are remarkably similar to the pronouncements of the realist movement and acting theorists right up to the present day (Clifton 2016; Chubbuck 2005; Donnellan 2005; Stafford-Clark 1991).

For example, the latter emphasises truthfulness to 'nature' in the sense of responding to surroundings: 'Adaptation is a response to habitat and situation. An actor's transformation is a truthful response to imagined habitat and situation' (Clifton 2016: 78). The second strand is theorised through reference to the work of great actors or canonised works of art or both. This, the bulk of the practical texts, gives codified examples of movements, gestures and positions, often with the use of line drawings, which literally provide the 'solutions' to the interpretation of texts.

Thus, the job of the actor is theorised as understanding the interpretive need of the text and then selecting the 'correct' visual signs to communicate that need. The authority for this is provided by the fact that great performers move audiences greatly, and that works of art are a correct distillation of emotional states into (frozen) facial gestures, stances and gestures. In this framework, tronies[4] of an artist such as Rembrandt represent an outstanding body of work, which could be, and was, mined by the illustrators of acting manuals.

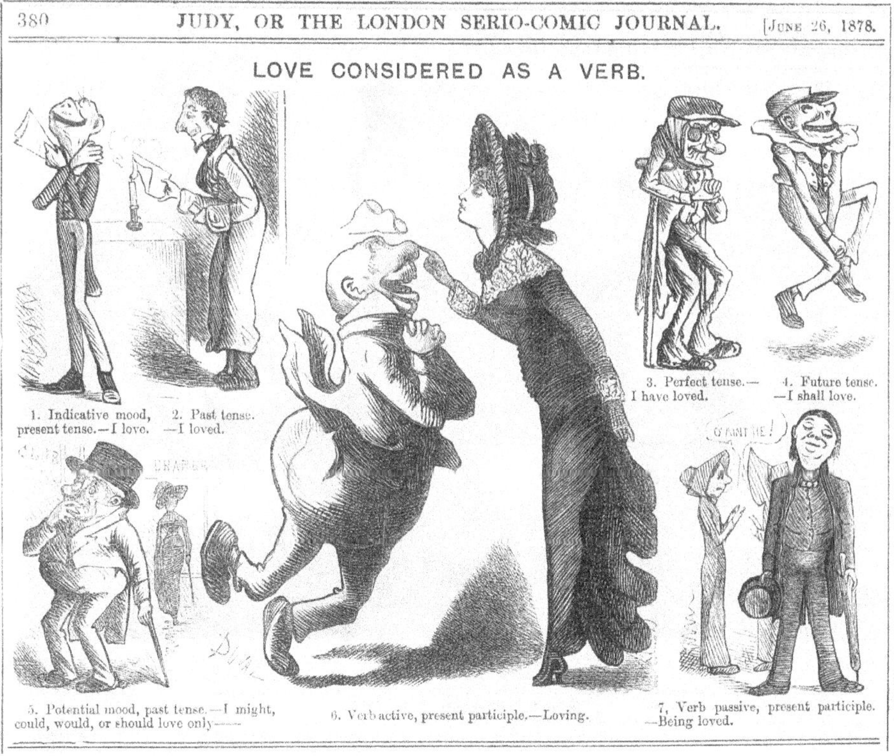

7.1 Marie Duval (1878) 'Love Considered as a Verb', *Judy, or the London Serio-comic Journal,* Volume 22, p. 380

It would be possible to relate this to the early nineteenth-century convention of 'points', the moment in acting when a climactic (usually) emotional moment is marked and held as a pose (Duval 1878f, Figure 7.1). However, it is beyond the scope of this chapter to examine the gradual emergence of realism, which was taking place and overlapping with romanticism precisely in Duval's time. In fact, commentators, and indeed actors, in the 1870s and 1880s were every bit as aware that they were living at a time when actors presented a mixture of styles exacerbated by the concurrent repertoire of older melodrama, contemporary melodrama, 'cup and saucer' realism[5] and Shakespeare – the latter being a canonical figure whose texts supported both different styles within individual productions. Shakespeare was also edited to foreground the particular skills or tastes of the 'star' performing the work. Thus, Hugh Moss reflects in his diary (Moss 1880) on the differences between the plays he is mostly required to perform, a revival of one of the first hit melodramas, which was still in the repertory, and a new melodrama:

> Rehearsal of the 'Corsican Brothers' today. Very long and uninteresting. Thought how what with this play & the 'Bells' Psychological phenomena are perhaps the best ingredients of the true melodrama. (Moss 1880: 3 November)

Moss reveals that his taste reflects the current interest in psychological character whilst amply demonstrating that (as in twenty-first-century analysis) melodramas of 1852 and 1871 were easily classed together, but that by 1880 actors were finding more interest in character interaction than stage 'sensation'. As Taylor has demonstrated in his germinal study of performances across the Victorian period, acting styles undoubtedly changed, but within a framework where the actor was making the gestural lexicon their own (Taylor 1989).

In 1875 Lewes was very careful to make this point in his essay on Salvini.[6] He stresses a clear distinction between an interpretation of the typology of a character in a play, where opinions may validly differ, and the need 'correctly' to represent that typology (or, in a specific scene, emotional state). Thus the actor may form their own view of the 'reality' of Hamlet's madness, a point which Shakespeare's text leaves in 'great uncertainty', but 'whether Shakespeare meant him to be mad, or feigning madness, nothing can be less equivocal than the indication of a state of cerebral excitement in speech and conduct, and this the actor ought to represent' (Lewes 1875: 265–6).

The manuals of writers such as Siddons or Garcia take this as their foundation and set out to catalogue possible states of mind and provide illustrations as to how these states indeed 'ought' to be represented. For Lewes and his other contemporary reviewers, it was not so much how these attributes should be represented but the power with which the performer achieved the representation, and the recipe of their choices. Victorian actors considered their art to consist of the satisfactory organisation of vocal and physical elements, derived from 'life' and 'nature' into a coherent and effective pattern, based on universal (rather than culturally specific) codified signs which, most significantly for us, could usefully and didactically be condensed into still images in the form of line drawings.

These influences are concisely demonstrated by the collaboration represented by the makers of *The Actor's Art: a Practical Treatise*, Amedee Forestier and Gustav Garcia (1888). Forestier, who provided the illustrations, was a French Academy trained artist from the Ecole des Beaux Arts. Garcia, who wrote the text, was primarily a musician working at both the London Academy of Music and Guildhall School of Music. The anonymous illustrator of Siddons's *Practical Illustrations of Rhetorical Gesture and Action* (1822) 66 years earlier is, like Siddons, both lifting from the German original and adding illustrations based on fine art. Thus, the depictions of 'False Gesture' (Siddons 1822: 224–7) opposite pages 224 and 226 are a slight redrawing of the illustrations placed together opposite page 28 of Engels's *Ideen zu einen Mimic* (Engels 1795: 28–9). There is no deception here. Rather Siddons acknowledges his work to be an adaptation 'to the English drama' (Siddons 1822: v) from Engels's work, and as well as redrawing, his illustrator adds a very large number of extra images, both as plates in the style of Engels's book, but also and entirely originally as small cartoon-like drawings that punctuate the 'letters' out of which the work is constructed. These would appear to be illustrations of actual performances with naturalised settings, which nonetheless suggest stage sets.

This internal evidence shows that like Forestier, Siddons's illustrator was versed both in classical models (his plate 14 opposite page 78 is a copy of a character from Velazquez's *Apollo in the Forge of Vulcan*) and able to reproduce scenarios from contemporary performance either implicitly or explicitly. Thus, in the appendix of the work Siddons cites specific scenes and even identifiable actors, his illustrator showing the performers frozen in their roles: for example the actor who played Bajazet at the Opera House in 1806 is illustrated in plate 61 (Siddons 1822: 384–5).

In both Siddons and Forestier/Garcia the images 'freeze' the performer in a moment, which summarises the action of both a sequence of events and an aspect of the personality of the character. Needless to say, it is not possible to evince the full 'meaning' of the image without the gloss provided by the text but, once married together, text and illustration, in the manner of cartoons,[7] complement each other to provide a plausible summation. Thus, for example, the Siddons illustration of 'Vulgar Triumph' is of a woman smirking (Figure 7.2). The text identifies a character from Thomas Morton's comedy *Speed the Plough* (produced in 1874 at the Theatre Royal Covent Garden) who, as Siddons explains, takes more delight from discomforting her neighbour following her daughter's socially advantageous engagement than she does in the happiness of her daughter. The facial expression is indeed entirely appropriate for this notion, combining as it does in one image the suggestion of a thoughtless or, as the text puts it, 'vulgar' character with the storyline to which the expression provides the background and summary.

In this respect this illustrator's achievement, and behind that we must assume the achievement of the actor, is remarkably close to later theatrical theorisations of character summations more associated with the realist tradition. Thus Michael Chekhov (himself a very fine naturalistic actor best known for his performance in Hitchcock's *Spellbound* 1945) urges the actor to find a 'psychological gesture', which summarises the character and provides a grounding for the actor to produce artistic consistency within the play as a whole (Chekhov 2014: 63–84). This gesture, like the image of 'Vulgar Triumph', is to be found with the whole body, although unlike Siddons's illustration it may not, or rather almost certainly won't, ever appear onstage but will remain part of the actor's internal preparation.

Since the beginning of the twentieth century, the notion of cataloguing external facial expressions, however, has been completely rejected in drama theory, and a 'slavish' imitation of a facial gesture would be considered not only unnecessary, but positively unhelpful. This is consistent with the notion of a psycho-physical methodology, since the impulses are conceived as receiving an unconscious and holistic expression in the performer, with which a conscious mimicry would interfere. However, the idea of copying facial expressions or gestures is pervasive and, in some traditions, still standard training, for example in Kabuki or Noh theatre, the acting student learns by copying the master (for example, see Leiter 2001, or *Onnagata and the Fan* (1999) where Gojo Masanosuke models Kabuki moves).

Indeed, in the Western tradition, aspects of performance craft may still involve copying and checking that copy in a mirror. Thus, Antonio Fava's training for commedia dell'Arte at *Lo Stage International di Commedia dell'Arte* (Fava 2019; Rudlin 1994: 226–31) and Soum and Wasson's training for mime corporel (Soum and Wasson 2019) involve initial copying of gestures followed by more independent explorations (Waite 2008: 123–31). With Soum and Wasson this consists of initial exercises in front of a mirror, followed by the teacher drawing a curtain over the mirror for improvisations, where the rote learning is then perceived as integrated into exercises which rely on the attention being directed away from the self and towards the other performers in improvised scenes. In contemporary drawing training there is a parallel practice, with a number of specific works containing photographs or line drawings of a large range of facial and postural tropes (Faigin 2008; Simon 2003; Rogers Peck 1990) designed to be copied for internalisation or used as reference for illustration. These are very similar in appearance to Siddons and Garcia resting as they do in the same tradition as the classical tronie.

Therefore in the mid-nineteenth century a young actor would almost certainly perceive their craft as characterised by the following: something to be learned by watching experienced practitioners and practice; fundamentally consisting of a codified catalogue of gestures that could be taught, but which when executed would need to be organised and performed with a level of precision and skill. The 'genius' with which this was accomplished would reflect the genius with which the actor was received. Thus Peter Paterson reports that the 'old stagers [...] with whom I was associated' disabused his youthful belief that he could launch straight into performing Hamlet, pointing out that 'there were certain rules and conventionalities, which, according to them, must be observed' (Paterson 1864: 33).

As a performer specialising in male attire roles, Duval would have known these rules and conventions. However, far from any awareness of theatrical rules and codifications resulting in her seeking an academic training in drawing, she instead brought her untutored drawing style unapologetically to the pages of *Judy*. This is entirely consistent with an

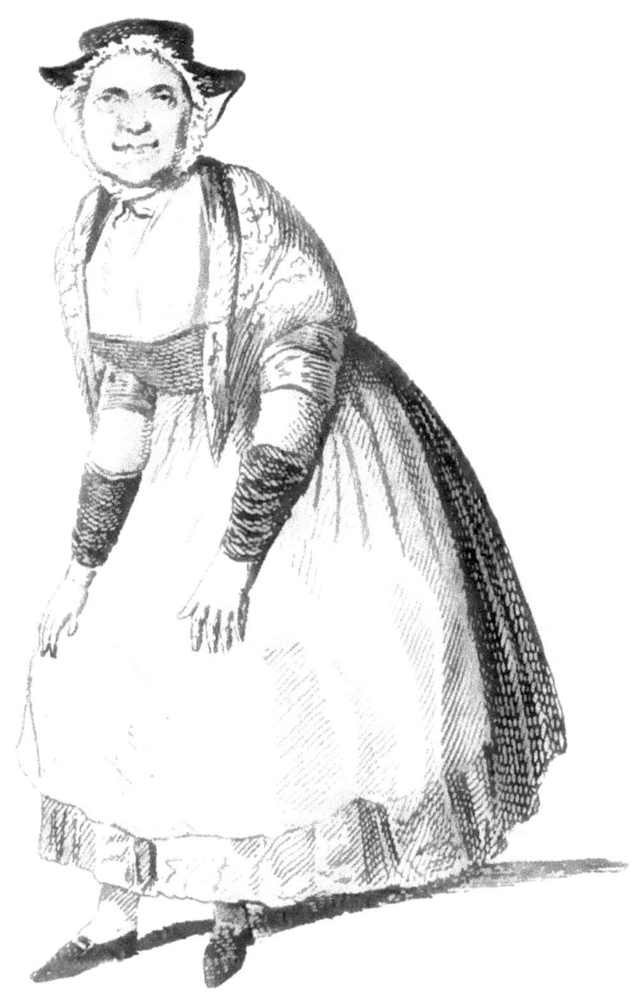

7.2 Henry Siddons (1822) 'Vulgar Triumph', *Practical Illustrations of Rhetorical Gesture and Action*, London: Sherwood, Neely and Jones. Plate 56, opposite p. 378

'actorly' frame of mind, since for the performer the individual or even maverick personality of the actor was deliberately sought after within the conventions of performance.[8] Paterson, writing about actor/manager William Henry Murray who he worked for in Edinburgh, situates his acting entirely within types (emphasising as an additional excellence the fact that Murray could succeed in such a wide range of types) but is able to account for Murray's effect on an audience only by recourse to hyperbole rather than description:

> Every character sustained by Mr Murray was a portrait painted by an artist – full of excellence – a living, walking personation of the character no matter what it might be. A foppish footman, an eccentric citizen, a jealous husband, a doting father, or an old worn-out roué, all came alike to Murray. The flash of his genius vivified and lighted up the part, and placed it before his audience a breathing type of what such an actor was capable of realising. (Paterson 1864: 74)

This emphasis on archetypes is something Duval understood and translated into line with all her characterisations, not just, and yet most famously, with Ally Sloper. The entirely practical training of the theatre may have been the internalised convention that allowed her to develop and present her vision of her characters and conventions, drawing in a naive style that came from her internal impulses rather than a 'stepping down' from expertise manifest in an artist like Edward Lear.

The frequent use of art as a metaphor, used by Paterson here, again suggests the symbiotic relationship between the two disciplines, which Duval would undoubtedly have been steeped in as a performer. Painted settings were, at this period before the structural reforms of Appia and Gordon Craig, firmly based on renaissance perspective principles, and were admired by actors as works in their own right that contributed to the effect of performances, rather than integrated elements (Craig 2008; Appia 1981).

Thus Paterson admires the quality of the scenery even of a 'booth' theatre, touring in a fair by writing: 'the scenery in particular was beautiful, and had been painted by an artist of note specially for its present owner' (Paterson 1864: 110), whilst Moss as a utilities actor is occasionally involved in working on scenery alongside his rehearsal duties: 'Worked hard all day from 10 – 4.30. Cleared stage – painted snow scene' (Moss 1880: 28 April). Later, in July, he paints a steamboat scene for *Uncle Tom's Cabin* (Moss 1880: 21 July).

Although there is no evidence Duval ever did this, there is an interesting cross-over between performer and scenic artist reported in Moss, where the scenic artist Hemsley also appears in the bill as 'the rapid caricaturist' (playbill in Moss 1880: 9 April), a role which survives in contemporary circus, for example in the Blackpool Tower Circus (Endresz 2019). It is therefore entirely consistent that Duval would put herself forward as an artist to *Judy*, possibly following success in tasks assisting the artists in the pantomimes and burlesques of her early career.

One other notable feature of Duval's practice, which emerges in the course of her career, is her facility with storytelling in successive panels. In fact, it is possible to relate the interest in depicting a specific summary moment of a narrative, as represented by the sort of drawings which focus emotion or a combination of emotion with narrative such as the illustration of 'Vulgar Triumph' in Siddons (1822: 378; Figure 7.2), with a sequence of drawings which progress a narrative through fixed 'points'.

This is the foundation of a theory of acting which in the early part of the century celebrated those moments as virtuosic, but which by Duval's period no longer accepted that, whilst continuing to understand that narratives require specific pointing of key information. This interest is, in 2019, represented very strongly in the storyboard, demonstrating that a film narrative can usefully be perceived as a series of key points read by the audience which is organised systematically and clearly carries the sense of the narrative without the need for the intervening material.

This is an also aspect of the methodology of the comics register (although comics also excel in indexing other types of time), and a key part of contemporary narrative theatre and storytelling practice (see, for example, Alfreds 2013). Thus, remarkably, Siddons includes a sequence where individual expressions are linked into a narrative sequence (Figure 7.3). Here a young man's facial and (more importantly) physical gestures and body positions show a narrative where the man gradually becomes more interested in the document his fellow actor is reading. The positions are highly legible to a twenty-first-century reader. The actor faces out initially ('Indifference') and gradually makes eye contact with the page ('Expectation'), then his fellow actor ('Excited interest') and finally his head gets so close as to encompass both ('Gratification' Siddons 1822: 334–5; Figure 7.3). The sequence is an exceptional example demonstrating the principles of a lost methodology, showing the way an actor might have linked together the tropes that appear unacceptably stylised in isolation into something that is recognisable as the clear charting of a narrative journey. The sequence looks something like a strip cartoon, and to a practising actor such as myself would be entirely usable as a 'score' to provide a structure for an improvisation. Surprisingly, the images are relevant in details as much as in broad effect – thus the flat hand in 'Excited Interest' suggesting tension, and the curved fingers in 'Gratification' (Siddons 1822: 335) implying a sense of physical relief, could be utilised by an actor as suggestive physical triggers. This receives resonance with Mike Alfred's seminal work on narrating, where he emphasises the importance of movement to narrative:

> how [actors] move has to be connected with and motivated by the inner life of the characters […] The tuning of their bodies must be so fine that they instinctively respond to the subtlest of thoughts and feelings with the most delicate expressiveness: an intake or breath or tilt of the head, flick of an eyelid or straightening of the spine. (Alfreds 2013: 220)

Duval shows this sensibility within her unorthodox style. *Back Gardening in April (from a Sloperian Point of View)* (Duval 1876h; Figure 7.4) is typical. The drawings are in naive style, although on this occasion the text doesn't specifically claim they are drawn by Sloper himself. Duval regularly, as here, draws with a wide format which itself suggests a stage, whilst the progression of the characters across a frieze of flowers is clearly influenced by progressing backdrops. Aside from these obvious theatrical suggestions, the characters, although very roughly drawn, entirely obey the theatrical need to convey character through posture. The conceit is that Sloper has a pretence that he is working

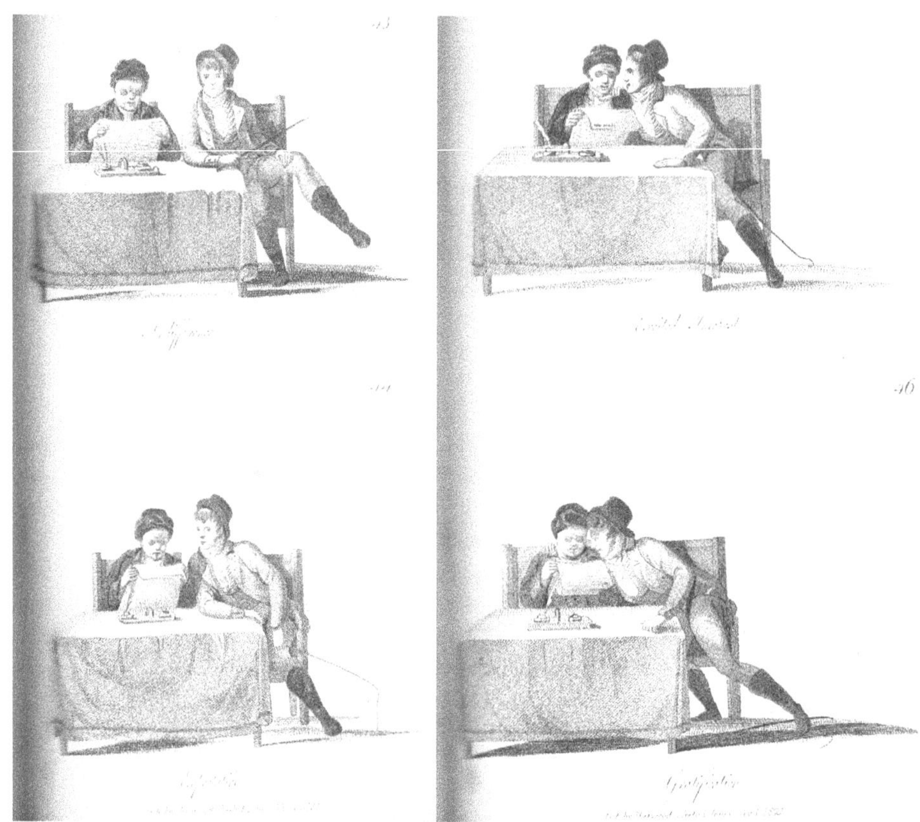

7.3 Henry Siddons (1822) 'Indifference, Expectation, Excited Interest, Gratification', *Practical Illustrations of Rhetorical Gesture and Action*, London: Sherwood, Neely and Jones. Plates 43–6, opposite p. 334

in his garden whilst in fact his wife is doing the work. This is represented by the props of pipe and bottle (in Sloper's hands) as opposed to watering can and bucket (Mrs Sloper). Gesturally, Sloper has an arched back flowing into pert head and through to his pert hat, whilst his pointed toes are likewise suggestive of relaxed energy. Simultaneously, the arm holding the bottle is bent, suggesting lightness and active use. In contrast, Mrs Sloper is all weight, the curve of her spine continuing into her neck being concave, emphasised by drooping hair and eyebrow, whilst her feet sit flat and arms slope directly downwards in an inverted 'V'. Even the 'chorus' of flowers subtly contribute to the effect – Sloper's have more relaxed curved stems, Mrs Sloper's straight with heads that appear like wakeful staring eyes. As with Garcia's chapter on walks, an actor could use the visual information here to animate a character (Figure 7.5), with the exception that Duval's

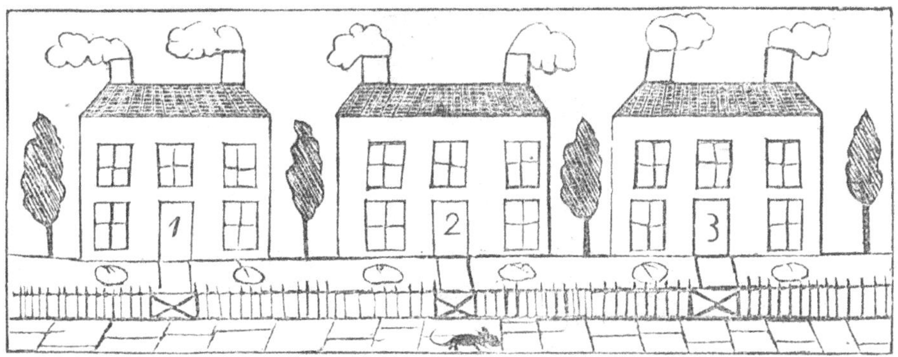

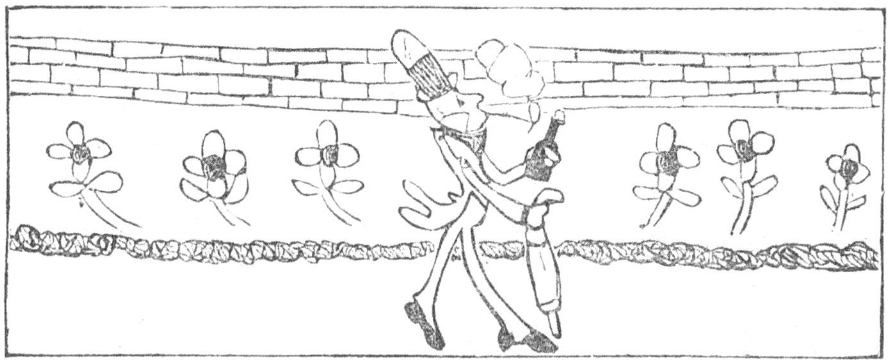

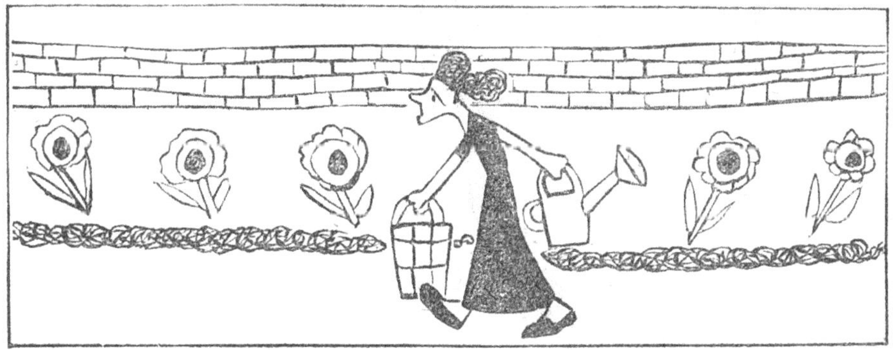

7.4 Marie Duval (1876) 'Back Gardening in April (from a Sloperian Point of View)', *Judy, or the London Serio-comic Journal*, Volume 18, p. 261

171

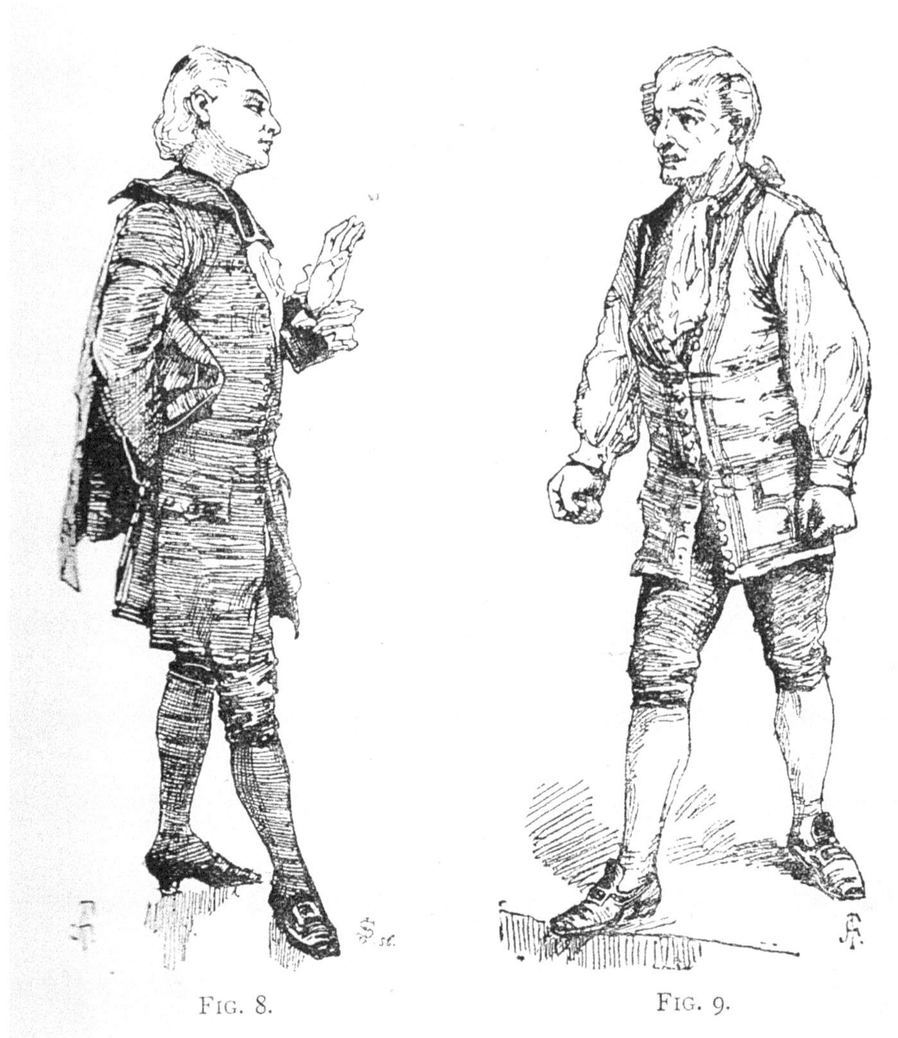

7.5 Gustave Garcia (1822) *The Actor's Art: A Practical Treatise On Stage Declamation, Public Speaking and Deportment, for the Use of Artists, Students and Amateurs*, London: Simkin, Marshall & Company, p. 39

visual information is incomparably more expressive and both specific and emblematic where Forestier's illustrations, although beautifully achieved and undoubtedly based on a similar use of physical gesture, suggest a specific archaeology of movement that is of its period and would require translation.

Gestural drawing

In this section I raise a number of ideas relating to conceptions of drawing, and attempt to make some tentative connections and suggestions regarding the connection between processes of acting and processes of drawing. This section therefore presents a number of 'lenses', and invites the reader to look and ponder, rather than presenting a finished argument. The first of these is Ernst van Alphen's adoption of Barthes's notion of 'transitive' and 'intransitive' to drawing. The second, longer section, relates the way that drawing has been understood as the record of performance, and ponders the notion that the controlled abandon of performance (allowing acting to 'happen') may illuminate Duval's ability to suggest the spontaneity of the drawing body. Third, since this section principally considers Duval's 'performance' of 'Ally Sloper drawing', I consider the idea of performing the role of (imperfect) artist. It is in this sense that I put forward the idea of synaesthesia, an interaction between drawing and performance.

Transitive/intransitive drawing

A number of Duval's Sloper drawings, such as Figure 7.6, explicitly offer the conceit that they are by Sloper himself. They are also highly gestural. They 'write' the representation (often a self-portrait of Sloper himself) but distort, disfigure and spiral away into scrawl. In this section I use van Alphen's notion of 'transitive' and 'intransitive' drawing to suggest a way that Duval's gestural drawings might be understood and investigated. Being 'by Sloper' these drawings in particular foreground the idea of drawing as performance, both in the conceit and in the fluidity and abandon of their execution. For further discussion of Duval's use of pseudonymous styles of drawing, see Chapter 6 (pp. 153–9).

Van Alphen summarises fifty years of academic thought on drawing practice by referring to Barthes's terms transitive and intransitive. Whereas an image can be transitive (of something) or intransitive (revealing itself only as its own self, perhaps as 'marks') van Alphen explains that the 'gesture of drawing is transitive and intransitive at the same time. The gestures of the moving hand register, one could say, the movement of the thinking eye'. Thus 'when the gestural traces of the hand result in a representation the lines become transitive; if not they are intransitive, and the resulting lines can be read as indexes of gesture or as echoes of the body' (van Alphen 2018: 110). Our interest arises precisely because as a performer/dancer we may wonder if that practice informs the clearly transitive (in van Alphen's definition) illustrations Duval produced. Her distortions, her adoption of various naive styles and personas strongly suggest she provides something of a bridge between those 'transitive' artists cited by van Alphen (such as Holbein) and those who are described as 'artists [...] whose practice of concepts foreground the gesture of drawing as intransitive' (van Alphen 2018: 110). Alongside abstract artists Armando, Britta Huttenlocker and Cy Twombly, van Alphen places Durer, whose work seems to him to suggest a straddling of these foci. Thus, Durer is perceived as being depictive but also in his processes prepared to reveal, utilise and incorporate the record

CRIMES AND DISASTERS.
(From a Sloperian Point of View.)

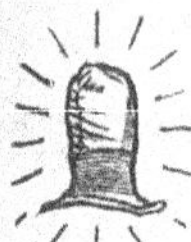

I AM given to understand that it has been put about that this article is illustrated by engravings " from sketches taken by A. SLOPER." I hereby give notice that A. SLOPER will legally proceed against any party or parties who in future make such statements in any way whatsomedever. A. SLOPER has not taken any sketches from any one. The works of art adorning these observations are traced in front of a window-pane. They are perfectly original, and no trouble or expense has been spared by A. SLOPER in producing them, and I don't like such things to be said.

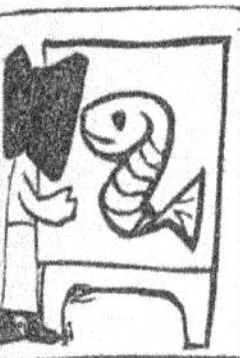

I AM glad to see that one important question has been settled satisfactorily. It is highly proper to eat boiled fish on a Friday, but it is wicked to look at raw fish on a Sunday. In future the Octopus at the Brighton Aquarium will have to spend his Sabbath solitarily. A tract will, however, be dropped into the top of his tank to keep him cheerful and improve his mind.

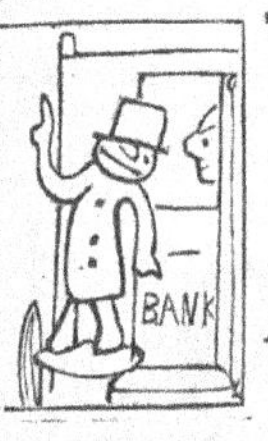

THE attention of energetic active young men is respectfully directed to a recent Old Bailey case. It would appear that five shillings a day can be easily nicked by the conductor of a London omnibus, and the robbery will never be discovered unless the thief splits on himself. Let's all be conductors.

A YOUNG man who had taken too much MOODY and SANKEY unmixed, recently went down to Bristol, thinking he had got a call to preach in the public streets there, and impede other less serious business. Some medical man thought something was wrong with his head, and it has been shaved since then.

IT may be very poetical to say to a sweet young girl, " Whisper what thou feelest," but after being a good bit married, you like the missus to speak distinctly, so that you have not to ask two or three times over what the dickens she's talking about.

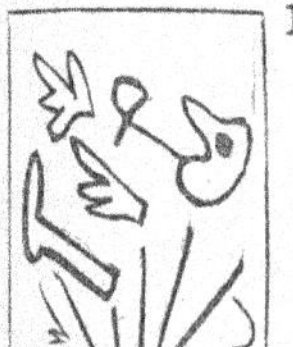

I WOULD not for the world advise kind-hearted persons who like to give money to the sufferers from a colliery explosion to withhold their charity; it would be almost as unreasonable as if we interfered with a collier who removed the top of his lamp when he wanted to light his pipe, as one JONES, of Merthyr Tydvil, did within a few yards of a " blower." JONES has been summoned, but is missing just now; but he might have been more missing still, and it would not have surprised me.

SLOPER,
Pictorial Moralist.

7.6 Marie Duval (1875) 'Crimes and Disasters (From a Sloperian Point of View.)', *Judy, or the London Serio-comic Journal*, Volume 17, p. 39

7.7 Marie Duval (1877) 'To a Michaelmas Goose', *Judy, or the London Serio-comic Journal*, Volume 21, p. 254

of his gestural and therefore abstract thought-journey. 'What is 'modern' about Durer is the way in which the hand is no longer directed by the idea but by perception in time' (van Alphen 2018: 113). Van Alphen goes on to explain that this is both an abstract and almost metaphysical manifestation (related to Durer's own notion of a kind of divine inspiration imbuing drawing in particular) and also simply the practice of incorporating what another artist might suppress: 'Durer [...] makes the most of the effects of mistakes; he allows all his lines, both the successful and unsuccessful, to breathe life into his self-portrait' (van Alphen 2018: 113).

One might well observe the same practice in Rembrandt's drawings or Pontormo's graphic investigations and I argue that it is present in Duval's work and this accounts for the effect of modernity when viewing her cartoons on the pages of *Judy* among her more precise contemporaries. In this sense, as with Durer, Duval's gestural drawings can be usefully investigated by reference to the intransitive work not only of cartoonists/fine artists such as Purple Ronnie or David Shrigley but also of recent abstract expressionists such as Cy Twombly.[9]

Drawing as performance

In his discussion of Cy Twombly, Barthes observes: 'The artist [...] is a performer of gestures by definition. He wants to produce an effect, but at the same time he couldn't care less' (Del Roscio 2002: 90). This is precisely what Duval achieves here and in the Sloper drawings, giving a vivid sense of the performance of her hand creating the fluid lines, but upholding the conceit that Sloper is wanting to enhance his verbal reporting whilst, in terms of the 'quality' of the drawing, simply not caring (or even noticing its chaotic relationship to draughtsmanship).

This itself is the result of Duval's artful puppetry of the narrative: the visual image is the result of Sloper's carefully delineated character and the alcoholic haze in which he permanently lives and therefore inevitably draws.[10] However, there is something even more theatrical in Duval's work, since the line has a sense of unfolding without 'caring less' but also with a gauche artfulness. As Barthes writes of Twombly, 'the essence [of his images] is neither form nor usage but simply gesture – the gesture that produces it *by allowing it to happen*: a garble, almost a smudge, a negligence' (Del Roscio 2002: 89).

This typically insightful comment suggests the acting commonplace that a theatre performance cannot be executed 'consciously'. Rather, the preparatory work must be done but the performance will only unfold in a convincing way quite specifically by allowing it to happen.[11] In this sense Duval's work is a perfect graphic expression of archetypal character in performance, as in the structure of her drawing she enshrines the principle of letting go, the nexus at which as Barthes suggests that drawing intersects with performance (in contrast to painting, which can be manipulated 'post hoc').

Another contemporary artist who illuminates this area of practice is Trisha Brown. Unlike Pollock, whose movement while dripping paint was subsequently defined as dance-related, Brown is a dancer who consciously transcribes her physical movement into gestural drawing. Kertess writes tellingly about her ability to write 'page space as stage space' (cited in Butler and De Zegher 2010: 193). Brown makes videos of her performing her artworks and defines her work as evolving 'into a practice separate from her dance work but parallel with it and originating kinaesthetically in the same place: her body' (Butler and De Zegher 2010: 192).

If Duval's sweeping lines resolve into figures, or at the least represent the abstract nature of explosions or falling bodies, there is nonetheless a sense that in their freedom they are translating a dancer's sensibility into a graphic form just as 'Brown developed a kind of drawing made using her body to push charcoal around on large sheets'. The almost crude or primitive coupling of body against and on paper, the use of the limbs literally as tools is both romantic, in its desire to give mark making a status of authenticity, and oddly transgressive, yielding a visual object that is genetically part drawing, part performance' (Butler and De Zegher 2010: 193). This practice is clearly far more consciously determined than Duval's (and in some measure an investigation of the free female form as mark maker). Nonetheless, within the cultural signifiers of Duval's drawn world her manipulation of line is undoubtedly 'transgressive', and it is arguable that through this combination of transitive fluidity and conceptual character drawing she also achieves 'a visual object [...] part drawing, part performance'.

Where Butler describes Brown's marks with approval as 'almost crude or primitive', Duval's shapes are likewise crude. Barthes, again in relation to Twombly, provides insight into the notion that the abstract or in this specific case graffiti-related lines he is reviewing are not childish, but rather the result of a sophisticated application of graphic freedom. Writing of the lettering which appears in Twombly's works he points out that the drawing is not childish as 'a child applies himself, presses carefully, rounds things out, sticks out his tongue' (Del Roscio: 89). Neither Ally Sloper nor his shadow amanuensis is being childish in this sense. Rather, the drawings in rejecting artistic convention in favour of gestural fluidity, succeed in abandoning worked structure in favour of the gestural mark. The drawings are eloquently inexpert, in the service of character, rather than childish: a negligence depicting Negligence.

Yet within this, just as Barthes gives Twombly's work the designation 'extremely delicate' there is a consistent appropriateness to Duval's 'crude' sketches, which communicates exactly the information required for the effect. Therefore, like the contemporary cartoonist and fine artist David Shrigley (who on the one hand has published in popular newspapers and on the other exhibited at the Hayward Gallery) Duval has also created a graphic style for her character, which 'communicates as simply and directly as possible' (Lausen 2012: 27). Lausen could easily be talking about Duval when he writes of Shrigley 'rather than appropriating the existing comic genre for use in art, he defines his own aesthetic' (Lausen 2012: 27). More strikingly still, Shrigley has often referred to his graphic personality as a 'character' in a way that is startlingly like Duval's strategy in the Sloper drawings 150 years earlier. In an interview with David Eggers, Shrigley made the following comments:

DAVID SHRIGLEY:
I don't really understand why anybody is really that interested in me either. I think the parts that I create are more interesting. They generally are kind of, you know, slightly psychotic, dysfunctional, sociopaths.

DAVID EGGERS:
You said before that when you're drawing, you're taking on a role. That is, that there's a persona, almost, that you've generated who is behind your work. That's something that not everyone knows about or assumes – that the artist is often shaping a persona that's different than the artist's everyday self. (Lausen 2012: 149)

Shrigley is perceived by press as well as critics, as making 'a kind of visual ventriloquism' (Cumming 2012). The phrase, as Grennan emphasises in Chapter 6, describes Duval's strategies well. Thus, the fact that aside from these drawings, Duval cultivated a persona that manifested in her making work under the pseudonym 'Noir' (or rather a second pseudonym since Duval was an already adopted stage name) as well as consistently dressing in black (Clayton 1876: 332), suggests strongly that she was indeed one of the artists 'shaping a persona' that Eggers, perhaps curiously, suggests happens 'often'.

In a very real sense Shrigley is here describing 'acting drawing'. This is a specific reduction of the idea of gesture in drawing. In one of the clearest expositions of this notion, that is, of gesture in drawing as the expression of performance, Newman explains her ideas in a conversation with Catherine De Zegher from 2003. Newman defines two types of gesture in drawings: 'I would want to make a distinction between the actions of gesture as encountered in theatre and in images depicting theatrical acts, on the one hand, and as registered in drawings, on the other' (De Zegher 2003: 75). What she means is that there is a theatricality in certain drawings, which refer to, and in a sense are frozen as, potential theatrical acts. She gives an example of a Barbara Hepworth drawing of a medical operation. Whilst this is not theatrical in a literal sense, Hepworth arranges the figures in a theatrically gestural set-up.

Duval does this very frequently in many of her drawings, both in the sense of being influenced by specific theatrical spectacle (see Chapter 8) but also by her placement and setting of characters in entirely Hepworthian theatricalised configurations. Duval frequently uses this strategy, for example in 'Another Bad Case at a Barbers' (Duval 1877b) where characters are carefully juxtaposed in stillness with slight differences in the first three frames followed by a sudden contrasting closeness as the barber leaps forward to shave the unfortunate customer's head. Another notable use of imagery derived specifically from stage proxemics occurs in the earlier 'A Tale of a Tooth' (Duval 1870r; Figure 7.8). Here in a strip clearly inspired by Wilhelm Busch's 1862 *Der hohle Zahn* (Grennan, Sabin and Waite 2018: 10), Duval creates far more theatrical imagery than her source, especially in the two lower central images. These depict action hidden by the back view of the actor and subsequently as the 'torture' gets worse the action, farce-like, is hidden behind a curtain out of which arm and foot flail.

However, according to Newman, the other way that gesture emerges is in the more Barthesian sense of it being 'registered in drawings'. Newman is thinking of the way the mark registers the gesture in the rich tradition of abstract expressionist work initiated by Pollock and including Twombly. She goes on to give a further insight by suggesting that certain gestures registered in drawing incite a kind of 'audience participation'. She refers to Leger's drawing *Mechanical Elements 101* where the shape and position of a handle specifically invites an imagined gesture from the viewer, movement that is 'gesturally implied in the object for the viewer to grasp' (De Zegher 2003: 76). Her interviewer agrees, adding that since language invites gesture, 'we gesture when we speak', so does the visual (De Zegher 2003: 76).

One gesture that is specifically invited in the reader by the Sloper character drawings is that of the wandering, spontaneous line, a line which depicts play and children at play that is particularly vividly. Thus we see Sloper often being teased and chased by children, when 'taking one of those walks of his' (Duval 1876g; Figure 7.9 and see Duval 1875h), impotently berating the cheeky office boy and being followed in mock procession. In such drawings, as Newman suggests, we are invited mentally to abandon ourselves through the traversing of her lines into the amoral world of desires. It is in this play that we become in Newman's terms 'gesturally implied' (De Zegher 2003: 76).

Tormey goes even further than Newman in suggesting that, at a fundamental level, the very process of drawing is performative. She considers all drawing can be defined as performative, saying she and her colleagues have chosen to exhibit drawings 'with an emphasis on how the process of making the drawing contributes to its content, a concept

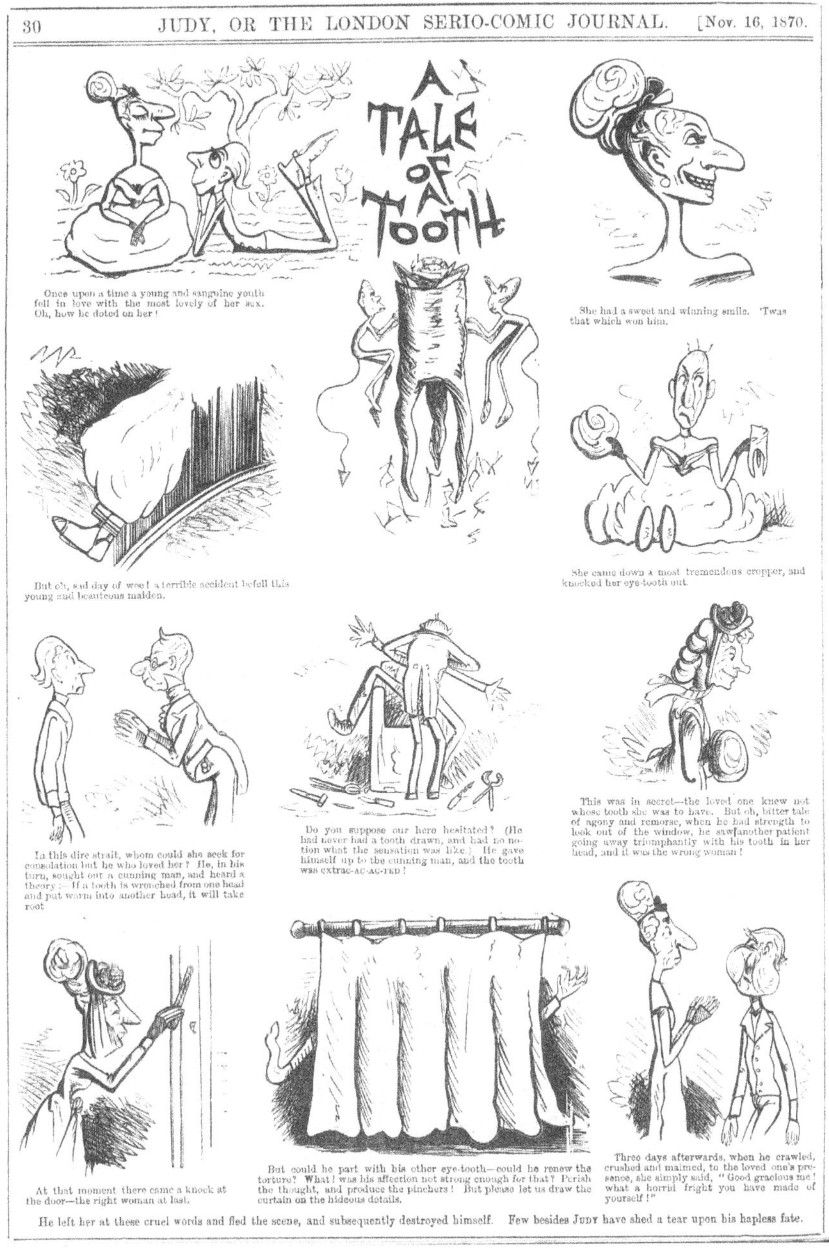

7.8 Marie Duval (1870) 'A Tale of a Tooth', *Judy, or the London Serio-comic Journal*, Volume 8, p. 30

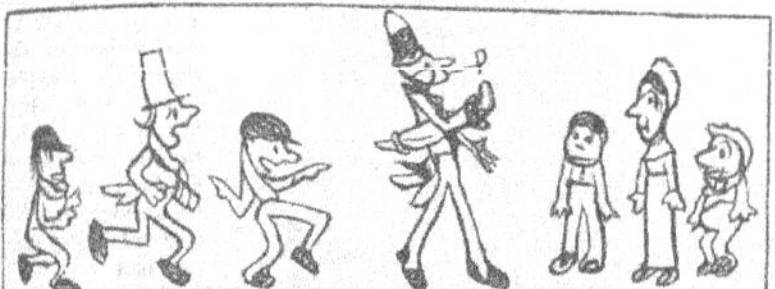

MAR. 22, 1876.] JUDY, OR THE LONDON SERIO-COMIC JOURNAL. 235

CRIMES AND DISASTERS.
(From a Sloperian Point of View,)

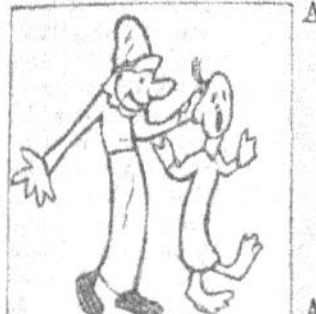

A FEW remarks about things generally may come in here. There has been another fasting girl lately. A. SLOPER is informed that, at the instigation of a local authority, she has been pulled out of bed by the ear and well slapped. She now calls for her five meals a day quite regular.

A BOY at Blackheath stole a penny-worth of figs the other day, and when pursued by the police, jumped out of a third-floor window· He promised not to do it again, so he was not prosecuted.

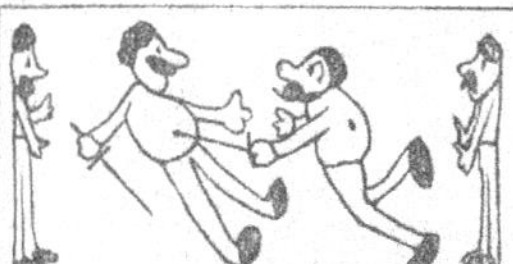

THE French correspondent of the *Daily Telegraph* recently gave a terrible account of a duel to the death between two French noblemen, one a duke, who having slain him, dipped his handkerchief in the gore of his antagonist, and smearing his face with it, fell down dead, saying that he left it as an heirloom to his children. The names of the noblemen are not given, but I am told, upon first-class authority, one of them was le Duc DE BRUMMI, who thus perished tragically beneath the green-wood tree.

I CALL this rather a hard case. A gentleman in the iron trade took it into his head the other day to borrow an organ-grinder's organ, and go about playing tunes. Some one with no music in his soul looked up the iron merchant, and the inspector (also with no music in his soul) said the prisoner was drunk. The prisoner denied this indignantly, and paid for a surgeon to attend, and the surgeon who attended certified that he *was* drunk. That was a nice thing for the surgeon to do, after getting his good money. Perhaps it was true, though; I never thought of that.

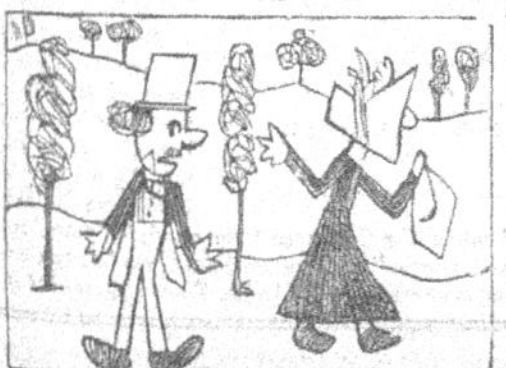

WHERE'S Chivalry? What has become of Romance? Has anybody lately heard anything of Love's young dream? The young man who invited the young woman to fetch a walk alonger him amidst the flowery 'edges-rows and shady by-lanes of 'Ighgate, and then gave her in charge for stealing his purse, with three pounds ten and two-pence three farthings in it, and went home afterwards to find it was on his own mantelpiece all the while, says he is sorry; but I ask again, What about Chivalry, Romance, and Love's young dream? I'm anxious to know.

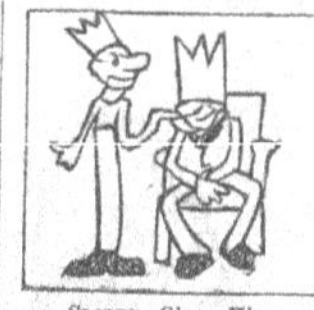

IT would appear, from a recent romantic divorce case, that gipsy brides give a good bit of trouble sometimes taming. The days when A. SLOPER went gipsying are not of recent date. At the time the Gipsy Queen was fond of A. SLOPER, and wanted to make him a Gipsy King, but Mrs. SLOPER didn't like it.

SLOPER, *Zingarilar Moralist.*

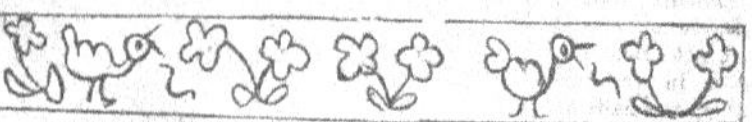

7.9   Marie Duval (1876) 'Crimes and Disasters (from a Sloperian Point of View)', *Judy, or the London Serio-comic Journal*, Volume 18, p. 235

which we describe as "performative"' (Tormey 2007: ix). In terms of our consideration of the connection between Duval as performer and Duval as actor this presents a curious problem. If all drawing is performative, then the literal status of the graphic artist as actor or non-actor arguably becomes entirely irrelevant.

However, Tormey's words also suggest a link between the way in which making a drawing is 'performed' and the 'object' of the drawing, and that would seem highly relevant to an artist who is, like Duval, finding a form to express the character of the fictional persona she is representing. The form she exploits, that is a naive scrawl made by the character himself, suggests a fine correlation between object and process, where she has 'enacted' the process of the character making a drawing and therefore memorialised it in the documentation of this process.

In this sense these particular drawings head towards the notion of drawing as memory, an idea expounded in the much referenced Derridean exposition of drawing as blindness from his *Memoirs of the Blind*. Duval makes particularly manifest the idea of drawing as 'a *memory of a trait* that speculates, as in a dream, about its own possibilities' (Derrida 1993: 3). Indeed, Derrida's emphasis on the process of drawing as movement and feeling, expressed through the metaphor of the blind, seems particularly appropriate in connection with Duval's fluid exploratory lines imagined as the scribblings of the semi-conscious drunken self-portraitist. In all her drawings, but pre-eminently in these, we see how her work 'coordinates the possibility of seeing, touching and moving' (Derrida 1993: 4). Derrida calls the moments when this is manifest 'rare and theatrical' (Derrida 1993: 4) and gives as a personal example a moment such as writing a scrawl when his attention is elsewhere. This recalls Brown's notion of allowing a gesture to happen.

Barthes's examination of line also includes some important statements of the significance of the body in relation to the drawn mark. He suggests the importance of the artist's body in art and indeed the commercialisation of art, not in the sense of carnal art, but of the mark made fundamentally by the body as constituting an 'individuality'. 'In other words' he writes, 'what one buys when one buys the work of an artist is in fact the body of the artist – we're dealing with an exchange in which we are forced to recognize contract of prostitution [*sic*] [...] What's consumed [...] is a body' (Del Roscio 2002: 97).

There are strong shades of Trisha Brown here. Duval, on the other hand, both as cartoonist and performer sits in a liminal betwixt and between space, as her work was clearly entirely commercial and about consumption, yet it was also cheap, available, printed and disposable, requiring the churning out of hundreds of images at the zenith of her career. More like Shrigley, Duval 'effectively vexes the art/non art dialectic, functioning as a kind of interstitial category' (Lausen 2012: 82) and in simple terms, like Duval 'many of Shrigley's drawings were made with publication in mind [which is] important, both in terms of their design and distribution' (Lausen 2012: 27).

In terms of occupying interstitial categories, the notion of the artist selling their body actually embraces perfectly the other gap between 'respectability' and sex work occupied by the Victorian female actor, in which Duval's citation in an actor's divorce suit represents one aspect, and her common-law marriage to an established publisher and writer another. The jobbing actor Alma Ellerslie similarly represents the issue of female actors being perceived as sex workers, believing that just by being an actor she has 'put herself in a questionable position, and it is unjust to blame people if they think I am a questionable character' (Ellerslie 1885: 100. There is an authoritative contemporary discussion in Davis 1991: 137–63). From the reviews quoted at the beginning of Chapter 3, we can make the assumption that, at her best, Duval was onstage a compelling and charismatic figure. If anything, that part of her graphic work which gives the impression that it was the most hastily thrown off and executed with the least conscious commercial zeal, suggests most strongly the gestures and physicality of the artist/performer who made it.

Performing the role of (imperfect) artist

Of course, this is not to say Duval *did* make the Sloper 'autograph' images quickly (or any other of her naive-style drawings), but it is part of their effect that we must always believe she did. What she undoubtedly did, like a successful actor, is achieve Winnicott's 'play (which is free)' rather than 'game (which is strictly ruled)', in a passage cited by Barthes (Del Roscio 2002: 99). In the course of this playing, and especially in these drawings, Duval has freed herself from any constraints of perspective or academic design, through the device of the character drawing, but also (and this is true to some extent of all her work) due to the intrinsic removal of a specified pattern. The self-portrait of Sloper only has to look as much like Sloper that it is recognisable as Sloperian, and the trope of hat and umbrella often takes care of that, sometimes in an entirely metaphorical way.

In this Duval has removed the need for her line to achieve a predetermined goal. She has achieved full representation when the scrawl gives enough hints to determine what it is, but no more than is needed to suggest the complete lack of expertise and downright laziness of its fictional creator. In this she shares Twombly's ability, according to Barthes, to avoid any sense of aggression, because her drawings have 'no goal, no model, no exigencies. It is free from *telos* and therefore free from risk' (Del Roscio: 100). In this, as in so many places in his essay, Barthes suggests an aspect of the body as inscriber of movement in marks, which is beautifully congruent with the work of the actor.

The Victorian actor was pre-eminently the subject of a cult. Actors had to represent at one moment stereotypes from melodrama and at the next moment Shakespeare roles, both of which carried a similar baggage of signs and tropes to be either represented or rejected, and yet, within this the great actors of the day were adored for their particular individual personalities and personal idiosyncrasies. Thus, contemporary reviewers of Helen Faucit complain that she 'overdid her part' yet was 'eminently successful' (*The Times*, cited in Pascoe 1880: 135), whilst Edward Sothern's celebrated performance of

Lord Dundreary was exemplary in being perceived by audiences as both exaggerated and underplayed, 'so strange and yet so natural' as the American reviewer of *The Atheneum* wrote: 'We are, therefore, disposed to believe that Mr Sothern, as an eccentric actor, is a man of no ordinary genius' ('Haymarket' 1861: 12).

In these drawings the conceit of Sloper's authorship removes the 'telos' of realism. By doing so, Duval allowed herself to let go. In an analogous way, Victorian actors give themselves the freedom simultaneously to be themselves and to be someone entirely other. Because of this, we can ask, how could performers 'correct themselves' when there was no original that they were working to be: the audience has come to see Helen Faucit, Mrs Kemble, Henry Irving or Edward Sothern and not someone else. Similarly, for Duval in drawing these works, we can ask with Barthes, 'How could one 'correct oneself' when there is no drawing master?' (Del Roscio 2002: 100).

Shrigley also allows himself complete freedom from correction. His practice (described in detail in Lausen 2012) consists of making hundreds of drawings at a sitting. He never corrects or redraws any of these ('there are certain rules to what I do, like I'm not allowed to re-draw or anything, it just is what it is', Lausen 2012: 150) but instead chooses the small number that work from this extensive production of 'first thoughts'. Thus far from correcting himself he deliberately publishes works that 'are often a bit haphazard, slightly misshapen, or like parodies of ideal forms' (Lausen 2012: 30). Another word, which seems appropriate to describe Duval's work, 'amateur', is used with approval by Lausen in describing Shrigley's work:

> The overall impression of these works is thus one of amateurism, of a certain degree of technical competence, but with an accidental or deliberately imperfect aesthetic. For Shrigley, it is a way of animating the inanimate, of breathing life into his objects: 'I like the personality of things being a bit half-finished, of basically *having* a personality'. (Lausen 2012: 30–1)

Duval exploits exactly the same device to give a personality to the Sloper drawings, but in her work the meanings are layered: the drawings have a personality owing to their being (apparently) spontaneous, but are also, theatrically, presented as the productions of a specific personality, that of the character Sloper himself. Several of the images reveal further levels of parody, such as in the images of paintings at Royal Academy Summer Exhibitions seen by Sloper (see Chapter 6) or in the depictions of narratives, which themselves parody contemporary social or political events (for example 'The Kenealy Procession'; Figure 7.10).

As a cartoonist of social mores and, in a broad sense, political events, Shrigley exploits similar levels of meaning and interpretation in his newspaper cartoons and popular collections. In both we see what Dillon calls 'an absence of attitude – a cultivated innocence, a tireless indolence, and openness to discovery' (Dillon 2009: 8) and what Barthes summarises as conjoining 'infancy and culture, drift and invention' (Del Roscio 2002: 94).

For Tormey it is a theme of the whole of contemporary drawing that there is 'a leaning towards a conscious naivety, perhaps, and a denial of the signs of "good drawing"' (Tormey

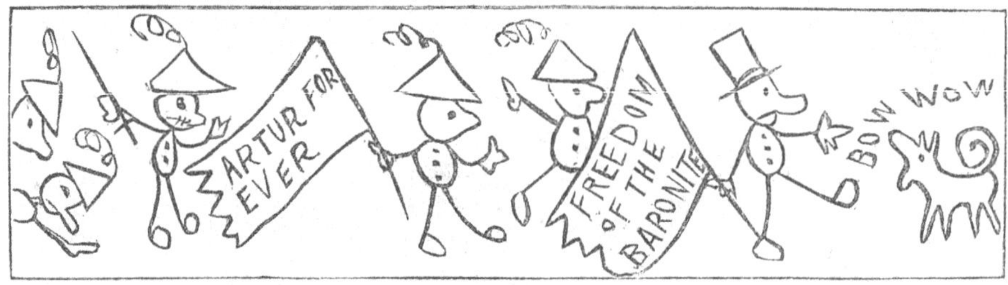

The first part of the Procession bearing Banners, breathing defiance.

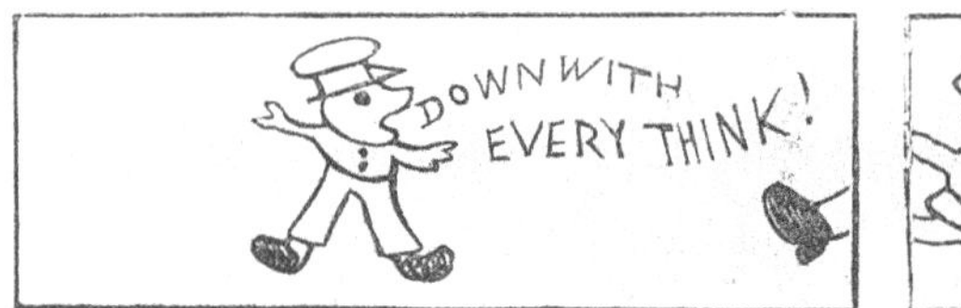

The Populace excited.

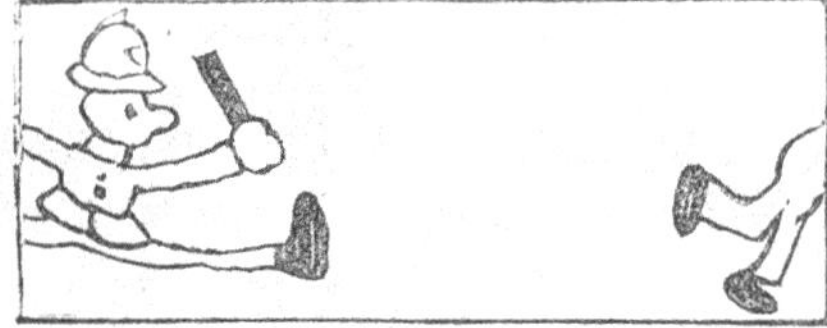

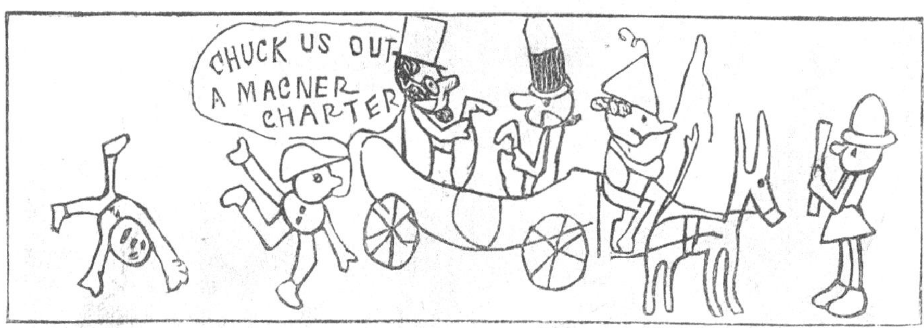

SLOPER and K. borne onwards 'midst deafening cheers.   The meddlesome Police interfere.

7.10   Marie Duval (1876) 'The Kenealy Procession – From a Sloperian Point of View', *Judy, or the London Serio-comic Journal*, Volume 18, p. 185

2007: ix). It is arguable that Duval's appeal to the twenty-first-century reader lies in this area. Her familiarity with the 'great' art of her period shown by her journalistic tendency to report (through parody) on contemporary fine artists showcasing themselves in the Royal Academy Exhibitions, is combined with a career in contemporary popular culture strictly comparable to the practice of Shrigley, Saul Steinberg or Marcel Dzama. Like them she brought word and image together in the same frame, bringing lettering to life (Duval 1881c; Figure 7.11), incorporating characters into the titles of panels, such as 'The Very First Original Oyster Eater' (Duval 1873q), or inscribing words in visual images (Duval 1877c; Figure 7.7).

FEB. 2, 1881.] JUDY, OR THE LONDON SERIO-COMIC JOURNAL. 57

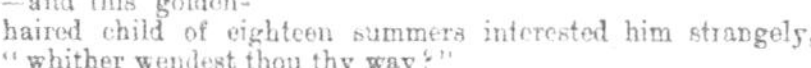

CRIMES AND DISASTERS
FROM A SLOPERIAN POINT OF VIEW.

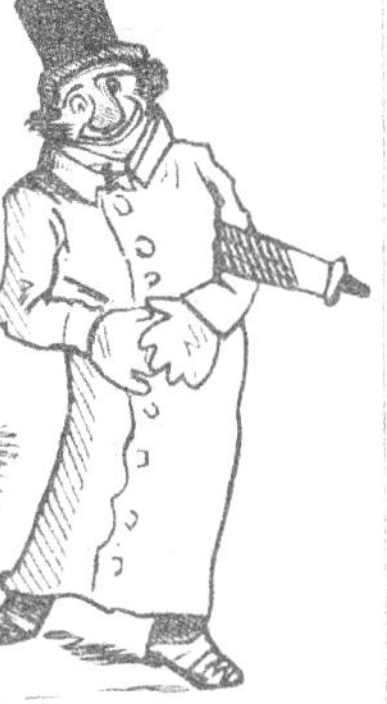

"THIS," said he, "is the kind of weather that I thoroughly enjoy."

He was a hale and hearty fellow. His chest was broad. His big cheeks as red as pippins. His voice sonorous and deep. A JOHN BROWDIE sort of man, and it did your heart good to look at him and listen to what he said. The snow was falling fast, the north-east wind was raging, and the frost-bitten *littérateur* stood knee deep in a drift and listened.

The JOHN BROWDIE man was on the other side of the drift, stamping his thick boots upon the pavement and beating together his warmly gloved hands—the picture of health.

"I am told that it comes inconvenient to the poorer class of people," murmured the Eminent. "According to the newspapers they're here and there subjected to a certain amount of annoyance in consequence of the continued frost, but most likely it's their nasty perverseness. Nothing ever suits the lower orders."

"You are perfectly right," said JOHN BROWDIE. "If they're cold, why don't they keep on the move, sir, as I do?"

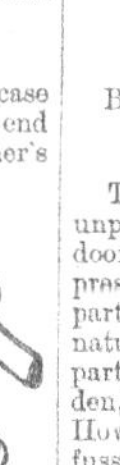

"It's their brutal obstinacy in persisting in not wrapping themselves up I can't get over," said the Eminent.

"Splendid weather," cried JOHN BROWDIE. "Healthy, appetizing weather. It's freezing again, I'm glad to see. Good-day to you."

Saying which he strode forward, stepped on the round iron lid of a coal cellar, and—yesterday A. SLOPER saw them take his leg off at St. Thomas's.

When Mr. BOFFIN took his seat on Monday last, the first case brought before him was that of a man who had bitten the end of another man's nose off. It was argued by the prisoner's counsel that the man's nose was even now of abnormal length, and that, in fact, what had happened had improved his appearance rather than otherwise. His Worship, however, who is himself pretty well off for nose, thought that this was a matter of opinion, and asked the man with the half nose what he had to say about it. The man said he had no idea, not being in the habit of looking in a glass once in a month. He had, in point of fact, quite forgotten what he used to look like when he had all his nose. He, however, was not prepared to say upon his oath that he thought much of his personal appearance with the sticking plaster on. Mr. BOFFIN said he thought the man seemed a very undecided sort of man, and that, perhaps, he had better go home and ask his wife.

The case was here adjourned until the afternoon, when the man came back to say that he hadn't got a wife and had been unsuccessful in the attempts he had made to get married since the morning. Mr. BOFFIN reprimanded the man severely for wasting the time of the Court and bound the biter over to keep the peace for six months. The bitten man then asked whether he couldn't have the piece back a little sooner, the biting man having stated that he, himself, had really no use for it. Here the Court was cleared and the Usher shut out by accident.

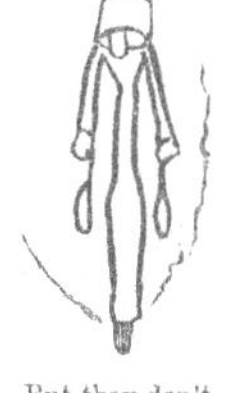

'Twas afternoon time and the sun was shining on the beauteous snow-covered earth, and A. SLOPER, coming out of one of them, was wiping his mouth upon his sleeve, as 'tis his wont to do. Then she passed. "Fair Skatist," the old man said in soothing tones—he was in a paternal mood—and this golden-haired child of eighteen summers interested him strangely, "whither wendest thou thy way?"

She said, "Mamma says I'm not to talk to strangers."

He answered, "Your mamma is evidently a superior woman; I should like to be acquainted with her. But 'tis but a simple question I would ask thee, maiden. Where art thou going, and wilt thou skate when thou gettest there?"

She said, "If you don't go away I will speak to a policeman."

And thus is it ever. The simple object of the *littérateur* was to ascertain whether the young lady really had any intention of using the skates she carried. He is convinced she had not. This is not the first time that the *littérateur* has stopped and questioned the fair carriers of skates, but upon no occasion has he ever been able to obtain a straightforward answer. If all the young ladies about who carry skates really skated there wouldn't be ice enough to hold them. It's a big sham.

But they don't.

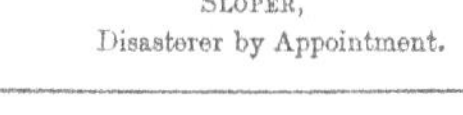

There has been, as was anticipated, unpleasantness about that man next door's speckled hen's egg. The present Mrs. SLOPER is particularly partial to a new-laid egg, and very naturally, as the hen flew over the party wall and laid it in our garden, had the egg for breakfast. However, as the man made such a fuss about it, we said he should have his egg restored to him, and sent out for a nice one from the shop. This, unfortunately, Mrs. SLOPER broke whilst endeavouring to give the shell a new-laid look with the nail-brush. And now the man is holloaing over the wall, about another egg we had to buy. There are people you can't get on neighbourly with, try what you will.

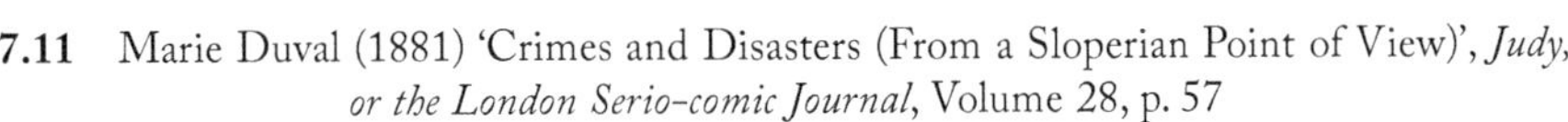

SLOPER,
Disasterer by Appointment.

7.11 Marie Duval (1881) 'Crimes and Disasters (From a Sloperian Point of View)', *Judy, or the London Serio-comic Journal*, Volume 28, p. 57

Notes

1 Del Roscio 2002: 97.
2 For clarity, I have added the original publication dates of these works to that of the latest modern editions. The latter dates can be found in the Bibliography.
3 Stage proxemics is the study of the placing of actors and use of space onstage.
4 A portrait showing a clear or exaggerated emotional expression.
5 A term for the domestic dramas of Thomas Robertson, of which *Caste* (1867) is perhaps the best known today, which were produced by the Bancrofts at the refurbished Prince of Wales's Theatre. Duval makes reference to these in one of her cartoons (see Figure 3.11).
6 Salvini was an actor who inspired Stanislavski to develop his system. The Russian director quotes him and refers to his performance of Othello extensively in *Building a Character* (2013b).
7 I would argue a relationship to cartoons here, or at least illustrations in narratives such as novels or short stories, rather than other text/image combinations such as explanatory manuals, railway timetables or advertisements; the reason being that the image is designed to develop both character and narrative, regardless of its stylistic genre, which here is realist rather than 'cartoony'.
8 The 'respectability' or otherwise of female actors particularly was not simple at this period, and the pattern of relationships enjoyed by a celebrity such as Ellen Terry shows how Duval's private life was far from unique. As is suggested by Moss's diary, bending the proprieties of marriage was no bar to ultimate respect and even ennoblement (Terry, Duval's exact contemporary, was made a dame in 1925).
9 Playing Devil's advocate, of course all marks bear the trace of their maker. I understand van Alphen to be expressing the ends of a useful spectrum from marks where the movement of the author's 'hand' is foregrounded, to where it is worked over, smoothed out, concealed.
10 Simon Grennan has described this as 'sensational ventriloquism' and gives a detailed analysis of the effect in Chapter 6.
11 Stanislavski's description of the 'conscious/unconscious' process of acting is in my experience universally understood by creative practitioners in any field. His 'system' is designed to provide a conscious structure to support it, but fundamentally Stanislavski requires an unconscious unfolding of performance, moment to moment: 'Sometimes [feelings, will and mind] go into action spontaneously, subconsciously. On such favourable occasions we should give ourselves up to the flow of their activity' (Stanisvaski 2013a: 233–4). The notion is similar to Csikszentmihalyi's celebrated notion of 'flow' (see Csikszentmihalyi 1992).

8

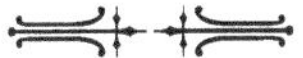

The role of spectacle in
Marie Duval's work

Julian Waite

Fascinated by spectacle, the Victorians flocked to the ring to see acts that spoke to the eye. (Assael 2005: 1)

Speaking to the eye

In Chapter 3 I examined the literal influences of the theatre on Marie Duval's drawings, considering her biography, stage appearances and knowledge of front and backstage life and how this influenced the subject matter of her work. In this chapter I consider more archaic forms of theatre, which have now either disappeared or remain in altered or fossilised forms. In doing so I concentrate on several popular forms of theatre, most of which involved spectacle either in terms of stage mechanics or human athleticism, not because Duval is known to have worked in these areas (since, apart from pantomime, there is little evidence she did) but because such theatre forms involved the manipulation of bodies in a way entirely unrecorded in the usual drawing tropes of the nineteenth century, arising as they did from classical training and fine art models.

I not only intend to show that Duval has left an important historical record of Victorian spectacle but also suggest how she might have been influenced by the spectacular per-formances of her day in developing her vivid gestural style. As an actor and dancer, Marie Duval would have been aware of how her body spoke to the eyes of her audience. She was also intimately acquainted with the stage mechanics which allowed her (and her fellow performers) to display themselves in public. Her drawing explicitly and, I argue, implicitly references the performativity of bodies in display and in motion. Consistent with this, we find in her work themes and structures which relate more or less directly to spectacular and sensational theatrical activity, such as falling bodies (often depicted as if suspended from wires) and panels which may owe their structure to the tableaux of 'poses vivants' or pantomime transformation scenes.

187

The transformation scene

Pantomimes in Duval's period often involved complex transformation scenes at the end of the piece where producers vied to out-stage competitors. Duval, with her background in pantomime (see Chapter 3) would certainly have taken part in transformation scenes, although neither of the pantomimes she is recorded as performing in, *The Sleeping Beauty in the Wood* (1868) and *The Beast and the Beauty* (1869), used the convention. The pantomime that followed her first success at the Surrey Theatre (performing in *Ruth* in 1871) on the other hand, undoubtedly did. This 'Grand Pantomime', which was called *My Son Jack*, continued the tradition of pantomime for which, along with melodrama, this theatre was particularly known (Davis and Emeljanow 2001: 32).

Reviewers found the transformation scene especially satisfactory, the *Daily Telegraph* writer reporting that this 'most elaborate transformation scene, effectively closed the entertainments' ('Surrey Theatre' 1871a: 3) and the *Illustrated Times* critic, who presumably travelled from north of the river, declaring that: 'The transformation scene of the Surrey pantomime is worth the trouble of a long journey. It is certainly the best I have seen this year' ('The Theatrical Lounger' 1871: 123). The *Evening Standard* reviewer was even more effusive:

> The pantomime forms the second feature of the programme, terminating with the grand transformation scene entitled the Nativity of Venus. Anything more elaborately gorgeous than this specimen of Mr Charles Brew's scenic powers would be hard to conceive, and every lover of fairy splendour would be well repaid by a visit to the house if even this were the only attraction. ('Surrey Theatre' 1871b: 3)

What the lover of fairy splendour was actually seeing was a slow reveal of an entire fairy landscape, gradually peopled, accompanied by music and lighting effects and ending with some sort of tableau where a central figure was surrounded and supported by lesser figures. This unfolding is obviously difficult to depict graphically in a single image, and nineteenth-century illustrations often show only the arrangement of the final tableau. There is a contemporary verbal description by Percy Fitzgerald from *The World Behind the Scenes*:

> All will recall in some elaborate transformation scene how quietly and gradually it is evolved. First the 'gauzes' lift slowly one behind the other – perhaps the most pleasing of all scenic effects – giving glimpses of 'the Realms of Bliss', seen beyond in a tantalizing fashion. Then is revealed a kind of half-glorified country, clouds and banks, evidently concealing much. Always a sort of pathetic and at the same time exultant strain rises, and is repeated as the changes go on. Now we hear the faint tinkle – signal to those aloft on the 'bridges' to open more glories. Now some of the banks begin to part slowly, showing realms of light, with a few divine beings – fairies – rising slowly here and there. More breaks beyond and fairies rising, with a pyramid of these ladies beginning to mount slowly in the centre. Thus it goes on, the lights streaming on full, in every colour and from every quarter, in the richest effulgence. In some of the more daring efforts, the 'femmes suspendus' seem to float in the air or rest on the frail support of sprays or branches of trees. While, finally, perhaps, at the

back of all, the most glorious paradise of all will open, revealing the pure empyrean itself, and some fair spirit aloft in a cloud among the stars, the apex of all. (Fitzgerald 1881: 89)

An example of this final figure is provided by a contemporary engraving of the final scene from the 1851 production of *Mr and Mrs Briggs: or Punch's Festival* at Astley's (Figure 8.1). Originally published in the *Illustrated London News* ('Christmas Pantomimes, Burlesques, Etc' 1851: 8), this shows a regal figure on a globe surrounded by chariots led by horses and ostriches, with genuflecting maidens in attendance.

As an image this is stilted and rigidly symmetrical, but the viewer can imagine that in reality this would have been astonishing, especially given the close proximity of the proscenium arch, which indicates the height these actors achieved. It becomes clear that many of Duval's panels made for festive occasions (particularly Valentine's Day and Christmas) are parodies of these final ascensions, often but not exclusively featuring Ally Sloper rather than the chief fairy or Venus of the originals.

The imagery of these transformations hint at classical models, whilst also being structured by the stage mechanics of the day. For example Fitzgerald explains that aside from 'irons'

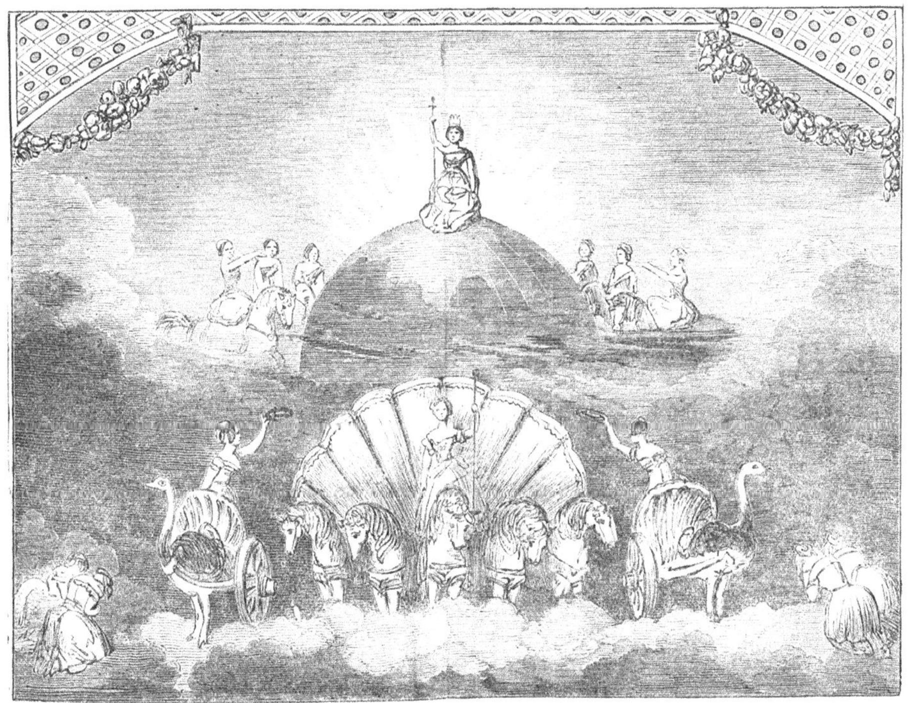

8.1 Anonymous (1851) 'Astley's – Scene from the Pantomime of 'Mr. and Mrs. Briggs; or, Punch's Festival', *Illustrated London News*, Saturday 27 December 1851, p. 8

to hold individuals suspended 'large platforms [...] are the essential portions of every "transformation", consisting of a vast stage rising slowly from below, and suspended by ropes and counterpoises', and it is clearly evident that the composition of the Astley's scene is to a great extent governed by this (Fitzgerald 1881: 90).

Similarly, Duval herself, whilst referring no doubt to suspended scenes she had witnessed or even taken part in, might have combined in her imagery reference to classical imagery (or contemporary imagery which referred to the classical) or indeed be unconsciously referring to a classical influence from the stage designer whose work she is parodying. So in *Judy* on 14 February 1877 (Duval 1877d; Figure 8. 2) she takes the opportunity of Valentine's Day to parody Ally Sloper as Cupid, surrounded by tumbling women.

Her Christmas image the same year (Duval 1877e) shows a more naturalistic character: Pettigrew, surrounded by a ring of floating fairies, which is explicitly related to pantomime 'fairy visions' in the text. Both these images show floating figures reminiscent of Baroque cupids but actually consisting of flying barmaids, creditors, bags of money and Christmas puddings. Thus, the most immediate reference for Marie Duval would surely have been the pantomime tableau, and may even have been her own experience of being suspended, strapped in a theatrical 'iron' as described by Fitzgerald:

> The ingenuity exhibited in the aerial displays – girls apparently floating in the air at great heights – has to be supplemented by extraordinary precautions to prevent accidents. These 'irons' as they are called, to which the performers are strapped, are [...] secured by extending them below the stage in the shape of long levers, which take their share of the weight. (Fitzgerald 1881: 90)

Although a little distorted by camera tricks, which mar the charm of the sort of effects which entranced the audiences at The Surrey, an idea of this sort of imagery and technology can be seen in the British Film Institute's compilation of early twentieth-century French shorts in *Fairy Tales: Early Colour Films from Pathe* (Pathe 2012). For example, a rising tableau of fairy women can be seen in *Le Faune* (1908) using imagery that still resembles Fitzgerald's descriptions, despite being performed thirty years later.

The use of tinting in these early films reflects the care with which colour was utilised in stage presentations, as Fitzgerald shows in his account of the final moments of a pantomime transformation. His description reveals that these scenes clearly functioned as autonomous moments of spectacle and were applauded in order to credit their creators:

> Then all motion ceases; the work is complete; the fumes of crimson, green and blue fire begin to rise at the wings; the music bursts into a crash of exultation; and, possibly to the general disenchantment, a burly man in a black frock steps out from the side and bows awkwardly. (Fitzgerald 1881: 90–1)[1]

The Pathe films, presumably through technological restraints, fail to convey the size of the spectacle that is being described here. Not only would these scenes require the whole depth and width of the stage (Southern 1970: 24ff) and a corresponding 'carpenter scene' whilst they were erected[2] (Fitzgerald 1881: 96) but for pantomime or Shakespeare

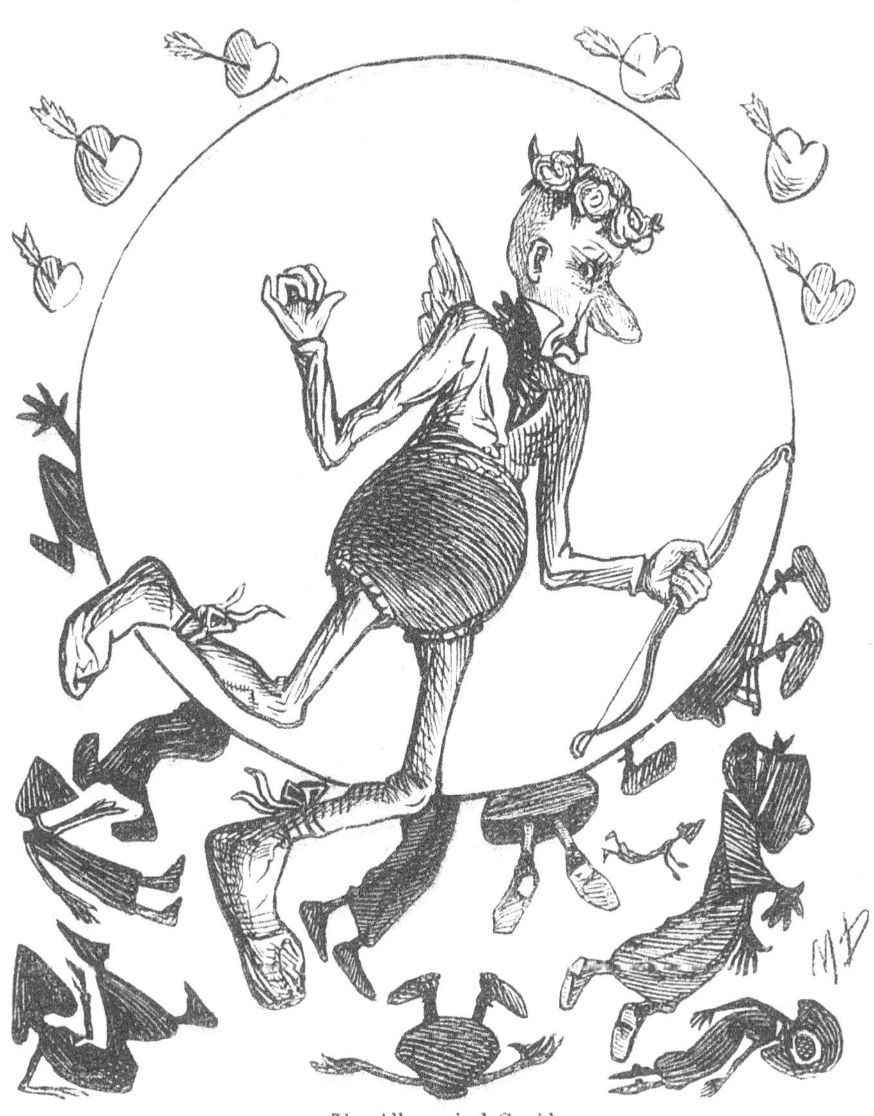

8.2 Marie Duval (1877) 'Valentines From a Sloperian Point of View', *Judy, or the London Serio-comic Journal*, Volume 20, p. 182

productions featuring crowd scenes and effects, literally hundreds of seasonal staff would be employed, both as supernumeraries and to operate stage machinery (Booth 1991: 34–5).

Fitzgerald reports that a particular effect in Offenbach's *L'Africaine* appears to the audience to have required 'seven or eight hundred [...] to produce this effect; and yet on counting it proved that there were little over two hundred' (Fitzgerald 1881: 106). Sometimes such extravagant effects lasted 'but a few minutes' (Fitzgerald 1881: 109). This sense of crowding is strong in Duval's work, where she will often provide numerous flying figures. So, in *Judy* on 4 March 1885 (Duval 1885b) she draws masses of stick men to convey something akin to the description of a particularly effective crowd scene from Covent Garden's *Babil and Bijou:*

> Then all descended and entered on a kind of fantastic promenade, crossing and recrossing – people of the early centuries finding partners in those of a later age. It was half a dream, half a nightmare. (Fitzgerald 1881: 109)

Pantomime characters

Aside from her tableaux, which may be an indirect reference to her work in pantomime, there are a number of Duval's cartoons that reference pantomime effects more or less explicitly. She is particularly fond of the girl as butterfly or other winged insect, which features not only in her pantomime parodies, but also in more elegant form in several of her Noir[3] drawings. A particularly interesting case of the former is her cartoon 'Pantomimical' from 22 December 1875 (Duval 1875e; Figure 8.3), the year that *Cinderella* was the pantomime staged at Drury Lane. A formal illustration by David Friston of a scene from this performance appears in the *Illustrated Sporting and Dramatic News* of 8 January 1876, showing fairy-like characters being menaced by a tribe of insects (Friston 1875; Figure 8.4). Given that Duval also drew insects it seems possible that she was referring to this very pantomime and it is tempting to think her backstage observations might be based on life. It is particularly appealing to think of the character of the cricket with her little son dressed as a beetle being a piece of observation.

In contrast to Friston's image, where the evil insects are dehumanised, the illustrator conspiring with the costume designer to make their feet and hands impossibly insect-like, Duval presents the actors backstage in wrinkled costumes and showing human weariness. Sloper, also as a cricket, seems to be springing up through some sort of trap (although the meaning of the multiple lines around his feet is obscure), whilst Duval's other characters express a curiously twentieth-century interest in motivation (an actor asking what her insect is supposed to do with its outstretched wings when tired), tired children (the beetle mentioned above) and the disgruntlement of performing as a vegetable.

Indeed, the range of activity depicted in this single set of drawings is quite remarkable, covering authors, costume designers and comedians as well as adult and child actors. Actors in 'skin' roles are even present in the shape of the three monkeys. Elsewhere Duval

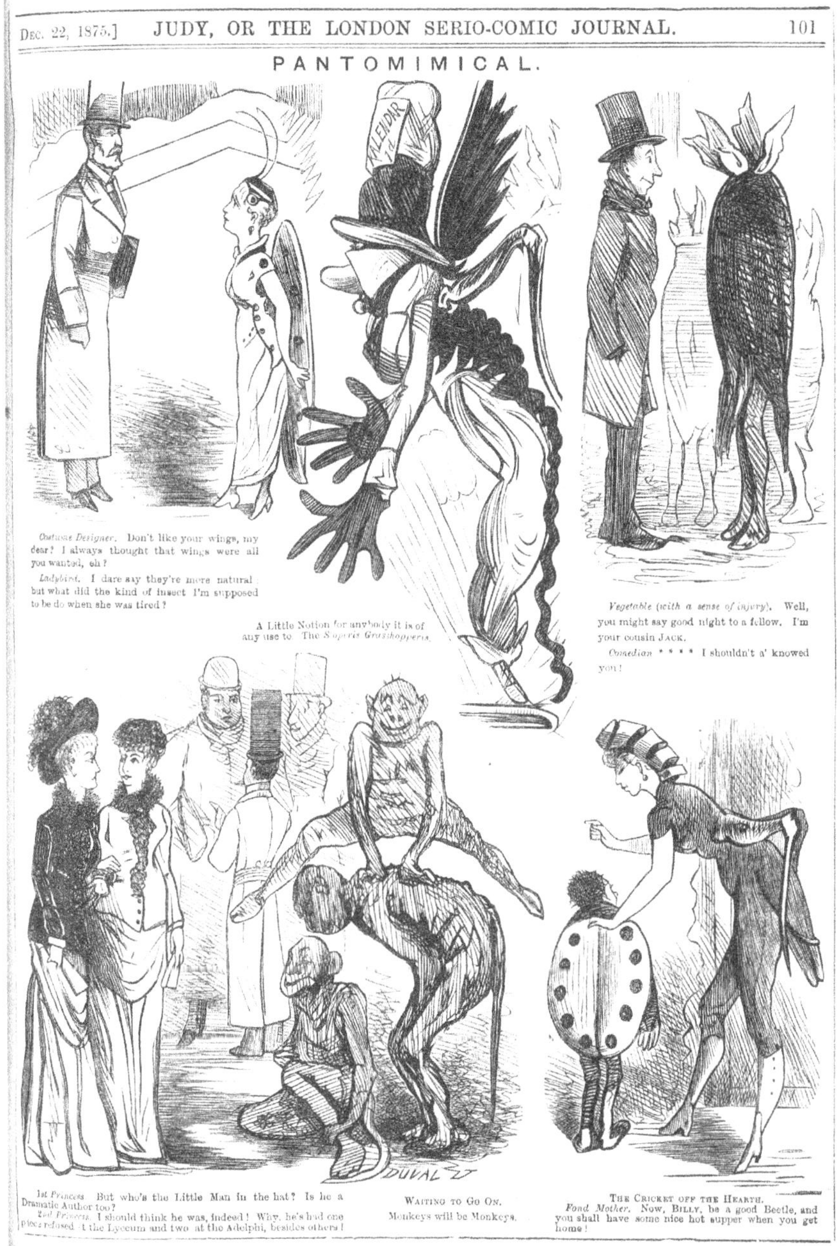

8.3 Marie Duval (1875) 'Pantomimical', *Judy, or the London Serio-comic Journal*, Volume 18, p. 101

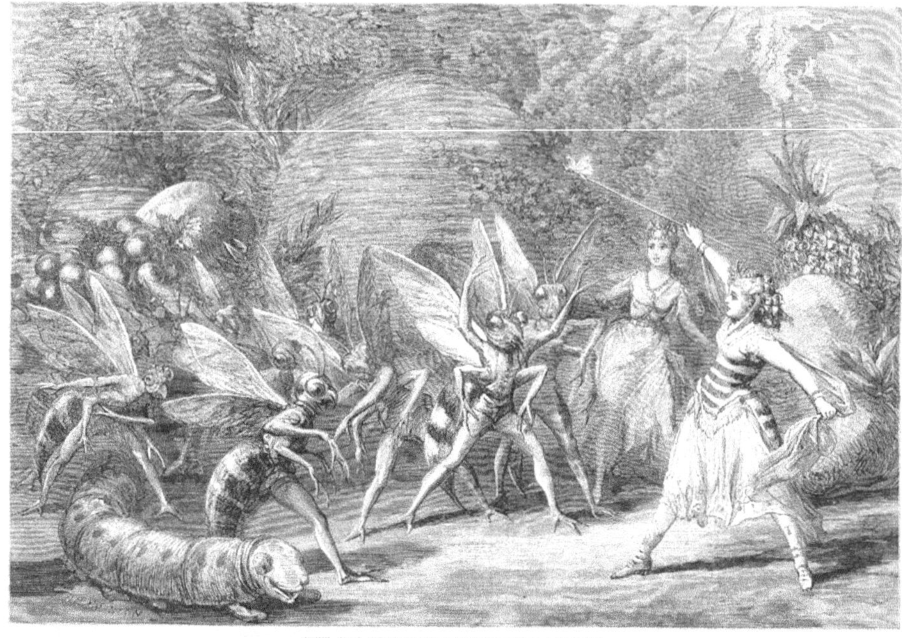

8.4 David Friston (1875) 'Scene from "Cinderella", the Covent Garden Pantomime, *Illustrated Sporting and Dramatic News*, 8 January 1876, p. 263

shows anthropomorphic monkeys as well as other inanimate objects. For example, the London locations Monument and St Paul's are embodied in her cartoon for *Judy*, 8 August 1877 (Duval 1877f).

A favourite comic device of Duval's is to present bottles and puddings with legs (for example Duval 1874c; Figure 8.5, image bottom right) where bottle and pudding nurse hangovers. This seems to be a classic pantomime trope, to judge from a rare backstage image from the *Illustrated London News* some twenty years later, which shows a realistic rendering of exactly the costume Duval seems to be depicting, being painted by a scenic painter surrounded by typical characters (Figure 8.6).

Figure 8.6 also shows two classic mainstays of pantomime on a shelf in the background, that is, characters with big heads. These occasionally make their way into Duval's drawings – for example in 'Sloper does the Derby' (Duval 1872d) where in the second image down on the right two characters have large heads, and in 'The False Friends' (Duval 1877g) where, exceptionally, the entire strip features big heads since generally Duval's distortions are not as consistent as this.

Her contemporary, and sometimes imitative, artist Archibald Chasemore, on the other hand, exploited the idea of an oversized head frequently and it occurs dissociated perhaps

194

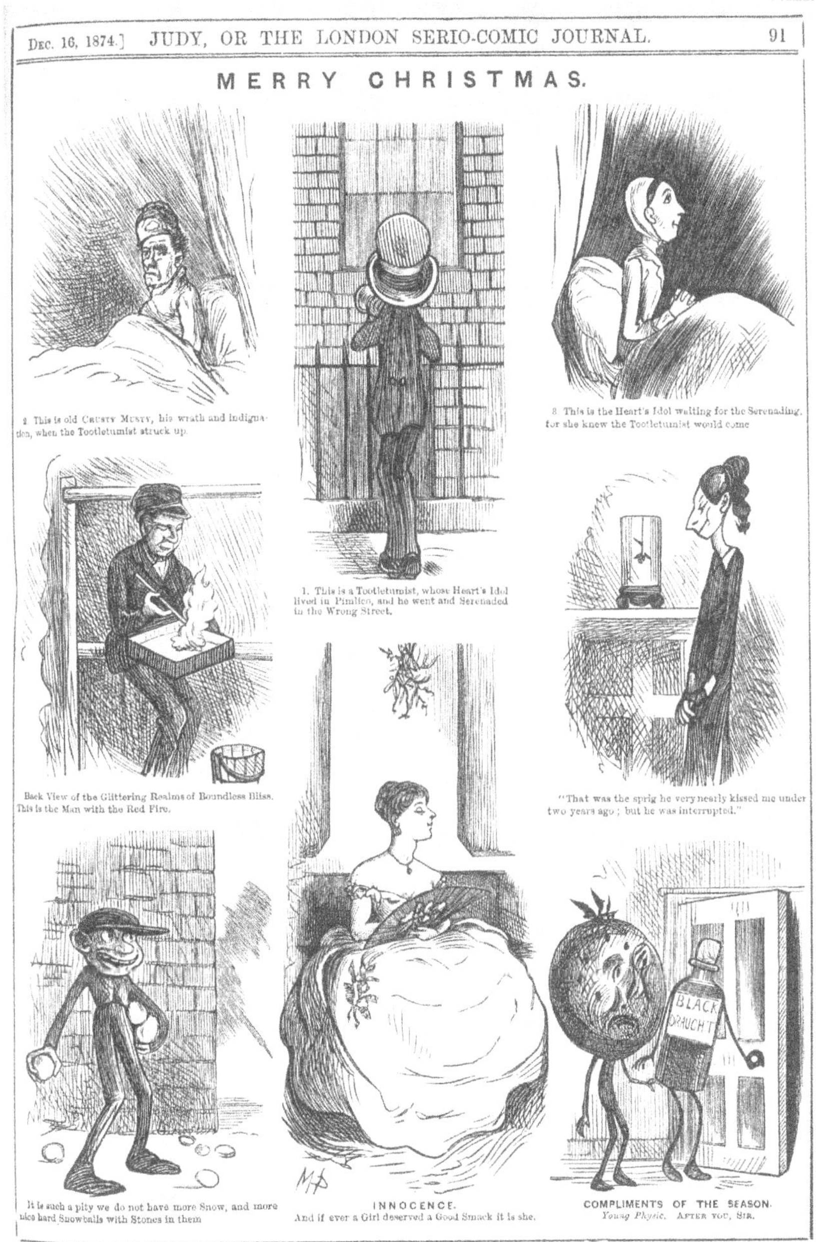

8.5 Marie Duval (1874) 'Merry Christmas', *Judy, or the London Serio-comic Journal*, Volume 16, p. 91

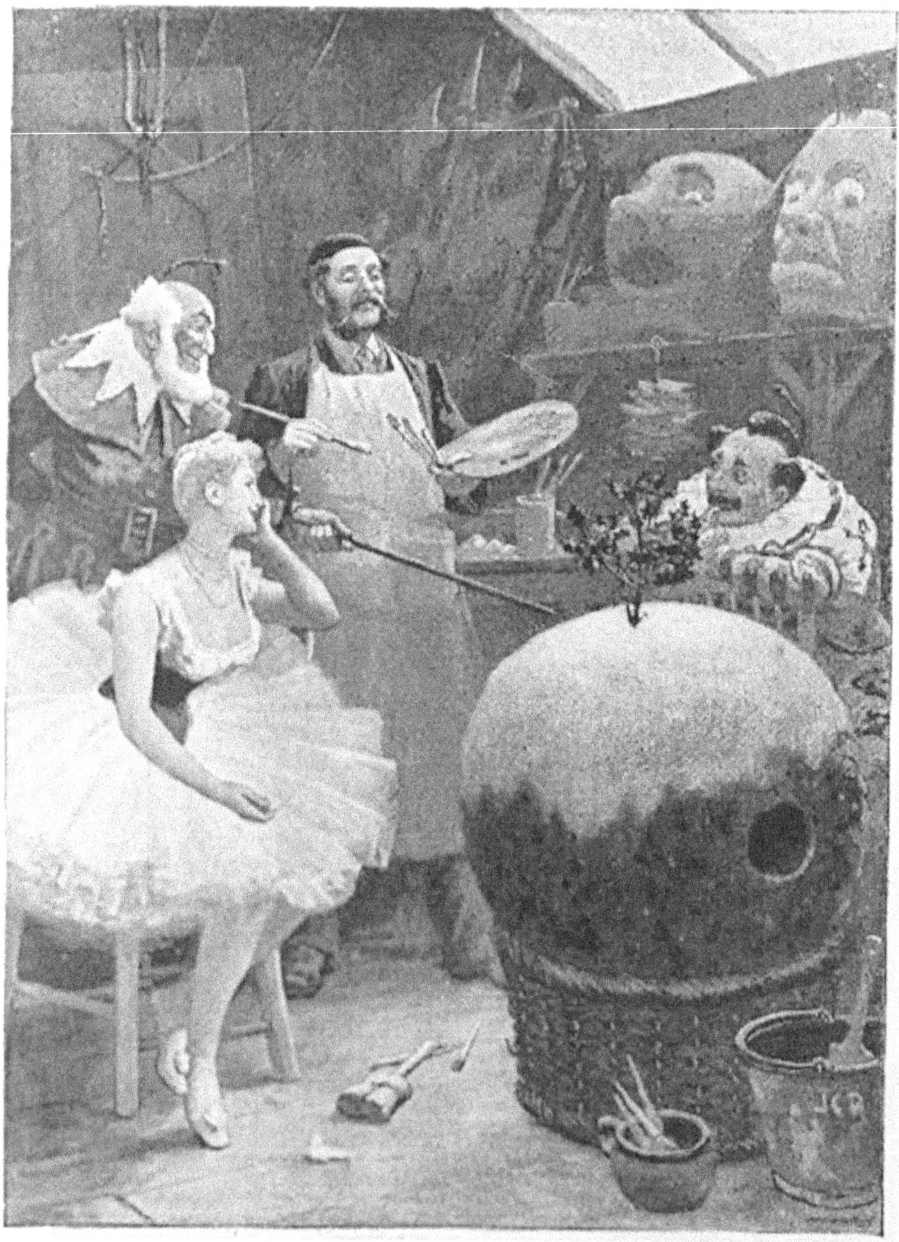

8.6 JCD. (1893) 'The Pantomime Pudding – A Private View', *Illustrated London News*, 23 December 1893, p. 12

from its pantomime origins in many Victorian cartoonists and, most famously, in Tenniel's *Alice's Adventures in Wonderland* illustrations (for example the Duchess and the Mad Hatter).

Flying bodies

It would seem that by 1871 with her appearance as Lord Fernfield in *Ruth* at The Surrey Theatre Duval had some status as an actor (see Chapter 3), although it is clear from her non-speaking roles, only a few years earlier, that at other times in her career, and certainly early on, she may have worked in less prestigious forms of performance. It is possible she was employed as a singer (Clayton recording that she was musical; Clayton 1876: 333) or as a dancer, which may have been in chorus lines, and did indeed work in burlesque in trouser roles (Claude Duval in *The Beggar's Uproar*, Morice 1870), something she might have done in music halls in the years 1864 to 1868 (see Figure 3.12).

However, there is no evidence of her working in music halls, or in physically virtuosic forms of popular entertainment such as circus, acrobatics, clowning or the combinations of these forms with drama which emerged in an integrated form in the second half of the nineteenth century. This kind of entertainment was presented extensively in music hall as individual 'acts' and there is no doubt that Duval saw such performance and she occasionally drew it although, as with her performance illustrations in general, there is no emphasis in her work on such popular forms. However, there are two significant images of circus in her illustrations for 'The Goings on of Gran'papa' (Duval 1883d and 1884b) both set in a historical context to which we shall return.

Here I argue that Duval's interest in the physical movement of the body is revealed more significantly through the frequency and graphic style of her depictions of bodies moving in space than through literal depictions of circus skills. In this regard a striking number of her images involve the body falling, rolling, suspended and flying through the air in a way that has visual echoes of, but also goes beyond, nineteenth-century imagery of the body in motion.

Some photographs exist of circus and other physical performers, but for technical reasons there were no contemporary photographic images of performers actually in flight, in the sort of poses that Duval or other contemporary artists employ. An image of Zazel, the 'human cannonball', sitting on her cannon in the circus tent, is exceptional in even being posed outside a studio let alone in motion. However, there was a great deal of imagery of the human body in flight or suspension appearing in magazines, fine art (for example in the work of Edgar Degas, who documented trapeze artists) and poster artwork. Posters for Zazel's appearances at the Royal Aquarium show her mid-flight, as would be expected given the purpose of the image, whilst advertising for other circus-based acts are often compilations of key images from their performances and show numerous examples of bodies in flight.

In the period that Duval was drawing, circus was performed in a wider variety of venues than today, the tent being only one possibility. Indeed, even touring circuses would often stay in the same area for a number of months. Bratton and Featherstone describe 'portable circuses' as resident for three months in various towns across the North West as close as Frodsham and Warrington (Bratton and Featherstone 2006: 21) and most circuses set up in permanent buildings in a way that survives in Blackpool today (Bratton and Featherstone 2006: 28). One reason for this was the presence of animals (menageries were often a permanent feature of the circus, viewable during the day) and another reason, the fact that the spectacles of direct performances of skill are more amenable to repeated viewing than even the stage spectacle of pantomime. Once a plot is known there is little reason to return, but human daring is always a thrill.

Historically, Assael cites Speaight (1980) in giving 1768, when Astley's circus was founded, as the date 'when the modern circus was born' (Assael 2005: 3). Her contemporary illustration shows a theatre which looks more like a classic London theatre, with a clearly identifiable stage behind a ring which is embraced by the standard boxes creating an architecture similar to today's Covent Garden rather than the circus ring of the Blackpool Tower. Indeed, the building-based survivor in Blackpool is actually less like most Victorian building-based arrangements, since the Blackpool Tower site is modelled on a reproduction of a circus tent rather than a theatre. This arrangement allowed particularly for the presentation of equestrian acts, as in Assael's illustration, and circus in the early part of the century was dominated by gymnastic feats on horseback (Assael 2005: 3). By the time Duval was drawing, the circus was modulating into a more theatrical entertainment of the sort in which Duval herself might well have participated:

> Variety acts overshadowed elaborate equestrian dramas in [...]1860–80. Commenting on the metropolitan scene in particular, the dramatic critic Edward Dutton Cook was moved to write in 1876 that 'of late years a change has come over the equestrian drama. The circus flourishes, and quadrupeds figure now and then [...] but the 'horse spectacle' has almost vanished.' (Assael 2005: 4)

Circus acts at this period found their place as comfortably in the rising music halls, such as the Cambridge Music Hall (Shoreditch), where in 1868 Munby watched Zuleilah, one of the female artists he admired, in her trapeze act (Hudson 1971: 254). Thus, if Duval took roles either as dancer or 'en travestie' in music halls early in her career, she would have not only seen, but also shared the dressing room and stage with, trapeze artists and clowns. One aspect of the staging arrangement of such performances is the close proximity of the artists to the audience and the fact that they would be seen from all angles including directly underneath as well as the more oblique angles from which we are likely to see such performers in a ringside arrangement today. Thus, Munby describes how a performer at the Oxford Music Hall in 1870 not only swings over the audience but actually has to push through the entire hall to reach the starting point for her final trick:

> But this was not all: for the 'chairman' got up & said 'Ladies and Gentlemen, Mlle de Glorion will now take her daring leap for life, along the whole length of the hall.' And the fair acrobat went down from the stage, among the audience, alone, and walked, half naked as she was,[4] through the crowd, to the other end of the long hall, and there went up a staircase into the gallery [...] and climbed the rope ladder that led up from the gallery to

a small platform [...] And she had to swing herself, high over the heads of the crowd, across that great space of eighty feet or so, and leap through the two discs and alight in his inverted arms, which she could not even see. (Munby's diary cited in Hudson 1971: 286)

As with the vast majority of acts of the period, Mlle de Glorion had no safety net (and the audience no protection should she have fallen on them). The sight of a body flying through space with such complete vulnerability must have been a part of the spectacle and thrill for the audience. Indeed, the gradual introduction of safety nets was often rejected as defeating the point of such acts and it was only the introduction of a child act by the Great Farini which began to make safety nets acceptable.

Duval's gestural drawings of figures in flight suggest something of the visceral nature of this experience described by Munby. Duval drew a number of panels where many figures tumble in varied positions throughout her career, from the flight of black-clad women published on 18 April 1877 (Duval 1877h) or those surrounding Ally Sloper on 14 February the same year (Duval 1877d; Figure 8.2), to the chaos of stick figures in the Late 'London Town Upside Down' of 4 March 1885 (Duval 1885b).

She also showed single figures in flight or falling helplessly such as her image of 10 November 1869 where a walker plummets comically but spectacularly from a mountain (Duval 1869k). The contrast between figures soaring and falling uncontrolled was of interest to Duval and may well reflect her experience of seeing choreographed aerialists who occasionally and disastrously made mistakes, so well depicted in the Lulu cartoon I examine later.

However, it is possible to identify material where Duval depicted movements that seem to come from circus acrobatics in domestic situations. For example, between 18 July and 6 August 1873, Duval drew four cartoons with unusually distinct circus imagery but in non-circus contexts, two being of children. So, in 'Judy's Fashions 1873' (Duval 1873k) she drew an image of a boy in clown attire doing a handstand. The same week she used stilt walking (Duval 1873l). Just a month before she had drawn a particularly striking set of three images of a boy playing on a single bar fence in 'The Earliest News from the Seaside' (Duval 1873m). Although set at the seaside these bear a remarkable resemblance to an artist performing on a trapeze bar. Shortly after the boy clown (again not in a circus context) she drew Mr Potterbury attempting horticultural support in 'All About a Scarlet Runner' (Duval 1873n; Figure 8.7) in a way that appears to be a parody of the trapeze artist. He is held dangling by his feet by one woman (herself being held by a third character) and in another frame hangs by his toes from a window ledge in precisely the way a trapeze artist would hang from the bar.

Indeed, 'All About a Scarlet Runner' is particularly interesting in putting imagery from physical entertainment into a narrative context. Physical entertainment was a feature of music hall acts in the United Kingdom and vaudeville in the United States, which would later make its way into the medium of film in the hands of artists such as Buster Keaton early in the next century. Duval's most famous contemporaries in this convention were undoubtedly the Hanlon-Lees Brothers.

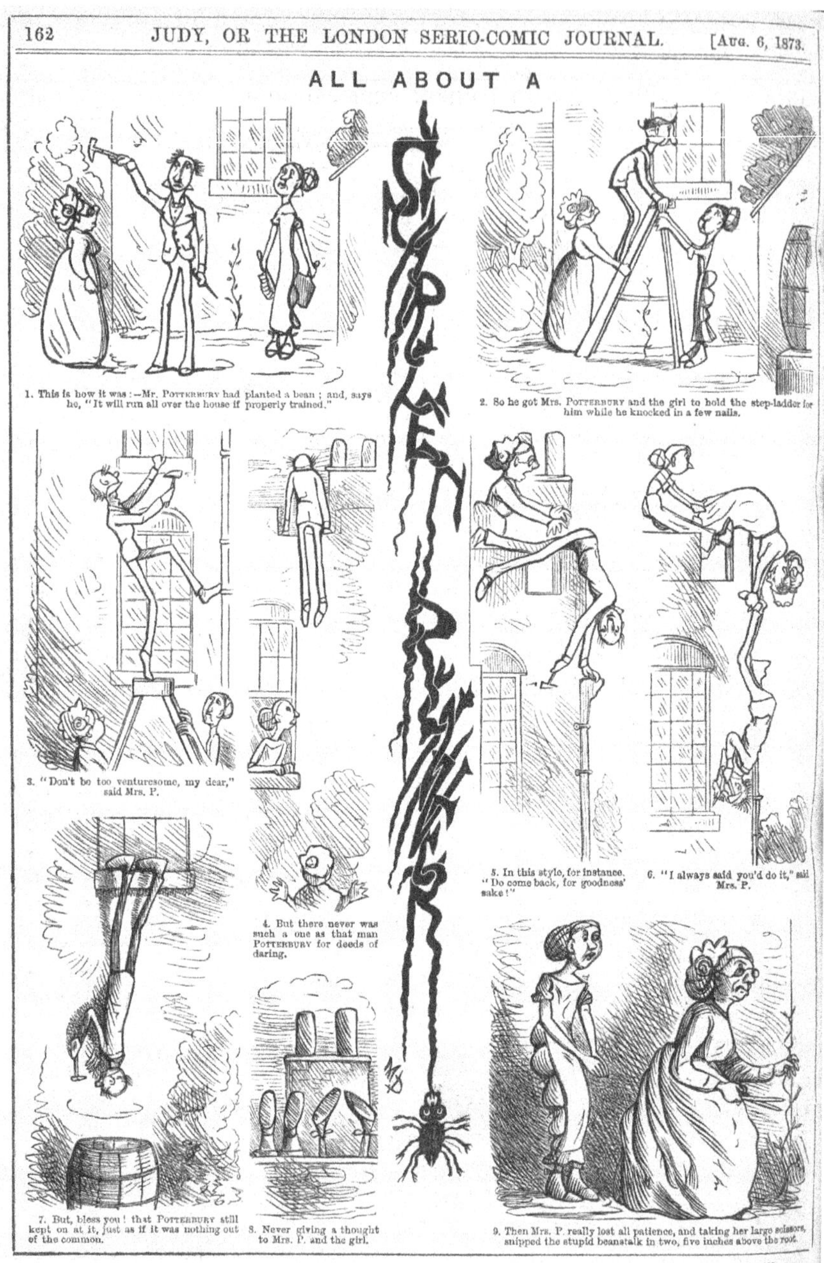

8.7 Marie Duval (1873) 'All About a Scarlet Runner', *Judy, or the London Serio-comic Journal*, Volume 13, p. 162

Spectacle and narrative in the Hanlon Troupe

The Hanlon-Lees Brothers were clowns and circus athletes who also incorporated tumbling in theatrical performance. They turned to theatrical ventures as they grew older and withdrew from trapeze work, utilising their technical skills of physical theatre and impeccable timing in the creation of short and full-length performance pieces (in effect, set pieces sustained by a thin plot) which, exactly like 'All About a Scarlet Runner', exploited and incorporated the spectacle of suspended and falling bodies into a loose containing narrative.

The British-born brothers were performers who after extensive, world-wide touring in their youth, settled principally in the United States and France. They regularly toured Britain and the year before 'All About a Scarlet Runner' were performing a compilation of the sort of pantomime scenes featuring 'extreme' acrobatics which they had made their speciality at the Folies Bergère in Paris. This included '*Echelle Perilleuse* (comedy acrobatics on the ladder) [...] [and] *La Salle a Manger* (a dignified dinner scene in which the acrobats upset all laws of politeness)' (McKinven 1998: 31). Both these scenes are illustrated in *La Vie Parisienne* of 9 November 1872 in a style far more restrained than Duval's but showing something of her penchant for depicting the body in extremis as shown in an illustration in McKinven (1998: 32). Here the body shapes foreground the tumbling skills that are being advertised, and in this way reveal the purpose of the images, to evoke the spectacular gymnastics which will be entertainingly displayed.

On the other hand, Duval in 'All About a Scarlet Runner' and other such drawings is, in effect, truer to the conceit of this sort of entertainment. Her images foreground the narrative, so that Mr Potterbury does seem to be getting into these positions accidentally (in the way that, at their best, Keaton and Chaplin appear to in their early films). However, the images correspond with great accuracy to material she would have had the opportunity to see in the circus or music hall, or borrowed from publicity material for such performances.

In 1879 the Hanlons created one of several full-length performances containing some of their cabaret and music hall scenes along with new material that was moulded into a full-length loosely designed plot. *Le Voyage en Suisse*, which Towsen has called 'one of the most significant productions in the history of popular entertainment', opened in Paris, and transferred to The Gaiety Theatre in London in March 1880 (Towsen 1976: 66). The plot, which is a mixture of farce and melodrama, entails the thwarting of the heroine's forced marriage during her journey to Switzerland where her inappropriately interfering guardian lives. In the course of the journey the Hanlon brothers, in the guise of servants, reinstate the hero to a position of favour (McKinven 1998: 49–54). The plot manages to encompass two set pieces of explosive destruction – the arrival of a carriage and a train accident. For the first:

> the coach [is] drawn by a live horse [and] halfway across the stage the carriage overturns in a violent smash-up. Carriage, gentlemen, English trunks – everything is demolished into a hundred pieces. But to relieve the audience's horror, the Hanlon-Lees come sliding down

the wreckage landing in a perfect row at the footlights, calmly smoking cigars, with one brother sitting on another's shoulders. (McKinven 1998: 49)

This is highly Duvallian in its mix of demolition and surrealism. Explosions feature in two later scenes, one involving the wreck of a train, the other an explosion which 'blows' a character down through the ceiling to land on the table of the onstage dinner party. The former, as with the coach crash, features performers on wires so that they could travel and land in safety: 'In the ensuing explosion the railroad car splits in two on the stage, blowing the terrified passengers safely into nearby trees' (McKinven 1998: 52).

Visual evidence of these scenes survives in publicity brochures and posters and in the programme for the performance (a concertina book of eight lithographs), and, as with the publicity for the Folies Bergère, the style of these clearly reflects the gymnastic tumbling and wire work of the performance (Figure 8.8).

Figures flying away from wreckage or explosions are neatly delineated, all four limbs spread with angled joints. The hero, Finsbury, disguised as a train guard catching the beautiful Julia from the train explosion, takes precisely the attitude of the flying trapeze

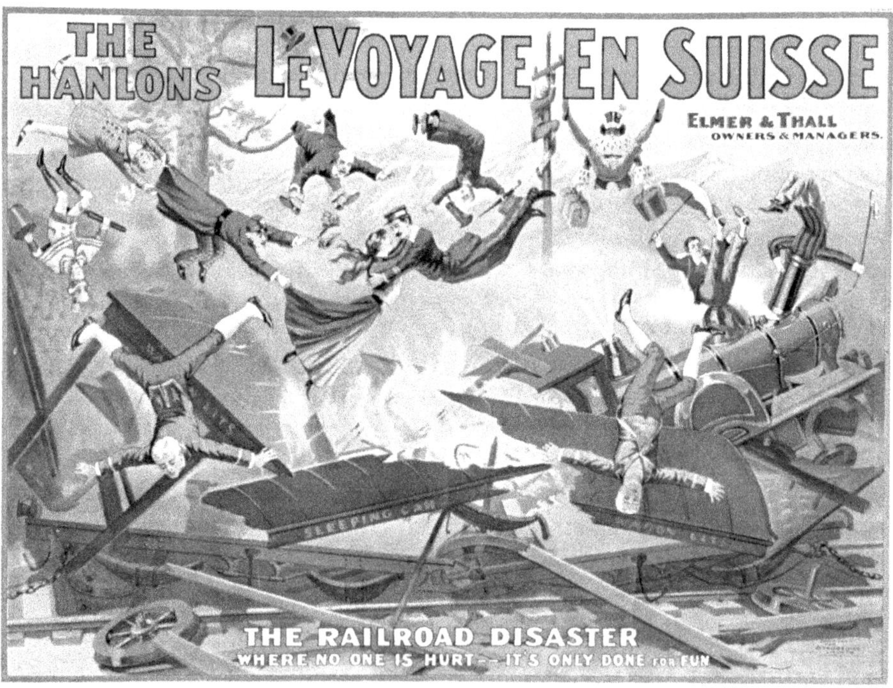

8.8 Anonymous (1879) 'Le Voyage en Suisse', *Theatre poster*, Strobridge Lithographic Company.

artist so memorably pictorialised in publicity for the first ever man on the flying trapeze, Jules Leotard. The latter, who first performed at The Alhambra in 1860, was the source of the Hanlons' work and would undoubtedly have been known to Duval both through his reputation as a performer and the music hall song still known today, *The Daring Young Man on the Flying Trapeze* (Leotard 1860; Busby 1976: 12).[5] The illustration on the cover of Leotard's contemporary *Memoires* is the earliest example of what would become the trope clearly shown in the Hanlons' publicity (Figure 8.8).

Duval's flying bodies are diverse and spread throughout her work. She regularly depicts fairies and other characters on visible wires, often with a satiric purpose. So, in *Judy* of 22 January 1873 in the panel 'Behind the Scenes' (Duval 1873d; Figure 8.9) we see a fairy with a visible wire or rope hovering in a slightly undignified way, with a caption that is surely based on experience: 'Calculated to give Terrestrial Bodies a bad attack of Pins and Needles.' In *Judy* four years earlier, the suspension is even more satiric, as a woman hangs by her hair in order to make her chignon rise ever further upward: 'Young ladies should begin early. It doesn't hurt so much when you're used to it' (Duval 1869m).

However, as with the Hanlons' conceit, if not in their imagery, she also depicts bodies flying that, in the context of the narrative, are falling or hovering. For example, on 2 February 1881, the year after *Le Voyage en Suisse* opened, for her regular panel, 'Crimes and Disasters (from a Sloperian point of view)', Duval draws the title itself – a literal verbal disaster in the form of stick men (Duval 1881c; Figure 7.11). Here the gestural positions of her little figures are more varied than in the Hanlon publicity, but it is curious that several feature the trope of divided bent legs, so prevalent in her contemporaries' illustrations, and the letter 'A' appears in exactly the same pose as the figure on the extreme left foreground of the Hanlons' English poster (Figure 8.8). That the gesturally energetic and seemingly randomised nature of Duval's line leads to a highly successful and much more vivid sense of falling figures is amply demonstrated by the boys tumbling away from the Mad Chemist in her 1883 illustration for 'The Dying Moments of a Suburban Beauty IV' (Duval 1883e).

Duval does not use the precise delineation of bodies evident in most of her contemporaries and in the work of the Hanlon illustrator, but instead creates figures who are not only falling more satisfactorily, but whose descent is emphasised by distorted depictions of limb and body length. Indeed the coy byline of 'The railroad disaster where no one is hurt – it's only done for fun' (Figure 8.8) is far from the literal obliteration of Duval's many exploding figures, of which the 5 October 1870 depiction of Ally Sloper being shot is typical (Duval 1870s). In July 1883 we find him exploding with laughter (Duval 1883f) whilst in 'A Pinch of Snuff Judy' explodes 'after taking a deuce-and-all of a pinch' (Duval 1874d).

In Duval's world it seems people sometimes simply get blown up on mountains ('A Few Recollections of Foreign Climbs', image extreme right, Duval 1869k).[6] It is possible that Duval saw onstage pyrotechnics up close, and there is evidence that performers were involved in accidents with explosives, such as, for example, the tragic case of James

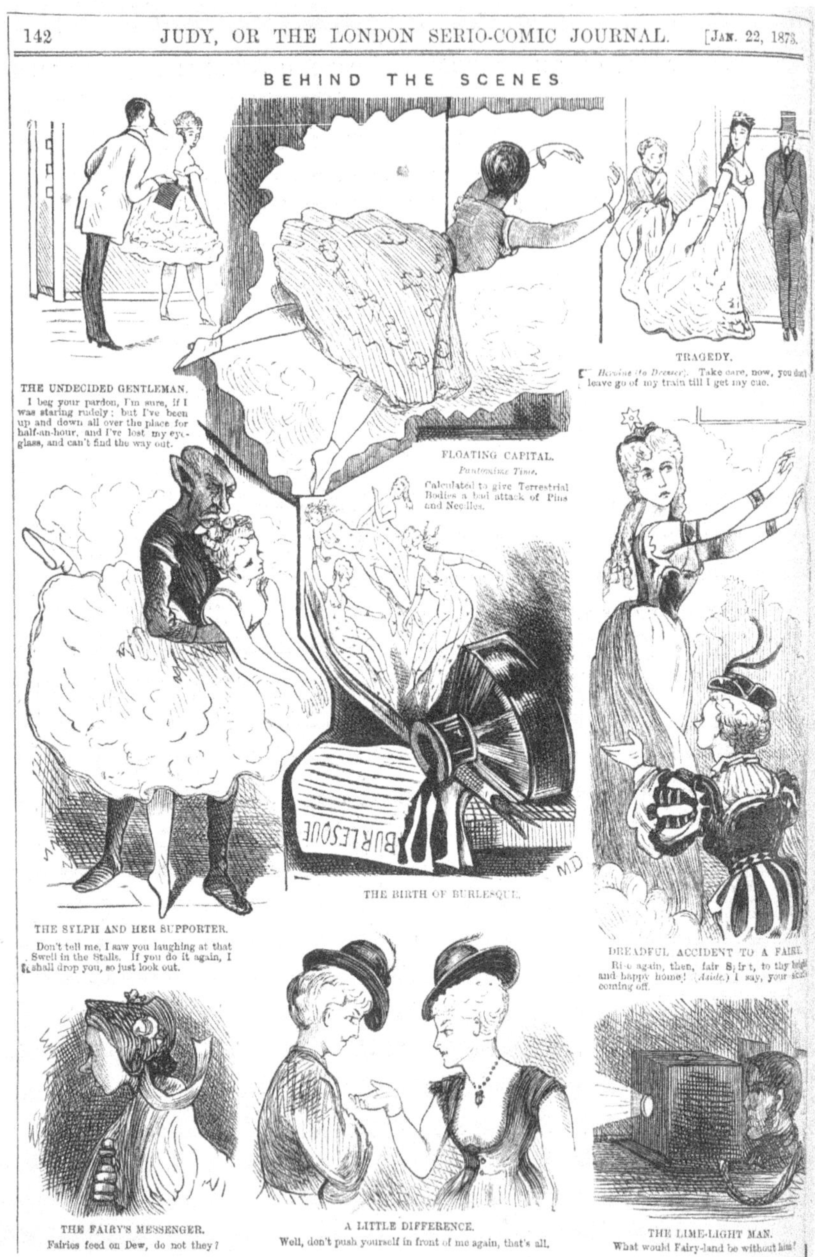

8.9 Marie Duval (1873) 'Behind the Scenes', *Judy, or the London Serio-comic Journal*, Volume 12, p. 142

Frowde's grandmother, a horse rider and pyrotechnic artist, who was killed in an explosion of fireworks in her home (Bratton and Featherstone 2006: 44).

Both the large-scale disasters in *Le Voyage en Suisse* were frequently exploited as stage effects in the 1880s and real horses and train carriages were utilised onstage regularly. A particular favourite with circuses and music halls was Millner's *Dick Turpin or the Death of Black Bess* (1836), which featured an onstage leap over a turnpike gate by a real horse in the depicted ride to York (Bratton and Featherstone 2006: 51–4). The animated train in *Le Voyage en Suisse* was clearly a piece of technology that went beyond even that spectacle, and in a sense introduces the train as a character in the drama, its spectacular destruction being the final apotheosis.

Duval seems also to have had a love affair with trains and their characterful progress and comic destruction (perhaps encouraged by living near a railway line, as Roger Sabin points out in Chapter 9). Thus, the flying train she draws for 'The Deed of Darkness' (Duval 1873o) is still in her visual repertoire twelve years later, weaving through 'London Town Upside Down' (Duval 1885c). In the intervening years trains climb unfeasibly steep hills and tumble off, in 'Rigi-Lections' (Duval 1874e) or simply explode and fall from the sky at the end of the summer seaside season, in 'After the Season is Over' (Duval 1873p). The conception revealed here, of carriages splitting apart and figures independently falling from them, is more theatrical than any accurate depiction of the ground-based twisted metal of a real train disaster. Perhaps we can assume that Duval's visual reference was based more on theatrical imagery of explosions and collisions, with its use of wires and dis-assembly of the stage setting, than reportage or early photography in the aftermath of such serious disasters.

Indeed, the use of flying to give spectacle and beauty to moments that in fact depict visceral carnage survives in contemporary theatre practice. The National Theatre of Scotland's production of *The Black Watch* (Tiffany 2006) features a scene in which soldiers are blown up by a mine in Iraq. The staging uses slow-motion flying on wires to show the actors' bodies flying through the air, and whilst beautiful is not perceived as melodramatic or sentimental in context. In fact, critics have universally found it a satisfying climax. For example, David Smith in the *Guardian* wrote that the realist basis of the play is 'interspersed with set pieces that are sensational eruptions of light, sound and high octane physical theatre' (Smith 2008).

As with trains, so with boats. In the 1870s the Hanlon brothers developed stage scenery for a spectacular sequence where a large sailing boat leaves dock and puts out to sea, climaxing in a storm where the characters are thrown about the wildly rocking boat.[7] The final sequence of what must have been an astonishing spectacle consisted of the boat in the open sea rocking whilst acrobats slid about, fell from the deck and were even hurled through a piano using a version of the 'leap trap' (or 'trappe anglaise' as it was called due to it originating in Britain but being used extensively in France).[8] Like her trains, Duval's boats are characterfully puppet-like, for example her 1870 cartoon of Ally on board a boat which finally rocks to a degree which makes him seasick or as the caption says 'the rest of SLOPER, dreadfully ill, somewhere in the background' (Duval

1870t). Whilst we don't see Sloper, we do see Duval's literally revolving boat, clearly conceived theatrically like a cut-out on a stick, puppeteered on a painted ocean. At the end of the sequence the boat even disappears between a major waveform and the mass of waves behind, exactly as a theatrical effect would work dropping between two painted surfaces (Duval 1870t).

Hoops, traps and springs

If there are shades of the theatrical here, then Duval's images of bodies falling through things, such as paper hoops, ice, walls or simply into clouds of dust, seem to show a particular visual reference to the skill of the tumbler or a troupe such as the Hanlon-Lees. A number of images in her corpus are directly those of a character leaping through a hoop. Perhaps foremost among them the frontispiece for *Judy*, Volume 16 (Duval 1874f) which shows Ally Sloper as a clown holding a papered hoop through which the character Judy has already jumped so that we see only her skirts and boots. This image is highly suggestive of both this leap through a hoop and the use of the English Trap in Keaton.[9] An earlier surviving example of the latter, as a theatrical, rather than gymnastic leap, survives in Méliès' *L'Auberge du Bon Repose* (1903) where tumblers leap through paintings rather than traps, but with exactly the speed and expertise that is suggested by Duval's many drawings of bodies disappearing into holes (Figure 8.10).

Thus we have Sloper diving in through a window to escape cannon fire (Duval 1870u, Figure 8.11); people who have tumbled off an insecure seating stand in (Duval 1872e, 'Thanksgiving Day', image bottom right); Sloper's feet disappearing into a river having been tossed by a bull in 'Ally Sloper Goes a-Fishing' (Duval 1874g, also bottom right); a

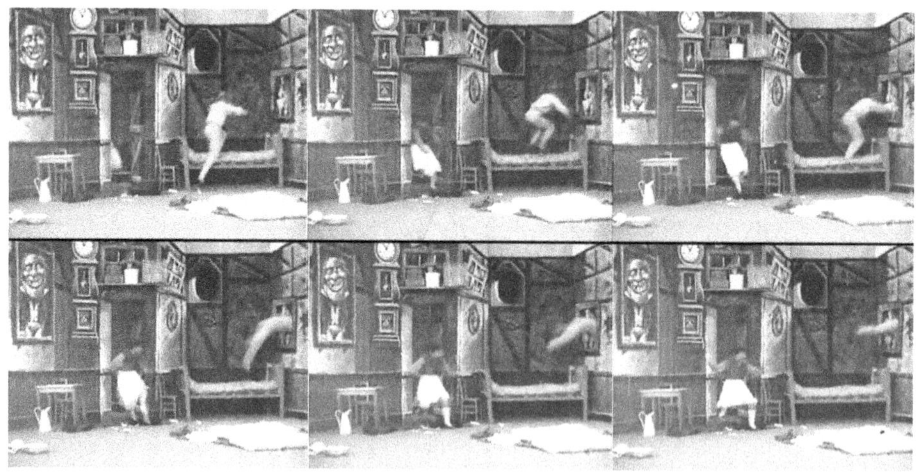

8.10   Georges Méliès (1903) *L'Auberge de Bon Repos*, American Library Association

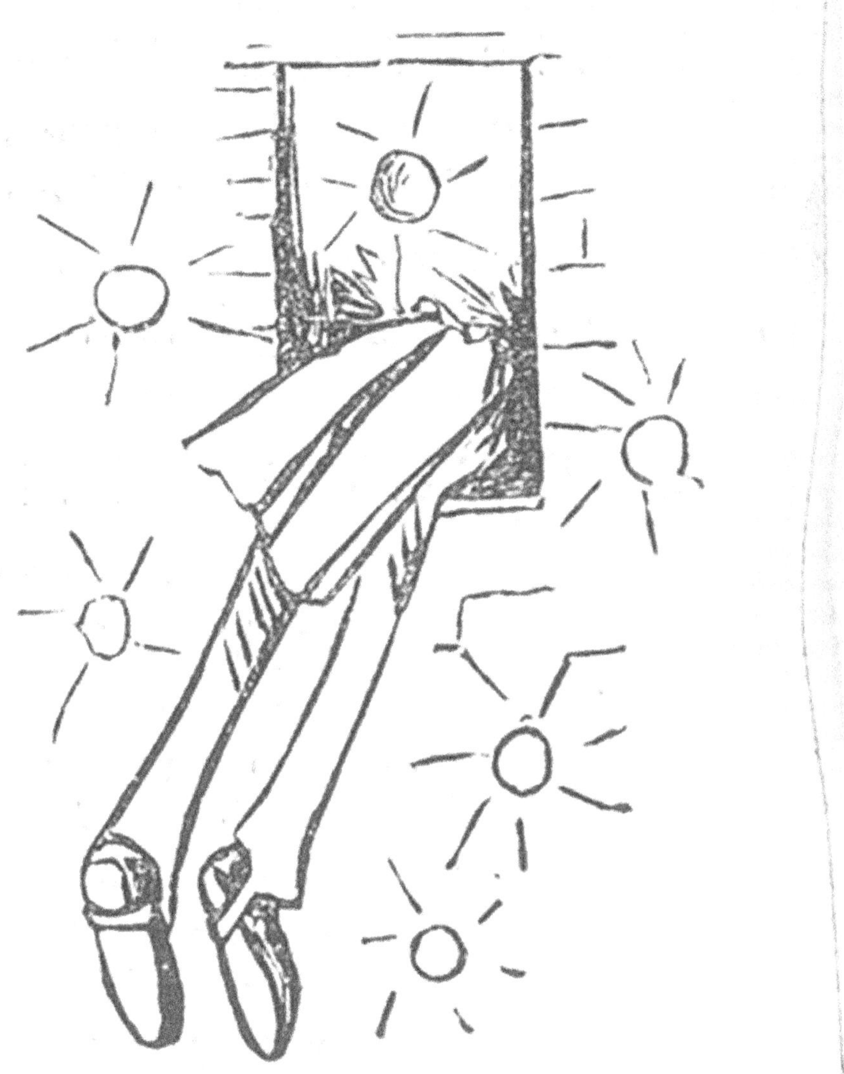

8.11   Marie Duval (1870) 'Ally to the Front' (detail), *Judy, or the London Serio-comic Journal*,
Volume 7, p. 172

young man falling into ice in 'New Year Nonsense 1875' (Duval 1875f); more pantomime hoops in 'Spring, Summer, Autumn, Winter' (Duval 1875g, image upper centre) and so on.

Given her stage career, it is highly probable that Duval saw performers jumping through hoops because she specifically depicted them, and likely she saw the use of a leap trap. She also drew traps in the floor, for example in the sequence of cartoons entitled 'Tragedy'. Here an actor who refuses to die on cue is seen finally dropping into a stage trap (Duval 1878e).

In terms of flying bodies, there were two mechanisms for stage traps, one which would raise or lower a performer smoothly and elegantly, and one much faster designed to give the performer an impetus to leap upwards onto the stage (Southern 1970: 32 and 108, the former giving an illustration of the mechanism, the latter of such a trap in use). However, there is another unique image made by Duval of a particular invention of the period designed to make such entrances even more vivid.

On 13 June 1871 William Hunt, using his stage name William Farini, was granted a United States patent for his invention of a spring projector, which would hurl an acrobat 30 feet up into the air. The principle was the same as that used in human cannons, where the artist was not propelled by the small pyrotechnics, which were only for visual effect, but usually by a spring action within or below the cannon (this is the mechanism of the cannon which Zazel is shown sitting on in a contemporary photograph, and which she used for the first ever presentation of the trick in 1877).

A large amount of material survives on Farini in the theatre collection at the Victoria and Albert Museum, which shows that he was a tightrope walker and trapeze artist and developed an act with his adopted son Samuel Wasgate. A number of photographs in the Guy Little collection now housed in the Victoria and Albert museum show Wasgate, for example. Initially, Wasgate was billed as El Niño Farini but by 1870 he was performing under the stage name Lulu, cross-dressing as a successful piece of deception in the interests of enhancing the spectacle. As Lulu, Wasgate used his father's spring-loaded platform, described in publicity as a catapult, and was billed as 'the Eighth Wonder of the World!!!!' ("'Lulu!" "Lulu!"' 1875: 13), an expression widely used by newspaper reviewers, picking up the phrase from Hunt's advertising for the act, for example in *The Era* 17 October 1875 ("'Lulu!" "Lulu!"' 1875: 13), in an advertisement for a national tour following the Holborn run.

At Holborn 'she' was seen on 20 February 1871. A show card for the performance is held in the Victoria and Albert collection showing Lulu flying upwards with a backdrop of moon and stars (Concanen 1871; Figure 8.12). Later that year Duval drew Ally Sloper taking his usual Christmas panto engagement 'at one of the London theatres. This time he was to do the Lulu trick at the Great Sahara' (Duval 1872f; Figure 8.13).

Duval shows Ally soaring into the air 'as per poster' (Duval 1872f) with stars and even a suggestion of low cloud as in the show card from the Victoria and Albert Museum's collection (Figure 8.12), suggesting she was either recalling the staging from the performance or referring to this image. If the latter, her talent for energetic, gestural depictions is greater than the artist of the show card and she provides a telling contrast between the

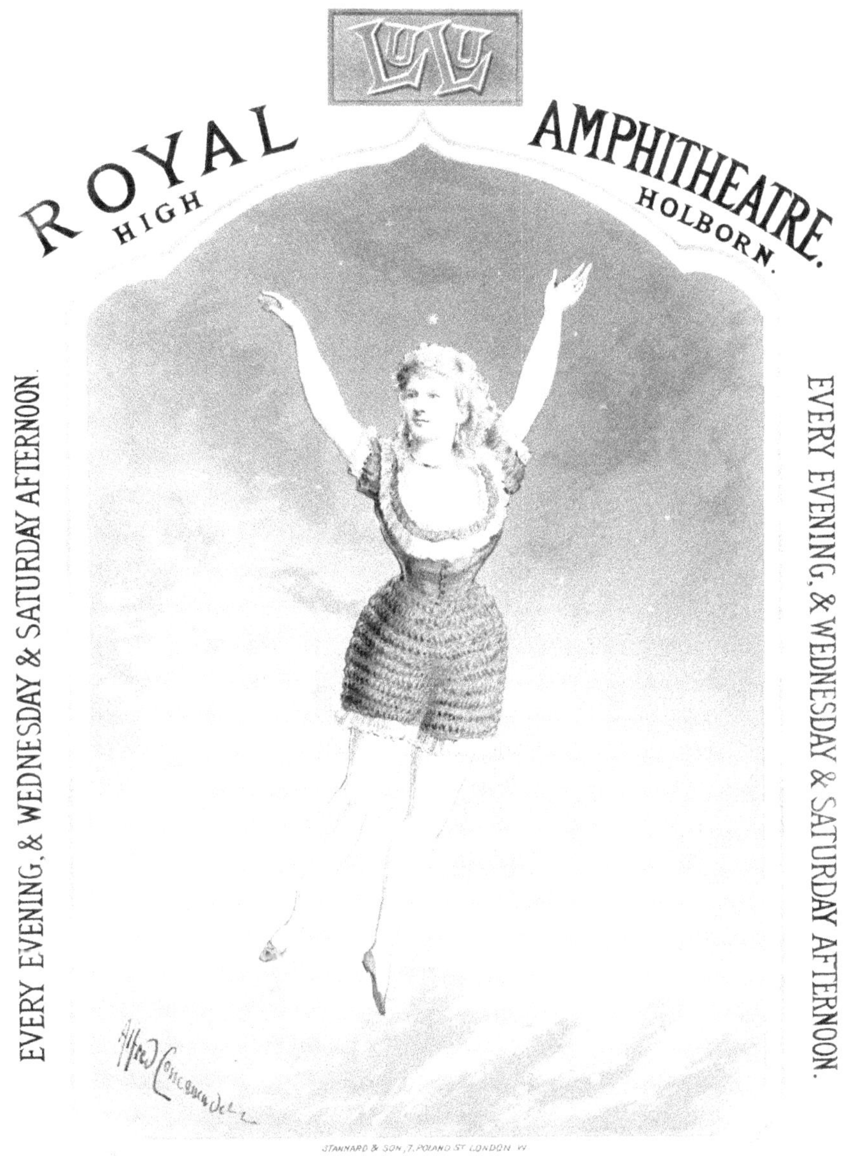

8.12 Alfred Concanen (1871) *Lulu as she appeared before their Royal Highnesses the Prince and Princess of Wales, 20 Feb 1871*, London: Stannard & Son

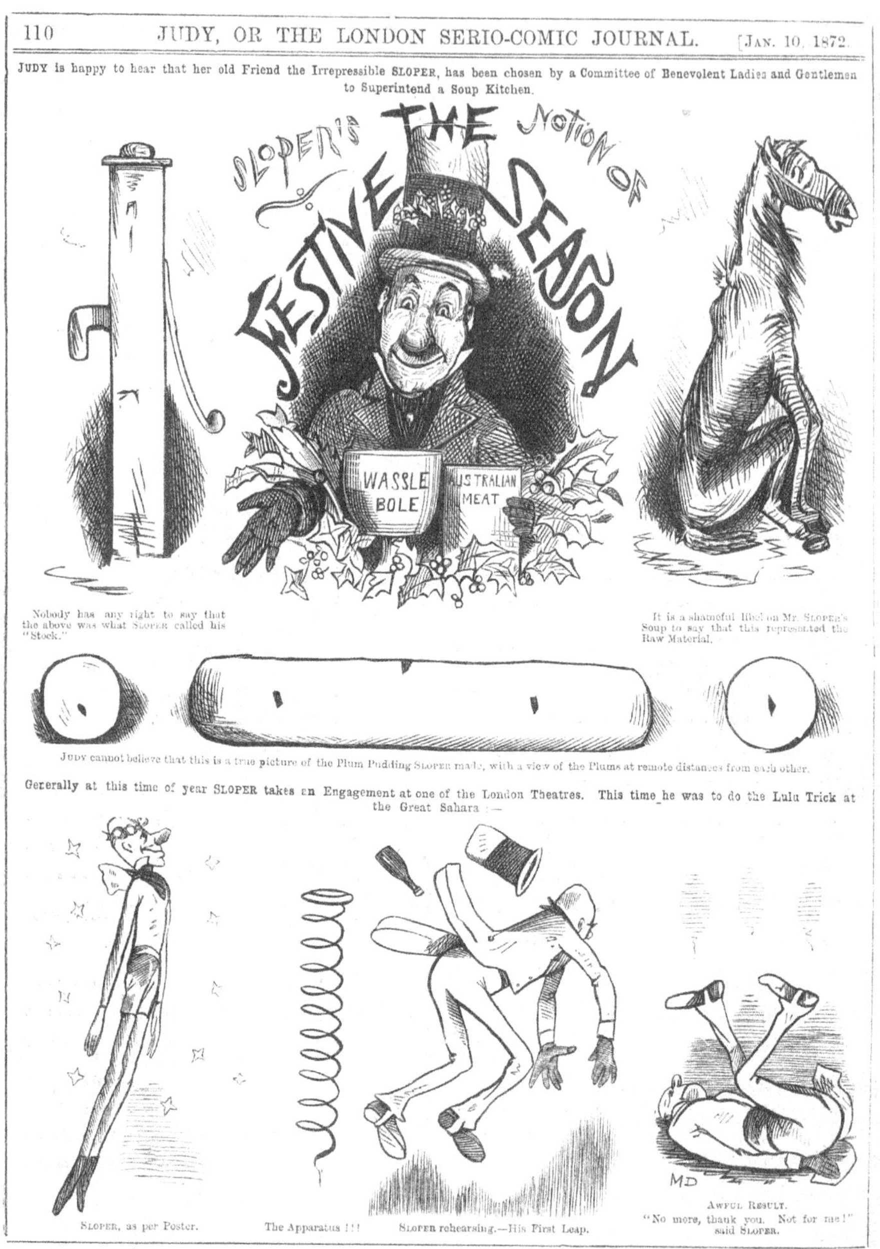

8.13 Marie Duval (1872) 'Sloper's Notion of the Festive Season', *Judy, or the London Serio-comic Journal*, Volume 10, p. 110

serene bullet-like Ally in the first frame and the usual tumbling figure showing the final results of his disastrous 'first leap'. Ironically, but perhaps unsurprisingly, his fall is prophetic. Although Hunt actually pioneered the use of a safety net (it was first used when he introduced the child Wasgate in 1860) and as Lulu Wasgate continued to use one, he suffered a dislocated hip in Dublin in 1875. This was reported extensively, for example in *The Sunday Times*:

> In the leap to the roof of the circus, the spring of the machinery by which she is impelled upwards failed to send her the requisite height and she missed the cross bar. The netting, which should shoot out under her, failed to work and she fell on the edge of the platform with great violence. ('Serious accident to an Acrobat' 1876: 5)

A month later *The Evening Star* in Washington also reported the accident adding the detail that 'the attending physician discovered that Lulu is a man!' ('The Centennial regatta furnishes the last rows of summer' 1876: 3) a revelation that a number of Lulu's reviewers and audience continued to disbelieve despite Wasgate's almost conventional masculine appearance in presentation cards of the time.

Circus in the late drawings

The most explicit depictions of circus and clowning occur late in Duval's oeuvre as two episodes in a narrative series called 'The Goings on of Gran'papa', published from 1883 to 1884. In these two cartoons Duval depicts a composite of the plot of the story in a number of separate images. The story is not contemporary but set in 1835, and part of the conceit is that Gran'papa meets various celebrities on his travels. So in the 16 January 1884 storyline he meets 'a comic writer called "Boz"' (Duval 1884b) and in the previous instalment he is amused by Sam the Boots and, presumably in a reference to Sam Weller, notes that 'This Sam is a character and I shouldn't be a bit surprised if some fellow some time or other doesn't put him into a book' (Duval 1883d).

It is less clear whether the description of the two performances is meant to be a parody of contemporary theatre-going or that there are differences that Duval's audience would have perceived between 1835 and 1883 which they would have found amusing. Certainly, the mention of a performance of hunting a zebra, bullfighting and an emphasis on equestrian acts is consistent with a historical setting (Assael places equestrian acts and re-enactments in her 'second phase' of circus history, which she gives as 1820–60; Assael 2005: 4).

The cast mentioned is certainly historical, including the clown Ducrow who was legendary by 1883, and the master of ceremonies Widdicomb (1813–68) who was involved with Ducrow's circus and performed regularly at the Vauxhall Gardens being appointed Master of Ceremonies there in 1842 (Coke 2017). John Ducrow, who was Astley's clown and the performer both referred to and illustrated here (he used make-up similar to the more famous Grimaldi) died in 1834 (Highfill, Burnim and Langhans 2006: 494). The author of the story Duval is illustrating may be thinking of a spectacular pantomime of *St George and the Dragon* which was performed by Astley's in January 1834, and either misremembering the date or fudging the issue, having committed her/his character to the date of 1835 earlier in the sequence.

Duval's illustrations are a whistle-stop tour of historical circus practices (in the way that these were performed onstage by 1834 and still were in 1883) including and emphasising clowning and physical movement. The conceit of the storyline also allows Duval to depict consecutively the world of circus viewed by the audience followed by the view backstage. Having come to London, Gran'papa visits Astley's in the third episode and watches the performance from a box (Duval 1883d); in the fourth he is taken to Drury Lane by his 'friend the M.C.' (Duval 1884b) who attempts to get him in free to the performance and then at the interval succeeds in getting him backstage to watch where he gets in the way to the extent that he is thrown out. Thus, the fourth episode revisits backstage mechanisms Duval has depicted earlier such as the stage trap.

These two panels are done in Duval's 'formal' style and depict moving bodies far more 'realistically' than any referred to earlier in this chapter. In this respect it is likely that, as in her fashion work, Duval may have been referring to picture references, some of which may have been historical for her. Thus, Ducrow is shown in his classic make-up apparently bursting through a hoop, but his posture is actually that of a figure walking forward rather than in flight through the hoop headfirst. Similarly, the beautiful Miss Woolford, shown twice, is accurately rendered with her horses in formal perspective. The personal reference to Gran'papa's splitting headache the following morning allows Duval to create an anthropomorphic bottle and a distorted, tiny Ducrow hitting Gran'papa's sleeping head with a hammer, exploiting her interest in the surreal.

The drawing of 16 January, depicting Drury Lane, is less historically constrained (Duval 1884b; Figure 8.14). The performance is a double bill of play and pantomime. The play, *George Bramwell or the London Merchant*, would have been a revival even in 1834 or 1835 of George Lillo's 1731 tragedy. Gran'papa is relieved when this is over and he is taken backstage for the pantomime, and it is this which Duval exclusively shows. Thus we see the clown diving through the scenery and crashing into Gran'papa, the 'spill and pelt' scene,[10] which he gets inadvertently involved in, the beautiful Columbine (who turns out to be an elderly actress drinking porter) and even the stage hands who he stands drinks, shown by Duval operating a trap for a fairy and presumably working a lantern. The final image, of another clown in Ducrow-style make-up, who is literally juggling live chickens, is perhaps the beginning of the spill and pelt scene.

Duval's individual style is represented most clearly by the drinking actress and the Duvallian chickens being apparently juggled by the clown. This drawing would appear to be evidence of the longevity of these tropes, since spill and pelt scenarios remained staple fare through the Hanlon brothers' work and into the vaudeville-inspired films of 'Fatty' Arbuckle, Chaplin and Keaton in the first part of the twentieth century (for example 'The Complete Buster Keaton Short Films 1917–1923' 2016). Indeed, the Hanlons were notable for introducing violence into their slapstick scenarios, as Thomas Walton writing

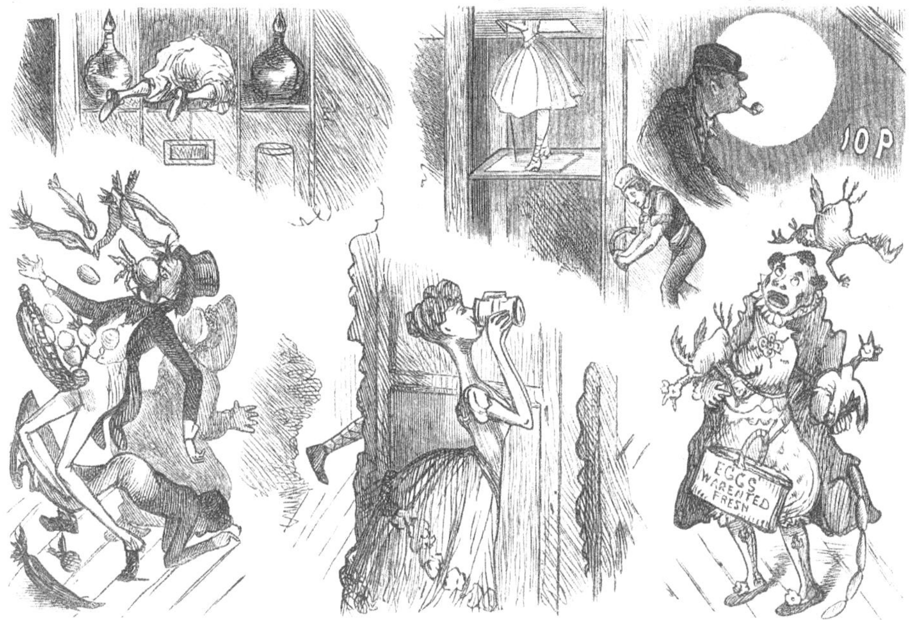

8.14 Marie Duval (1884) 'The Goings on of Gran'papa', *Judy, or the London Serio-comic Journal*, Volume 34, p. 27

in 1943 and cited in McKinven emphasises: 'For over a century English pantomimists had been celebrated in France for their eccentricity, their awe-inspiring rough and tumble. The Hanlon-Lees startled even English audiences [...] [and] violence was characteristic of their work from the very beginning; it was one of their greatest attractions in the eyes of Parisians' (McKinven 1998: 34). The casual violence of Arbuckle's vaudeville-inspired spill and pelt scenes seems both shocking by today's standards and highly likely to have left Gran'papa 'badly bruised and black and blue all over' as he reports (Duval 1884b).

Conclusion

Thus, over the sixteen years of her drawing, Duval provides us with a wide range of images which depict the physicality of her profession as an actor. Reference to contemporary images and documentation suggest that aspects of theatrical activity such as transformation scenes in pantomime influenced the layout and conception of some of her work. Similarly, her interest in the movement of bodies through space and in the distortions of our perceptions of rapid movement, results in a large body of visual imagery that may be associated with tumbling and clowning.

This is especially the case when, like performers such as the Hanlon-Lees Troupe, she is putting extreme physical actions into everyday settings. There is also a small but significant documentary aspect to her work, and some of her images are specifically about spectacular aspects of theatre including flying and other stage mechanics, and extravagant and comic costumes. The overall dynamism of her drawing suggests that her knowledge of spectacle and her work in inevitably close proximity to circus, music hall acrobatics and other physically demanding performance, allowed her to depict the actions and presence of bodies in space through a unique gestural, graphic style that communicates movement, and theatrical movement at that, more vividly than many of her contemporaries trained in the visual arts.

Notes

1 In the British Film Institute's *Fairy Tales* there are several occasions where the Pathe tinters have reproduced this specific coloured smoke effect.

2 A shallow scene taking place at the front of the stage whilst the bulk of the stage behind was being prepared by the carpenters of the theatre. A simple drop curtain was also used for this.

3 Another of Duval's pseudonyms. She signed herself Noir for a sequence of carefully worked drawings with much use of black, which she made in 1875. See Introduction to this volume.

4 An example of Munby's mixture of prurience and prudery often pointed out by contemporary feminist theorists. See for example Day in Gardiner and Rutherford 1992: 140–6.

5 There is a delightful account of Leotard's premiere in London in the Australian newspaper the *Sydney and Sporting Chronical* of 1860, 'Lyotard at the Alhambra' 1861: 4. The effect of seeing a flying trapeze act for the first ever time is described with breathless excitement and may make the reader realise how such art forms are now taken for granted, but how impossibly virtuosic they actually are.

6 Although it seems entirely arbitrary and is unexplained, I offer the suggestion that the climbers are being blown up by a chance volcano vent.

7 I have so far been unable to determine in which production this appeared. McKinven writes that it was 'a fantastic play involving a shipwreck' (McKinven 1998: 40) and Southern, incorrectly, that it was the opening sequence of *Le Voyage en Suisse* (Southern 1970: 105). McKinven is relying on Georges Moynet's extraordinary 1893 work *Trucs et Décor* which gives descriptions and imagery of stage machinery of the period in incredible detail but fails to give the name of the particular performance. Thus, it is certain is that the stage machinery was used by the Hanlons in Paris in about 1880. Moynet does say that it was produced as part of a pantomime by the Hanlons in Paris 'not long ago': 'Nous allons mettre sous les yeux du lecteur les équipes d'un paquebot, qui se produisit, il n'y a pas longtemps, su las scene d'un théâtre parisien. La pièce a ait été écrite avec une partie de pantomime jouée par une troupe d'acrobates agiles et amusants, celle des Hanlon-Lee' (Moynet 1893: 81). It is also certain that William Hanlon took out an American patent (No. 263900) for the same stage machinery in September 1882, which is consistent with the troupe's subsequent activity in the United States (McKinven 1998: 92).

8 This was a vertical trapdoor in scenery, such that a performer would leap through it flying horizontally and disappear, rather than the better-known trapdoor in the floor of a stage, which

would propel a performer upwards or downwards. The leap trap consists of two flaps hinged at top and bottom. It is used in a number of early films, for example Keaton's 1923 *Sherlock Junior* ('Sherlock Junior' 2001) and there is an image of one from *Punch* 1852 (reproduced in Southern 1970: 34).

9 In an earlier sequence in *Sherlock Junior* (1923) Keaton jumps through a papered hoop set in a window, which contains a dress, combining the leap with a costume change (1970: 34).

10 A graphic name for, as might be expected, a routine where comedians spill things and throw them at each other!

9

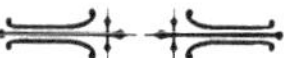

A women's cartoonist?

Roger Sabin

Duval's female characters present a puzzle. If we ask whether she was a women's cartoonist, this points to several supplementary questions. Was her work aimed at a female readership, and did she emphasise 'female issues' and female characters? (After all, must not there be a difference between strips and cartoons that happen to have been drawn by a woman, and 'women's cartooning', which purposefully concerns itself with the expression of women's experience?) And was she 'for women' in the sense of being pro-women's rights? In other words, was she a feminist, with all the definitional problems that the term implies?

This chapter provides a selective survey of strips, cartoons and illustrations in order to look for clues. It functions as a complement to Chapter 2, but takes a different perspective based on historicising the work in relation to nineteenth-century expectations of behaviour, and what it meant for Duval to work in a 'serio-comic' mode.

By way of introduction, it is helpful to position Duval in a history of women's cartooning. It is clear that she was not the first funny woman to make drawing her chosen mode. Within the eighteenth- and nineteenth-century print tradition, and especially regarding caricatures, women were present as patrons, publishers and artists (albeit in far smaller numbers than men). In the eighteenth century the most prominent was Mary Darly (1756–79), who, according to one historian, was 'the first to recognise the commercial potential of the fashion for caricature' and whose *A Book of Caricaturas* was aimed at 'young gentlemen and ladies' (O'Connell 2018: 11).

Moving on to the nineteenth century, and as the extension of the print industry into magazine publishing heralded new opportunities, so women's magazines became a genre, with some specialising in humour. *The Comic Offering*, the subtitle of which was 'The Ladies' Melange of Literary Mirth', lasted from 1831 to 1835 (published by Smith, Elder and Company); it had a female editor, Louisa Henrietta Sheridan, who may also have contributed illustrations (Hunt 1996).[1] General humour magazines later in the century saw women's names appearing more frequently. *Punch* (1841) had female writers from

216

1856, and its most prominent early illustrator was Georgina Bowers, who became known for her hunting scenes (see also Chapter 6).[2] The post-*Punch* boom in magazines made space for women to contribute to various titles, sometimes simultaneously, and names included sisters Adelaide and Florence Claxton.

Such rudimentary scoping of the past is necessary because the details are not well known, and in the context of the large amount of published drawing in the period, the historical record relating to women is sparse to the point of near invisibility. This is partly due to prejudice. Not only have commercial artists been ignored, but women's efforts to assume a comedic role have been doubly marginalised, because of a pervasive prejudice that humour was out of bounds (see Wagner-Lawlor 2000 and Chapter 6). The first major history of *Punch* (1895) states that 'women, as a rule, are humourists neither born nor made' (Spielmann 1895: 392).

How this relates to Duval is obvious. She was pushing against this environment every day of her working life. Because she was prolific and successful, it seems fair to call her a 'pioneer'. But this epithet, too, comes freighted with assumptions. For example, a pioneer of what? The answer to that usually means later comics. The modern conflation of 'cartooning' with the making of comic strips functions to her advantage because so much of her output was in this mode (see Chapter 1). Similarly, a significant proportion of twentieth- and twenty-first-century comics production has been devoted to slapstick laughs, and she can be seen as part of this tradition.

Also, Duval's status as a 'pioneer' is salient partly as a result of the huge expansion in women's cartooning in particular (mostly in comics and graphic novels).[3] Today, it is still true that women creators are a minority, and are severely marginalised in some sectors of the comics industry, but they are active as writers and artists, and as editors and proprietors. Some of the most important and successful comics of recent times have been by women.[4] This phenomenon has led to the asking of new questions about the past, including about the value of reclaiming hidden voices – Duval's among them.

But retrospective judgements are problematic, and we need to be mindful of the paradigm shift within Comics Studies in the way 'firsts' are approached. To summarise, many scholars now believe that hybridity is the key theme in media evolution, and that change is a constant. Technology and style fluctuate and alter at a rate that is uneven, and ideas are constantly travelling from one media form to another. This unstable terrain suggests that, theoretically speaking, settling on a 'first' or a 'pioneer' is controversial at best, and impossible at worst.

None of which background should distract us from the questions about Duval that opened this chapter, and which prompt the focus of it. The gendered nature of her work reveals a story about not just her, but where 'women's cartooning' and 'cartooning by women' fitted into the broader picture of the nineteenth-century entertainment industry. This brings us back to *Judy*, and we need to ask whether this was a publication that actively courted a female readership. Its relationship with *Punch* is key here, because it was going for a slice of its market, which meant men (see also Chapter 1). This was the demographic who traditionally bought humorous magazines, and who had the disposable income to do so. The main editorial thrust at *Judy* was therefore to cover 'male issues' and satisfy the male gaze.[5]

Just how far *Punch* was defined by a masculinist approach needs to be emphasised. As Patrick Leary has pointed out, it was put together in 'a sea of talk' among men conspiring together in a manner that was exclusive: 'Every Wednesday evening the staff would gather [...] and over [...] many glasses of champagne and the inevitable cigars, proceed to fire off puns, reminisce, trade gossip [...] tell dirty jokes, pontificate and argue about matters sexual, political and religious' (Leary 2010: 1). It was a self-styled literary brotherhood, which traded in a kind of humour that excluded women on a variety of levels: for example, coarse jokes and matters of high politics were not considered 'their business'. This, then, was a specific culture, and as comedy theorist Andrew Stott notes, 'the question of how or why things come to be funny is determined by culture' (Stott 2004: 15).

The producers of *Judy* had no intention of going this far, and indeed the magazine differentiated itself by taking a more feminised approach, as symbolised by having a woman in its title. The idea of courting a female readership made business sense: if men could be persuaded to buy *Judy* instead of *Punch*, or along with *Punch* (or, indeed, along with any of the other *Punch* copyists on the market), then it could be sold on the basis that it was appealing to 'the man and the lady of the house'. As for women purchasers per se, by the final decades of the century women had more disposable income, and greater numbers from all classes were reading in general (which meant changes in the book, magazine and newspaper markets). If *Judy* was never 'dual address' in the modern sense of that term, then at least women were part of the plan.

Female readers themselves were subject to certain restrictions. The home was the default venue for reading; pubs and cafes could often be male spaces, and the same went for clubs: working men's clubs and more middle-class clubs mostly excluded women, and the rise of women's clubs did not take place until the 1890s. Middle-class women would have had more opportunity to read because they would have had servants and were therefore freed from domestic labour; they also had more opportunity to read by gas-lamp and later electric lighting (both of which were expensive). As for *Judy* capturing women readers from the lower classes, this was not as improbable as it once might have seemed. As we have noted, cheap publications circulated in ways that were ubiquitous and 'democratic' (see Chapter 1), and literacy levels were relatively high. By the end of the century, jokey accounts were appearing of slaveys (maids-of-all-work) reading cheap periodicals, sometimes having been discarded by their employers.[6]

But during the first two decades of *Judy*'s existence, things were changing rapidly for women, as the more severe patriarchal strictures were challenged, and employment possibilities increased. This was the period of the rise of the lower-middle class, and the first sightings of the New Woman. As women became a new consumer market, so they partook more in the business of leisure, and there is evidence for the expansion of women's publications, clothes and cosmetics, as well as their rising presence in the audiences at theatres and music halls, and as spectators at certain kinds of sport.

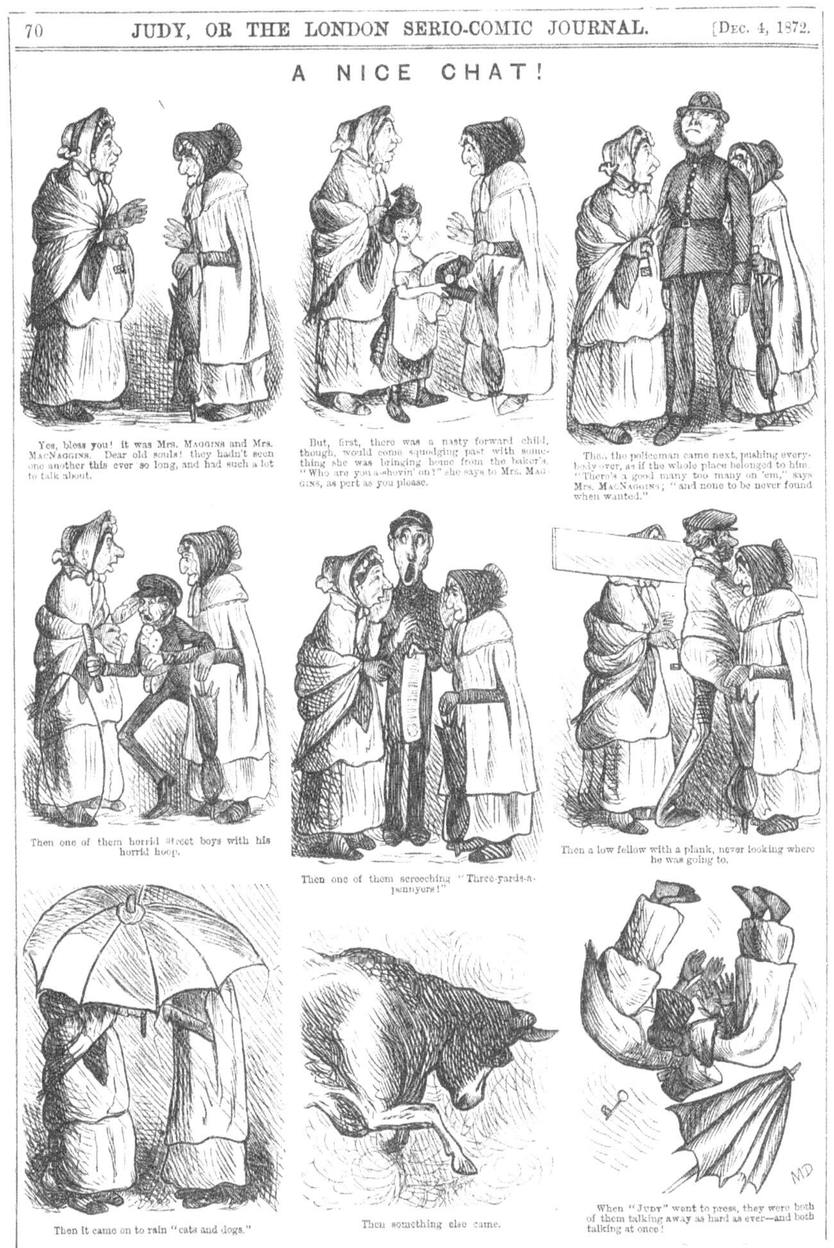

9.1 Marie Duval (1872) 'A Nice Chat!', *Judy, or the London Serio-comic Journal*, Volume 12, p. 70

In response, *Judy*'s female-friendly spin became more marked over time. The content was one thing, but it was undergirded by the fact that women were a prominent part of the creative team, thereby pre-empting any notion of a 'brotherhood' (we have noted the presence of Bowers and others at *Punch*, but *Judy* was more inclusive). There was Duval, of course, but also Clotilde Graves (who would garner a reputation as a New Woman) and Ellen Clayton, both of whom were primarily writers, though Graves did produce spot illustrations.[7] There was also Adelaide Claxton, who produced complex and mannered cartoons about upper-middle-class and upper-class life. By 1880, the contributors to the *Almanack* included Florence Marryat, Kate Field and Annie Thomas (all writers). There were no doubt more, but because so much material was anonymous it is now hard to tell.

Did these women have a significant influence on *Judy*'s editorial direction? This is arguable. And it is true that the model of the 'male club' was not eschewed entirely, especially in the sense of the way the magazine was conceived. There is evidence that the old ways endured, and that the pub was the favoured place for editorial meetings, specifically, the Cheshire Cheese, off Fleet Street. We can only conjecture as to whether female creative practitioners were invited, or, indeed, would have wished to go along. All existing portrayals of the Cheshire Cheese indicate that it was a smoky, testosterone-fuelled dive – indeed, the only time Duval herself depicted it, it was full of men (Duval 1877i).[8]

However, the very presence of women on the creative team had profound consequences for *Judy*. Even if they were being pushed down a particular editorial path (or were required to pull their punches in what they had to say, which is debatable in some cases), they affected the tone of the magazine as well as reader expectations.[9] Mostly, this process would have been subtle: the way a topic was approached, the people referenced, how clothes were drawn. But sometimes their presence was more overt, and this would have been a powerful signal. For example, both Duval and Claxton signed their work prominently, in many cases.

As *Judy* added more female-oriented content over time, so its nature became more refined. Of course, it would be wrong to assume that women readers were uninterested in high satire or reports on Westminster. Or that images designed for the male gaze did not also have an appeal to the female gaze. Nevertheless, the idea that 'women's issues' existed was an accepted part of entertainment and consumer culture, and one historian has noted that 'regardless of their economic or social status, Victorian women liked to read about love, marriage, children, fashion, hobbies, personal enrichment, and other women' (Ledbetter 2016: 274). *Judy* was more ambitious than this and included a smorgasbord of content for its (implied) culture-savvy readership.

So, for example, in terms of prose fiction, the review columns included female authors who were both established and up-and-coming and who were not always producing 'high-end' literature. A column from 1879 gives the thumbs-up both to Frances Burnett's *Haworth's* (a 'lifelike and stirring' melodramatic tome with characters that included working-class women and the illegitimate daughter of a fallen woman) and Mary Elizabeth Braddon's *Vixen* (a 'sensation' story about a gritty tomboy dealing with bereavement and romance) ('Thumbmarks' 1879a). The theatrical coverage similarly featured a range from high to low (from West End theatres to less-than-salubrious East End music halls), and focused on favourite performers like Ellen Terry (actress), Nelly Farren (singer), Nelly Power (singer) and Harriet Coveney (actress).

Similarly, *Judy* took a particular interest in fashion. Clothing was described in close detail, often as a digression in comedic stories; and the cartoon depictions were lavish, usually of a particular look that happened to be in fashion, or a parodic version thereof. One of the more flamboyant portrayers of women's fashion was Archibald Chasemore, who had a parallel career as a costume designer for the theatre. As one edition put it: '*Judy* is the one and only reliable authority on ladies' dresses, and [insists] that every pretty fashion now in vogue has long previously been foreshadowed in her sprightly pages' ('Thumbmarks' 1879b).

When it came to 'women's politics', the magazine's position was complex. In so far as it hove to a Conservative Party line (see Chapter 1), this meant taking into account the huge range of opinions that existed within the party. For example, on suffrage, there were plenty of 'anti' hardliners, but also powerful voices in the 'pro' camp, including Disraeli himself. On issues such as employment, education and marriage, there was similarly no unified Conservative voice, meaning that *Judy*'s gags tended towards *Punch*-style mockery, but with plenty of room for ambiguity and change over time.

The magazine's matriarch was, of course, Judy herself.[10] She was not just a totem; she was given a 'personality' that could appeal to women without alienating men. This meant making her assertive, which in turn meant subverting her role in the traditional puppet show, which would have been well known by readers. In the show, she is Mr Punch's wife, and is beaten up by him on an extended basis. She is essentially a battered spouse. But now, Judy was her own woman, and in no way inferior to Punch, a statement about both the status of the magazines, and of the sexes. The very first issue set the tone. Judy is pictured on a platform labelled 'Protection of Women', giving her 'Opening Speech', in which she entreats women to 'grind [men] to dust' (which, of course, amusingly played into fears of women taking over the world). Meanwhile, in the 'Correspondence' section that follows, there's a 'backlash' to her speech, wherein a letter-writer who signs '[A] Woman Who Knows Her Place' begs Judy to 'listen to the voice of [...] Punch' (A Woman Who Knows Her Place 1867).

This new iteration of the Judy character was developed over the years, and her connection with the country's women reinforced. In 1872, a column began, 'It is needless to say that Judy is an advocate of women's rights' ('Miss Field and Women's Rights' 1872), and this was a sentiment repeated constantly, sometimes in ironic fashion, and sometimes not. Her status as powerful and in control was underlined by the way in which the magazine frequently associated her with another, rather well-known, powerful and ageing woman: Queen Victoria. In a cheeky move, the connection with Empress Victoria was made clear when Judy was pictured as the 'Empress of Fleet Street' (Boucher 1876a).

As time went on, the textual clues as to readership became more obvious. There were more images of women reading periodicals, and as reader competitions became fashionable, so more of the names of the winners were female. Above all, advertising was indicative. This became more important to the economy for *Judy* over time (as competitor publications multiplied), with the appearance of advertisements for everything from sewing machines to laundry starch in the main magazine, and corsets to recipe books and children's medicinal powders in the spin-off volumes. As an aside: the nature of these advertisements suggest that however sophisticated the female readership may have been in reality, whoever was responsible for the advertising provision still saw them as feminine and domestic.

It would be nice to be able to corroborate what we can learn from the text itself with evidence from diaries, letters, biographies and autobiographies. Unfortunately, no such records survive. There are scrapbooks made up of *Judy* content, however, and in so far as scrap-booking was coded as female in the nineteenth century, this may be an indicator of readership. However, it is not much, and just as female cartoonists have been forgotten, so too have female readers, accounting for why, in the words of one historian, 'The laughing woman is the least remembered woman of the Victorian period' (Stetz 2000: 219).

So, how did Duval fit in? She was, unsurprisingly, a major part of *Judy*'s female orientation. Even the way she drew can be seen as making a gendered point: her art was in complete contrast to the male-dominated, *Punch*-style, satirical tradition. As shown in Chapters 1 and 6, the contrast was deliberately provocative, and, indeed, became one of her selling points. This is not to say her drawing style was intrinsically 'female', in the sense of being associated with intimacy and a heightened (female) reader connection: this idea has been superseded.[11] Instead, it mattered because it made a statement, one which was underscored by the existence of a signature, growing over time from a shy 'MD' in a corner to a full-blown 'MARIE DUVAL' in upper-case lettering.

Indeed, her name itself can be seen as a signifier. Duval was known as an actor (although her fame as such was eclipsed considerably by her fame as a cartoonist) and, originally, Tessier would have taken the name presumably so as not to embarrass her family, because the acting profession was not respectable. Indeed, in the less tolerant corners of the Victorian imagination, as expressed in some of the newspapers, female actors were sometimes equated with sex workers: both were nocturnal, put on make-up and 'displayed themselves for money'. Some theatres and halls were notorious pick-up spots for sex workers, and some actors did indeed moonlight in this profession – which was not yet illegal.

The obvious Frenchness of the Duval name was another factor, and would have pushed these associations into further erotic territory. This was both because Paris was the place where sexual taboos were (in the minds of the British) being broken by the week, and because French books and plays were often seen as semi-pornographic: '[Britons have] got to look upon the portrayal on the stage of the passions and vices existing all over the world [...] as French', complained *Judy*'s theatre critic ('The Only Jones' 1875). Duval may not have been seen by readers as a libertine, but for some she might have been reckoned to be heading in that direction.[12]

We can extrapolate that the Duval name had an impact on how her strips and cartoons were received, and possibly gave her permission to explore territory that might ordinarily have been seen as out of bounds. If we follow the logic of pseudonymity as a kind of performance, that is, as a role that can be assumed, then Duval was playing a game with gendered identity.[13] The signature, her style and her 'Duval-ness' were all part of a self-conscious performance, undertaken with a knowing audience in mind. Looked at in this light, she was a performer on the page, as well as on the stage.

As for the subject matter of Duval's work, she was, by default, the most prolific chronicler of women's lives at the magazine. Because of the volume of her output (outlined in Chapter 1), women feature not just prominently, but in all manifestations – young and old; tall and short; fat and thin; clever and stupid; fashionable and unfashionable; British and foreign (European, Japanese, African, Polynesian); upper-class, middle-class and lower-class; white and ethnic; Christian and non-Christian; workers (slaveys, performers, writers, artists) and non-workers (mothers and the equivalents of 'ladies who lunch' [maintained women]); contemporary and historical (medieval queens and princesses); and 'realistic' and fantastical (fairy-tale characters).

Because of *Judy*'s editorial emphasis, however, especially on current cultural affairs in London, women of two kinds were foregrounded. The first was the young beauty (unmarried, demure, heterosexual, white). This stereotype was useful because it created a space for cartooning about performing sexiness, complemented by jokes about 'mashing' (and other kinds of manners within the 'sex war'), and about fashion. The second category was the older woman ('old' being an appellation that could start around 40 in the Victorian period): hunched, black-clad, bespectacled, often witch-like. This type was contrasted with her younger sisters and played off against them; it provided space for commentary on ageing, and especially roles for chaperones, 'spinsters' and matriarchs.

A sidebar here about that word 'mashing'. It is a term that was ubiquitous in late Victorian culture, but has since disappeared from the English language, at least in its original meaning.[14] It translates roughly as 'flirting', but could be a synonym for an infatuation, as in 's/he's a mash', or 's/he is mashable'. It also seems to have been used more vaguely, in the sense of dressing up to go out, specifically with the intention of attracting a romantic partner. The context for mashing involved the strict rules of Victorian courtship, whereby men were expected to treat women of every social class according to a code of chivalry, and women were never expected to take the lead in social discourse.

We will look at these two kinds of female stereotype, but first it is necessary to posit some supplementary questions. For example, how did Duval observe her women? One method was in her role as a kind of visual journalist, as Simon Grennan argues in Chapter 5. In this regard, she can be counted among a growing number of female journalists (overwhelmingly writers) in the UK press, and although their contribution is only just beginning to be fully understood, still it was true that, to quote historian Barbara Onslow, 'On almost every issue, from vivisection to the penal system, from fashion to astronomy, women had their say' (Onslow 2000: 3). Indeed, within the pages of *Judy* itself, a number of pioneering women journalists 'had their say', albeit in comedic mode (Clotilde Graves being the prime example; see Onslow 2000: 3 and Bloodworth 2013).

Duval's visual journalism also had much in common with the *flâneuse*, in the sense that this figure was being constructed in contemporary culture.[15] The idea of the female city-walker implied a different kind of spectatorship than that engaged in by men: according to one historian, whereas the *flâneur* was 'dispassionate [...] disinterested and clinical', the *flâneuse* was 'engaged and sympathetic, preoccupied with the interplay of human relationships' (Musgrove 2009: 160, quoted in Hall and Grennan 2019). Duval's was not a respectable kind of *flânerie*, either. Such walking-and-observing had famously been described by Balzac as concerning women promenading on boulevards and shopping, never stopping to chat with anybody. Duval, however, was interested in 'ordinary' women, going about their business. She was an observer of everyday city life, and this made her transgressive (also see Chapter 2).[16]

Her observations of London women had idiosyncrasies. For example, she lived by the railway (near Clapham Junction) and it is noticeable how many of her strips and cartoons involve what historian Peter Bailey has termed 'railway erotics' – young women being propositioned on a train, mashed on a platform, kissed in a tunnel and so on (Bailey 2004). Duval was also a stage performer, and that entailed an intimate knowledge of the goings-on in front of the theatre curtain and behind it. The adventures of her actors, singers, ballerinas, stage-hands and audience members have a ring of truth, and, indeed, sometimes she was specific about her sources, as in the case of the strip 'The Beast and the Beauty at the Royalty' (Duval 1869c; Figure 3.2), which was about a pantomime at a Soho theatre (a venue which happened to be managed by a woman).

As for fashion, the rhythm of changing London looks was something that would have been visible to her on a day-to-day basis, especially if she made the trip to the *Judy* offices on Shoe Lane. London was the Number Two fashion centre of the world, and Duval worked on a serial publication with a particular interest in the subject. The Number One fashion centre was Paris. The growth of couturier houses, the fashion press and fashion shows was cementing its reputation, and the term 'haute couture' originated in the 1860s. Duval's French heritage was clearly useful in giving her fashion-inflected stories a Gallic twist. For example, she produced a pair of collage-style pages entitled 'Encore des Bêtises' (Duval 1874h and 1876e), a phrase which roughly translates as 'More Nonsense', involving women's hand-held fans and kinds of dresses.

But if Duval was a journalist, she was a *comedy* journalist. Her other key influence was modes of humour, especially as performed on the stage. This meant absorbing received notions of performative types and comedy scenarios, particularly derived from the burgeoning music hall scene. It is hard to overestimate how far *Judy* was bound up with the performance industry, and Duval continued to be part of it for many years into her cartooning career. Thus, comedy stereotypes borrowed for the page were convenient because they were 'pre-loaded' with information.

Again, the types would have been London types (female examples include the slavey, the coster's girlfriend, the fashionable flirt, the fearsome landlady, the chaperone and performers of various kinds), and the mode of comedy quite localised. Rendezvous points for romance tended to be famous London sites (for example, London Bridge, St Paul's Cathedral, Covent Garden). Dialect was location-specific, and when one young woman declares her pal to be 'a perfick lady', there is little question to which social class they belong or where they live (Duval 1876i).

The politics of Duval's work are unsurprisingly complex. For her women readers, it would be tempting to argue that her stories were part of a wider 'culture of consolation', a balm for the soul, rather than a questioning of the status quo. In most of her work, she does not veer away from the 'two spheres' theory of society, and the other hierarchies of Victorian behaviour are respected. She makes (ostensibly) simple comedy out of everyday affairs. A housewife leaves the children in charge of the laundry and chaos ensues; a lonely tripper on a visit to the beach scrapes 'What Is Love' in the sand; four young women wearing long dresses negotiate puddles on a rainy day (Duval 1872a; 1873f; 1875i).

Her stories are often about 'quotidian women' trying to enjoy themselves, at the seaside, at the music hall, at the races, at the skating rink or at home. She captures their trials and tribulations, and winds up with a punchline. Such narratives are not necessarily jabbing at men, though some do; and they seemingly do not represent an activist ('feminist') 'spur to action'. What they do is say 'this is how life is, and occasionally it can be funny'. Or, in other words, 'the two spheres exist, so let's laugh at them'.

Is this conservatism 'reactionary'? For some observers, then and now, no doubt. But why does observational humour have to be seen as negative? Put another way, what is so wrong with consolation? Andy Medhurst (2007: 65) asks this question in relation to class-based comedy, adding that consolation works: 'Especially for audiences whose working day consisted of […] repetitive and soul-destroying labour.'[17] The general point can be applied to all women's lives in the nineteenth century, at least to some measure.

Thus, if we step back, Duval's work is about the laughs available in a bigger context of male suppression, and of the frequent grimness of everyday life in a patriarchal society. Such a reading can be seen as politically significant in its own terms, in so far as the stories give women a profile, and suggest that their lives matter: 'comedy [of this kind] is primarily a politics of defence, not attack, of refusal not uprising, of embracing your own, of consolation against condescension' (Medhurst 2007: 69).

But there are other ways of looking at Duval's work, and a close reading of some of the strips (and strips, in particular) reveals resistive strategies that are hard to ignore. When it comes to depicting women, Duval's output is characterised by a tension between seemingly conservative storylines, often supported by cartooning modes that reinforce gender norms, and comedic 'tweaks' that undercut them. This is a double-edged process that gathers power from being repeated week after week, and which can be argued to result in a cumulative subversion of socio-political expectations.

The best way to make this process evident is to look at some examples, and for the purposes of analysis, I concentrate on the two prominent kinds of female representation identified: the young, mashable woman and the old hag. The former fitted into ostensibly conservative scenarios quite comfortably: these were flirtatious young things, brides-to-be and brides, and their stories are correspondingly unexceptional, involving flirting, formal courting, and then marriage and family. Duval's depictive mode is also 'standard' in the sense that these women are portrayed as being doll-like. Such representation was typical in Victorian cartooning, and fed into narratives about how women were assumed to be 'pure', morally angelic, demure and goddess-like, but also how they were somehow child-like and obsessed with frivolity. It conveniently fed the male gaze, since such a construction of femininity was undoubtedly erotic.

But the 'Duvallian tweak' is never far away. For example, 'Expression!' (Duval 1872g, Figure 9.2) features a typically glacial doll-like portrait that invites the viewer to contemplate the insouciant expression on her face. The caption, however, explains: 'This sweet thing let her Mother die in the Workhouse.' This simple act of ironic juxtaposition undercuts not just the idea of young women's supposed moral superiority, but also a whole cartooning tradition. It is possible to imagine the gag working on stage, as well, with a comedian observing a beautiful actress and commenting in much the same way in an aside to the audience.

Moral purity is again the subject of 'The Latest Horror at the Old Bailey' (Duval 1877j), a strip which starts off, unremarkably, with a 'young lady of fashion' eager to get somewhere unspecified before she misses an unnamed event. However, as the story unfolds it is clear that it is about how young women – pretty/vacant – are flocking to the public gallery of the famous courthouse to watch trials involving unspeakable crimes. Their 'absolute necessities' for the trip are a bottle of sherry and a box of sandwiches, and we now realise that the one in the first panel was holding a pair of binoculars. The final panel is a postscript, and imagines an old man asking his granddaughter what she would like as a present on her birthday, and her replying: 'Take me to see them hanged, grandpapa, please!'

In 'Spring, Summer, Autumn, Winter', the trope of idealising marriage is under attack. It starts off as 'an allegorical picture' of some young 'dears' being pestered by cupids and fantasising about romance (marriage, wealth, a cottage in the countryside). However, the final panel is of a young wife in bed next to her husband: she is wide awake, unable to sleep, while he snores loudly. This, we are told, is the 'reality of Love's young dream' (Duval 1875g).

This riff is returned to in 'Dreams. And the Awakening'. A little girl dreams of marrying a handsome dancing instructor; a schoolgirl dreams of marrying a dashing corsair; a wealthy young lady dreams of marrying a peer of the realm. But, lo! The reality is a rather ordinary man who is short of stature and has a receding hairline ('What it all ended with: Mr Tompkins!'). The final panel is of an older lady waiting forlornly with a candle for Mr Tompkins to come home after a night on the tiles (Duval 1878i).

As for young women supposedly exhibiting demure behaviour, strips often start in conservative fashion and then become something more wild. For example, in 'Such Young Things Too' a couple visit Paris on a tourist excursion and slip away from the tour group in order to dance the cancan at a club (Duval 1878j, Figure 9.3). Here, Duval's dancing

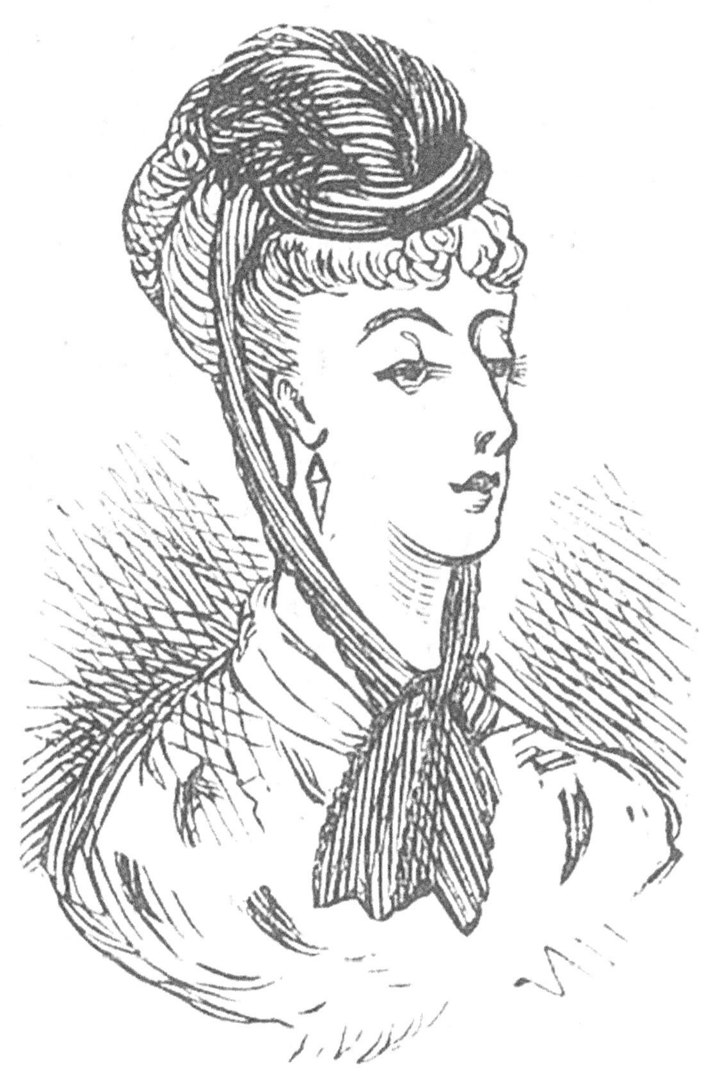

9.2 Marie Duval (1872) 'Expression!', *Judy, or the London Serio-comic Journal*, Volume 12,
p. 60 (detail)

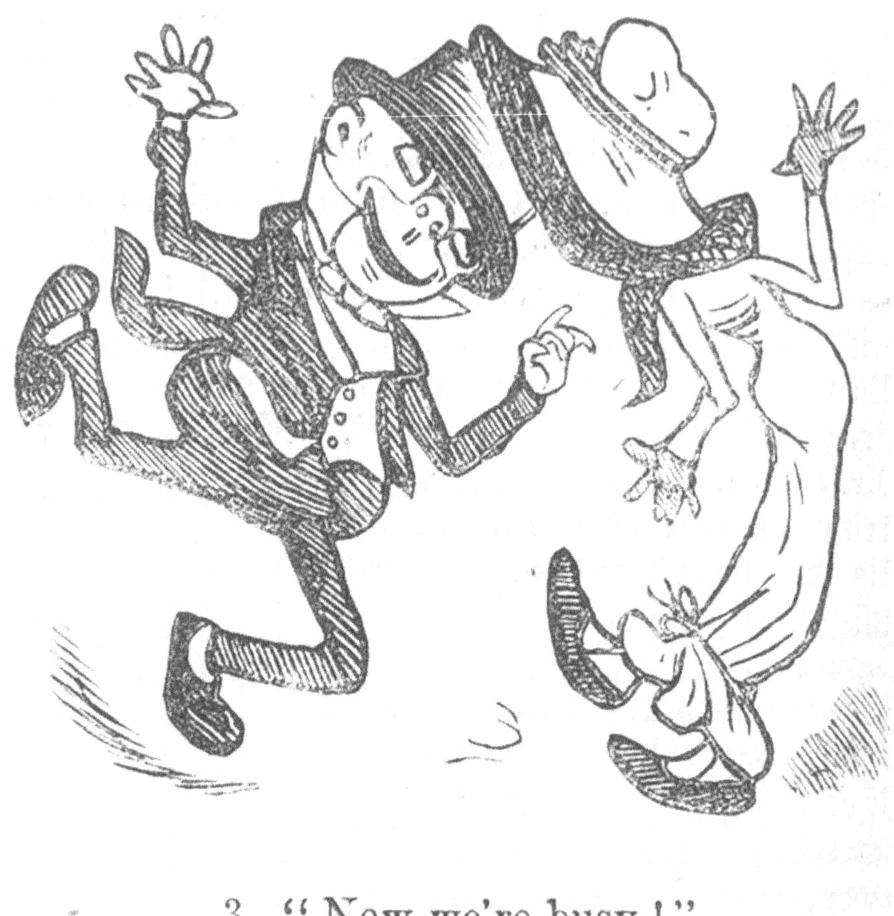

9.3 Marie Duval (1878) 'Such Young Things Too', *Judy, or the London Serio-comic Journal,*
Volume 23, p. 122 (detail)

woman, still dressed in a long skirt and a bonnet, is a thing of elastic, abandoned, joy.
She is a subversion both of repressed manners and how the female body 'should' be
displayed (see Butler 1990; 1993; Rowe 1995).

The same kind of trick is applied to stories about the supposed 'weakness' of young
women (a function both of their state of 'purity' and their distance from the world of
labour). Thus, in terms of physical weakness, there are many Sloper stories in which
women end up putting him to shame, or, indeed, beating him up. In 'Romeo and Juliet.

228

(From a Sloperian Point of View)' (Duval 1876j), the first image is of a conventionally shy woman being wooed by him, while the second is an image of his inert body, having been stabbed by her with his own umbrella. In 'Ally Sloper: Slayer of Wolves!!!' (a three-parter – Duval 1875j; 1875k; 1875l), he is sent on a mission to rid a French village of a marauding wolf, and fails miserably: in the end, it is down to a skinny female villager to strangle it. Meanwhile, in terms of mental weakness, 'Recent Occurrences' pictures a young woman sobbing, apparently due to a broken heart: in fact, it is because she has pricked her nose when accidentally sniffing a cactus (Duval 1873r).

Duval's subversions of the role of young women in the workplace depended on social class. At one end of the scale, slaveys were a favourite concern. Domestic service was by far the biggest employer of working-class women in London, and Duval's slaveys were defined by their distinctive bonnets, plain dress and underfed appearance. In amongst the 'conventional' stories (where they get on with their jobs in the background, or are foils for the amorous attentions of the master of the house) there are glimpses of other scenarios, where they skive off, for instance, or break the house rules. When they are left in charge of children, this is particularly disastrous: there is a recurring Duval image of a slavey holding a child by the ankles and dangling them upside down (the reason could be anything from 'getting some colour into their cheeks', or dunking them in the sea to get used to the water). Such a striking image was not only a subversion of the job, but of the stereotype of the 'nurturing woman'.

In one strip, Duval goes further, and imagines a world turned upside down, where slaveys go on strike and gain the upper hand, resulting in the house being controlled by them. Here, slaveys can entertain any number of gentleman callers; they get to eat the best cuts of meat before sending the remnants upstairs; and the mistress has to swap clothes: 'That Missus should wear the [servant's] cap' (Duval 1872b).

When it came to middle-class workers, the twist was more subtle. Again, most of the narratives seem at first sight to be standard gags that uphold gender norms: the women are either satirised, or shown to be failing at their job in some way, with the protagonists invariably portrayed in familiar doll-like fashion. Politically, the message seems to be that women are not fit for work, and their place is in the home. The very act of depicting women in employment is making a point, however, especially when they are seen in a wide range of jobs. In other words, these characters are making their own money (like Duval) and are therefore challenging the 'two spheres' theory, sometimes to the point of being 'independent' or, at least, as independent as Victorian society would allow.

One particularly good example involves a strip about the middle-class 'authoresses' working on *Judy* itself. Duval depicts four of them, all pretty-looking and posing in standard coquettish fashion, with captions saying that one 'complains that Judy [as editor] cuts her [copy] down and crowds her dreadfully', while another charges too much for her corner of a page. The inference is that they are just playing at journalism, and are not really very good at it, either by failing to hit a word-length (by dint of being verbose, in turn, by dint of being a woman) or by being unaware of the going rates of pay (by dint of having no idea about money, by dint of being a woman). Such a narrative obviously looks conservative and plays into gender stereotypes. However, the fact that 'authoresses' existed at all at *Judy* was a powerful signal. The extra inference, for the reader, was that the story or poem they had just read on the page before might well have been written by one (as discussed in Chapter 2). The fact that the strip itself was by a woman added yet another layer of meaning. Whether the depictions were based on real people is unknown (Duval 1869l).[18]

When it came to young women and fashion (again usually middle-class women), Duval also had critical things to say. Here, they are again depicted in an ostensibly stereotypical mode: obsessed by frivolity; narcissistic to the point of being detached from the real world; and spending money on clothes and cosmetics that could be better spent on the household. They are invariably attractive individuals, and their fashion choices make them more so. Duval's subversions therefore had to work in a context in which, according to one historian, 'Victorian dress [...] equally licensed or discouraged particular forms of clothing, fantasies and moralities about men and women, as well as distinctions between generations' (Hatter and Moody 2019: cover description).

The way clothes deform bodies became a focus. The biggest culprit was crinolines, and Duval returned to them again and again. The vogue for this mode of dress had lasted from the late 1850s to the mid-1860s, and Duval's commentaries date from a few years later, when it was still fashionable, but when its political meaning was less discussed. Put simplistically, whereas previously crinolines were overtly linked to the question of women's control over money (Thomas 2004), and could be interpreted as a tool for emancipation for the way they symbolised taking up more space (physical and social), now they were starting to be seen as nostalgic signifiers of domesticity and restriction (Thomas 2004; Mitchell, 2016). Therefore, Duval's work speaks to this latter context, and can be seen as subversive of it. For example, in '"The Human Form Divine" – A Study', there is an image of a woman wearing the architecture of a diaphanous skirt, with the caption: 'How much was woman, and how much wire-work?' (Duval 1872h). In 'Encore des Bêtises', a distraught woman, head in hands, is having her body lassoed by wire hoops, by nothing other than a 'Crinoline Monster' (Duval 1876e, Figure 9.4).[19]

Corsets are similarly a target. In the *Judy* spin-off *Ally Sloper's Book of Beauty* (1872), a two-panel cartoon pictures a portly woman on the left, and the same woman with a minute waist, this time looking very unhappy, on the right, with the caption reading: '[the] baneful effects of tight lacing' (Duval 1872i). Hair extensions get the same treatment in 'Some Fashions for the Hair', where the central panel depicts 'what a small connection there is between the human skull and the inhuman Chignon' (Duval 1872j). Headgear, in general, is not the woman's friend: 'What are We Coming To?' (Duval 1872k) has an image of a coal scuttle at the centre with different versions of bonnets circling it, while 'Hats and Heads' is an entire strip about over-elaborate chapeaux: 'how could such a nice little woman like that make such a fright of herself?' (Duval 1873s).

Fashion is also a source of fun for the way women make mistakes. What is 'in' and 'out' of fashion offers opportunities for gags about taste distinctions, and these generally seem to support gender stereotypes. But here, too, there is room for critique. In 'A Little

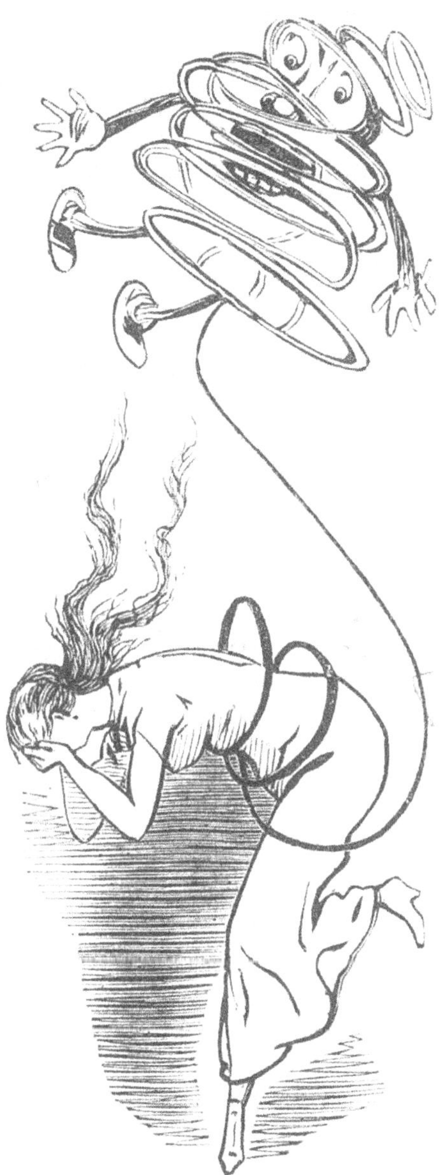

9.4 Marie Duval (1876) 'Encore des Bêtises', *Judy, or the London Serio-comic Journal,*
Volume 19, p. 100 (detail)

Dear From This Month's Fashion Books …', two 'little dears' are pictured modelling the latest headgear. The first has on a bonnet, described as 'a la something-or-other, trimmed a la so-and-so', and this bored tone continues to the second example, who has on a hat, described as 'ditto, ditto'. Her utterly fed-up demeanour is captioned 'Expression of countenance quite equal to the occasion' (Duval 1872l).

But fashion could have other meanings, and when Duval chose to depict dresses and hats in detail, doubtless on occasion tracing from fashion catalogues (and sometimes signing as 'Noir'), it is hard at first to see any subversive element. Typically, the wearers are glamorous and middle class, and the message seems to be that they are dressing to please men, and that their tastes indicate an obsession with consumerism (at a time when the rise of the department store was revolutionising this notion). Christopher Breward adds that such women were 'expected to communicate their families' social positions through their clothing and appearance' (Breward 1994: 75). We can speculate that female readers of *Judy* were 'using' such images as vicarious window-shopping: a variant on the 'culture of consolation' idea.

However, looking more closely, Duval's 'fashionable ladies' are women in public places. They are out in the world: at the theatre, at the races, on the station platform, at the ice-skating rink or – yes – at the courthouse. This is a vision of independence and freedom, and the women in the stories generally have agency. This out-in-the-worldness is emphasised by the fact that the backgrounds to such images are typically drawn in a contrastingly 'cartoony' style, with much less attention to detail, wherein action and chaos ensue (see Chapter 6). The storylines themselves were also often nuanced in political ways, as we have seen.

If these examples make a point about the 'Duvallian tweak' in relation to young women, then equally it is possible to find instances among her depictions of their older sisters. Again, most narratives are predictable. Older women are surplus to requirements: they are represented as washed-up, un-marriageable and hag-like. Either this, or they are out-of-touch old dears who take up everybody's time. It is true that Duval often goes for the quick laugh, with no effort at subversion in evidence. To give two examples: in 'The Teaseful Toy: A Seaside Story' an eager suitor mistakes a pretty young woman for her ugly old chaperone and duly pays the price (Duval 1880d). 'The Adventures of a Poor Old Lady Up for the Cattle Show at the Oxford Circus' mercilessly lampoons a hard-of-hearing oldster who takes over an hour to travel a short way across London (Duval 1875m).

But even old women sometimes have their day.[20] In 'The Bar Young Lady', an 'elderly female person' wanders into a bar and is immediately contrasted with the sexy young barmaid. She is desperate to eat something, in this case one of the buns on a platter on the bar counter. There is a man ahead of her in the queue (an upper-middle-class man with a monocle), so she waits patiently. But, eventually, 'she loses patience' and hits him over the head with her umbrella. The final image sees her fleeing the scene and dropping the bun she has grabbed (Duval 1876d). Similarly, in 'Almost Another Explosion!' an elderly female Sloper relative is snoozing and about to be blown up by a firework planted by Sloper's son; she gets wise to the ruse, and goes after him with the birch (Duval 1884c).

The ultimate sassy old lady is, of course, Judy. I've talked about her here, but it is worth pointing out that Duval essays her constantly and she forms a significant constant in the chapters in this book. In line with other representations, Duval's version is elderly by Victorian standards (sixty-something), but full of vigour. For example, on one frontispiece for a collected volume, she is seen riding an ostrich (Duval 1876k). In this regard, she is referred to wryly as 'the Ever Young and Lovely Judy' (Duval 1876l). But Duval adds other dimensions, such as Judy's relationship with other women, which sometimes takes literally her role as 'protector' (as flagged in the first issue of the magazine). In one strip, Judy looks after the women attending the Derby, which was an event somewhat notorious for sexual harassment (Duval 1876m). Here she is more than just a chaperone, and perhaps better described as an all-seeing defender.

How are we to think about Duval's sense of humour involving women? Of course, the aforementioned jokes can be interpreted in any number of ways.[21] But if we accept that subversive twists are a Duval trope, then this is interesting on a number of levels. It fits neatly into the idea of the 'serio-comic', for example, a term previously defined in this book as meaning a mix of serious and funny content, but which I now want to suggest had an alternative meaning denoting specifically women's comedy, and not only this but women's comedy which customised conservative storylines via subversive modes of delivery. This idea had its origins in music hall: evidence from *The Era Almanack*, the annual supplement to the weekly theatrical trade paper, suggests that 117 'London music hall artistes' identified as 'serio-comic' in 1868, leaping to 384 in 1878 (Beale 2018: 33). It is unthinkable that Duval, with her theatrical background, would not have been aware of this. Similarly, *Judy*, as the *London Serio-comic Journal*, was making a deliberate link.

Samantha Beale (2018) has explored the concept of the serio-comic extensively, and identifies certain characteristics. Above all, she emphasises how performers could imbue ostensibly conservative narratives with new and often oppositional meanings via strategies such as ironic counterpoint. For example, a female performer might say one thing and do another; this was a remarkably common device in the halls, often used in the service of routines about marriage. It could also imply moral ambiguity. This was because stage performers were associated with being sexually promiscuous in the public imagination. In other words, it translated as slightly racy; slightly knowing; slightly adult. In the context of her professional drawing, Duval, with her stage background, and her French heritage, chimed with these risqué associations perfectly.

'Serio-comic' had yet other possible definitions. Music hall routines (by women) could contain elements that were both serious and comic, but in such a way that suggested humour infused by tragedy. This comedic mode would have been described as 'grotesque' at the time, and invited the viewer to acknowledge hardship and laugh, despite it. Again, some of the Duval strips fit this description very well: slaveys in a cycle of never-ending drudgery; young women stuck in disappointing marriages; women in poverty looking to a trip to the seaside as their once-in-a-year escape; and so on.[22] This sounds like Medhurst's culture of consolation, but when combined with the other aspects of the serio-comic it becomes something else.

But if Duval's subversive tricks had close resonances with a serio-comic performing mode, so too they had parallels with themes in other kinds of popular culture. In the world of literature, one particular genre was appealing to women partly as a result of its willingness to question traditional female roles. Sensation novels were so-called because of their emphasis on high drama, typically meaning a mix of ripped-from-the-headlines topicality and Gothic atmospherics. Women characters are prominent, and exhibit unprecedented agency; stories involve them trying to escape from stultifying circumstances, such as work and marriage, or end with a twist in which they turn out to be not what they seem. Sensation novels became a craze in the 1860s and 1870s, and a significant number of authors were female, the best-known being Mary Elizabeth Braddon, as featured in *Judy*'s book reviews. Indeed, some *Judy* contributors themselves were sensation novelists, such as the aforementioned Florence Marryat.

Duval's strips often exhibited sensation-style elements, albeit in a comedic mode. As we have seen, her passive women are often not that passive, and there is commonly a twist in which they get the upper hand. In one remarkable strip, Duval references the Sensation novel craze directly. 'Heroines' (1876n) states that it takes its cue from Rhoda Broughton's novel *Nancy* (a torrid tale about a trophy wife), and pictures several heroines doing heroically romantic things and getting into difficulties. One tries to faint in her suitor's arms, but he fails to catch her; another flounces out of the room and accidentally knocks the china flying; and so on. It is simple satire on one level, but the women are the ones with agency, and by referencing the sensation trend at all, it was influencing *Judy*'s tone.

If we accept that Duval could be subversive about women's issues, did this make her a feminist? This is a much harder proposition to argue. It is axiomatic among historians that the past is gone, and we can only hope to create a subjective impression from the fragments that are left. History, in other words, is the stories that historians tell about the past. From here, it is a small step to acknowledging that any judgement about what might have been 'progressive' in a political sense in the nineteenth century can only be attempted from a particular vantage point and is, therefore, philosophically compromised (so much so, in fact, as to make the effort redundant). To give one small example, nineteenth-century women commonly held views that seem contradictory today, but which were perfectly logical then: such as supporting advances in education, employment and property rights, but opposing suffrage.

When Duval does address the world of women's politics directly, the results are ambivalent. There are two main examples of this. One is the strip 'Ally on the Rights of Women' in which Sloper addresses a meeting of women, and gesticulates wildly with his umbrella, thereby jabbing them in the face and knocking them over (Duval 1872m). On one level, it is the uncomplicated story of an idiot 'mansplaining', and the emphasis is squarely on Sloper. However, the subject matter was of its time, and was indicating a profound societal shift. Whether the women depicted are activists is not clear, but suffrage

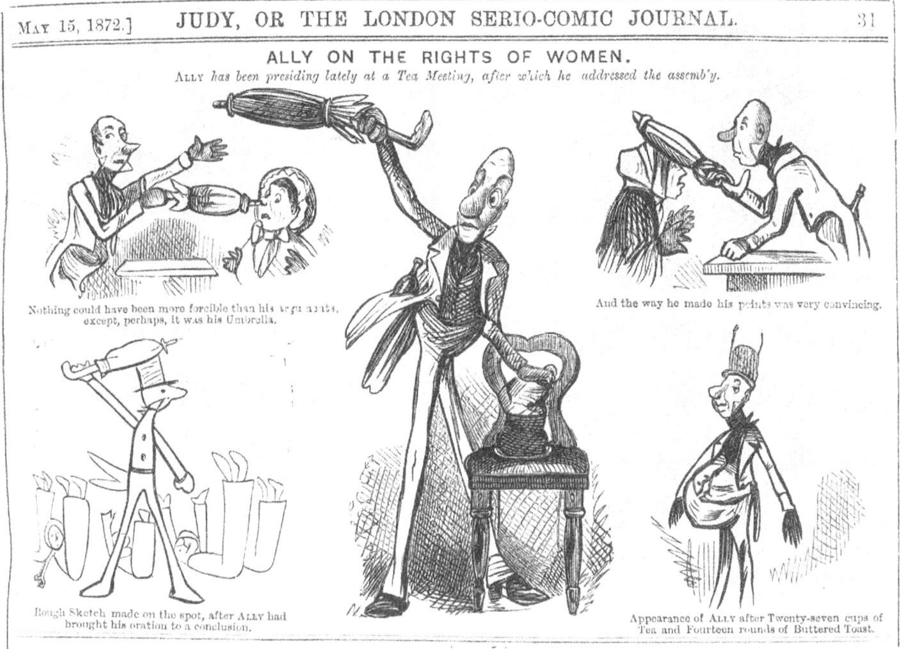

9.5   Marie Duval (1872) 'Ally on the Rights of Women', *Judy, or the London Serio-comic Journal*, Volume 11, p. 31

groups were becoming more popular in the 1860s and 1870s, and it is likely that this was another part of urban life that Duval was observing.[23] The strip's inclusion in her oeuvre is political by its very nature.

The other example is a strip about rational dress, entitled 'In Re "The Dual Garments"'. The context here was the Dress Reform movement, which promoted 'rational' clothing for women, that is, clothing that was not extravagant, or which did not restrict their bodies (like Duval's much-hated corsets and crinolines). Such attire included bloomers (baggy trousers, gathered at the knee) and 'sensible jackets'. Such 'feminist' fashion was argued to be symbolically and physically freeing.[24] In the strip, the reform movement in America is parodied, and various fashionably dressed young ladies are sarcastically applauded for sticking to their guns and wearing ridiculously inappropriate clothing (for example, a huge dress with a train to go to church). However, rational dress itself is also attacked in the last panel, where it is lampooned as 'loose-fitting trousers and [a] sack' (Duval 1876o).

In conclusion, amongst Duval's more straightforward material involving women, she imagines scenarios in which they go wild and let themselves go, are bored by fashion, behave badly with children, fantasise about worthier suitors and superior marriages, and beat up stupid men; and in which slaveys get the better of their masters and mistresses. It may have been comedy, but it was saying something serious and doing cultural work. As countless cultural theorists have argued, the worlds imagined in texts give permission for readers to imagine alternative futures. It is important to recognise that the same goes on those occasions when explicit politics might be ambiguous. On this reading, Duval's strips and cartoons can be seen to represent small revolutions, week after week, contributing to a bigger one. The walloping signature, 'MARIE DUVAL', with its message that 'women can do this', only helped things along.

Notes

1 Hunt asserts that she did, but gives no source. Further research by Brian Maidment could find no illustrations that were signed. (Private correspondence with Maidment, 7 January 2020).

2 See the *Punch Historical Archive*, put together by Gale Cengage and Liverpool John Moore's University, which identifies contributors: www.gale.com/intl/c/punch-historical-archive (accessed on 13 August 2019).

3 The most notable recent initiative to map (and celebrate) women's cartooning in the UK per se was *The Inking Woman* exhibition and book. See Streeten and Tate (2018).

4 Examples of graphic novels include Alison Bechdel's *Fun Home*, Marjane Satrapi's *Persepolis* and Nicola Streeten's *Billy, Me and You*. The list of creative jobs might be expanded to include pencillers, inkers, colourists and letterers.

5 The idea of the male gaze is associated with Laura Mulvey and later finessed by Judith Butler.

6 For example, the anonymous 'Patty – a Sketch' from *All the Year Round* (1893), which tells the story of the master of the house trying to 'improve' Patty by giving her some Shakespeare to read – but she prefers *Ally Sloper's Half-Holiday* (quoted in Banville 2008).

7 As a biography of Graves, Bloodworth (2013) is excellent, though skimpy on her *Judy* career.

8 In one account, the regulars are described by one of their number thus: 'We are a close, conservative, inflexible body [...] no new-fangled notions, new usages, new customs or new customers for us. [...] there is nothing new, gaudy, flippant or effeminately luxurious here. A low-planked ceiling [...]. High, stiff-backed settles [seats] [...] sawdust covers the floor [...] there are men in this [pub] who have dined here every day for a quarter of a century' (quoted in Thornbury 1873).

9 The influence of women contributors on *The Idler* magazine is explored by Anne Humpherys (2005).

10 The other recurring strong female figure in the magazine was Britannia. Duval never pictured her, but Boucher did.

11 Eszter Szép, 'Lynda Takes the Line for A Walk: Attitudes and Philosophies of Drawing in Lynda Barry's Comics', paper delivered at Transitions 8 (conference) on 10 November 2018, Birkbeck, University of London.

12 This impression may have been reinforced by the scandal of her affair with Herbert Such in 1871, which resulted in the divorce of Such from his wife, and which was reported in the national papers (see Introduction and Chapter 3, pp. 90–1). How far *Judy* readers would have scoured the small print of the court reports, or have been interested, is debatable.

13 Judith Butler has famously argued that gender is not fixed but rather performed – a constructed identity. See *Gender Trouble* (1990) and *Bodies that Matter* (1993).

14 Twenty-first-century dictionaries of slang offer dozens of modern examples, including everything from female masturbation to driving fast to 'getting smashed up'.

15 This construction happened mostly in fiction, but some dictionary definitions were gender-neutral. For example, in the 1866–79 edition of the Larousse *Grand Dictionnaire*, '*Flâneur/euse*' is 'a person who strolls' (though the rest of the text refers to men). See Iskin (2006: 114).

16 As Simon Grennan and Leo Hall observe, 'As the flâneuse is neither victim; nor sexually available; nor a 'fallen woman'; and her economic security protects her, she becomes classed as dangerous, a deviant, transgressive, or subversive' (Hall and Grennan 2019: 17).

17 The idea of a 'culture of consolation' is associated with historian Gareth Stedman-Jones, and how, in his view, the music halls became progressively more conservative in the late nineteenth and early twentieth centuries.

18 The strip is an oddity in that it is split by two cartoons in the middle, one by an unknown cartoonist and one by Phiz. The Phiz example depicts a slavey washing a man's clothes – again, a comment on women's work. The strip is not signed by Duval, but other illustrations of women in the same issue of the magazine are, meaning that readers could in theory make the connection.

19 Duval's work involving crinolines would probably merit a chapter on its own, and we need to remember that some of it was intrinsic to strips and cartoons presumably penned by herself, and some was illustrating text by other writers. What we can say is that it fed into a rich tradition of such satire: see Thomas (2004) and Mitchell (2016). I am not a fashion historian, and am grateful to the anonymous peer reviewer of this book's manuscript for suggestions.

20 For an excellent account of attitudes towards older people, see Chase (2009).

21 For a capsule tour through some relevant aspects of comedy theory (incorporating Kant, Marx, Bourdieu, Marcuse, Adorno, Jameson, Rancière and Žižek) see Holm (2017: 181–205).

22 'Grotesque' is a word Clayton (1876) uses to describe Duval's work (Clayton 1876: 332).

23 The strip's other dimension is that Sloper is a boozer and this is a 'tea meeting', presumably connected to temperance. He ends up drinking all the tea and eating all the toast.

24 Bloomers were actually a revival of an 1850s fashion, when they were also associated with women's rights.

Appendix 1

Questions of attribution

Simon Grennan, Roger Sabin, Julian Waite

In revealing and analysing a body of work that has remained largely obscured and unconsidered for 135 years, the researcher faces a number of challenges. In the case of Marie Duval, the conditions in which she worked militated against clear attributions and claims to ownership from the very start: both Duval's professions as actor and humorous artist were low status, precarious and, consequently, largely unrecorded. Her chosen media were ephemeral and inexpensive to produce and consume. Immediately after the event (either a performance or a publication), no one was really interested. The next entertainment beckoned both the artist and the audience. Hence, evidence for the attribution of drawings to Duval raises challenges unknown to the historians of artists who are more successful, more lauded by posterity and, crucially, more completely recorded. These are not methodological challenges, in fact, but rather involve the degree to which established methods are relatively unproductive when applied to a search for Duval.

In compiling *The Marie Duval Archive*, writing this book and producing the other academic and public activities associated with our endeavour to reveal and contextualise Duval's work, we have applied a number of methods to the challenges of attribution. We considered her signed work and attempted to evaluate the significance of her signatures in the context of her recorded professional life, on stage and in periodical publishing. We considered the functions of anonymity and pseudonym, in creating and manipulating reader expectations, in the development of a professional life, which exploited mutable gender roles. We considered the status of the written components of her drawings, relative to the historic contingencies of undertaking visual journalism, within the team production that constituted Victorian periodical printing businesses.

We undertook visual stylistic analysis, ultimately grounded in the large task of viewing every known publication in which Duval appeared and many others that we discovered. We viewed every page of *Judy* magazine, from its launch in 1867 to Duval's death in 1890 (numbering approximately 11,500 pages, that is 46 volumes of approximately 260 pages each), in order to try and identify unsigned drawings by understanding and enumerating the particular ways in which Duval produced them.

Finally, we searched for contemporaneous historical commentary, particularly from those who worked alongside Duval. Part of this task was complicated by the contradictory content of this commentary and the repetition of inaccurate comments by subsequent commentators and scholars, until very recently.

What emerges is not a definitive body of work, but rather one with changing horizons, according to the period in which the drawings appeared. We cannot substantiate or contradict differences in authorship between text and drawings, for example. Neither can we establish the complete chronology of Duval's life relative to the drawings. Such a chronology is required to enable any scholar to substantiate her single and unqualified authorship in every case. Further, we believe that these methodological activities are the only grounds on which we can identify Duval as author of the work, or part of the work, or as a collaborator in the work. Simply put, this process is a way of identifying a corpus. This is not the same as claiming that Duval had an unqualified authorial role in every drawing and every text that form this corpus, identified in retrospect. We recognise this. In the absence of other evidence, we believe that this retrospective process identifies a corpus, distinct from others.

Duval's work in *Judy* was most commonly signed 'D', 'MD', 'M. Duval', 'Duval' or 'Marie Duval'. The way in which these signatures changed over time, in terms of their prominence and size, has been expertly tracked by David Kunzle, with emphasis on her Ally Sloper work (Kunzle 1986). Additionally, she signed 'Noir' for a number of cartoons published in 1875. Not every *Judy* contributor was allowed an authorial signature: for an artist to sign was a marker of status, and for a woman, it was doubly striking. But Duval's signed work is sporadic and the appearance of a signature followed no rationale, with the exception of the series of drawings signed 'Noir', in which it appears to be a concerted attempt to establish a visible pseudonym for a slightly different type of drawing to those recognisable to readers as by Duval.

The act of fictionalising the author had been a significant marketing device since the 1830s, as Bill Bell has shown (Bell 1993). Most obviously, anonymity or a pseudonym could be used to disguise ethnic background, nationality, social class and gender.[1] But it could also be used to suggest associations which were attractive to particular readers, as a niche marketing strategy or as a strategy to maintain continuity: a number of authors could work under the same name, for example, or the life of the pseudonym could be extended beyond the death of any single contributor. Elsewhere in this book, Simon Grennan argues that Duval visually fulfilled the role more usually taken by text journalists, as a member of the teams producing periodical print. She provided visual content for engraving in the same way that journalists provided written content for typesetting.

As Duval's surviving body of work is exclusively print, it appears that Duval drew directly onto wood blocks or provided drawings on paper for transfer, and the engraver's job was key to how the final illustration turned out. In a sense, all Duval's cartoons could be attributed to anonymous engravers, based on designs by the artist. However, such a radical rethinking of cartoon attribution is beyond the scope of this book. Suffice it to say that Duval's engravers had licence to interpret what they saw, but that in fact she was being engraved by the best in the business so we can reasonably assume verisimilitude to her wishes. The Dalziel Brothers, who published *Judy*, were a long-established engraving firm as well as a publisher, and staked their reputation on the quality of the former (see Chapter 1, note 18).

Duval drew single-frame cartoons with legends, strip cartoons (some of ongoing characters) and illustrated comic articles, stories and books. For the cartoons and strip cartoons we might ask about the attribution of the writing that often accompanies the drawings as an integral part. Conventional wisdom has it that because an artist made the drawing, they also came up with the scenario, joke and written text. In the standard histories, a Tenniel image will be credited to Tenniel, including the written component: that is what the caption would say in a book or gallery. We consider the same to be likely with Duval. In the case of her book *Queens & Kings and Other Things* there is little doubt that as sole author she wrote the text, whilst our assumption would be that the longer texts to which she provided illustrations are most safely considered not hers. There are a number of books in which she collaborated with other writers where they are specifically credited as author and she as illustrator and there seems no reason to question this in the vast majority of cases.[2]

In attempting to assess the presence of different hands and minds in drawings and writing, there are available a number of methods of stylistic analysis: at the story level, comparative analysis of topics, treatments and structures; with printed texts, benchmarked comparisons of the frequency and proximities of words, for example; with printed wood engravings, benchmarked comparisons of the types of cut lines utilised in an identified range of tactic situations combining both depicted story and the locations of ink marks on the page. But these techniques do not indicate any primary distinction between registers. In Duval's work, when words are present, both the drawings and the words produce the story. We might be tempted to think of the distinction between registers as indicative of a distinction between authors. Indeed, in twentieth-century anglophone comics in particular, the tasks of scriptwriting and drawing were habitually devolved. However, approaching attribution from the starting point of a distinction between registers is largely tendentious. In fact, we might as easily ask if different authors made some parts of a text or some parts of a drawing.

As we considered the possible drawings of Duval, in her named and unnamed productions, signed works and the thousands of pages of *Judy*, we reflected on the competing definitions of stylistics, the study of comparative methods of production for the purpose of analysis. In every instance, this production encompasses the material and formal properties of an image, the story and the discursive ecology of an image, thereby relating how it was made to when and where it was made and how it was used.

For the purpose of identifying Duval's work, a capsule description of stylistics would be: the study of the distinctive forms found in the works of individual artists and writers. This approach has its roots in a technique developed by Giovanni Morelli (1816–91) whereby identification of a work relies on extrapolating to the whole from a part. In other words, the key to identifying authorship is found in the comparative analysis of the formal properties of an image. Morelli believed that every artist has a distinct style, or method of production, which reveals itself in the smallest details, and that this is evident even when the artist is working in an adopted style.

These ideas were later supplemented by those of art historian Bernard Berenson (1865–1959), who argued that not only the artist's hand but also their personality could be discerned in a work of art: in other words, that mark-making is an expressive gesture that reveals the body and environment of the artist in the artwork. These notions together have been extremely influential, and have led to the idea of the line being central to aesthetics. However, for all its sophistication, this kind of stylistic reasoning remains an inexact science. It can also be questioned on theoretical grounds. For example, the approach has been superseded by a more holistic methodology that locates stylistic analysis within a systematic analysis of discursive relationships.

Finally, we might have presumed that commentary on Duval's work by her contemporaries, such as journalistic pieces, and quotations by editors and publishers and, later, the work of historians, would provide more-or-less accurate guides to what she produced. This was not the case. The secondary sources turned out to be just as slippery as the primary sources, and the pattern was, unsurprisingly, that mistakes made in the nineteenth century were repeated in the twentieth and twenty-first centuries.

The historic commentaries fell into three phases. First, during the period Duval was active, a range of surviving, repeated activity promoting publications featured her drawings to readers, as an attraction, notwithstanding the early hint that they were part of an editorial joke on the part of Ross, denied by Ross. Central to this period was Clayton's biography of Duval in *English Female Artists*. Second, after 1884 and her final published drawing in *Judy* in 1885, Duval's drawings were reused (and often dismembered) in *Ally Sloper's Half-Holiday*, and her signatures erased. Third, after the death of Ross in 1897, published reminiscences in 1901, 1922, 1927 and 1930 (some by writers who must have known Duval personally, due to their daily proximity in business), stated or repeated that Duval either assisted Ross in making drawings or that Ross was their author.

In the first phase, Clayton's *English Female Artists* praised Duval for being an autonomous artist of note, identifying her authorship of 'drawn caricature subjects' under several pseudonyms, including Noir in *Judy* and in 'several books' (Clayton 1876: 332). In 1888 another account stated approvingly that she was 'the first lady comic artist' (Hone 1888: 274). *Judy* editor Ross himself came to Duval's defence in 1869: in a letter to *The Theatrical Journal*, in response to an article suggesting that it was 'difficult to determine, with any degree of correctness, which sketches are by Miss Duval and which by Mr Ross'. He wrote: 'her pictures are not imitations of Mr C. H. Ross's absurd style and can very easily be distinguished from that gentleman's production, because Mademoiselle is an artist and C. H. R. is not' (Ross 1869b).

Alongside these affirmations of Duval's authorship, over the course of her fifteen-year drawing career, small commercial advertisements in a range of periodicals announced

Duval's drawings in numerous publications for sale. Further, Duval's contribution of drawings was frequently announced boldly in these publications.

Throughout the 1870s and 1880s, the Ross-devised character Ally Sloper greatly increased in popularity, through Duval's development of a complete storyworld in which he had his adventures. The second phase began after 1883, when Ross sold his Ally Sloper copyright to the Dalziel Brothers, who established a company with nephew Gilbert Dalziel, to publish a new comic with Sloper as the star. *Ally Sloper's Half-Holiday* (1884) became a bestseller in the 1880s and 1890s. Duval was excluded from the new comic. She was never mentioned, and when her *Judy* work was reprinted therein, she was never credited and her signatures were erased, for example in 'Zee Englishe Sommaire' (*sic*) (Duval 1886).

In the third phase, in 1901, Duval's own publisher, Dalziel Brothers, made the statement that 'His [Ross's] pages of humorous pictures, which appeared in *Judy*, were generally signed "Marie Duval"' (Dalziel and Dalziel 1901: 320). The Dalziels' sister, Margaret Dalziel, a significant figure in the firm for four decades, was described in the same reminiscence as an assistant to the Brothers (Dalziel and Dalziel 1901: 19–21).

In 1922, the *Half-Holiday* (then no longer under the control of Dalziel Brothers, but still associated with them) stated that Ross was 'assisted by his wife, Marie Duval' (Boswell Jnr 1922: 11), a claim repeated in the same column in the following week's issue.[3] In 1927, the theatrical journal *The Referee* published a letter by Gilbert Dalziel crediting Ross, and adding that he 'no doubt availed himself of her [Duval's] artistic tendency in helping him with his 'Sloper' drawings. Often these would be signed 'M. D.' or 'Marie Duval'; but they were, in reality, the creations of Ross himself' (Dalziel 1927: 10).[4]

In 1930, an anonymous writer in *The Yorkshire Evening Post* stated that: 'Charles Ross, who was Editor at *Judy*, invited Ms. Duval to do a series of drawings, the jokes for which he invented' ('Ally Sloper Memories' 1930). Subsequent academic study of Duval's work constitutes quite a different type of activity to the historic commentaries. The change in the historic commentaries, from promotional during Duval's life to erasing and denying, after her death and Charles Ross's death, is now the topic of academic study and evaluation, rather than media manipulation and memoir.

We believe that it is impossible to draw conclusions about Duval without looking at the wide scope of her oeuvre, which we have been fortunate enough to identify and collate. Our creation of *The Marie Duval Archive* has meant that scholars and members of the public can view Duval with fresh eyes. With over 1400 drawings collected in one place for the first time, it is now possible to see patterns and make judgements that were simply impossible before. For example, we now know that Duval was not just a routine contributor to *Judy*, but a mainstay, over period of fifteen years. We can also see that her Sloper work was, approximately, only 15 per cent of her overall output. These observations make it easier to evaluate the extent to which she was ignored in later years, when her work (now freshly identified in many cases) was reprinted in the *Half-Holiday* and how she was pivotal to that publication's early success.

There is more Duval to be discovered. We remain tantalised by a mention in Clayton that Duval contributed to French and German magazines, about which we have been able to discover nothing (Clayton 1876: 331–2). There are also Duval works that we know existed, but which we have not been able to find, including an illustrated periodical published by Lynes and Sons for which she contributed illustrations to two volumes, *Smiles and Styles* and *Mirth and Modes* (see Chapter 3, note 7, p. 97), *The Archive*, and our Duval research in general, is an ongoing project.

Notes

1 See 'How Did You Choose Your Pseudonym?' by Dora D'Espaigne, *The Girl's Realm*, Volume 6, September 1904 (wherein female authors such George Egerton, George Paston, John Oliver Hobbs, Lucas Malet and John Strange Winter, discuss their 'masculine disguises').

2 For example, *Ally Sloper's Guide to the Paris Exhibition* (1878) states: 'By Charles H. Ross and many pictures By Marie Duval'. In the case of some other books with Duval content, her name is left off the credits. Very occasionally, authorship is more complex: for example, *Ally Sloper: A Moral Lesson* (1873), states '750 pictures by Marie Duval' with 'The words by Judy's Office Boy'. When it comes to the drawings, it turns out that not everything is by Duval: some is by Ross in a solo capacity (including Sloper's debut 'Some of the Mysteries of Loan and Discount', originally from 1867). When it comes to the writing, a fair speculation would be that, so far as the strips per se were concerned, Duval scripted most of them. However, as well as the examples by Ross, there were others that were collaborations between the two of them. Finally, the text narrative that holds the strips together, which is the bigger prose story into which they are embedded, numbering many thousands of words, is by somebody else entirely. This is the uncredited Arthur Pask, a jobbing writer for *Judy*.

3 The first quotation is interesting because it speculates that Duval did the foregrounded female figures while Ross did the cartoony material in the background, that is, 'the funny ones'

4 Gilbert Dalziel had made this claim privately some years earlier. In a recently discovered letter dated 20 February 1920, Dalziel wrote to a certain Mrs Callcott about the circumstances of creating *Queens & Kings and Other Things*. The relevant passage reads: 'It was a Dalziel venture, Charles H. Ross being paid by us for his part, & Chatto & Windus being paid for publishing the Book. I have <u>all</u> the original designs by Ross' (Dalziel 1920). There are cogent reasons for questioning the claims of the letter – many covered in Chapter 4 (not least the explicit attribution of the book to Duval by Clayton) – and this is something to which we shall return in a forthcoming academic publication. With thanks to Harrison-Hiett Rare Books for providing photographs of the letter.

Appendix 2

Questions of terminology and historicisation

Simon Grennan, Roger Sabin, Julian Waite

If it is true that 'reading is a transaction, a relation between the cultural vocabulary of the text, and the cultural vocabulary of the reader', to paraphrase Catherine Belsey (2002: 31), then any discussion of the nineteenth century has to take into account that both vocabularies shift over time. The following few paragraphs are not intended as explanations of terms or of problems with historicisation, but function to illuminate areas where misunderstandings may arise, specifically to do with Duval's main preoccupations (as we have identified them, such as class, gender and comedy) and her employment (as an actor and artist). There is an added layer of complexity due to the fact that the book is interdisciplinary (incorporating periodical studies, Victorian studies, theatre studies, Comics Studies, drawing studies, comedy studies, media studies, cultural studies, and women's studies) because not all these disciplines and fields agree on definitions.

First is the issue of class. This book has refrained from defining 'working class' and 'middle class'.[1] The categories are contentious and constructed differently at different times (Munt 2000). For example, in the Duval epoch (late 1860s to mid-1880s) most 'working-class' people were rural and labour was agricultural: the great migration to the cities was still ongoing. Further, the 'lower-middle class' was coming into being as a distinct group, entailing more than just creating a space away from the crowding, smog and disease of the inner city, and initiating a lifestyle.

Further, we can say that wealth (capital) is not a reliable guide to class stratification. For example, membership of the middle and working classes was not entirely based on earnings: as historian Liza Picard points out 'a skilled London coach-maker could earn up to five guineas […] a week – considerably more than most middle class clerks' (Picard 2009). However, education and tenure (a bank clerk's job was for life) defined the middle classes, and social mobility was usually seen as both possible and desirable.[2] This meant that poverty conversely was often seen as a matter of personal fault, with the poor as feckless and therefore responsible for their own plight, which in turn justified the workhouse system. Many of the adventures of Duval's character Ally Sloper are a parody of lower-middle-class aspirations (Sabin 2014; Kunzle 1985).

When it comes to taste distinctions (cultural capital), the difficulties over class definition are multiplied (Gunn 2005). Commonly referred-to signifiers such as clothes, food choices, speech and social manners do not always provide instantly recognisable clues, and there have been changes in the historical forms which cultural capital has inhabited. The number of Duval stories with working-class people using 'chivalrous' (supposedly middle-class) language, wearing 'bourgeois' garb (for example, Sloper's suit and hat), or eating 'genteel' food, are many.

Thus, class distinctions in Britain were obvious towards the end of the nineteenth century in theory, if less clear cut in practice. The rise of socialist ideas in the period served to solidify the language of class, and to question assumptions around the 'age of capitalism' and the 'undeserving poor'. (The downturn in the economy from 1873, known at the time as the 'Great Depression', and the rise of trade unions, made this questioning more urgent.) The notion of class struggle was therefore an ever-present backdrop to Duval's work (Waters 1990).

As for Duval's own class status, this is debatable. In terms of upbringing, her father was a schoolteacher or private tutor (it is not possible to ascertain which), which were undoubtedly middle-class professions. Also, when she and Charles Ross were living together, it would seem likely that they would have defined themselves as middle class, especially given his status as editor, playwright and producer. As Picard points out a '£100-a-year clerk and his wife could find a cottage to rent in a suburb within walking distance of his work [...] His wife might employ a 'slavey' or maid-of-all-work, for only £6 a year' (Picard 2009). This would have been well within Ross and Duval's joint means and would have placed them in the middle class, according to Rowntree's 1901 definitions.

In terms of Duval's employment, she might be said to hover between working class and middle class. Picard gives three layers in the Victorian working class, namely 'working men' or labourers, the 'intelligent artisan' and the 'educated working man' (Picard 2009).[3] As a periodical journalist, Duval might be an 'educated working woman'. However, whilst journalism is widely if loosely referred to as a profession throughout the era, and the education required would seem to equate it with the middle classes, the job brought with it social stigmas which militate against a simple class definition. Thus historian Martin Conboy explains how 'despite well-documented liberal accounts of journalists as operating within a politically important forum of communication, daily journalists themselves suffered from a reputation as scoundrels with no scruples, in great part, on account of their need to get a story, meaning that bribery and blackmail were frequently imputed to them' (Conboy 2016: 743). For Duval, as a visual journalist, working in a mode that was distinct from the *Punch*-style satirical tradition, and which was typically seen as inferior to it, these prejudices would have been exacerbated (see Chapter 1).

Duval the actor was a worker in a different field, but this too had stigmas attached, and as a woman, she would have been viewed as transgressive, partly because of the job's associations with sex work (see Chapters 2, 7 and 9). On the question of class positioning, it has been argued that performers (and managers) belonged to a kind of class of their own, on account of the nature of their self-supporting community, and the liminal nature of the employment, which was becoming more professionalised in the period (Bailey 1986; Rutherford 1986). This professionalisation was given credibility by coverage in magazines such as *Judy*.

Second, there is the issue of gender. This book has assumed that 'men' and 'women' were (and are) constructed categories. The Victorian period was dominated by the 'two spheres' theory of society, discussed by Simon Grennan in Chapter 2. In other words, according to Lisa Tickner, masculinity and 'femininity became associated with a division between the rational, competitive, and public world of production on the one hand, and the affective, nurturing, and private sphere of the [...] home on the other' (Tickner 1987: 213). This meant that women were typically seen as inferior biologically and emotionally, as 'under-developed men'. Within the system, their place in the home was therefore obvious, and their main function, to look after their spouses and raise children, was supposedly the bedrock upon which the modern British state was founded. This logic explained their position as second-class citizens, denied certain legal and property rights, as well as being excluded from the vote and positions of power.

Certainly, the late nineteenth century saw challenges to the patriarchy, and a questioning of the 'natural' hierarchy of the sexes. Important educational, legal, professional and personal changes were instigated. But how far this translated into any real loosening of power structures is debatable, and gender equality was as distant at the end of Duval's life as it was at the beginning. The law still enforced dependency, and men never relinquished their right to provide financially, or to be 'served' within the family. Similarly, the vote remained a utopian dream.

Duval's work has to be seen in this wider context, and how far it conformed to received gender politics, or offered symbolic opportunities for women's self-fashioning, is a constant theme of this book. As such, the usual concerns about historical revisionism are acknowledged. For example, her comedy of manners often revolved around 'mashing', a ubiquitous term that is explored in Chapter 9, and which encompasses a wide range of flirting: but from a twenty-first-century perspective, it is possible to see its more extreme manifestations in the light of twenty-first-century social phenomena such as https://everydaysexism.com/ and #MeToo.[4]

This book appears at a time when concepts of masculine and feminine are hotly contested, as they were in the nineteenth century, a debate motivated by the keen imperatives of different opinions, traditions and ways of life and thought. Compiling, reflecting and commenting upon Duval's work, we recognise that we are unavoidably historicised by our own experiences, concepts, capacities to influence and motivations, compared to others'. In researching, reflecting upon and representing the work of a nineteenth-century woman, our own work on Duval identifies our historicised position. Our work has contributed to the creation of our own identities, as much as reflecting upon Duval's.

Moving on to the issue of comedy and humour. Towards the end of the nineteenth century, words like 'wit', 'irony' and 'satire' were being defined afresh in the face of new pop cultural forms, George Meredith's *An Essay on Comedy and the Uses of the Comic Spirit* being an example (Meredith: 1898). From today's vantage point, the historian has to 'rebuild the joke' in order to understand it, and to apprehend why people at the time might have thought it funny (Wagner-Lawlor 2000: 43). By decoding a gag's reference points and unpacking its dynamics, we can in theory 'restore its energy'. But we have to ask how far this is possible. The past is gone, evidence is missing, and all we can do is make a 'best guess'. Therefore, because we can never restore the energy altogether, Duval's work can never appear quite so hilarious as it did to her Victorian fans.

To modern eyes, Duval's output is often immediate, voguish and already seems 'energetic'. It is frequently 'cartoony', and not layered with symbolism like contemporaneous satirical ('*Punch*-like') work, and the captions often tell a story that is easily graspable. However, elsewhere her humour has become detached from the cultural, social and political contexts that underpinned it, and is harder to understand. Take, for example, her illustrations for the continuing text series 'A Conscientious Chronicle of Pretty Women's Prettiest Frocks', which was about fantasy women from history and their wardrobes, as filtered through a music hall imagination ('Egyptian style', 'Roman style') (Duval 1875n). This requires us to understand the Victorians' complicated relationship with antiquity, with fashion, and with music hall; and that is before trying to unravel what 'pretty women' might mean in the context of prevailing gender norms.

The politics of the jokes are therefore difficult to unravel. For example, in the same way that we might seek to understand a gag by relating it to a modern context, so it is tempting to look for 'progressive' signs. Thus, one legacy of 1970s and 1980s approaches in cultural studies is to look for 'radical' and 'resistant' moments. They are present in Duval's work if we look for them. But applying a retrospective lens can be misleading, and what is 'progressive' today may not have been in the 1860s or 1880s. This is a point taken up in Chapter 9.

If unpacking the humour can help us to access the minds of readers in fresh ways (therefore offering new insights into their shifting concerns, tastes and attitudes) then we have to ask how far they were passive consumers. Peter Bailey has argued (in the context of music hall) that pop culture audiences were far more 'knowing' than is often assumed. They were proactive and were licensed to 'fill in the gaps and complete the circuits of meaning' (Bailey 1998: 185). He goes on to note that in the halls, 'sexual knowingness was a highly developed second language' (Bailey 1998: 186). Bearing in mind Duval's closeness to the stage, and the 'gaps' she leaves in her drawings, this is an extra dimension to her humour that is worth considering (and, indeed, the issue of 'serio-comic' address is covered in Chapter 9).

Finally, there is drawing. The general background to Duval's work involves the repeal of the so-called 'taxes on knowledge', improvements in printing technology and increases in literacy rates, resulting in a proliferation of cheap publishing, both fictional and non-fictional. This shift in the culture is explored in Chapter 1, and has been well covered elsewhere (Scully 2018; Easley, King and Morton 2017).

The term 'cartoonist' was not in common usage in the late nineteenth century, and Duval was usually referred to as an 'artist' or 'illustrator'. The other frequently used term was 'caricaturist', but today this has associations with a bygone era of the late eighteenth- and early nineteenth-century print tradition. Today, Duval is sometimes referred to as a 'comics creator', but this is again placing her in a particular tradition, this time with modern associations, which assumes definitional boundaries around the primacy of strips, and to which, therefore, she can only be said to tangentially belong.

By contrast, 'cartoonist' is derived from 'cartoon', a word which itself went through a swift evolution in meaning following the publication in *Punch* of Leech's 'Cartoon No 1' in 1843, which heralded the twin ideas of a mix of journalism and art, and a drawing (or series of drawings) with humorous intent, which moved the word away from previous associations with a preliminary drawing for paintings (Leech 1843). 'Cartoonist', according to Richard Scully, 'is an even more recent coinage, appearing only in the 1860s' (Scully 2018: 31). By 1893, the word was current enough to be included in the first edition of the *Oxford English Dictionary*.

Notes

1 Except in the context of household income relative to the capacity to employ a domestic servant, which was a measure used by Rowntree in 1901.
2 Samuel Smiles's bestseller *Self Help; with Illustrations of Character and Conduct* (1859) was effectively a manual of how to achieve social mobility through industriousness, aiming to show how to use education and hard work to get on.
3 Of course the role of the working woman, as described by Simon Grennan in Chapter 2, was a matter of social disturbance and anxiety to male-dominated structures and philosophies, as working-class women (and children) worked extensively following the industrial revolution alongside, and often in the same jobs as, men.
4 At the time of writing, a CFP (call for papers) has just gone out for the Summer 2020 special issue of *Nineteenth-Century Gender Studies*, around the topic of 'Victorian Literature in the Age of #MeToo', stating: ' For decades, feminist scholars have been identifying and analyzing scenes of sexual assault and harassment in Victorian imaginative literature. In the age of #MeToo, it is no longer tenable to simply cast such actions or literary scenes as products of a different time.'

Bibliography

A Woman Who Knows Her Place (1867) 'Correspondence', *Judy, or the London Serio-comic Journal*, Volume 1, p. 4

Adcock, John (2010a) 'Judy's "Jolly Books"', *Yesterday's Papers* (accessed 13 August 2019) https://john-adcock.blogspot.com/2010/01/judys-jolly-books-part-i.html

—— (2010b) 'Charles Henry Ross (1835–1897)', *Yesterday's Papers* (accessed 13 August 2019) https://john-adcock.blogspot.com/2010/09/charles-henry-ross-1835–1897.html

Agarwal, Sudhir and Sebastian Rudolph (2008) 'Semantic description of distributed business processes', Stanford: AAAI Spring Symposium. Unpublished paper

Alchian, Armen and Harold Demsetz (1972) 'Production, Information Costs, and Economic Organisation', *The American Economic Review*, Volume 62, Number 5, pp. 777–95

Alfreds, Mike (2013) *The What Happens? Storytelling and Adapting for the Theatre*. London: Nick Hern Books

Allen, Robert (1994) 'Real Incomes in the English Speaking World 1879–1913' in Grantham, George and Mary Mackinnon (eds) *Labour Market Evolution: The Economic History of Market Integration, Wage Flexibility and the Employment Relation*. London: Routledge, pp. 107–38

'Ally Sloper Memories' (1930) *The Yorkshire Evening Post*, np

Altick, Richard (1958) *The English Common Reader: A Social History of the Mass Reading Public 1800–1900*. Chicago: University of Chicago Press

Anderson, Gregory (1988) 'The White Blouse Revolution' in Anderson, Gregory (ed.) *The White Blouse Revolution: Female Office Workers since 1870*. Oxford: Oxford University Press, pp. 1–26

Antinucci, Raffaella (2015) 'Sensational Nonsense: Edward Lear and the (Im)purity of Nonsense Writing', *English Literature*, Volume 2, Number 2, pp. 291–312

Appia, Adophe (1981) *The Work of Living Art and Man is the Measure of All Things*. Miami: University of Miami Press

Aries, Philippe (1965) *Centuries of Childhood*. New York: Random House

'Art, Literature, and Music' (1872) *Globe*, 9 November, p. 2

Assael, Brenda (2005) *The Circus and Victorian Society*. Charlottesville: University of Virginia Press

'Astley's – Scene from the Pantomime of 'Mr. and Mrs. Briggs; or, Punch's Festival'' (1851) *Illustrated London News*, Saturday 27 December, p. 8

'Babil and Bijou' (1872) *The Spectator*, 28 September, p. 12

Bailey, Peter (1986) 'Chapter 2: A Community of Friends' in Bailey, Peter (ed.) *Music Hall: The Business of Pleasure*. Milton Keynes: Open University Press, pp. 33–52

—— (1998) *Popular Culture and Performance in the Victorian City*. Cambridge: Cambridge University Press

—— (2004) 'Adventures in Space: Victorian Railway Erotics, or Taking Alienation For a Ride', *Journal of Victorian Culture*, Volume 9, Number 1, np

Baker, Cathleen (2012) *From the Hand to the Machine: Nineteenth-century Paper and Mediums – Technologies, Materials and Conservation.* Ann Arbor: The Legacy Press

Balliet, Barbara J. (2007) '"Let Them Study as Men and Work as Women" – Georgina Davis, New Women, and Illustrated Papers', *Commonplace: The Journal of Early American Life*, Volume 7, Number 3, np

Bancroft, Squire and Marie Bancroft (1889) *Mr. and Mrs. Bancroft on and off the Stage.* London: Richard Bentley and Son

Bannerjee, Jacqueline (2007) 'Ideas of Childhood in Victorian Children's Fiction: The Child as Innocent', *The Victorian Web* (accessed 13 August 2019) www.victorianweb.org/genre/childlit/childhood1.html

Banville, Scott (2008) 'Ally Sloper's Half-Holiday: The Geography of Class in Late-Victorian Britain', *Victorian Periodicals Review*, Volume 41, Number 2, pp. 150–73

Barr, John (1986) *Illustrated Children's Books.* London: British Library Board

Baudelaire, Charles (1964) *The Painter of Modern Life.* New York: Da Capo Press

Beale, Samantha (2018) 'Gagging for It: Irony, Innuendo and the Politics of Subversion in Women's Comic Performance on the Post-1880 London Music-Hall Stage and its Resonance in Contemporary Practice'. PhD thesis, Middlesex University (unpublished)

Beegan, Gerry (2018) 'Researching Technologies of Printing and Illustration: Clement Shorter, Phil May and Photomechanical Reproduction in the *Sketch*' in Easley, Alexis, Andrew King and John Morton (eds) *Researching the Nineteenth-Century Periodical Press: Case Studies.* London: Routledge, pp. 115–30

Beetham, Margaret (1996) *A Magazine of Her Own: Domesticity and Desire in the Women's Magazine 1800–1914.* London and New York: Routledge

Beckett, Sandra (ed.) (1999) *Transcending Boundaries: Writing for a Dual Audience of Children and Adults.* Abingdon: Routledge

Bell, Bill (1993) 'Fiction in the Marketplace: Towards a Study of the Victorian Serial' in Myers, Robin and Michael Harris (eds) *Serials and their Readers 1620–1914.* Delaware: Oak Knoll Press, pp. 125–44

Belsey, Catherine (2002) *Critical Practice.* New York: Routledge

Bernstein, Robin (2013). 'Toys Are Good for Us: Why We Should Embrace the Historical Integration of Children's Literature, Material Culture, and Play', *Children's Literature Association Quarterly*, Volume 38, Number 4, pp. 458–63

Bernstein, Susan and Elsie Michie (2009) 'Introduction' in Bernstein, Susan and Elsie Michie (eds) *Victorian Vulgarity – Taste in Verbal and Visual Culture.* Farnham: Ashgate, pp. 1–19

Bingham, Madeleine (1978) *Henry Irving and the Victorian Theatre.* London: Routledge

'Birmingham' (1870) *The Era.* 18 September, p. 11

Blair, Margaret (2004) 'Locking in Capital: What Corporate Law Achieved for Business Organisers in the Nineteenth Century', *51 UCLA Law Review 2003–4*, pp. 387–455

Blake, Robert (1960) *Disraeli.* London: Faber & Faber

Bloodworth, Jenny (2013) 'Clotilde Graves: Journalist, Dramatist and Novelist. Writing to Survive in the Late Nineteenth and Early Twentieth Century'. PhD thesis, University of Leicester (unpublished)

Boleslavsky, Richard (2013) *Acting: The First Six Lessons.* Connecticut: Martino Press

Booth, Michael (1991) *Theatre in the Victorian Age*. Cambridge: Cambridge University Press

Boswell Jnr. (1922) 'Chats at "The Cheese"', *Ally Sloper's Half-Holiday*. New series, Number 2, p. 11

Boucher, William (1870a) 'Six of One – Half-a-dozen of the Other', *Judy, or the London Serio-comic Journal*, Volume 7, pp. 146–7

—— (1870b) 'At Bay!', *Judy, or the London Serio-comic Journal*, Volume 7, pp. 166–7

—— (1870c) 'The Voice of the Peacemaker', *Judy, or the London Serio-comic Journal*, Volume 7, pp. 176–7

—— (1870d) 'Civilisation's Lament', *Judy, or the London Serio-comic Journal*, Volume 7, pp. 186–7

—— (1870e) 'Modern Warfare', *Judy, or the London Serio-comic Journal*, Volume 7, pp. 196–7

—— (1870f) 'Between Two Stools', *Judy, or the London Serio-comic Journal*, Volume 7, pp. 216–17

—— (1870g) 'Birds of Prey', *Judy, or the London Serio-comic Journal*, Volume 7, pp. 226–7

—— (1870h) 'About Time!', *Judy, or the London Serio-comic Journal*, Volume 7, pp. 236–7

—— (1870i) 'Non-interference Policy', *Judy, or the London Serio-comic Journal*, Volume 7, pp. 246–7

—— (1870j) 'The French Sinbad; or, "Irregular" Warfare', *Judy, or the London Serio-comic Journal*, Volume 7, pp. 256–7

—— (1875) 'Extraordinary Change in the Weather', *Judy, or the London Serio-comic Journal*, Volume 17, p. 163

—— (1876a) '*Judy*, Empress of Fleet Street', *Judy, or the London Serio-comic Journal*, Volume 18, frontispiece

—— (1876b) 'True Blue First – Where's the Other?', *Judy, or the London Serio-comic Journal*, Volume 18, pp. 252–3

Brake, Laurel (1994) *Subjugated Knowledges: Journalism, Gender & Literature*. Basingstoke: Macmillan

Brake, Laurel, Bill Bell and David Finkelstein (2000) 'Introduction' in Brake, Laurel, Bill Bell and David Finkelstein (eds) *Nineteenth-Century Media and the Construction of Identities*. Basingstoke: Palgrave, pp. 1–13

Brake, Laurel and Marysa Demoor (eds) (2009) *Dictionary of Nineteenth Century Journalism in Great Britain and Ireland*. Gent: Academia Press

Bramston, Mary (1885) *A Woman of Business*. London: Society for Promoting Christian Knowledge

Bratton, Jackie and Ann Featherstone (2006) *The Victorian Clown*. Cambridge: Cambridge University Press

Breward, Christopher (1994) 'Femininity and Consumption: The Problem of the Late Nineteenth-Century Fashion Journal', *Journal of Design History*, Volume 7, Number 2, pp. 71–89

Burnham, Sandra (ed.) (1979) *Fit Work for Women*, London: Croom Helm

Bury, Stephen (ed.) (2012) *Benezit Dictionary of British Graphic Artists and Illustrators*. Oxford: Oxford University Press

Busby, Roy (1976) *British Music Hall: An Illustrated Who's Who from 1850 to the Present Day*. London: Paul Elek

Butler, Judith (1990) *Gender Trouble*. Abingdon: Routledge

—— (1990) 'Performative Acts and Gender Constitution: An Essay in Phenomenology and Performance Theory' in Case, Sue-Ellen (ed.) *Performing Feminisms: Feminist Critical Theory and Theatre*, London: Johns Hopkins University Press, pp. 270–82

—— (1993) *Bodies That Matter*. London: Routledge

Butler, Cornelia H. and Catherine de Zegher (2010) *On Line: Drawing Through the Twentieth Century*. New York: Museum of Modern Art

Campbell, Kate (2000) 'Journalistic Discourses and Constructions of Modern Knowledge', in Brake, Laurel, Bill Bell and David Finkelstein (2000) *Nineteenth-Century Media and the Construction of Identities*. Basingstoke: Palgrave, pp. 40–53

Campbell Orr, Clarissa (1995) 'Introduction' in *Women in the Victorian Art World*. Manchester: Manchester University Press, pp. 1–32

'Cardiff' (1873) *The Era*. 28 September, p. 5

Chadwick, Edwin (1962) *Report from the Poor Law Commissioners on an Enquiry into the Sanitary Conditions of the Labouring Population of Great Britain, 1842*. Edinburgh: Edinburgh University Press

Chapman, Theodosia (1896) 'A Dialogue on Vulgarity'. *The Nineteenth Century*, Number 39, pp. 624–35

Chase, Karen (2009) *The Victorians and Old Age*. Oxford: Oxford University Press

Chasemore, Archibald (1873) 'The Office Boy's mother at The Royal Academy', *Judy, or the London Serio-comic Journal*, Volume 13, p. 109

Chekhov, Michael (2014) *To the Actor: On the Technique of Acting*. Connecticut: Martino Press

Cherry, Deborah (1996) *Painting Women: Victorian Women Artists*. London and New York: Routledge

Chubbuck, Ivana (2005) *The Power of the Actor: The Chubbuck Technique*. New York: Gotham Books

'Christmas Books' (1874) *The Graphic*, Volume #, 26 December

'Christmas Pantomimes, Burlesques, Etc' (1851) *Illustrated London News*, 27 December, p. 8

Clarke, Ambrose (Marie Duval) and Charles H. Ross (1875) *Rattletrap Rhymes and Tootletum Tales. A Big Book for Babies ….* London: Office of *Judy*

Clarke, Anna (1997) *The Struggle for the Breeches: Gender and the Making of the Working Class*. Berkeley: University of California Press

Clayton, Ellen (1876) *English Female Artists, Volumes II*. London: Tinsley Brothers

Clement, Elizabeth (2006) *Love for Sale: Courting, Treating and Prostitution in New York City 1900–1945*. Chapel Hill: University of North Carolina Press

Clifton, Alex (2016) *The Actor's Workbook A Practical Guide to Training Rehearsing and Devising*. London: Bloomsbury

Coke, David (2017) *Vauxhall Gardens 1661–1859 Full Chronology* (accessed 4 August 2019) www.vauxhallgardens.com/vauxhall_gardens_fullchronology_page.html

Conboy, Martin (2016) 'It is Nobbut (Only) an Oligarchy that Calls Itself a 'We': Perceptions of journalism and journalists in Britain 1880–1900', *Journalism Studies Journal*, Volume 17, Issue 6, pp. 730–46

Concanen, Alfred (1871) *Lulu as she Appeared Before Their Royal Highnesses the Prince and Princess of Wales, 20 Feb 1871*. London: Stannard & Son. Victoria and Albert Museum catalogue number S.2760–1986

Craig, Edward (2008) *On the Art of the Theatre (Routledge Theatre Classics)*. London: Routledge

Crossick, Geoffrey and Heinz-Gerhard Haupt (1995) *The Petite Bourgeoisie in Europe, 1780–1914*. London: Routledge

Cruikshank, George Jr (1867) 'Royal Academy Sketches', *Judy, or the London Serio-comic Journal*, Volume 1, p. 115

Csikszentmihalyi, Mihaly (1992) *Flow: The Psychology of Happiness*. New York: Harper & Row

Cumming, Laura (2012) 'David Shrigley: Brain Activity – review', *The Observer*, Sunday 5 February (accessed 14 August 2019) www.theguardian.com/artanddesign/2012/feb/05/david-shrigley-brain-activity-review

Dalziel, Gilbert (1927) 'Who Invented Ally Sloper?' *Referee*, 15 May, p. 10

Dalziel, Gilbert (1920) *Letter to Mrs Callcott*. Unpublished letter: Private Collection

Dalziel, Gilbert and Edward Dalziel (1901) *The Brothers Dalziel; A Record of Fifty Years' Work in Conjunction with Many of the Most Distinguished Artists of the Period, 1840–1890*. London: Methuen and Company

Darby, Nell (2017) *Life on the Victorian Stage: Theatrical Gossip*. Barnsley: Pen and Sword Books

Davidoff, Leonore (1979) 'The Separation of Home and Work: Landladies and Lodgers in Nineteenth- and Twentieth-century England' in Sandra Burnham (ed.) *Fit Work for Women*, pp. 57–90

Davidson, Cathy (1988) 'Towards a History of Books and Readers', *American Quarterly*, Volume 40, Number 1, pp. 7–17

Davis, Jim and Victor Emeljanow (2001) *Reflecting the Audience: London Theatregoing, 1840–1880*. Hertford: University of Hertford Press

Davis, Tracy C. (1991) *Actresses as Working Women: Their Social Identity in Victorian Culture*. London: Routledge

De Maré, Eric (1980) *Victorian Wood-block Illustrators*. London: Gordon Fraser Gallery

De Tocqueville, Alexis (1840) *Democracy in America*. London: Sanders and Otley

De Vere (1865) *E. Danvers as Scampa in Ernani at the Highbury Alexandra*. London: De Vere. Victoria and Albert Museum catalogue number S.148: 265–2007

De Zegher, Catherine (2003) *The Stage of Drawing: Gesture and Act: Gesture and Art*. London: Tate Publishing

Del Roscio, Nicola (2002) *Writings on Cy Twombly*. Munich: Schirmer/Mosel Verlag

Delap, Lucy (2012) *Knowing Their Place: Domestic Service in Twentieth-century Britain*. Oxford: Oxford University Press

Demoor, Marysa (2000) *Their Fair Share: Women, Power and Criticism in the Athenaeum, from Millicent Garrett Fawcett to Katherine Mansfield, 1870–1920*. London: Routledge

Derrida, Jacques (1993) *Memoirs of the Blind: The Self-Portrait and Other Ruins*. Chicago: University of Chicago Press

Dierick, Charles and Pascal Lefèvre (1998) *Forging a New Medium: The Comic Strip in the Nineteenth Century*. Brussels: VUB Press

Dillon, Brian (2009) *The End of the Line: Attitudes in Drawing*. London: Hayward Publishing

Donnellan, Declan (2005) *The Actor and the Target*. London: Nick Hern Books

'Dramatic and Musical Gossip' (1880) *The Referee*, 11 July, p. 3

Du Maurier, George (1898) *Social Pictorial Satire*. London: Harper & Brothers

Duval, Marie (1869a) 'Au revoir Rose Anna' in Ross, Charles and Ambrose Clarke, *The Story of a Honeymoon*. London: J. C. Hotten, p. 303

—— (1869b) 'At Bolong', *Judy, or the London Serio-comic Journal*, Volume 5, p. 150

—— (1869c) 'The Beast and the Beauty at the Royalty', *Judy, or the London Serio-comic Journal*, Volume 5, p. 260

—— (1869d) 'The Moulsey Hurst Paper', *Judy, or the London Serio-comic Journal*, Volume 4, p. 200

—— (1869e) 'The Story of a Lady who Married a Walking Gent', *Judy, or the London Serio-comic Journal*, Volume 5, p. 242

—— (1869f) 'Some of the Latest Fashions', *Judy, or the London Serio-comic Journal*, Volume 5, p. 252

—— (1869g) 'The Siren', *Judy, or the London Serio-comic Journal*, Volume 6, p. 60

—— (1869h) 'Lover of His Art', *Judy, or the London Serio-comic Journal*, Volume 5, p. 172

—— (1869i) 'Pictures from Fairyland (Not by Richard Doyle)', *Judy, or the London Serio-comic Journal*, Volume 6, p. 80

—— (1869j) 'The Last New Burlesque', *Judy, or the London Serio-comic Journal*, Volume 6, p. 80

—— (1869k) 'A Few Recollections of Foreign Climbs', *Judy, or the London Serio-comic Journal*, Volume 6, p. 11

—— (1869l) Untitled, *Judy, or the London Serio-comic Journal*, Volume 5, p. 262

—— (1869m) 'Chignons', *Judy, or the London Serio-comic Journal*, Volume 6, p. 18

—— (1870a) *Smiles and Styles: A. Lynes & Son's Summer Magazine*. London: A. Lynes & Sons

—— (1870b) 'Some Selections From What Wasn't Accepted', *Judy, or the London Serio-comic Journal*, Volume 7, p. 28

—— (1870c) 'Anarchy in Islington', *Judy, or the London Serio-comic Journal*, Volume 8, p. 40

—— (1870d) 'Ally Sloper off to the Wars', *Judy, or the London Serio-comic Journal*, Volume 7, p. 152

—— (1870e) 'Ally to the Front', *Judy, or the London Serio-comic Journal*, Volume 7, p. 172

—— (1870f) 'Sloper a Prisoner', *Judy, or the London Serio-comic Journal*, Volume 7, p. 182

—— (1870g) 'Sloper's Retreat', *Judy, or the London Serio-comic Journal*, Volume 7, p. 192

—— (1870h) 'After the Battle', *Judy, or the London Serio-comic Journal*, Volume 7, p. 202

—— (1870i) 'Sloper and Moses Reunited', *Judy, or the London Serio-comic Journal*, Volume 7, p. 222

—— (1870j) 'Sloper and Moses go into the Spy Business', *Judy, or the London Serio-comic Journal*, Volume 7, p. 232

—— (1870k) 'At Dead of Night', *Judy, or the London Serio-comic Journal*, Volume 7, p. 242

—— (1870l) 'In Re Sloper', *Judy, or the London Serio-comic Journal*, Volume 7, p. 252

—— (1870m) 'Sloper Sends Round the 'Hat'', *Judy, or the London Serio-comic Journal*, Volume 7, Almanack, p. 2

—— (1870n) 'At a Burlesque', *Judy, or the London Serio-comic Journal*, Volume 6, p. 242

—— (1870o) 'Not Entirely a Fancy Sketch', *Judy, or the London Serio-comic Journal*, Volume 7, p. 30

—— (1870p) 'At the Theatre Royal and at a Hall', *Judy, or the London Serio-comic Journal*, Volume 7, p. 82

—— (1870q) 'Mr Blank's Dramatic Agency', *Judy, or the London Serio-comic Journal*, Volume 8, p. 68

—— (1870r) 'A Tale of a Tooth', *Judy, or the London Serio-comic Journal*, Volume 8, p. 30

—— (1870s) 'At Dead of Night at 73', *Judy, or the London Serio-comic Journal*, Volume 7, p. 242

—— (1870t) 'Ally Sloper on his Travels', *Judy, or the London Serio-comic Journal*, Volume 7, p. 112

—— (1870u) 'Ally to the Front', *Judy, or the London Serio-comic Journal*, Volume 7, p. 172

—— (1871a) 'Ally Sloper's Night Cap', *Judy, or the London Serio-comic Journal*, Volume 9, p. 92

—— (1871b) 'Another to Sloper', *Judy, or the London Serio-comic Journal*, Volume 8, p. 232

—— (1871c) '*Judy*'s Valentines', *Judy, or the London Serio-comic Journal*, Volume 8, p. 162

—— (1872a) 'Round the Corner', *Judy, or the London Serio-comic Journal*, Volume 10, p. 140

—— (1872b) 'The Slaveys' Strike', *Judy, or the London Serio-comic Journal*, Volume 11, p. 38

—— (1872c) 'The Drama of 1872', *Judy, or the London Serio-comic Journal*, Volume 12, p. 83

—— (1872d) 'Sloper does the Derby', *Judy, or the London Serio-comic Journal*, Volume 11, p. 61

—— (1872e) 'Thanksgiving Day', *Judy, or the London Serio-comic Journal*, Volume 10, p. 180

—— (1872f) 'Sloper's Notion of the Festive Season', *Judy, or the London Serio-comic Journal*, Volume 10, p. 110

—— (1872g) 'Expression!', *Judy, or the London Serio-comic Journal*, Volume 12, p. 60

—— (1872h) '"The Human Form Divine' – A Study', *Judy, or the London Serio-comic Journal*, Volume 12, p. 40

—— (1872i) *Ally Sloper's Book of Beauty*. London: Offices of Judy

—— (1872j) 'Some Fashions for the Hair', *Judy, or the London Serio-comic Journal*, Volume 10, p. 220

—— (1872k) 'What Are We Coming To?', *Judy, or the London Serio-comic Journal*, Volume 11, p. 163

—— (1872l) 'A Little Dear from This Month's Fashion Books …' in *A Book of Comicalities: Selected From The Pages of Judy*. London: Offices of *Judy*, p. 125

—— (1872m) 'Ally on the Rights of Women', *Judy, or the London Serio-comic Journal*, Volume 11, p. 31

—— (1873a) 'Sloper Among the Artists', *Judy, or the London Serio-comic Journal*, Volume 13, p. 30

—— (1873b) 'Still Among the Pictures', *Judy, or the London Serio-comic Journal*, Volume 13, p. 40

—— (1873c) Untitled, *Judy, or the London Serio-comic Journal*, Volume 13, frontispiece

—— (1873d) 'Behind the scenes', *Judy, or the London Serio-comic Journal*, Volume 12, p. 142

—— (1873e) '*Judy* Medal, Pencil and Quill', *Judy, or the London Serio-comic Journal*, Volume 14, frontispiece

—— (1873f) 'The Earliest News from the Seaside', *Judy, or the London Serio-comic Journal*, Volume 13, p. 92

—— (1873g) 'Behind the Scenes', *Judy, or the London Serio-comic Journal*, Volume 12, p. 142

—— (1873g) 'Ally Sloper: A Moral Lesson' in Ross, Charles Henry *Some Playful Episodes in the Career of Ally Sloper*. London: Office of *Judy*

—— (1873h) 'After the Holidays', *Judy, or the London Serio-comic Journal*, Volume 12, p. 152

—— (1873i) 'Popular Plays Properly Reported. No. 1 – Charles I', *Judy, or the London Serio-comic Journal*, Volume 12, p. 139

—— (1873j) 'Passing Events', *Judy, or the London Serio-comic Journal*, Volume 12, p. 224

—— (1873k) '*Judy's* Fashions 1873', *Judy, or the London Serio-comic Journal*, Volume 13, p. 133

—— (1873l) 'Podger on Stilts – A long Legged Love Story', *Judy, or the London Serio-comic Journal*, Volume 13, p. 142

—— (1873m) 'The Earliest News from the Seaside', *Judy, or the London Serio-comic Journal*, Volume 13, p. 92

—— (1873n) 'All About a Scarlet Runner', *Judy, or the London Serio-comic Journal*, Volume 13, p. 162

—— (1873o) 'The Deed of Darkness', *Judy, or the London Serio-comic Journal*, Volume 13, p. 72

—— (1873p) 'After the Season is Over', *Judy, or the London Serio-comic Journal*, Volume 13, p. 260

—— (1873q) 'The Very First Original Oyster Eater', *Judy, or the London Serio-comic Journal*, Volume 13, p. 202

—— (1873r) 'Recent Occurrences', *Judy, or the London Serio-comic Journal*, Volume 12, p. 162

—— (1873s) 'Hats and Heads', *Judy, or the London Serio-comic Journal*, Volume 13, p. 182

—— (1874a) 'How Mrs Todgers Tackled the Ocean', *Judy, or the London Serio-comic Journal*, Volume 15, p. 212

—— (1874b) *Queens & Kings and Other Things*. London: Chatto & Windus

—— (1874c) 'Merry Christmas', *Judy, or the London Serio-comic Journal*, Volume 16, p. 91

—— (1874d) 'A Pinch of Snuff', *Judy, or the London Serio-comic Journal*, Volume 14, p. 264

—— (1874e) 'Rigi-Lections', *Judy, or the London Serio-comic Journal*, Volume 16, p. 50

—— (1874f) '*Judy's* Skirts', *Judy, or the London Serio-comic Journal*, Volume 16, frontispiece

—— (1874g) 'Ally Sloper Goes a-Fishing', *Judy, or the London Serio-comic Journal*, Volume 15, p. 92

—— (1874h) 'Encore des Bêtises', *Judy, or the London Serio-comic Journal*, Volume 15, 112

—— (1875a) 'Among the Painters', *Judy, or the London Serio-comic Journal*, Volume 17, p. 40

—— (1875b) 'The Statues of London. From a One-eyed Point of View', *Judy, or the London Serio-comic Journal*, Volume 17, p. 38

—— (1875c) 'Papillonis Sillibillis: or, Sillybilly Butterfly', *Judy, or the London Serio-comic Journal*, Volume 17, p. 21

—— (1875d) 'Another Mediaeval Love Affair', *Judy, or the London Serio-comic Journal*, Volume 17, p. 83

—— (1875e) 'Pantomimical', *Judy, or the London Serio-comic Journal*, Volume 18, p. 101

—— (1875f) 'New Year Nonsense 1875', *Judy, or the London Serio-comic Journal*, Volume 16, p. 123

—— (1875g) 'Spring, Summer, Autumn, Winter', *Judy, or the London Serio-comic Journal*, Volume 18, Almanack p. 13

—— (1875h) 'Crimes and Disasters (From a Sloperian Point of View)', *Judy, or the London Serio-comic Journal*, Volume 17, p. 39

—— (1875i) 'When it Used to Rain', *Judy, or the London Serio-comic Journal*, Volume 17, p. 184

—— (1875j) 'Ally Sloper: Slayer of Wolves!!!', *Judy, or the London Serio-comic Journal*, Volume 17, p. 212

—— (1875k) 'Sloper: Slayer of Wolves – (Continued.)', *Judy, or the London Serio-comic Journal*, Volume 17, p. 232

—— (1875l) 'Sloper: Slayer of Wolves – (Conclusion.)', *Judy, or the London Serio-comic Journal*, Volume 17, p. 252

—— (1875m) 'The Adventures of a Poor Old Lady Up for the Cattle Show at the Oxford Circus', *Judy, or the London Serio-comic Journal*, Volume 18, p. 78

—— (1875n) 'A Conscientious Chronicle of Pretty Women's Prettiest Frocks', *Judy, or the London Serio-comic Journal*, Volume 17, p. 2

—— (1876a) 'The Royal Academy. (From a Sloperian Point of View.)', *Judy, or the London Serio-comic Journal*, Volume 19, p. 39

—— (1876b) 'The Royal Academy. (From a Sloperian Point of View.)', *Judy, or the London Serio-comic Journal*, Volume 19, p. 59

—— (1876c) 'The Kenealy Procession. – From a Sloperian Point of View', *Judy, or the London Serio-comic Journal*, Volume 19, p. 185

—— (1876d) 'The Bar Young Lady', *Judy, or the London Serio-comic Journal*, Volume 19, p. 80

—— (1876e) 'Encore des bêtises', *Judy, or the London Serio-comic Journal*, Volume 19, p. 100

—— (1876f) 'Some Naughty Nursery Rhymes. Wholly Unsuitable for Any Well-Regulated Nursery', *Judy, or the London Serio-comic Journal*, Volume 18, p. 234

—— (1876g) 'Crimes and Disasters (from a Sloperian Point of View)', *Judy, or the London Serio-comic Journal*, Volume 18, p. 235

—— (1876h) 'Back-Gardening in April (from a Sloperian Point of View)', *Judy, or the London Serio-comic Journal*, Volume 18, p. 261

—— (1876i) 'Crimes and Disasters (From a Sloperian Point of View)', *Judy, or the London Serio-comic Journal*, Volume 18, p. 153

—— (1876j) 'Romeo and Juliet. (From a Sloperian Point of View)', *Judy, or the London Serio-comic Journal*, Volume 19, p. 121

—— (1876k) Untitled, *Judy, or the London Serio-comic Journal*, Volume 18, frontispiece

—— (1876l) 'More Playful Episodes in the Career of A. Sloper', *Judy, or the London Serio-comic Journal*, Volume 18, p. 194

—— (1876m) 'Derby Tips', *Judy, or the London Serio-comic Journal*, Volume 19, p. 71

—— (1876n) 'Heroines', *Judy, or the London Serio-comic Journal*, Volume 20, p. 18

—— (1876o) 'In Re "The Dual Garments"', *Judy, or the London Serio-comic Journal*, Volume 19, p. 256

—— (1877a) 'The Annual Outing!', *Judy, or the London Serio-comic Journal*, Volume 21, p. 174

—— (1877b) 'Another Bad Case at a Barber's', *Judy, or the London Serio-comic Journal*, Volume 22, p. 82

—— (1877c) 'To a Michaelmas Goose', *Judy, or the London Serio-comic Journal*, Volume 21, p. 254

—— (1877d) 'Valentines from a Sloperian Point of View', *Judy, or the London Serio-comic Journal*, Volume 20, p. 182

—— (1877e) 'Dreams', *Judy, or the London Serio-comic Journal*, Volume 22, p. 96

—— (1877f) 'The Annual Outing', *Judy, or the London Serio-comic Journal*, Volume 21, p. 174

—— (1877g) 'The False Friends', *Judy, or the London Serio-comic Journal*, Volume 21, p. 204

—— (1877h) 'Spring Fancies', *Judy, or the London Serio-comic Journal*, Volume 21, p. 10

—— (1877i) 'A. Sloper, War Correspondent', *Judy, or the London Serio-comic Journal*, Volume 21, p. 38

—— (1877j) 'The Latest Horror at the Old Bailey', *Judy, or the London Serio-comic Journal*, Volume 21, p. 254

—— (1878a) 'Pictures', *Judy, or the London Serio-comic Journal*, Volume 22, p. 301

—— (1878b) 'England, Home and Beauty', *Ally Sloper's Comic Kalendar for 1879*, p. 20

—— (1878c) 'Ally Sloper's Effigy (on a Stick)', *Ally Sloper's Comic Kalendar for 1879*, p. 6

—— (1878d) 'Krikketekrakkle', *Judy, or the London Serio-comic Journal*, Volume 23, p. 92

—— (1878e) 'Tragedy', *Judy, or the London Serio-comic Journal*, Volume 22, p. 280

—— (1878f) 'Love Considered as a Verb', *Judy, or the London Serio-comic Journal*, Volume 22, p. 380

—— (1878g) 'Personally Misconducted', *Judy, or the London Serio-comic Journal*, Volume 23, p. 162

—— (1878h) 'The Fatal Ending of a Flirty Fly', *Judy, or the London Serio-comic Journal*, Volume 23, p. 182

—— (1878i) 'Dreams. And the Awakening', *Judy, or the London Serio-comic Journal*, Volume 22, p. 362

—— (1878j) 'Such Young Things Too', *Judy, or the London Serio-comic Journal*, Volume 23, p122

—— (1879a) 'July August September', *Ally Sloper's Comic Kalendar for 1879*, p. 14

—— (1879b) 'Nature and Art', *Ally Sloper's Comic Kalendar for 1879*, p. 15

—— (1880a) 'Rejected, But Why?', *Judy, or the London Serio-comic Journal*, Volume 26, p. 226

—— (1880b) 'The Royal Academy Much Improved Upon (From a Sloperian Point of View.)', *Judy, or the London Serio-comic Journal*, Volume 26, p. 238

—— (1880c) 'More of the Academy. (From a Sloperian Point of View.)', *Judy, or the London Serio-comic Journal*, Volume 26, p. 274

—— (1880d) 'The Teaseful Toy: A Seaside Story', *Judy, or the London Serio-comic Journal*, Volume 27, p. 12

—— (1881a) 'Sloper in Knots', *Judy, or the London Serio-comic Journal*, Volume 28, p. 318

—— (1881b) 'Sloper's Mixture', *Judy, or the London Serio-comic Journal*, Volume 29, p. 9

—— (1881c) 'Crimes and Disasters (From a Sloperian point of View)', *Judy, or the London Serio-comic Journal*, Volume 28, p. 57

—— (1882) 'Ikey Moses's Mummy', *Judy, or the London Serio-comic Journal*, Volume 31, p. 226

—— (1883a) 'A Mean Way of Mashing', *Judy, or the London Serio-comic Journal*, Volume 32, p. 83

—— (1883b) 'Nobody all Right at Last', *Judy, or the London Serio-comic Journal*, Volume 32, p. 111

—— (1883c) 'The Dying Moments of a Suburban Beauty. II. – The Cruel Irony of Fate' (1883) *Judy, or the London Serio-comic Journal*, Volume 33, p. 183

—— (1883d) 'The Goings on of Gran'papa', *Judy, or the London Serio-comic Journal*, Volume 33, p. 306

—— (1883e) 'The Dying Moments of a Suburban Beauty IV.', *Judy, or the London Serio-comic Journal*, Volume 33, p. 207

—— (1883f) 'Awful Accident!', *Judy, or the London Serio-comic Journal*, Volume 33, p. 23

—— (1884a) 'Herny Brodrib as a Kettle Holder', *Ally Sloper's Comic Kalendar for 1884*, p. 6

—— (1884b) 'The Goings on of Gran'papa', *Judy, or the London Serio-comic Journal*, Volume 34, p. 27

—— (1884c) 'Almost Another Explosion!', *Judy, or the London Serio-comic Journal*, Volume 34, p. 287

—— (1885a) 'London Town Upside Down. Part I. – (Continued). – Somewhere in the City. Crisis!', *Judy, or the London Serio-comic Journal*, Volume 36, p. 50

—— (1885b) 'London Town Upside Down. Part IV. – In the Presence of Danger', *Judy, or the London Serio-comic Journal*, Volume 36, p. 98

—— (1885c) 'London Town Upside Down. (Continued). – Somewhere in the City. Crisis!', *Judy, or the London Serio-comic Journal*, Volume 36, p. 14

—— (1886) 'Zee Englishe Sommaire' (reprinted from 1873 'Ze Englishe Sommaire'), *Judy, or the London Serio-comic Journal*, Volume 13, p. 152), *Ally Sloper's Half-Holiday*, Volume III, Number 124, p. 29

Easley, Alexis, Andrew King and John Morton (2017). *Researching the Nineteenth-century Periodical Press*. Oxford: Routledge

Ellerslie, Alma (1885) *The Diary of an Actress, or, Realities of Stage Life*. London: Griffith, Farran & Co.

Elliot, Joseph and Clarence Fry (1866) *Miss Martha Oliver*. London: Elliot & Fry. Victoria and Albert Museum catalogue number S.141: 104–2007

Endresz, Laci (Dir.) (2019). *Circus Carnival*. Blackpool Tower: Laci Endresz Snr.

Engels, Johan (1795) *Ideen zu einer Mimic*. Berlin: Berlin Selbstverlag

Epstein Nord, Deborah (1995) *Walking the Victorian Streets: Women, Representation, and the City*. New York: Cornell University Press

'Exhibition of the Royal Academy' (1876) *The Pall Mall Gazette*, 28 April, p. 12

F. H. (1894) 'Women's Work: Its Value and Possibilities', *The Girls' Own Paper*, Number 27, p. 51

Faigin, Gary (2008) *The Artist's Complete Guide to Facial Expression*. New York: Watson-Guptill

Fava, Antonio (2019) *Lo Stage International di Commedia dell'Arte* Fava (accessed 14 August 2019) www.antoniofava.com/it/corsi/

Feather, John (1988) *A History of British Publishing*. Abingdon: Routledge

'Feminine Humour' (1871) *The Saturday Review*. 15 July, pp. 75–6

Fetterley, Judith (1978) *The Resisting Reader: A Feminist Approach to American Fiction*. Bloomington: Indiana University Press

Fitzgerald, Percy (1881) *The World Behind the Scenes*. London: Chatto & Windus

Flood, Catherine (2013) 'Contrary to the Habits of their Sex? Women Drawing on Wood and the Careers of Florence and Adelaide Claxton' in Hadjiafxendi, Kyriaki and Patricia Zakreski (eds) *Crafting the Woman Professional in the Long Nineteenth Century: Artistry and Industry in Britain*. Farnham: Ashgate, pp. 107–21

Fradelle, Albert and Eugenia Leach (1872) *Harry Paulton as Roi Carotte in 'Le Roi Carotte' at the Alhambra Theatre*. London: Fradelle & Leach. Victoria and Albert Museum catalogue number S.141: 999–2007

Fraser, Hilary, Stephanie Green and Judith Johnson (2003) *Gender and the Victorian Periodical*. Cambridge: Cambridge University Press

Friston, David (1875) 'Scene from "Cinderella", the Covent Garden Pantomime', *Illustrated Sporting and Dramatic News*, 8 January 1876, p. 263

Garcia, Gustave (1888) The Actor's Art: a Practical Treatise on Stage Declamation, Public Speaking and Deportment. London: Simkin, Marshall & Company

Gardiner, Viv and Susan Rutherford (eds) (1992) *The New Woman and her Sisters: Feminism and Theatre 1850–1914*. London: Harvester Wheatsheaf

Gifford, Denis (1971) 'The Evolution of the British Comic'. *Historical Journal*, 349–58

—— (1975) *Victorian Comics*. Crows Nest, AU: Allen & Unwin

Gillies, Mary Ann (2007) *The Professional Literary Agent in Britain, 1880–1920*. Toronto and London: University of Toronto Press

Girouard, Mark (1977) *Sweetness and Light: The Queen Anne Movement, 1860–1900*. Oxford: Clarendon

Gitelman, Lisa (2006) *Always Already New: Media, History and the Data of Culture*. Cambridge, MA: MIT Press

Goldman, Paul (2005) *Beyond Decoration: The Illustrations of John Everett Millais*. London: Oak Knoll Press

Greenwood, Emma (2015) 'Work, Identity and Letterpress Printers in Britain, 1750–1850'. PhD thesis, University of Manchester (unpublished)

Grennan, Simon (2017) *A Theory of Narrative Drawing*. New York: Palgrave Macmillan

—— (2018) 'Memory and the Development of the Comic Strip Canon' in Ahmed, Maaheen and Benôit Crucifix, *Comics Memory – Archives and Styles*. New York: Palgrave Macmillan pp. 251–58

Grennan, Simon, Roger Sabin and Julian Waite (2016) *The Marie Duval Archive* Guildhall Library (accessed 22 February 2019) www.mariedual.org

—— (2018) *Marie Duval*. London: Myriad

Gretton, Tom (2008) 'Not the *Flâneur* Again: Reading Magazines and Living the Metropolis around 1880' in D'Souza. Aruna and Tom McDonough (eds) *The Invisible Flâneuse? Gender, Public Space and Visual Culture in Nineteenth-Century Paris*. Manchester: Manchester University Press

Gunn, Simon (2005) 'Translating Bourdieu: Cultural Capital and the English Middle Class in Historical Perspective', *The British Journal of Sociology*, Volume 56, Number 1, pp. 49–6

Hague, Ian (2014) *Comics and the Senses*. Abingdon: Routledge

Hall, Leo and Simon Grennan (2019) 'Literary and Historic Flâneuses: Observation, Commentary, Enterprise and Courage in Late-Nineteenth-Century Women's Professional Lives', *Journal of Victorian Culture*, Volume, 20, Number 20, pp. 1–19

Hadjiafxendi, Kyriaki and Patricia Zakreski (2013) 'Introduction' in Hadjiafxendi, Kyriaki and Patricia Zakreski (eds) *Crafting the Woman Professional in the Long Nineteenth Century: Artistry and Industry in Britain*. Farnham: Ashgate, pp. 1–18

Hatter, Janine and Nickianne Moody (eds) (2019) *Fashion and Material Culture in Victorian Fiction and Periodicals*. Brighton: Edward Everett Root Publishers

'Haymarket' (1861) *The Atheneum*, 16 November, p. 12

Heyman, Michael and Kevin Shortsleeve (2011) 'Nonsense' in Nel, Philip and Lissa Paul (eds) *Keywords for Children's Literature*. New York: New York University Press, pp. 96–8

Heywood, Colin (2017) *A History of Childhood*. London: Polity Press

Highfill, Philip, Kalman Burnim and Edward Langhans (2006) *A Biographical Dictionary of Actors, Actresses, Musicians, Dancers, Managers and other Stage Personnel: 1660–1800*. Illinois: Southern Illinois University Press

Hobbs, Andrew (2016) 'Provincial Periodicals' in King, Andrew, Alexis Easley and John Morton (eds) *The Routledge Handbook to Nineteenth-Century British Periodicals and Newspapers*. Abingdon: Routledge

Holcombe, Lee (1974) *Victorian Ladies at Work: Middle-class Working Women in England and Wales 1850–1914*. London: Archeon Books

Holm, Nick (2017) *Humour as Politics: The Political Aesthetics of Contemporary Comedy*. New York: Palgrave Macmillan

Hone, Annie M. (1888) 'Women's Enterprise and Genius', *Myra's Journal of Dress and Fashion*, Number 5, 1 May, p. 274

Hood, Tom (1875) *From Nowhere to the North Pole*. London: Chatto & Windus

Hopkins, Tighe (1889) 'Anonymity?' *The New Review*, Volume 1, Number 6, pp. 513–31

Hoskin, Dian Marie and H. Peter Dachler (1995) 'The Primacy of Relations in Socially Constructing Organisational Realities' in Hoskin, Dian Marie, H. Peter Dachler and Kenneth J. Gergen (eds) *Management and Organization: Relational Alternatives to Individualism*. Aldershot: Avebury, 29–50

Houfe, Simon (1981) *Dictionary of British Book Illustrators and Caricaturists 1800–1914*. Woodbridge: Antique Collectors' Club.

'Housekeeping' (1875) *Harper's Bazaar*, Volume VIII, Number 48, pp. 767–8

Howard, Diana (1970) *London Theatres and Music Halls 1850–1950*. London: The Library Association

Howes, Craig (2016) 'Comic/Satiric Periodicals' in King, Andrew, Alexis Easley and John Morton (eds) *The Routledge Handbook to Nineteenth-Century British Periodicals and Newspapers*. Abingdon: Routledge, p. 323

Howitt, Mary (1865) 'Woman's Mission' *Bow Bells*, n. s., Volume 3, p. 235

Hudson, Derek (1972) *Munby: Man of Two Worlds*. London: Murray

Humpherys, Anne (2005) 'Putting Women in the Boat in The Idler (1892–1898) and TO-DAY (1893–1897)', *19: Interdisciplinary Studies in the Long Nineteenth Century*, Volume 1, np

Huneault, Kristina (2002) *Difficult Subjects – Working Women and Visual Culture, Britain 1880–1914*. Aldershot: Ashgate Publishing

Hunt, Tamara L. (1996) 'Louisa Henrietta Sheridan and the Critics – Gender and Humour in the Early Victorian Period', *Victorian Periodicals Review*, Volume 29, Number 2, pp. 95–115

Huxley, Leonard (1923) *The House of Smith Elder*. London: Printed for private circulation

Iskin, Ruth (2006) 'The Flaneuse in French fin-de-siècle Posters: Advertising Images of Modern Women in Paris' in D'Souza, Aruna and Tom McDonough (eds) *The Invisible Flaneuse*. Manchester: Manchester University Press

Jackson, Lee (2019) *Palaces of Pleasure: From Music Halls to the Seaside to Football, How the Victorians Invented Mass Entertainment*. New Haven: Yale University Press

James, Henry (1963) *The Portrait of a Lady*. London: Penguin

Jameson, Anna (1844) *Companion to the Most Celebrated Private Galleries of Art in London*. London: Saunders and Otley

Johnstone, Christian Isobel (1834) 'Women of Business', *Tait's Edinburgh Magazine* (n.s.i), p. 596

Joseph, Marissa (2019) *Victorian Literary Businesses: The Management and Practices of the British Publishing Industry*. London: Palgrave Macmillan

'Judy's Opening Speech' (1867) *Judy, or the London Serio-comic Journal*, Volume 1, p. 3

King, Andrew (2016) 'Periodical Economics' in King, Andrew, Alexis Easley and John Morton, *The Routledge Handbook to Nineteenth-century British Periodicals and Newspapers*. New York: Routledge, pp. 60–74

Kooistra, Lorraine Janzen (2002) *Christina Rossetti and Illustration: A Publishing History*. Athens: Ohio University Press

—— (2011) *Poetry, Pictures and Popular Publishing: The Illustrated Gift Book and Victorian Visual Culture, 1855–1875*, Athens: Ohio University Press

Kunzle, David (1985) 'The First Ally Sloper: The Earliest Popular Cartoon Character as a Satire on the Victorian Work Ethic', *Oxford Art Journal*, Volume 8, Number 1, pp. 40–48

—— (1986) 'Marie Duval: A Caricaturist Rediscovered' *Women's Art Journal*, Volume 7, Number 1, pp. 26–31

—— (1990) *History of the Comic Strip, Volume 2*. Oakland: University of California Press

—— (2019) 'Review: Simon Grennan, Roger Sabin and Julian Waite, "Marie Duval" (Oxford: Myriad editions, 2018)', *European Comic Art*, Volume 12, Issue 2

Lausen, Cliff (2012) *David Shrigley: Brain Activity*. London: Hayward Gallery Publishing

Lawrence, Thomas, Roy Suddaby, and Bernard Leca (2011) 'Institutional Work: Refocusing Institutional Studies of Organization', *Journal of Management Inquiry* 20, Number 1, 52–28

Leary, Patrick (2010) *The Punch Brotherhood*. London: The British Library

Ledbetter, Kathryn (2016) 'Periodicals for Women' in King, Andrew, Alexis Easley and John Morton (eds) *The Routledge Handbook to Nineteenth-Century British Periodicals and Newspapers*. Oxford and New York: Routledge

Ledger, Sally (1997) *The New Woman: Fiction and Feminism at the Fin de Siècle*. Manchester: Manchester University Press

Leech, John (1843) 'Cartoon No. 1. Substance and Shadow', *Punch; Or, The London Charivari*, Volume 4, Issue 23

Leighton, Mary Elizabeth and Lisa Surridge (2019) *The Plot Thickens: Illustrated Victorian Serial Fiction from Dickens to Du Maurier*. Athens: Ohio University Press

Leiter, Samuel L. (2001) *A Kabuki Reader: History and Performance*. London: Routledge

'Letter to the Editor' (1869a) *The Theatrical Journal: A Weekly Review of Public Amusements*, Volume 30: 1557, 9 October, p. 325

'Letter to the Editor' (1869b) *The Theatrical Journal: A Weekly Review of Public Amusements*, Volume 30: 1558, 16 October, p. 331

Levin, Jennifer (2009) '"Ruby Pride of the on the floor naked": Fetishizing the Circus Girl in Joyce's *Ulysses*', *Joyce Studies Annual*, Volume 2009, pp. 125–58

Lewes, George Henry (1875) *On Actors and the Art of Acting*. London: Smith, Elder and Company 'London Amusements'

Lewes Jane (ed.) (1984) *Women in England 1870–1950: Sexual Divisions and Social Change*. New Jersey: Prentice-Hall

'Literature of the Day: – the New Magazine' (1831) *Metropolitan: a Monthly Journal of Literature, Science, and the Fine Arts*, Issue 1, pp. 17–22

Linton, Eliza Lynn (1868a) 'The Girl of the Period', *Saturday Review*, Issue 25, pp. 339–40

—— (1868b) 'The Wild Women', *Nineteenth Century*, Issue 30, pp. 79–88

—— (1868c) 'Pushing Women', *Saturday Review*, Issue 25, p. 578

—— (1868d) 'Feminine Affectations', *Saturday Review*, Issue 45, p. 776

'London Amusements' (1871) *Clerkenwell News and London Daily Chronicle*, 21 February, p. 4

London Stereoscopic and Photographic Company (1871) *Henry Irving as Mathias in 'The Bells'*, *Lyceum Theatre*. London: London Stereoscopic and Photographic

London Stereoscopic and Photographic Company (1873) *Henry Irving as 'King Charles I*. London: London Stereoscopic and Photographic Company. National Portrait Gallery catalogue number NPGx160516

Lown, Judy (1990) *Women and Industrialization: Gender and Work in the Nineteenth: Gender and Work in the Nineteenth Century*. Minneapolis: University of Minnesota Press

'Lulu!' 'Lulu!' (1875) *The Era*. 17 October, p. 13

Lundin, Anne (1994) 'Victorian Horizons: The Reception of Children's Books in England and America, 1880–1900', *Library Quarterly*, Volume 64, Number 1, 30–59

Lyotard, Jules (1860) *Memoires de Lyotard*. Paris: Simon Bacon and Company

'Lyotard at the Alhambra' (1861) *Bell's Life in Sydney and Sporting Chronicle*, 21 July, p. 4

Maclean, Marie (1991) 'Pretexts and Paratexts: The Art of the Peripheral', *New Literary History*, Volume 22, Number 2, p. 276

Macleod, Dianne S. (1996) *Art and the Victorian Middle Class: Money and the Making of Cultural Identity*. Cambridge: Cambridge University Press

Macmillan, George (ed.) (1908) *Letters of Alexander Macmillan: Edited with Introduction by His Son George A. Macmillan*. Printed for Private Circulation

'Mademoiselle Marie Duval' (1868) *The Era*. 27 December, p. 1

Maidment, Brian (2011) *Reading Popular Prints: 1790–1870*. Manchester: Manchester University Press

—— (2016) 'Illustration' in King, Andrew, Alexis Easley and John Morton, *The Routledge Handbook to Nineteenth-century British Periodicals and Newspapers*. New York: Routledge, pp. 102–23

Malcolm, Noel (1997) *The Origins of English Nonsense*. New York: HarperCollins

Marshall, Nancy Rose (2009) 'James' Tissot's 'Coloured Photographs of Vulgar Society' in Bernstein, Susan David and Elsie Michie (eds) *Victorian Vulgarity- Taste in Verbal and Visual Culture*. Farnham: Ashgate, pp. 201–22

Martin, Robert (1974) *The Triumph of Wit: A Study of Victorian Comic Theory*. London: Oxford University Press

Mayhew, Henry (1851) *London Labour and the London Poor*. London: Griffin Bone and Company

Maxwell, Richard (ed.) (2002) *The Victorian Illustrated Book*. Charlottesville: University of Virginia Press

Medhurst, Andrew (2007) *A National Joke*. Abingdon: Routledge

Meisel, Martin (1984) *Realizations: Narrative, Pictorial, and Theatrical Arts in Nineteenth-Century England*. Princeton: Princeton University Press

Méliès, Georges (1903) 'L'Auberge de Bon Repos', American Library Association version (accessed on 13 August 2019) https://archive.org/details/LeMerveilleuxEventailVivant

Meredith, George (1898) *An Essay on Comedy and the Uses of the Comic Spirit*. London: Archibald Constable and Company

McCloud, Scott (1993) *Understanding Comics: The Invisible Art*. New York: HarperCollins

McKinven, John A. (1998) *The Hanlon Brothers: their Amazing Acrobatics, Pantomimes and Stage Spectacles*. Illinois: Meyer Magic Books

Mitchell, Rebecca N. (July 2016) '15 August 1862: The Rise and Fall of the Cage Crinoline', BRANCH: Britain, Representation and Nineteenth-Century History, Dino Franco Felluga (ed.) *Romanticism and Victorianism on the Net* (accessed January 2020). www.branchcollective.org/?ps_articles=rebecca-n-mitchell-15-august-1862-the-rise-and-fall-of-the-cage-crinoline#_ftn13.end

Mitchell, Rosemary (2000) *Picturing the Past English History in Text and Image, 1830–1870*. Oxford: Oxford University Press

Miss Echo (Ed.) (1869) *Girl of the Period Miscellany*. London: J. Roberts

'Miss Field and Women's Rights', *Judy, of the London Serio-comic journal*, Volume 11, p. 69

'Modern periodical Literature' (1862) *Dublin Review*, Number 51, p. 277

'Modern Wood Engraving' (1838) *The London and Westminster Review*, Number 61, pp. 145–52

Moore, Tara (2009) *Victorian Christmas in Print*. Basingstoke and New York: Palgrave Macmillan

Morice, Herbert Jay (1870) *The Beggar's Uproar*. British Library Lord Chamberlain's Collection MS 53085 – P

Moss, Hugh (1880) *Diary 1880*. Unpublished manuscript: Collection Julian Waite

Moynet, Georges (1893) *Trucs et Décor*. Paris: La Librairie Illustrée

'Mr C. H. Ross' (1873) *The Era*. 13 July, p. 13

'Mr Charles H. Ross's Provincial Tour' (1870) *The Era*. 7 August, p. 1

Mullin, Katherine (2016) *Working Girls: Fiction, Sexuality and Modernity*. Oxford: Oxford University Press

—— (2016) 'Feminism and Women's Work 1776–1928', *Routledge Historical Resources: History of Feminism* (accessed 20 January 2020) http://dx.doi.org/10.4324/9781138641839-HOF3–1

Munt, Sally (2000) *Cultural Studies and the Working Class*. London: Cassell

Murray, Simone (2006) 'Publishing Studies: Critically Mapping Research in Search of a Discipline', *Publishing Research Quarterly* 22, Number. 4, pp. 3–25

Musgrove, Martha (2009) 'The Semi-Detached Flâneuse: Feminine Diversity in Romantic. London', *European Romantic Review*, Volume 20, Number 2, pp. 159–66

Nead, Lynda (2005) *Victorian Babylon: People, Streets and Images in Nineteenth-Century*. London and New Haven: Yale University Press

Nodelman, Perry (2008) *The Hidden Adult: Defining Children's Literature*. Baltimore: Johns Hopkins University Press

'Nonsense for Big and Little Babies' (1874) *Judy, or the London Serio-comic Journal*, Volume 16, p. 91

O'Gorman Francis (ed.) (2007) *Victorian Literature and Finance*. Oxford: Oxford University Press

O'Connell, Shiela (2018) 'Mary Darly' in Streeten, Nicola and Cath Tate (eds) *The Inking Woman*. Oxford: Myriad, pp. 10–11

Oliphant, Margaret (1876) 'The Royal Academy' *Blackwood's Edinburgh Review*, Volume 119, pp. 753–69

Onions, Oliver (2010) 'The Beckoning Fair One' in *The Dead of Night – The Ghost Stories of Oliver Onions*. London: Wordsworth Editions

Onslow, Barbara (2000) *Women of the Press in Nineteenth-Century Britain*. Basingstoke: Palgrave Macmillan

Palmer, Beth (2011) *Women's Authorship and Editorship in Victorian Culture: Sensational Strategies*. Oxford: Oxford University Press

Palmgren, Jennifer. and Lorretta Holloway (eds) (2005) *Beyond Arthurian Romances: The Reach of Victorian Medievalism*. New York: Palgrave Macmillan

Parsons, Deborah. (2000) *Streetwalking the Metropolis: Women, the City and Modernity*. Oxford: Oxford University Press

Pascoe, Charles (1880) *The Dramatic List: A Record of the Performances of Living Actor and Actresses of the British Stage*. London: David Bogue

Paterson, Peter (1864) *Glimpses of Real Life as Seen in the Theatrical World and in Bohemia: Being the Confessions of Peter Paterson, a Strolling Comedian*. Edinburgh: William P. Nimmo

Pathe (2012) *Fairy Tales: Early Colour Films from Pathe*. London: British Film Institute catalogue number N–132922

Patmore, Coventry (1857) *The Angel in the House*. London: J. Parker and Son

Pennell, Elizabeth. (1886) *The Contemporary Review*, Number 50, p. 521

Pettingell Collection, Templeman Library, University of Kent, Canterbury (uncatalogued)

Picard, Lisa (2009) 'The Working Classes and the Poor' (accessed on 13 August 2013) www.bl.uk/victorian-britain/articles/the-working-classes-and-the-poor

Piess, Kathy (1986) *Cheap Amusements: Working Women and Leisure in Turn-of-the-Century New York*. Philadelphia: Temple University Press

Planché, James (1840) *The Sleeping Beauty in the Wood*. London: Routledge and Sons

Poovey, Mary (ed.) (2003) *The Financial System in Nineteenth-century Britain*. New York: Oxford University Press

Poynter, Edward (1879) *Ten Lectures on Art*. London: Chapman and Hall

Purnell, Thomas (1861) 'Woman, and Art: The Female School of Design', *Art Journal*, Volume 76, pp. 107–8

Ramsay MacDonald, James. (1904) *Women in the Printing Trades*. London: P. S. King and Son

Reay, Barry (2002) *Watching Hannah: Sexuality, Horror and Bodily De-formation in Victorian England*. London: Reaktion Books

'Remarkable Case at the Melbourne District Court. Park and Boulton. Abridged from The Argus of Saturday' (1873) *The Sydney Morning Herald* (Sydney, Australia), 28 April, p. 6

Richards, Jeffrey (2014) *The Golden Age of Pantomime*. London: I. B. Tauris

Roberts, Elizabeth (1995) *Women's Work, 1840–1940*. Cambridge: Cambridge University Press

Rogers Peck, Stephan (1990) *Atlas of Facial Expression*. Oxford: Oxford University Press

Rossetti, Christina (1892) *Sing-Song. A Nursery Rhyme Book*. London: Macmillan and Company

Ross, Charles Henry (1865) *The Great Gun, An Eccentric Biography*. London: Ward, Lock & Tyler

—— (1867) *The Surprising Adventures of Clumsy Boy Crusoe*. London: unmarked

—— (1868) *The Book of Cats. A Chit-chat Chronicle of Feline Facts and Fancies*. London: unmarked

—— (1870) *Clam, a Romantic Drama*. Unpublished manuscript

—— (1871a) *Ruth, or a Poor Girl's Life in London*. Unpublished manuscript

—— (1871b) *Silence*. Unpublished manuscript

—— (1883) *Merry Conceits and Whimsical Rhymes*. London: Routledge

Ross, Charles Henry and Ambrose Clarke (1870) *The Story of a Honeymoon*. London: Chatto & Windus

Ross, Charles Henry and Dower Wilson (1882) *Flirting Made Easy: a Guide for Girls*. London: Dalziel Brothers

Rowe, Kathleen (1995) *The Unruly Woman*. Austin: University of Texas Press

Rowntree, Benjamin Seebohm (1901) *Poverty: A Study of Town Life*. London: Macmillan

'Royal Academy' (1876) *The Morning Post*. 29 April, p. 6

'Royal Academy' (1876) *The Examiner*. 6 May, pp. 16–17

Rudlin, John (1994) *Commedia Dell'Arte: An Actor's Handbook*. London: Routledge

Rummonds, Richard-Gabriel (2004) *Nineteenth-century Print Practices and the Iron Handpress*. London: British Library

Rutherford, Lois (1986) '"Managers in a Small Way": The Professionalisation of Variety Artistes, 1860–1914' in Bailey, Peter (ed.) *Music Hall: The Business of Pleasure*. Milton Keynes: Open University Press, pp. 93–117

Ruskin, John (1865) 'Of Queen's Gardens' in *Sesame and Lilies Part II*. London: The British Library archives

—— (1911) 'Fors Clavigera' in Cook, A. and Edward Wedderburn (eds) *The Works of John Ruskin*, Volume 29. London: G. Allen

Sabin, Roger (2003) 'Ally Sloper: First Comics Superstar?' *Image and Narrative*, Issue 7, np

—— (2009) 'Ally Sloper On Stage' *European Comic Art*, Volume 2, Number 2, pp. 205–25

—— (2014) 'Ally Sloper, Victorian Comic Book Hero: Interpreting a Comedy Type', *Visual Communication. Handbooks of Communication Science* 4. De Gruyter Mouton: Berlin, pp. 429–44

—— (2015) 'Comics Versus Books: The New Criticism at the Fin de Siècle' in Grennan, Simon and Laurence Grove (eds) *Transforming Anthony Trollope: 'Dispossession', Victorianism and Nineteenth-Century Word and Image*. Leuven: Leuven University Press

Sanders, Joe Sutliff (2013) 'Chaperoning Words: Meaning-Making in Comics and Picture Books' *Children's Literature*, Volume 41, pp. 57–90

Sausverd, Antoine (2011) 'Histoires de Pompiers', *Töpfferiana* (accessed on 13 August 2019). www.topfferiana.fr/2011/10/histoires-de-pompiers

Schwartz, Vanessa (1997) *Spectacular Realities: Early Mass Culture in Fin-de-Siècle Paris*. Berkeley: University of California Press

Scully, Richard (2018) *Eminent Victorian Cartoonists*. London: Political Cartoon Society

'Serious accident to an Acrobat' (1876) *The Sunday Times*. 13 August, p. 5

Seville, Catherine (1999) *Literary Copyright Reform in Early Victorian England: The Framing of the 1842 Copyright Act*. Cambridge: Cambridge University Press

Shanley, Mary Lyndon (1998) *Feminism, Marriage, and Law in Victorian England, 1850–1895*. Princeton: Princeton University Press

'Sherlock Junior' (2001) DVD. Stonevision 2001, Los Angeles: Metro Pictures Corporation

Shevelow, Kathryn (2016) *Women and Print Culture: The Construction of Femininity in the Early Periodical*. New York: Routledge

Siddons, Henry (1822) *Practical Illustrations of Rhetorical Gesture and Action*. London: Sherwood, Neely and Jones

'Sights in London' (1876) *Leicester Chronicle and Mercury*. 6 May, p. 10

Simmons, James Jr (2002) 'Industrial and Condition of England Novels' in Bratlinger, Patrick and William Thesing (eds) *A Companion to the Victorian Novel*. Oxford: Blackwell, p. 350

Simon, Mark (2003) *Facial Expressions: A Visual Reference for Artists*. New York: Watson-Guptill

Sinnera, Peter (2019) *Dynamics of the Pictured Page: Representing the Nation in the 'Illustrated London News'*. New York: Routledge

'Smiles and Styles Ready Oct. 3' (1870) *Daily Telegraph & Courier* (London), 13 September, p. 6

Smiles, Samuel (1859) *Self Help; With Illustrations of Character and Conduct*. London: Unmarked

Smith, David (2008) 'In bed with the boys from Fife', *The Guardian* online, 29 June (accessed 14 August 2019) www.theguardian.com/stage/2008/jun/29/theatre.reviews1

Smith, Shannon (2016) 'The Technologies of Production' in King, Andrew, Alexis Easley and John Morton. *The Routledge Handbook to Nineteenth-century British Periodicals and Newspapers*. New York: Routledge, pp. 29–41

Smith, Victoria (2017) *Between Generations: Collaborative Authorship in the Golden Age of Children's Literature*. Jackson: University Press of Mississippi

Smolderen, Thierry. (2014) *The Origin of Comics: from William Hogarth to Winsor McCay*. Jackson: University Press of Mississippi

'Some Amateurs' (1868) *Will-o'-the-Wisp*. 12 December, p. 11

Soum, Corinne and Steve Wasson (2019) *Theatre de L'Ange Fou*, Soum and Wasson (accessed 14 August 2019) www.angefou.co.uk/touringcompany.html

Southern, Richard (1970) *The Victorian Theatre: A Pictorial Survey*. Newton Abbot: David & Charles

Speight, George (1980) *A History of the Clowns*. London: Macmillan

Spielmann, Marion (1895) *The History of 'Punch'*. London: Cassell

Springhall, John (1998) *Youth, Popular Culture and Moral Panics: Penny Gaffs to Gangsta Rap 1830–1996*. London: St Martin's

Stafford-Clark, Max (1991) *Letters to George*. London: Nick Hern Books

Stanislavski, Constantin (2013a) *An Actor Prepares*. London: Bloomsbury

Stanislavski, Constantin (2013b) *Building a Character*. London: Bloomsbury

Stebbins, Genevieve (1885) *Delsarte System of Expression*. New York: Edgar S. Weiner

Stetz, Margaret (2000) 'The Laugh of the New Woman' in Wagner-Lawler, Jennifer (ed.) *The Victorian Comic Spirit: New Perspectives*. London: Taylor & Francis, pp. 214–37

—— (2001) 'The New Woman and the British Periodical Press of the 1890s', *Journal of Victorian Culture*, Volume 6, Number 2, pp. 272–85

Stillman William James (1891) 'Journalism and Literature'. *Atlantic Monthly*, Number 68, pp. 687–95

Stoker, Bram (1907) *Personal Reminiscences of Henry Irving*. London: Heinemann

Stott, Andrew (2004) *Comedy*. Abingdon: Routledge

Streeten, Nicola and Cath Tate (eds) (2018) *The Inking Woman*. Oxford: Myriad

'Surrey' (1870) *Illustrated London News*, 23 April, p. 18

'Surrey Theatre' (1870) *The Daily Telegraph*. 21 April, p. 3

'Surrey Theatre – (Last Night)' (1870) *The Era*. 8 May, p. 14

'Surrey Theatre' (1871a) *The Morning Advertiser* 20 February, p. 3

'Surrey Theatre' (1871b) *Daily Telegraph and Courier (London)*. 21 February, p. 3

Symons, Arthur (1896) 'Dieppe 1895' *Savoy* Number 1, pp. 86–8

Taylor, George (1989) *Players and Performances in the Victorian Theatre*. Manchester: Manchester University Press

'The Centennial regatta furnishes the last rows of summer' (1876) *The Evening Star*. 11 September, p. 3

'The Complete Buster Keaton Short Films 1917–1923' (2016) DVD. Hollywood: The Charlie Chaplin Studios, Eureka!

'The Holborn' (1871) *The Era*. 21 May, p. 11

The Mechanics' Magazine and Journal of Science, Arts and Manufactures (1871–72). London: Mechanics Magazine

'The Only Jones' (1875) *Judy*, Volume #, 1 September

'The Theatres' (1865) *Illustrated London News*, 27 May, p. 19

The Royal Academy (1876) *The Royal Academy Album: a series of photo-prints from works of art in the Exhibition of the Royal Academy of Arts*. London: Fine Art Publishing Company: Reeves & Company

'The Royal Academy' (1876) *Sheffield and Rotherham Chronicle*. 29 April, p. 6

'The Royal Academy' (1876) *The Ipswich Journal*. 2 May, p. 3

'The Royal Academy Exhibition' (1876) *The Yorkshire Herald*. 1 May, p. 6

'The Royalty' (1869) *The Era*. 10 October, p. 10

'The St. James's' (1868) *The Era*. 27 December, p. 13

'The Surrey' (1871) *The Era*. 5 March, p. 11

'The Theatres' (1871) *Illustrated London News*,13 May, p. 14

'The Theatrical Lounger' (1871) *Illustrated News*. 25 February p. 123

'The Women about Town' (1872) *The Sporting Times*, Number 380, 18 May, p. 156

The Young Clerk's Manual; or, Counting-house Assistant (1848). London: Cradock & Company

'Theatrical Divorce Case' (1873) *Liverpool Mercury, Issue* 7889, 03 May, p. 8

Thomas, Julia (2004) *Pictorial Victorians: The Inscription of Values in Word and Image*. Athens: Ohio University Press

—— (2016) 'Illustrations and the Victorian Novel' in Juliet John (Ed.) *The Oxford Handbook of Victorian Literary Culture*. Oxford: Oxford University Press

Thon, Jan-Noel and Lukas R. A. Wilde (2016) 'Mediality and Materiality of Contemporary Comics', *Journal of Graphic Novels and Comics*, Volume 7, Number 3, pp. 233–41

Thornbury, Walter (1873) *Old and New London*, Volume 1. London: Cassell, Petter and Galpin

'Thumbmarks' (1879a) *Judy*, Volume 25, p. 38

'Thumbmarks' (1879b) *Judy*, Volume 25, p. 192

Tickner, Liza (1987) *The Spectacle of Women: Imagery of the Suffrage Campaign 1907–14*. London: Chatto & Windus

Tilly, Louise and Joan Scott (1978) *Women, Work and Family*. New York: Routledge

Tormey, Jane, Andrew Selby, Phil Sawden et al. (2007) *Drawing Now: Between the Lines of Contemporary Art*. London: I. B. Tauris

Towsen, John (1976) *Clowns*. Boston: E. P. Dutton

Tuchman, Gaye and Nina Fortin (1989) *Edging Women Out: Victorian Novelists, Publishers, and Social Change*. New Haven: Yale University Press

Turner, Mark (2000) *Trollope and the Magazines: Gendered Issues in Mid-Victorian Britain*. Basingstoke: Macmillan

Tusan, Michelle (2004) 'Gender, Class, and the Printing Trade in Victorian Britain', *Journal of Women's History*, Volume 16, Number 1, pp. 103–22

Twyman, Michael (1998) *Printing 1770–1970: An Illustrated History of Its Development and Uses in England*. London: British Library

United Kingdom Census 1861: RG 9/84 f.79 p. 3

United Kingdom General Register Office Index to Births: 1847 December Quarter, Marylebone Registration District, 1: 156

United Kingdom General Register Office Index to Births: March Quarter 1875, Wandsworth Registration District, 1d / 598

United Kingdom General Register Office Index to Deaths: 1864 December Quarter, Marylebone Registration District, 1a / 398

United Kingdom General Register Office Index to Deaths: 1890 June Quarter, Wandsworth Registration District, 1d / 385

United Kingdom General Register Office Index to Marriages: 1861 June Quarter, St Martin Registry District, 1a / 608

United Kingdom National Archives 4 f.62 p. 23

Untitled (1872) *Judy, or the London Serio-comic Journal*, Volume 11, p. 134

Untitled (1876) *Judy, or the London Serio-comic Journal*, Volume 18, p. 113

Untitled (1883) *Magazine of Art* Number 6, pp. 128–9

Van Alphen, Ernst (2018) 'The Gesture of Drawing' in Grønstad, Asbjørn, Henrik Gustafsson and Øyvind Vågnes (eds) *Gestures of Seeing in Film, Video and Drawing*. New York: Routledge, pp. 110–22

Van Remoortel, Marianne (2015) *Women, Work and the Victorian Periodical: Living by the Press*. New York: Palgrave Macmillan

'Variorum Notes' (1876) *The Examiner*. 12 August, p. 21

Verdon, Nicola (2002) *Rural Women Workers in Nineteenth-Century England: Gender, Work and Wages*. Woodbridge: Boydell Press

Wagner-Lawlor, Jennifer (Ed.) (2000) *The Victorian Comic Spirit*. Aldershot: Ashgate

Wandsworth Cemetery Burial Register Index, np

Waters, Christopher (1990) *British Socialists and the Politics of Popular Culture 1884–1914*. Redwood City: Stanford University Press

Waite, Julian (2008) 'The Removal of Blocks to Effective Performance'. PhD thesis, University of Manchester (unpublished)

Walker, Lynn (1995) 'Vistas of Pleasure: Women Consumers of Urban Space in the West End of London 1850 – 1900' in Campbell Orr, Clarissa (ed.) *Women in the Victorian Art World*. Manchester: Manchester University Press, pp. 70–85

Waters, Christopher (1990) *British Socialists and the Politics of Popular Culture, 1884–1914*. Manchester: Manchester University Press

Watson, Edmund Henry Lacon (1906) *Hints to Young Authors*. London: Brown and Langham

Weber, Jean (2005) 'Cognitive Poetics and Literary Criticism: Types of Resolution in the Condition of England Novel', *European Journal of English Studies*, Volume 9, Number 2, p. 134

Weedon, Alexis (2003) *Victorian Publishing: The Economics of Book Production for a Mass Market, 1836–1916*, Aldershot: Ashgate

W. H. W. (1867) 'Provincial Notes' *Printers', Journal*, 5 August, p. 352

Wilson, A. J. (1927) 'Fun in fiction', *The Referee* 8 May, p10

'Women and Work' (1884) *Kidderminster Shuttle* 22 March, p. 2

Wolff, Janet. (2000) 'The Invisible *Flâneuse*' in D'Souza, Aruna and Tom McDonough (eds). *The Invisible 'Flâneuse'?: Gender, Public Space and Visual Culture in Nineteenth-Century Paris*. Manchester: Manchester University Press

Zakreski, Patricia (2013) 'Creative Industry: Design, Art Education and the Woman Professional' in Hadjiafxendi, Kyriaki and Patricia Zakreski (eds) *Crafting the Woman Professional in the Long Nineteenth Century: Artistry and Industry in Britain*. Farnham: Ashgate, pp. 145–65

Zola, Émile (2008) *The Kill*. London: Oxford University Press

Index

Note: 'n.' after a page reference indicates the number of a note on that page. Works by Duval are listed under their titles; other works are listed under their authors' names. Page numbers in *italic* refer to illustrations.

EU authorised representative for GPSR:
Easy Access System Europe, Mustamäe tee 50,
10621 Tallinn, Estonia
gpsr.requests@easproject.com

www.ingramcontent.com/pod-product-compliance
Ingram Content Group UK Ltd.
Pitfield, Milton Keynes, MK11 3LW, UK
UKHW051852150726
7214IPUK00021B/390